Additional Praise for *No More Police.*

"With *No More Police*, Mariame Kaba and Andrea Ritchie have written the definitive text on police abolition. The magic of this book is its ability to address the practical concerns of the present while strengthening our ability to craft ambitious and transformative freedom dreams for the future. Carefully researched, passionately written, and persuasively argued, *No More Police* is a must-read text for policymakers, activists, educators, and anyone else committed to imagining and building beyond the carceral world."

—**Marc Lamont Hill**, author of *We Still Here: Pandemic, Policing, Protest, and Possibility*

"In the powerful and generative tradition of Black feminist freedom-making, *No More Police* not only presents a compelling case for the abolition of police, but points us in the direction of building a safer and more just future. Ritchie and Kaba have worked for decades in transformative justice and abolitionist movements. The richness of that experience, the love that fuels it, and the brilliant insights that flow from it, shine brightly in this book."

—**Barbara Ransby**, activist, author, and historian

"An absolutely brilliant contribution. Black feminist abolitionists Kaba and Ritchie have issued a passionate mandate that we build relations and organizations that 'get it right' so that we avoid cooptation, learn from our mistakes, embrace an anti-oppression approach to the work, and never give up on the vision of a world where justice and safety live alongside each other. Generous and compelling, *No More Police* is a timely and critical intervention; essential reading as we continue to optimistically and faithfully fight for freedom."

—**Beth Richie**, author of *Arrested Justice*

"*No More Police* makes a sharp and compelling Black feminist case for a world without police, and without policing. Kaba and Ritchie are movement veterans, and their writing is as meticulously researched as it is grounded in practical knowledge gleaned over decades of abolitionist movement work. At once theoretically nuanced, analytically insightful, and highly accessible, *No More Police* is an essential, must-read book for this moment. It is sure to become a mainstay for longtime and new organizers, and for anyone invested in learning what it will take to build a movement and get free."

—**Robyn Maynard**, author of *Policing Black Lives: State Violence in Canada from Slavery to the Present* and co-author of *Rehearsals for Living*

"More than a synthesis and summation of the conditions of our movements' work over the last two years, and more than just an abolitionist movement timeline going back decades, Kaba and Ritchie weave together our collective stories, contradictions, tensions and all, and gift all of us and future generations with a map to a future free of cops and cages and full of care. This is a must-read in the abolitionist lexicon."

—**Ash-Lee Woodard Henderson**, Movement for Black Lives and co-director of the Highlander Center

"Kaba and Ritchie provide a much-needed primer on the demand to defund the police and how that demand can be leveraged toward an even more fundamental transformation of the violence of policing. The authors root their analysis in the reality of today's movements and offer practical, concrete recommendations that activists and organizers can put to work right now."

—**Rachel Herzing**, co-author of *How to Abolish Prisons*

"Kaba and Ritchie are such trusted souls in Black Liberation movements and *No More Police* passionately synthesizes the experiences and expertise necessary for building a new world with less violence on all fronts."

—**Raquel Willis**, author, activist, and board president, Solutions Not Punishment Collaborative

NO MORE POLICE.

Also by Mariame Kaba

See You Soon (illustrated by Bianca Diaz)

We Do This 'Til We Free Us: Abolitionist Organizing and Transforming Justice

Fumbling Towards Repair: A Workbook for Community Accountability (with Shira Hassan)

Missing Daddy (illustrated by bria royal)

Also by Andrea J. Ritchie

Invisible No More: Police Violence Against Black Women and Women of Color

Say Her Name: Resisting Police Brutality Against Black Women (with Kimberlé Crenshaw)

Queer (In)Justice: The Criminalization of LGBT People in the United States (with Joey L. Mogul and Kay Whitlock)

No More Police.

A Case for Abolition

Mariame Kaba and
Andrea J. Ritchie

With a foreword by Kandace
Montgomery and Miski Noor
for Black Visions

THE
NEW
PRESS

NEW YORK
LONDON

© 2022 by Mariame Kaba and Andrea J. Ritchie
Foreword © 2022 Kandace Montgomery and Miski Noor
All rights reserved.
No part of this book may be reproduced, in any form, without written permission from the publisher.

Requests for permission to reproduce selections from this book should be made through our website:
https://thenewpress.com/contact.

Published in the United States by The New Press, New York, 2022
Distributed by Two Rivers Distribution

ISBN 978-1-62097-678-4 (hc)
ISBN 978-1-62097-732-3 (pb)
ISBN 978-1-62097-730-9 (ebook)

CIP data is available

The New Press publishes books that promote and enrich public discussion and understanding of
the issues vital to our democracy and to a more equitable world. These books are made possible by
the enthusiasm of our readers; the support of a committed group of donors, large and small; the
collaboration of our many partners in the independent media and the not-for-profit sector; booksellers,
who often hand-sell New Press books; librarians; and above all by our authors.

www.thenewpress.com

Book design and composition by Bookbright Media
This book was set in Adobe Garamond, Rebrand Dis, and Interval Next

Printed in the United States of America

HC: 10 9 8 7 6 5 4 3 2 1
PB: 10 9 8 7 6 5 4 3 2 1

*To all the dreamers and organizers building new worlds,
in honor of all the people killed, criminalized, and harmed in this one.*

Once upon a time there was a dream. A dream of . . . turning the world all over.

—Pat Parker

Contents

Foreword • *xi*
Introduction • *1*

Cops Don't Stop Violence • 41
We Are Survivors • 71
Re-Form • 107
No Soft Police • 140
How Do We Get There? Toward a Police-Free Future • 177
Tricks and Tensions • 202
Experiment and Build • 240
Black Feminist Musings • 270

Acknowledgments • *287*
Resources • *291*
Notes • *299*
Index • *369*

Foreword

May 25, 2020, is a day we will never forget.

It was actually a nice day in Minneapolis on May 25 (not always guaranteed in the Midwest). Miski went to bed early with a migraine. Kandace sent her partner to the store to get supplies for a socially distanced cookout with their home pod. They almost went to Cup Foods, which sits two blocks from their front steps. At the last minute, Kandace asked them to get in the car instead so they could go to the grocery store and grab a few fresh ingredients. Not a day goes by that Kandace doesn't think about what could have happened if their partner had run that errand to Cup.

At 7:34 p.m. at Cup, a forty-six-year-old security guard who had lost his job during the pandemic showed up for a pack of cigarettes. Within hours, both of us received a flood of texts: Police had killed an unarmed Black man in front of Cup. By noon the following day, we knew his name: George Floyd.

We both navigated the familiar outpouring of love and concern from comrades and friends across the country. "Are you okay?" "I'm so sorry." "Can I support you in any way?" "What do you need?" Questions we never have the answer to but have to figure out quickly. Viral Black death meant the world knew about George's murder before Minneapolis got to process, let alone grieve. We were just coming to grips with the change happening around us. But the call to become a shaper of this change is strong and vital.

We both masked up and joined the massive protests starting at what is now George Floyd Square, marveling at the sheer number of people who braved the uncertainty of the pandemic to come together to march, shoulder to shoulder, in outrage, grief, and a powerful demand for justice.

In the days that followed, we'd be asked over and over: why is this moment different? We remember thinking that nothing and everything was different. The same cycle of emotions but against the backdrop of a pandemic. People no longer had the regularity of their life patterns, their activities, or their habits to distract them from the truth—the truth that capitalism is failing us, and failing us hard, the truth of the weight of the consistent violence and abuse that Black people experience at the hands of the state.

Organizing can never take credit for the energy and will of the community. What it can do is provide a container to understand the moment and build toward collective solutions to address our individual pain.

We got together with other organizers at Black Visions, a power- and base-building organization we, along with five others, co-founded, and allies at Reclaim the Block, another grassroots justice group in Minneapolis. Within twenty-six hours, we released a petition that demanded the defunding of the Minneapolis Police Department (MPD).

One month of organizing, agitating, and uprisings later, the movement in defense of Black lives achieved one of its first abolitionist wins: a veto-proof majority of the Minneapolis City Council supported an amendment to disband the MPD. The Minneapolis City Council is not particularly radical or visionary, and it was only after weeks of intense, Black-led, multiracial organizing that the council was forced to act.

That summer, we saw our righteous outrage at the death of George Floyd ignite a powerful movement that continues to create impact across the globe. With organizers in other cities, we've built a Black-led, multiracial coalition that recognizes how white supremacy harms all of us, particularly Black and Indigenous people of color, but also our Latinx, Asian, and white allies.

As many as 26 million people flooded the streets in the weeks after

George Floyd's murder. Black people organized our communities in the millions to vote out virulent white supremacy from the White House. Black women led the way in Georgia to flip the Senate's balance of power.

But May 25, 2021, the one-year anniversary of George Floyd's murder, was a painful reminder of the collective trauma the people in Minneapolis and across the country experienced in the summer of 2020, and too many summers before. We still have not received healing in the form of transformative justice.

Here in Minneapolis, a commission of unelected bureaucrats blocked the council's recommendation to defund the police. On April 30, 2021, our coalition delivered 21,000 signatures on a people's petition to replace the Minneapolis Police Department with a new Department of Public Safety to the city clerk. On November 2, 2021, over 40 percent of Minneapolis voters supported a ballot amendment that would clear a path for the city to do so by eliminating the requirement in the city charter that it maintain a police department. Yet today, the MPD continues to function using tens of millions of taxpayer dollars, while our calls for investment in true public safety have failed to be adopted.

We demand more. Our communities deserve more. We demand transformation.

We've spent the past two years getting familiar with the legal roadblocks thrown up by bureaucrats afraid of change, and devising methods to thwart them. We know that what we're doing in Minneapolis matters to other defund and abolition efforts, from New York to London to Los Angeles, and we are committed to the continued organizing it will take to make real this collective vision.

The transformative demand to "defund the police" moved abolition to the center of conversations and imaginations across the country and the world in 2020, but its roots run deeper. We would not have been ready that summer had we not been organizing and educating ourselves for years prior, following the brilliance of Ancestors and mentors and the teachings of our own experiences to shape our approach to dismantling systems of oppression.

For us, the journey of political education that led to the demand to defund the police began in 2014, after police in Ferguson, Missouri, killed

Michael Brown. Fifteen months later, the Minneapolis police killed Jamar Clark. After the death of Jamar Clark, who was shot by the MPD sixty-one seconds after they approached him, we were part of the response that established a No Cop Zone and the subsequent eighteen-day occupation of the Fourth Precinct police station.

By getting involved with this current iteration of the Black Freedom Struggle, Miski felt they had found the civil rights movement of our time. And just like civil rights activists of the 1950s and 1960s, we were shot at by white supremacists, who injured five people (while police looked the other way). At this early stage, our demands were not yet abolitionist. Rather than transform the existing system, we still sought to use its structures, calling for federal and state authorities to release the tape of Clark's killing, for a special prosecutor and not a grand jury to select the charges, and for the Department of Justice to investigate.

After the occupation, we began to connect across the Movement for Black Lives and other national movement formations, like Momentum and BOLD, that nurtured and developed our analysis as Black liberation and movement organizers. We have had the opportunity to train with some of the most brilliant and thoughtful Black organizers and leaders—including Denise Perry, Adaku Utah, adrienne maree brown—and read the work of people and groups such as Ruth Wilson Gilmore, Rachel Herzing, Critical Resistance, Project NIA, and Andrea Ritchie and Mariame Kaba, the authors of this book.

As we learned about abolition through a Black, queer, and transfeminist lens built on our own identities, we grew our transformative vision of true abolition. This is about recognizing that policing is a virulent force that must be addressed head-on—and about so much more: healing justice, transformative justice, and transformation toward a better world.

In summer and fall of 2017, holding this vision to push transformative change in Minneapolis, we co-founded Black Visions with Oluchi Omeoga, Sophia Benrud, Hani Ali, Yolanda Hare, and Ar'Tesha Saballos. We aimed to center our work in healing and transformative justice principles, intentionally developing the organization's "core DNA" to ensure sustainability and develop Minnesota's emerging Black leadership. We called for redirecting funding from police to community-led initiatives, such as support for houseless people, queer and transgender youth, and mental health services.

With our allies at Reclaim the Block, our organizing successfully pushed the Minneapolis mayor and city council in 2018 to move $1.1 million away from the police department to programs including a new Office of Violence Prevention that would provide community safety programs without police.

What we did not expect was for the mayor to join with the police the following year to stoke fears about a surge in crime, which was used to justify an $8.3 million increase in the police budget in early 2020. We learned from that pushback. When George Floyd was murdered, our prior organizing helped us move swiftly to make it clear to city government that we would not settle for less than transformative change.

As the uprising in the street continued, we worked with allies to push the city council from every side, sending them research, mobilizing their constituents to contact them, and, on May 29, 2020, giving them a twenty-four-hour deadline to sign our petition to defund. When they all failed to do so, we organized an action to leave art in memory of George Floyd in each of their yards. Members of Black Visions created mock tombstones with pictures of George Floyd, flowers, and the message: Defund. Four council members pledged after that. On June 6, 2020, we led a protest march to the home of Mayor Jacob Frey, a timid, play-it-safe politician. Kandace held a microphone to his face and asked a yes-or-no question: Would he commit to defunding the police? When he answered, "I do not support the full abolition of the police," the crowd booed him down.

Video of the confrontation went viral, and the rest of the council soon pledged to defund. On June 26, 2020, the Minneapolis City Council announced that all twelve of its members had voted to disband the police department.

But the devil remained in the details. The next step was to get the defund amendment on the ballot in fall 2020, so the people of Minneapolis could decide. An unelected body of Minneapolis bureaucrats and their pro-police allies stopped our efforts. The fifteen-member Charter Commission, appointed by the county's chief judge, rejected the proposal.

While proposals they reject can be put directly on the ballot by the city council or a citizen's initiative, the commission delayed its decision until it was too late for the proposal to go on the 2020 ballot.

As the people of Minneapolis and Minnesota called for justice, healing, and care, our city and state officials responded by spending millions of dollars on more police, as if preparing for war with the community—when the community is in the streets demanding justice for our people.

After the Charter Commission roadblocked the 2020 ballot measure to defund MPD, Black Visions and our allies formed the Yes 4 Minneapolis coalition to renew our fight to bring the issue to voters in November 2021. Unlike the city council proposal, the Charter Commission could not refuse to put our proposed measure on the ballot once we secured the necessary signatures. Having learned from the past, we were prepared for the city council and mayor's office to throw up other obstacles, such as utilizing their power to word the ballot measure to suit their agenda and, if the initiative passed, to write ordinances to interpret the law. We were ready, and successfully fought for language that would let the people of our city decide what safety looks like for our communities.

As Ruth Wilson Gilmore says, "Abolition is about presence, not absence. It's about building life-affirming institutions." In designing a plan for a new Department of Public Safety, we've been freedom-dreaming with community partners here in Minneapolis and around the country about what Black liberation will look like practically, in our daily lives.

We spent the eighteen months between the summer of 2020 and the end of 2021 working in the community to expand mental health crisis assistance, to generate resources for healers, elders, clergy, and community leaders to support restorative neighborhood-based practices, and to respond to the needs of our neighbors and loved ones.

We are inspired by all the historic and incredible ways the community has already shown up for one another. George Floyd Square organizers held down a police-free zone for more than a year, where people came together for joy and healing while providing community-led security and demanding justice and accountability from policymakers and institutions. Though the city has used dirty tactics to try and shut it down, organizers still gather and hold space, committing to not leave until our communities see true justice.

Part of our work has involved something we never would have expected: redistributing money. Before May 25, 2020, we were a tiny organization with Black, queer, and trans leadership, just beginning to talk about decision-making processes and membership growth. After May 25, as donations came in, our budget doubled very quickly, and doubled again, and again. In total, Black Visions and Reclaim the Block received $30 million after our call to defund the MPD. Together with Reclaim the Block, we established an Emergency Fund, which distributed $767,000 in immediate aid to meet the needs of the community reeling from George Floyd's murder and the pandemic, such as rent, health-care costs, and school supplies. The two organizations then joined with Nexus Community Partners, an organization that builds the capacity of community-based organizations to promote equitable and sustainable community change, to establish the Transformative Black-led Movement Fund to further redistribute donations. Nexus was able to organize and lead a community advisory to make decisions about grants. Another $1.1 million went to community members, and we awarded $6 million in grants to more than a hundred Twin Cities–based organizations, collectives, artists, and healers led by Black, Indigenous, and people of color. All of them are innovating alternatives to policing and real solutions for safety—from race-based therapy, art therapy, and yoga to providing affordable healthy food to transforming models for schools to organizing community members to take action. All commit to not using any of the money to collaborate with the police.

Now we are thinking about how to seed abolition work for the long term. Every year, just in Minnesota, far more than $30 million is needed for all our movements. We need philanthropy to step up, and we need a transformation of public investment in the people, not the police.

Not all of the solutions are clear right now; we are learning and innovating as we go. We recognize that the people most harmed by current unjust systems devise the most effective solutions. So we led a People's Movement Assembly process in Minneapolis to define safety together as a community, and continue to lead and explore more ways to center community participation in how we govern our city. Our assemblies are inspired by participatory self-governance practices in the U.S. South, in Kurdistan, and by the Zapatistas in Mexico. We've benefited from panels and trainings with Rukia Lumumba, an organizer with the Movement for Black Lives and the Malcolm X Grassroots Movement, who helps organize the Jackson People's Assembly in Jackson, Mississippi; Erica Perry, an organizer of the Black Nashville Assembly; and Mercedes Fulbright, organizing director with the Texas Working Families Party, who organized People's Assemblies in Dallas in 2020. Over the course of the summer of 2021, we moved from small to larger assemblies, in concentric circles of alignment building. The idea, as the Project South People's Movement Assembly Organizing Handbook puts it, is to avoid having "a single leader, organization or predetermined goal" and instead place trust and leadership in the hands of the people who convene to make decisions together.

As we move forward from here, we want to be clear about one thing: abolition is the goal. "Defund the police" is a clear rallying call based on an understanding that police and prisons do not keep us safe. It is an economic policy argument that recognizes the role of capital resources in fueling our oppression. And it is a call to budget and policymakers to invest in the care our communities need to create real safety. While Defund is a clear ask, it is not the destination but a step on the path to abolition. Taking away and reallocating capital resources opens the possibility of imagining what individual and community supports need to be in place to realize true and inclusive public safety. Divestment compels us to rethink the role and responsibility of our local, state, and federal governments in truly financing those supports. And it gives us space to center the leadership of Black people and people of color in determining that future.

This work lives beyond viral hashtags and beyond the moments when mainstream media is paying attention to the fruits of decades of Black-led organizing. In the aftermath of 2020, our communities face heightened threats, from co-optation to retaliatory violence, including militarized suppression of protesters. What we know too well in Minnesota is that these flash-in-the-pan moments are only coming more rapidly, with shorter periods of time to recover from the most recent—the near daily—trauma caused by the state.

If we know these moments are patterns, boomeranging back to us with slightly different characters and conditions, what must we do? We must build our people's resilience through strategy, organization, infrastructure, and care. If what brings you to this question is an authentic desire to win, to transform, to free your people, then the answer lies in the critical need to build beyond and throughout these moments of whirlwind.

What do we need to build our people up for the long-haul fight for liberation? Movements are built by organizations. Many people hear the story of Minneapolis in 2020 but don't know that organizers had been leading campaigns calling to defund the police since 2018. They don't hear that the campaign—which successfully moved $1.1 million from MPD in 2018, and $8 million in 2020—was built on the lessons learned from other campaigns. In our storytelling about how change happens, we need to talk about the work in between hearings, direct actions, and conversations with elected officials. It needs to be common knowledge that we are and must continue to build organizations capable of absorbing new people into our movements, educating them on the interconnectedness of the systems that oppress us, and honing the skills of new leaders.

People need organizations. Organizations need people. We must build political homes, places where our communities can practice self-governance and ways of being with each other that bring into the now what we envision for our society in the future. Organizations are our testing grounds, building our collective capacity to live more liberated lives. At the same time, people are the bones, blood, and meat of organizations. You cannot have one without the other—not authentically, at least. Too often, we learn in public, out loud, the ways we need to tend to the people who make up our formations for justice. As we fortify our struggle for the next transformative moment, we also need to create spaces and practices that center care and tend to the humans who fill up our streets or Zoom rooms. As the nonprofit industrial complex drives too many of us and our organizations away from practicing holistic sustainability and our own decolonization, we call on all of us to step deeper, right now, into a practice of holding these types of relationships amongst ourselves, of modeling the world we seek to build.

Reflection is a critical piece of the work. Space for reflection, especially collective reflection, can be rare in movement work. But in the midst of such violence, grief, hope, anxiety, progress, and regression, we must create and demand spaciousness to ask each other, what just happened? What was that like for you? Why did this happen? What are we doing together, and is it working? What does it mean for me to really show up for you, for us? Processing and learning in community is a necessary practice toward fortifying us for the work of building and imagining together. Abolition is a daily practice that is both individual and collective and that grows from holding space for our victories, our defeats, our sorrows, our joys.

We are in this work because our lives depend on it. We're building a world in which ALL Black lives matter, with a focus on the most marginalized people in our communities: people who are queer, trans, Indigenous, disabled, immigrant, and poor. Until we are able to live without fear, we'll keep pushing our bold vision.

Ultimately, our work is about building and centering Black power and leadership to move us toward Black liberation. We've each been organizers for years, and we know it's the day-to-day work that determines whether we succeed—the work that happens after the cameras have left, the fundraising dries up, and the attention fades. We invite communities across Minnesota and the nation to join us: get activated in our shared struggle for Black liberation, dignity, and equity for all.

We understand that abolition is the long game. We're in it for as long as it takes.

—Miski Noor and Kandace Montgomery, Black Visions,
February 2022[1]

NO MORE POLICE.

Introduction

When was the moment you first started to question the violence of policing?

Was it the brutal videotaped 1991 beating of Rodney King? The 1984 shooting of sixty-seven-year-old disabled grandmother Eleanor Bumpurs by New York housing police? The twenty-three shots Los Angeles police fired into Tyisha Miller in 1998 as she sat in her car in the throes of a seizure? Was it the forty-one bullets that felled twenty-three-year-old Guinean immigrant Amadou Diallo in the hallway of his Bronx apartment building in 1999? The killing of LaTanya Haggerty by Chicago police the same year? Or was it watching Oscar Grant be executed on an Oakland BART platform in 2010?

Every generation has their flashpoints—moments when the violence of policing overwhelms, when the stories we are told about cops and safety don't add up. For many in this generation, the catalyst was the sight of Michael Brown's body lying in the street for four hours after being shot by Ferguson, Missouri, police officer Darren Wilson, or the photo of Brown's father holding a cardboard sign saying "FERGUSON POLICE JUST EXECUTED MY UNARMED SON!!!,"[1] reminding the world that Brown had kin, he was loved, and his Black life mattered. Just weeks before Brown's death, a video came to light of Eric Garner saying "I can't breathe" eleven times as NYPD officer Daniel Pantaleo squeezed the life out of him using a banned chokehold. Stories of police violence continued to flood the headlines. In December 2014, the #SayHerName hashtag created by the African American Policy Forum began to increase visibility of the numerous stories of Black women, girls, and trans people killed and violated by police.[2] In April 2015, less than a year after Garner and Brown were killed, came the news that Freddie Gray's back was broken by Baltimore police who intentionally slammed his body around a police van during what they euphemistically termed a "rough ride," following an arrest prompted solely by the fact that Gray was trying to avoid an interaction with the cops who would go on to kill him. Just three months later, in July 2015, Sandra Bland died in a Waller County, Texas, jail cell after a violent traffic stop for not using her turn signal as she attempted to get out of the way of the cop car following her.

Many of us can point to the exact moment we realized there is something profoundly wrong with equating policing with public safety. For many people and communities targeted by police, it came with our own brutalization, sexual assault, criminalization, or humiliation by a cop, or when we were forced to witness a loved one killed, assaulted, or arrested by police, or when parents, family, and friends desperate to ensure our survival taught us that police represent danger, not safety. Or when we called for help and none came; or, worse yet, when the cops did come, they came for us. Or when we were confronted with the reality that police don't stop the shootings, domestic violence, sexual assault, or homophobic and transphobic violence that pervade our homes, neighborhoods, workplaces, and schools, and instead often simply add their own violence to the mix.

Research confirms that police are up to four times more likely to shoot Black people than white people, even when both groups are engaged in the same levels of criminalized activity, even when they are unarmed.[3] In the absence of reliable official statistics on how many people are killed by police,[4] the *Washington Post*, *The Guardian*, and volunteers at groups like FatalEncounters.org work to keep count, documenting over one thousand police-related deaths every year. According to the *Post*, police set a new record in 2021 for the total number of people they killed.[5] This gruesome accounting is complicated by misreporting. In fact, a study published in

The Lancet, a peer-reviewed medical journal, found that more than half of the estimated 38,000 deaths due to police between 1980 and 2018 were not reported as such.[6]

The violence of policing extends beyond killings to multiple forms of violence—including those we are told we need cops to protect us from. For instance, research by the *Buffalo News* found that a cop is caught engaging in acts of sexual "misconduct" every five days on average—a figure that represents only the tip of the iceberg on the systemic scale of police sexual violence.[7]

For decades, we have witnessed countless investigations, reports, and media exposés highlighting the breadth of harms caused by policing and mass criminalization, incarceration, detention, and deportation. The evidence that policing produces widespread violence and harm daily is overwhelming, repeatedly raising the question: what can we do to stop it?

A New Reckoning

The summer of 2020 brought a new moment of collective national reckoning with the violence of policing. It was prompted in large part by another suffocation of a Black man by a white cop (#GeorgeFloyd), the killing of a Black woman by police who invaded her home as she slept (#BreonnaTaylor), the shooting of a troubled Black trans man outside his apartment complex (#TonyMcDade), and the murder of a Black man jogging in a white neighborhood by three white men, one a former cop (#AhmaudArbery). These were, of course, not isolated incidents. In fact, more than three people a day have been killed by police on average since these cases made headlines.[8]

This national reckoning was also prompted by the fact that these spectacular acts of state violence against Black people took place against the backdrop of a devastating pandemic that claimed 100,000 lives in the U.S. in six short months (the death toll at the time this book went to print was over 1 million in the U.S., 6 million globally, and counting),[9] an economic crisis of unprecedented proportions, and a growing number of ecological crises caused by climate change—all disproportionately devastating Black communities.[10]

COVID-19 laid bare the deadly impacts of racist structural inequality and our collective failure to invest in an infrastructure of care: COVID-19 mortality rates for Black, Latinx, and Indigenous people in the U.S. were as much as double those of whites.[11] It also pushed individuals, families, and communities already living under precarious conditions to the edge of survival. During the pandemic, the scope of policing expanded through enforcement of public health orders, which also disproportionately targeted and impacted Black people.[12] Meanwhile, facing drastic revenue shortfalls, politicians slashed public programs and services desperately needed for survival while maintaining or increasing police budgets. By June 2020, 18 million people were unemployed and one in every five families was food insecure. Yet all the federal government offered people to meet these overlapping crises in that moment was a single $1,200 stimulus payment, while federal lawmakers made it a priority to fund over three thousand more cops.[13]

Against this backdrop, the world watched as George Floyd was choked to death by a white Minneapolis cop. For almost nine minutes, Derek Chauvin knelt on his neck while Floyd repeated that he couldn't breathe and called for his mother. Chauvin stared impassively into a cell phone camera held by eyewitness Darnella Frazier, a young Black woman, joined by others watching in horror. Frazier's footage, and the body cam video subsequently released at the behest of media outlets, set off a conflagration in the streets of the midwestern city.

Organizers had been up in arms in Minneapolis almost without pause since the killings of Michael Brown in Ferguson and Tamir Rice in Cleveland in 2014, and again after one of their own, Jamar Clark, was killed by the Minneapolis Police Department (MPD) in 2015. A year later, they flooded the streets again after Philando Castile was shot by a cop during a routine traffic stop filmed by his distraught girlfriend, Diamond Reynolds, as her four-year-old daughter watched from the back seat.

Floyd's murder blew the smoldering embers of community outrage at relentless police violence into a raging fire not unlike the one that consumed the city's Third Precinct. It also served as the match that lit the fuse of what has been called "perhaps the largest protest movement in United States history," bringing an estimated 15 to 26 million people into the streets in the weeks that followed, including half a million in 550 places on a single day.[14] But this massive movement didn't materialize overnight. At the time of Floyd's murder, Minneapolis organizers had already been locked in a battle with city lawmakers around the size of the police department's budget. They had won a substantial victory in 2018, diverting almost $2 million from the proposed police budget to an office of violence prevention,[15] only to see the police budget increase again the following year. In 2017, MPD150—a community initiative spearheaded by local organizers, researchers, artists, and activists to shift the discussion around police and policing in Minneapolis—completed and published an extensive, community-driven evaluation of 150 years of the MPD. A century and a half of evidence revealed that police violence against Black, Indigenous, youth, unhoused, migrant, and low-income communities remained intractable despite countless reforms. Their report, *Enough Is Enough*, concluded that the MPD should be abolished.[16]

Given the research and organizing community members were already engaged in, it was no surprise that, in the days after Floyd's murder the demands echoing in the streets focused on slashing the police department budget and reinvesting that money in meeting the needs of communities reeling from the pandemic. The call to action was shaped by Black Visions,[17] an "unapologetically Black organization with a Black queer feminist lens" and deep ties to queer, immigrant, and transgender communities, that grew out of protests following the killing of Jamar Clark, and its allies at Reclaim the Block,[18] populated by organizers who were part of the MPD150 crew and other abolitionist organizations. Both groups had been deeply engaged in protests, community outreach, political education, and budget advocacy around policing and public safety for several years. The summer of 2020 simply brought unprecedented attention to movements that had long been in motion. The long, hard work of local organizers was bearing fruit.

Within days of Floyd's murder, the University of Minnesota ended its contractual relationship with the MPD to provide law enforcement support. The Minneapolis School Board followed suit, voting to remove the MPD from public schools,[19] boosting decades-long campaigns for #Police-FreeSchools across the country.[20] A day after the school board's decision, the city's parks department officially cut ties with the MPD, which had provided security for park events. The parks department also barred park police from responding to MPD calls.[21]

At a rally held two weeks after Floyd's murder, Black Visions leader Kandace Montgomery addressed the crowd: "Minneapolis, we're here because now is the time to dismantle MPD. Black people, and queer people, and trans people, and Indigenous people, and disabled people, and immigrants, and poor people: We have never looked to the police for our safety. We have looked to each other for protection from the police. It shouldn't have taken this much death to get us here."[22] Montgomery was joined on stage by Andrea Jenkins, a Black trans woman elected to the Minneapolis City Council in 2018 who had long been on the frontlines of struggles for safety for Black trans women and their communities. A supermajority of Minneapolis city council members stood behind a banner citing the failure of decades of reform and committing to beginning the process of ending the MPD through budget and policy changes while consulting with communities to develop a new, transformative model for cultivating safety.[23] The council president, Lisa Bender, declared, "Our commitment is to end our city's toxic relationship with the Minneapolis Police Department, to end policing as we know it, and to recreate systems of public safety that actually keep us safe."[24]

Montgomery responded by saying: "We just made history, y'all. This is just the beginning. The world is watching us, Minneapolis."[25]

Pushed by the power of the streets and overwhelming public opinion in favor of systemic change, Minneapolis council members moved to amend the city's charter, which requires the city to maintain and resource a police department with a specific number of cops tied to the city's population size. The requirement had been added in 1961 after an intensive lobbying campaign by the local police fraternal association to lock a minimum police budget into the city charter.[26] The initial effort to remove it and create a Department of Community Safety and Violence Prevention was stymied by a little-known, predominantly white unelected board charged with oversight of the city's charter. Eight months later, in April 2021, organizers bypassed the Charter Commission, delivering a petition with 21,000 signatures to the city clerk calling for a public vote on the elimination of the mandate to maintain a police department and the creation of a new department of public safety on the November ballot.[27] Pro-police forces immediately mounted aggressive legal challenges to the ballot initiative while fueling fear, trading on loyalty to a Black police chief, and sowing misinformation about the broad-based grassroots "Yes 4 Minneapolis" coalition championing the amendment.

Meanwhile, Black Visions and Reclaim the Block engaged community members in citywide conversations about what would produce greater safety for all Minneapolis residents. They coordinated a coalition of over twenty partner organizations that hosted People's Movement Assemblies, culminating in a citywide assembly in the fall of 2021. Yes 4 Minneapolis organizers went door to door throughout the summer and fall, talking with residents about safety and the future of their communities. In November 2021, 62,000 people, making up almost 44 percent of voters,[28] voted to uncuff the city's budget from the cops and create a new department of public safety that would adopt a public health approach. These numbers are even more significant in light of the degree of disinformation spread, the number of lawsuits filed, and the millions of dollars spent by opponents to defeat the ballot measure, and of Mayor Jacob Frey's effort to take the wind out of the Yes 4 Minneapolis campaign by agreeing to create a new Department of Public Safety without eliminating the mandate to maintain a police department. The vote made history, marking the first time almost half a city electorate voted against the notion that police represent the only path to public safety.

As the struggle for the elimination of the MPD unfolded in 2020, protesters across the U.S. and Canada took up the abolitionist demands emanating from Minneapolis: cut the police budget, commit to no future increases, "protect and expand current investment in community-led health and safety strategies, instead of investing in police," and stop police violence—in many cases cutting and pasting the demands into petitions to their own city legislators. Calls to reduce police budgets, police presence, and police contact grew louder, replacing the usual calls for reforms, personnel changes, and prosecutions. As pandemic-related shutdowns wore on, municipal budget hearings moved online, making them more accessible. Thousands of people called and wrote in with an overwhelming and simple message: stop funding the people and institutions that kill us; start funding the things we need to survive.[29]

In the days, weeks, and months that followed, the message spread like wildfire across the continent and echoed through the streets and the virtual halls of power: Defund the Police.

The Demand Is Defund the Police

While the call to defund the police struck some as radical and new, this was hardly the first time that communities had made this demand. In 2015, Black-led Oakland-based grassroots group the Anti Police-Terror Project, founded in the wake of the murder of Oscar Grant by Bay Area Rapid Transit (BART) police,[30] launched its Defund OPD (Oakland Police Department) campaign[31] following the disclosure of sexual violence and extortion by OPD cops. The same year, organizers in Chicago began calling attention to the fact that the police department consumes 40 percent of the city's budget. A Black youth-led campaign emerged to stop the construction of a $95 million police training facility under the banner, "#NoCopAcademy—give that money to community!"[32] Seattle organizers fought a similar battle to stop the construction of a $150 million police facility through the #BlocktheBunker campaign in 2016.[33] In 2017, BYP100, an organization of Black youth, formed following Trayvon Martin's 2011 murder; Law for Black Lives, a legal support group, formed to support the Movement for Black Lives following the Ferguson Uprising; and the Center for Popular Democracy released *Freedom to Thrive: Reimagining Safety and Security in Our Communities*.[34] The comprehensively researched report demanded an end to the $100 billion—now close to $130 billion by some estimates[35]—spent on policing every year, naming local police budgets as targets, and highlighting campaigns to reduce their size and increase investments in community safety in Atlanta, Baltimore, Chicago, Contra Costa County, Detroit, Houston, Los Angeles, Minneapolis, New York City, Oakland, and Orlando.[36]

While calls to defund are not new, 2020 *was* the first time that local demands to cut police budgets morphed into a national call to action and became a mainstream topic of conversation. Organizers across the country harnessed the power of the streets to push policymakers to cut over $850 million from dozens of police department budgets, end public school contracts with over twenty-five police departments, and invest over $160 million into community safety initiatives.[37] Perhaps more importantly, they engaged hundreds of thousands of community members in conversations about anti-Black violence, policing, public safety, and participatory budgeting to meet community needs.

The power of the demand, and the abolitionist visions behind it, prompted first an effort to dilute it, and then a rapid and forceful counterreaction. Throughout the summer of 2020, policymakers and pundits sought to seem like they were onboard with the call from the streets, while simultaneously undermining it. Sure, police budgets might need some trimming, maybe cops shouldn't be doing everything they are asking, but surely protesters don't really mean get rid of the police entirely, they claimed. In response, Mariame published a widely read *New York Times* op-ed entitled "Yes, We Mean Literally Abolish the Police," which served as the catalyst for this book.[38] At the same time, Andrea, who was hosting weekly calls with defund organizers, gathered collective demands and strategies from across North America into a toolkit we co-authored with Woods Ervin and released in June 2020 entitled *Defund Police, Fund the People, Defend Black Lives*, and updated it in January 2021.[39] She also coordinated the development of defundpolice.org and supported defund fellows in over a dozen cities across the country through the Community Resource Hub.

Our ongoing engagement in movements to defund and abolish police—and this book—are rooted in our own experiences and reckonings over the past three decades—as survivors of both police and interpersonal violence, as anti-violence advocates, as scholars, as organizers in movements for Black liberation, against state and gender-based violence, for transformative justice, and as Black feminists. While the lure of "reimagining" and "reforming" policing is powerful—both of us have fallen prey to it at various points—history, experience, and research all point to the reality that policing is not "broken," it is operating exactly as it was intended: dealing out daily violence to contain, control, and criminalize. We understand calls to defund the police as an essential first step toward a larger vision of reimagining and building a world where everyone has access to greater safety.

The power of this vision—and the degree to which it threatens existing structures of power that rely on policing—is evident in the response to it. As soon as Democrats won the 2020 presidential elections, they trotted out everyone from former president Barack Obama to Mark Warner, a moderate Democratic senator from Virginia, in an effort to discredit the demand—calling it dangerous, unreasonable, and irresponsible.[40] Democratic Whip James Clyburn traveled the country blaming defund demands for Democratic losses in local races,[41] despite the fact that none of the candidates who lost their seats supported them, while many who *did* won reelection. In fact, a contemporary analysis indicated that many more cities that cut police budgets saw increased support for Democratic candidates than the other way around.[42] Nevertheless, mainstream Democrats continue to promote the narrative that any effort to decrease police budgets or power will sound a death knell for the party in future elections.[43] True to his long history of pro-police policymaking, President Biden condemned defund demands in his 2022 State of the Union Address, saying "The answer is not to defund the police. It's to fund the police. Fund them. Fund them. Fund them with resources and training."[44]

Beyond the Democratic Party, critics continue to scold defund organizers for what they claim is an inept—or dangerous—wording of movement demands. In fact, what they actually oppose is the demand's central premise: divesting from policing and investing in nonpolice approaches to safety.[45] They urge us to "reimagine" policing instead of challenging our current approaches to public safety, ridiculing the notion of defunding and ultimately abolishing the police as both impractical and dangerous, some sort of ill-advised new fad. They purposely overlook the fact that defund campaigns call for large-scale investments in programs and infrastructure needed to produce genuine and lasting safety for all. They willfully ignore the fact that defund demands emerged from communities deeply impacted by multiple forms of violence, and from deep study and critical analysis of the long history of policing.

The notion of divesting from police and investing in community-based safety strategies did not, as its detractors claim, emerge from privileged white "liberals" and "gentrifiers" who don't experience the daily violence Black, Indigenous, and migrant communities face. To the contrary—it came from communities who have the greatest stakes in eliminating all forms of violence, who are both targeted for state violence and abandoned to conditions that produce greater violence in communities. Defund demands emerged from Black, queer, trans, disabled, and migrant communities who experience the highest rates of every form of violence, including police violence. Support for divestment from policing and investment in community safety continues to be almost twice as high among Black people as whites;[46] a 2021 Data for Progress poll showed majority support in Black communities for defund demands.[47] Even poll results cited as evidence of decreasing support for defund demands show that a majority of Black people surveyed supported reallocation of police funds to community safety initiatives.[48]

Nor do defund demands fail to take into account the experiences of survivors of violence as opponents claim. To the contrary, movements to defund police are *led* by survivors who want more safety for themselves and their communities, and are constantly thinking about what structures, resources, and tools are necessary to produce it. They are a manifestation of Black feminist politics focused on ending *all* forms of violence experienced by Black women—and all other people—living at what the Combahee River Collective Statement describes as interlocking systems of oppression that increase vulnerability to violence, deprivation, *and* criminalization.[49] Defund demands are rooted in Black feminist theory and practice, focused on collective survival, safety, and care. They are deeply informed by Black radical traditions and anti-capitalist movements,[50] and deeply rooted in anti-colonial struggles,[51] disability justice,[52] and queer and trans liberation dreams.[53] Given the role of the U.S. military as global police, defund demands are deeply connected to global struggles against settler colonialism, militarism, and imperialism, and for migrant justice.[54]

Nor is the idea of defunding the police "a radical new concept, idealistic, naïve, or undertheorized."[55] The question of how to achieve greater safety has been debated and discussed by social scientists, historians, philosophers, organizers, and community members for generations. The role of policing has been central to these debates.

There is also, of course, a long tradition of pro-policing forces perpetuating the false narrative that policing is essential to public safety—and
that spin machine revved up in full force in the face of the 2020 Uprising.
Facing the greatest challenge to its legitimacy in a generation, the police
state roared back with a vengeance, claiming that defund campaigns were
responsible for spikes in violence—even though the increase in homicides
cited by politicians and pundits took place before any funding was cut
from police departments. And while, as outlined in greater detail in the
"Cops Don't Stop Violence" chapter, homicides did increase in 2020,
experts point to pandemic stress, economic crisis, governmental abandonment, environmental catastrophes, social dislocation, and increased availability of guns as likely causes, not relatively miniscule cuts to the more
than $100 billion the U.S. spends annually on policing. Importantly, most
other forms of violence *decreased* in 2020—a fact that was *not* trumpeted
in the headlines. Nevertheless, police and politicians, with the media serving as a willing accomplice, continue to exaggerate and manipulate crime
data and statistics to serve police interests while refusing to address the
root causes of violence. Instead, states began to pass legislation that would
punish any city that sought to decrease its police budget, while federal legislators across party lines enthusiastically endorsed a resolution condemn-
ing efforts to reinvest police funding elsewhere.[56] President Biden urged
local policymakers to divert hundreds of millions of dollars in federal aid
intended for pandemic relief to police, and poured urgently needed federal
dollars into police programs.[57] In many places, police budgets cut in 2020
were restored and increased in 2021, sometimes using American Rescue
Plan Act (ARPA) funds desperately needed to mitigate the devastating
impacts of a pandemic entering its third year.[58]

Meanwhile, across the country, increasingly coordinated organizers
continued to fight and limit police budget increases, take away police
powers, and increase investments in nonpolice, community-based safety
strategies such as mental health crisis response; long-term, safe, quality,
accessible, and affordable housing; guaranteed income programs; violence
interruption and youth programs.[59] From New York City[60] to Philadelphia, Raleigh-Durham[61] to Miami, Louisville[62] to Nashville,[63] Dallas to
Salt Lake City,[64] Seattle[65] to Los Angeles,[66] groups mobilized communi-

ties to attend budget hearings, generate thousands of emails to city council members, and continue to make bold proposals to reallocate millions of dollars from police to community needs. They fought to keep ARPA funds out of cop coffers and in community hands.[67] Public safety task forces in Durham, Austin, and Oakland, among others, offered wide-ranging recommendations that would pave the way to building robust infrastructures of community safety.[68] Organizers invited more people to really wrestle with what safety looks like and requires, rather than just continuing to default to policing. They demystified bureaucratic budgeting processes, opening the door to greater public participation and fueling debates about allocation of collective resources, forcing police and policymakers to justify proposed increases to police budgets instead of demanding and receiving blank checks without significant public scrutiny.[69] In the face of growing backlash and increasing attacks, defund organizers continue to fight for a world where George Floyd, Breonna Taylor, and hundreds of others killed by police would still be here.

Of course, dismantling systems of policing and punishment is the work of generations, not of a budget season or two. Still, the organizing inspired by the 2020 Uprisings catapulted us into a continuing national conversation. Despite claims that the movement to divest from policing is dead,[70] #DefundthePolice remains a powerful call to a safer future for all.

The Demand to Defund Is the Floor, Not the Ceiling

Of course, the demand to defund police is not just about cuts to police budgets. It is also about limiting police contact, functions, weapons, legitimacy, and power—and uprooting surveillance, policing, punishment, and criminalization from every aspect of our lives.[71] As abolitionist scholars Dan Berger and David Stein put it, "The call to defund is best understood as an effort to revoke the political and economic power of the police—and of the larger criminal legal system it upholds."[72] Defund campaigns "approach local and national budgets with necessary urgency as a venue in which the status quo can either be reinforced or remade. . . ."[73] They are about freeing up the billions we currently spend every year on policing—

and much, much more.[74] The ultimate goal is to reorganize our society to meet material needs and to build and resource community-based safety strategies and infrastructure. While some groups are responding to the backlash against defund demands by shifting their focus away from cuts to police budgets to securing greater investments in meeting community needs, both are required. Police do harm every single day, including by looting resources from and sabotaging community safety programs to preserve their legitimacy. To successfully increase safety, we need to limit their power and resources to do harm.

Defunding police means investing the billions currently poured into policing and the prison industrial complex into community-based safety strategies: meeting basic needs that include housing, health care, access to care for disabled people, childcare, elder care, a basic guaranteed income, and accessible, sustainable living-wage jobs that enable people to prevent, escape, intervene in, and transform the conditions that make violence possible. It is a process of creating, building, and resourcing tools, skills, relationships, and institutions that will create genuine and lasting safety for all.

Defunding police is neither the beginning nor the end of the story. It is simply a step toward a longer-term abolitionist horizon of dismantling police departments and abolishing policing, the prison industrial complex (PIC) that requires it, the economic system that produced it, and the social order it fabricates, while rebuilding a society organized around meeting our individual and collective needs, as well as the needs of the planet. The demand to defund is just the basement floor, abolition is the sky we are reaching for.

Rooted in the Black radical tradition and the lived experiences of criminalized people and communities, PIC abolition is a structural analysis of oppression, a political vision of a restructured society, a "theory of social life,"[75] or how we relate to one another, and a practical organizing strategy. Simply put, PIC abolitionists want to end the whole system of mutually reinforcing relationships between surveillance, policing, the courts, and imprisonment that fuel, maintain, and expand social and economic oppression, structural racism, patriarchy, ableism, and imperialism. It's not just about prisons or even police, but the entire world they reflect and produce. It is based on an understanding that the PIC is a central feature and prerequisite to establishing and maintaining a system of racial capitalism. As Black trans abolitionist scholar Che Gossett describes, abolition ultimately "demands and envisions social emancipation, and the end of all forms of social exile, banishment, criminalization, or incarceration. Abolition remains an ongoing project against the general institutionalization of the afterlife of slavery . . . from the site of the prison to the site of the psych ward, from the neoliberal corporation of the university to the detention center and more." And, as Black feminist scholar and defund organizer Robyn Maynard, author of *Policing Black Lives*, reminds us, "The abolition of police can also be understood as a decolonial practice, as part of a broader strategy of land restitution and liberation for Indigenous communities."[76]

Abolition challenges the very existence of a society that spends hundreds of billions every year to police and punish, cage and criminalize people and communities while investing a tiny fraction of that amount in supporting them. Critical Resistance reminds us that:

> Abolition isn't just about getting rid of buildings full of cages. It's also about undoing the society we live in because the PIC both feeds on and maintains oppression and inequalities through punishment, violence, and controls millions of people. Because the PIC is not an isolated system, abolition is a broad strategy. An abolitionist vision means that we must build models today that can represent how we want to live in the future. It means developing practical strategies for taking small steps that move us toward making our dreams real and that lead us all to believe that things really could be different. It means living this vision in our daily lives.
>
> Abolition is both a practical organizing tool and a long-term goal.[77]

As conceptualized by sociologist Thomas Mathiesen, abolition can be described as an "alternative in the making."[78] It pushes us to break with the current order, to say, "Not this," while simultaneously forging new ground and building a different world. PIC abolition is a vision of a restructured society where we have everything we need to be safe, to not only survive but thrive: food, shelter, education, health, art, beauty, clean water, and more. As trans abolitionist scholar Eric Stanley writes: "Abolition is not simply a reaction to the [PIC] but a political commitment that makes the PIC impossible."[79] This means that our work is to create a world where prisons, policing, and surveillance are no longer normalized facets of our society.

Abolitionists are interested in doing away with the system rather than finding ways to make it work better, or to make it "kinder and gentler." We don't see the PIC as "broken"—we see it working very, very well—at surveilling, policing, imprisoning, and killing exactly the people and communities it targets, in service of the power structures that produce and require it. Based on this analysis, we work to diminish the scope and power of the PIC, while simultaneously increasing the ability of communities targeted by it to be safer, stronger, healthier, and more self-determined.

Practically speaking, abolition necessarily means that our social and economic relationships must be transformed. As abolitionist scholar Ruth Wilson Gilmore describes, "Abolition is a movement to end systemic violence, including the interpersonal vulnerabilities and displacements that keep the system going. In other words, the goal is to change how we interact with each other and the planet by putting people before profits, welfare before warfare, and life over death."[80] She also reminds us "that abolition isn't just absence; as W.E.B. Du Bois showed in *Black Reconstruction in America*, abolition is a fleshly and material presence of social life lived differently."[81]

There are countless experiments and projects across the country and the world practicing these new social relations now.[82] As scholar Mia Karisa puts it in a discussion of Gilmore's work, "Abolition . . . isn't a process that will one day reach success but hasn't yet. Instead it's something that's in constant process—and that is successful now. Abolition is working. Abolition has been working. It's just up against a monster. So, I mean, we can't see liberation everywhere, but we do see its fruits in many places, alive and well."[83]

There is no fixed roadmap to abolition; instead, we must spend time imagining, strategizing, and practicing other futures. There is, however, a clear case for why policing can play no role in that future—that is the case we make in *No More Police*.

Our Case for Police Abolition

Our argument for police abolition has three central elements: First, and foremost, police don't promote safety, they prevent it. We are abolitionists because we want more safety, not less—as abolitionist lawyer Erin Miles Cloud says, "everybody wants safety for someone, somewhere. Abolitionists want safety for everyone, everywhere."[84] We call for abolition of police because, despite all of the power, resources, and legitimacy we pour into them, they cannot and will not deliver safety. The vast majority of what police do has nothing to do with preventing or interrupting violence or harm, and a majority of people who experience violence neither seek nor receive protection from police.

Instead, police contribute to violence by capturing the resources communities need to survive and thrive, and by perpetrating violence daily, including the kinds of violence most often used to justify their existence. Far from distant history, the roots of policing in colonial militias, "Indian constables," slave patrols, and municipal police departments created to police gender, sexuality, poverty, and migration, quash labor organizing, and quell dissent continue to shape their present-day practices.[85] Cops kill over a thousand people a year,[86] and rape, beat, maim, Tase, assault, harm, harass, and criminalize hundreds of thousands more—all disproportionately Black, Indigenous, disabled, migrant, trans, queer. Police make over 10 million arrests a year,[87] each with profound effects—perpetrating rather than preventing violence, and forever changing the course of the lives of the people who are criminalized and the people cops fail to protect. Police in the U.S. consume over $100 billion a year, contributing to economic violence and widespread deprivation in one of the richest nations on Earth. These harsh facts illuminate the reality that the role of police is not to create safety, but to establish and maintain a violent social order rooted in white supremacy, patriarchy, wealth accumulation, and the protection of private property over public good.[88]

The second element of our case is that the violence of policing cannot be reformed—because violence is inherent to the institution itself. Over a century of investigations, commissions, recommendations, oversight, and policy change has failed for this reason. As elaborated in the "Cops Don't Stop Violence" and "Re-Form" chapters and throughout *No More Police*, police are violence workers: policing, at its core, is about securing compliance through force, threat of force, or deprivation. Laws, rules, and policies offer the illusion of a check on police power while enshrining police discretion to act as they deem necessary to maintain the existing order. We cannot eliminate violence or create genuine and lasting safety for everyone so long as policing—and the institutions and power relations that require it—continues to exist.

We also cannot create safety by replacing police with policing and criminalization in different forms. As explored in the "No Soft Police" chapter, police exist in virtually every public space and institution—medical professionals, social workers, and even community organizations are engaged in the project of policing. The goal is not to find Someone Else, if not police, to put people Somewhere Else, if not jails, prisons, and detention centers. The goal is elimination of the violence inherent in all forms of policing and incarceration, including those enacted by other institutions of the police state—and the violence they fail to prevent—and to create conditions under which needs are met, harm is prevented, and, when it occurs, addressed transformatively.

The third and final element of our case is that we can create safety beyond policing. As explored throughout *No More Police*, a growing number of people and communities are already reimagining safety, experimenting and building on existing skills, relationships, and infrastructure to create it through mutual aid, violence prevention and intervention, transformative justice projects and practices. Yet, by consuming a majority of our collective resources and colonizing our imaginations with the narrative that policing is the only path to safety, police stand in the way of these efforts to create greater safety. Ultimately, we don't need to have all the answers before we move forward. We know enough to know that what exists now is not working, and to shape our visions of a society that doesn't require policing and punishment, and instead is organized around cultures of care, mutual responsibility, and accountability. And we know enough to take the first steps forward, and to collectively generate the answers to the questions that arise along the way.

We make this case for police abolition as Black feminists whose paths have crossed and joined many times over the years. We are both survivors of state and interpersonal violence. We were both shaped by the radical Black liberation movements of the 1960s and 1970s, deeply engaged in anti-apartheid movements in the 1980s, and a part of what was then called woman of color organizing in the 1990s. Mariame was born in the U.S. and studied in Canada; Andrea was born in Canada and studied in the U.S. We are both children of migrants, giving us perspectives beyond the borders of the U.S. or North America.

Our paths converged in 2002 at Color of Violence II, a conference organized by INCITE!, a group of radical feminists of color dedicated to ending violence in all its forms.[89] The organization would serve as a political home for both of us for close to two decades, with Andrea serving on the INCITE! national leadership collective from 2003 to 2008, where she was part of the editorial team for the *Color of Violence* anthology and coordinated the organization's work on police violence, culminating in the release of a toolkit for organizers on *Law Enforcement Violence Against Women of Color and Transgender People of Color* in 2008. Mariame was formerly a member of the Chicago INCITE! chapter and a member at large. Mariame also brought members of the Rogers Park Young Women's Action Team to the Color of Violence III conference, which Andrea co-organized. We met again at the 2006 National Coalition Against Domestic Violence conference, where Andrea spoke on a plenary, making the case that criminalization is not only failing to prevent or interrupt gender-based violence, but is perpetrating and facilitating it.[90] During Andrea's subsequent workshop on police violence against survivors, Mariame jumped in from the front row as a welcome impromptu co-facilitator to address the increasingly forceful pushback coming from anti-violence advocates committed to collaboration with the cops, even at the expense of criminalized survivors. We both served, at different times, on the board of the Young Women's Empowerment Project, supporting the leadership of young women, girls, and trans youth in the sex trades in

Chicago as they engaged in mutual aid, research, and shaping local and national narratives about their lives, resistance, and resilience. Of course, there is much more to each of our stories than where they intersect. *No More Police* emerges both from the places our paths have crossed and where they've diverged.

Separately and together, we have been on the front lines of struggles against police and gender-based violence for over three decades. Andrea's work has primarily focused on documenting and organizing around how the violence of policing manifests through the lens of Black women, queer, and trans people's experiences, making the case for abolition by offering a more complete picture of the problem. Mariame's organizing and advocacy has focused primarily on making a case for abolition by demonstrating the way forward through transformative justice visions and practice. It is thanks in large part to Mariame's work, zines, exhibits, research, and organizing through groups such as the Chicago Alliance to Free Marissa Alexander (which later became the organization Love and Protect), Chicago Task Force on Violence Against Girls and Young Women, Survived and Punished, and the *No Selves to Defend* exhibition that more people know about the criminalization of survivors like Celia, an enslaved woman who killed the man who enslaved her; Tiawanda Moore; Marissa Alexander; Bresha Meadows; and so many more. Andrea's research, writing, organizing, litigation, and advocacy around policing of Black women, girls, queer, and trans people, summarized in *Invisible No More: Police Violence Against Black Women and Women of Color*, has made a significant contribution to laying the groundwork for increased visibility and action around their experiences in movement, policy, and legislative contexts.

We have collaborated in a number of ways over the years, including on a Chicago vigil for Sandra Bland on the one-year anniversary of her death, and on the exhibit *Blood at the Root: Unearthing Stories of State Violence Against Black Women*.[91] We co-presented a workshop on police violence against Black women, queer, and trans people at the founding conference of the Movement for Black Lives (M4BL), and both served on its Policy Table until 2021. As part of M4BL, Mariame co-created a bail reform curriculum, and Andrea coordinated updates and expansions of M4BL's policy platform, the Vision for Black Lives, to bring a deeper Black queer and trans feminist, disability justice, and migrant justice analysis to its demands.[92] Together, we contributed to an M4BL toolkit on reparations.[93]

In 2018, we joined forces to co-found Interrupting Criminalization. Our goal was to create a container in which to work individually and collaboratively to support movements to end policing, criminalization, incarceration, detention, and deportation of women, queer, and trans people of color.[94] In 2020, we found ourselves supporting organizations across the country—predominantly led by Black women, queer and trans people, and survivors—working to disrupt criminalization at its source through demands to defund police and invest in community safety. It is based on these experiences and more—as organizers, advocates, researchers, practitioners, and survivors—that we make a case for not only defunding police, but for abolishing policing altogether.

Importantly, we are both Black feminist abolitionists. Our work is rooted in the principles of Black feminism, and guided by the central principle that Black women, trans, and gender nonconforming people are inherently valuable—and therefore are entitled to a multiplicity of tools to be safe, survive, and thrive. Leading Black feminist abolitionist and INCITE! co-founder Beth E. Richie, who has been a teacher and touchstone to both of us, explains how abolition feminism emerged from anti-violence organizing and core Black feminist theories and practices, including (1) listening to the stories of people harmed by violence about what they need, (2) understanding that our work for safety must be rooted in support and freedom, (3) knowing that the master's tools will not dismantle the master's house—justice will not come from creating injustice, (4) organizing from the premise that the violence we face is intersectional, and (5) the knowledge that we need to be in the work for the long haul. These principles offer a clear pathway to safety and to building a world that disappears threats to safety, in which we respond to individual harms while building broad responses to systemic harms. "It is a practice that assumes a different world is possible," Richie concludes.[95] Black feminism is a politic that gets at the source of our problems and grievances, alleviates suffering, and uproots violence. The prison industrial complex represents one of the most concentrated forms of violence in the world, creating untold suffering. Black feminism therefore requires us to reject and dismantle it, and to create new forms of accountability, governance, and sociality that create the world we want.

A Deeper History of Defund Demands

We are certainly not the first to make the case that policing and punishment interfere with, rather than produce, safety, nor will we be the last. As Naomi Murakawa, professor of African American studies at Princeton, writes in Colin Kaepernick's *Abolition for the People* anthology:

> The call to shrink, dismantle, or abolish police and prisons—not improve them—reverberates though the Civil Rights Congress and [their 1951 petition to the United Nations] *We Charge Genocide*, through Bayard Rustin and the Journey of Reconciliation, through the Black Panthers and the Young Lords, through Marsha P. Johnson, Sylvia Rivera, and queer liberation movements, to the creation of Critical Resistance in the late 1990s.[96]

For instance, calls to divest from police, prisons, and prosecutions echo the demands of the Black Panther Party's 1962 ten-point platform for Black Liberation: "We want an immediate end to POLICE BRUTALITY and MURDER of Black people. . . . We want land, bread, housing, education, clothing, justice and peace."[97] They were articulated by former Panthers and political prisoners like Eddie Ellis, who drew a direct line between divestment from policing and achieving what he called "human justice."[98] They were among demands made by the North Carolina Prisoners' Labor Union in 1974, who called for an "end to the judicial-prison-parole industrial complex."[99] They are rooted in anti-apartheid struggles and calls for divestment from oppressive regimes around the world.

More recently, demands to defund police and prisons emerged in response to spikes in prison populations and the size, scope, and budgets of police departments, increasingly diverting money from community safety and well-being.[100] For instance, California's prison industry saw a boom in the '90s—fueled by newly enacted three-strikes laws imposing long sentences on people convicted of more than two felony offenses.[101] In 1995, writer Mike Davis published an article in *The Nation,* citing economists' predictions that, as a result, "the state will have to loot its higher education budget for dozens of new prisons."[102] A gubernatorial spokesperson Davis quoted agreed: "If these additional costs have to be absorbed, I guess we'll have to reduce other services. We'll have to change our priorities."[103] Davis also references a contemporaneous report from the conservative RAND corporation, which confirmed that "[t]o support implementation of the [three strikes] law, total spending for higher education and other government services would have to fall by more than 40 percent over the next eight years. . . . If the three strikes law remains in place by 2002, the state government will be spending more money keeping people in prison than putting people through college."[104]

These troubling predictions came to pass—not only in California, but across the country. Since the mid-'80s, jail and prison spending increased at three times the rate of elementary and secondary education. And while state funding for post-secondary education remained constant, spending on jails and prisons increased by 89 percent.[105] These skewed spending priorities were evident in the state of Illinois where, between 1985 and 2005, over 25 new prisons or detention facilities were built, yet no new public colleges or universities were established. Meanwhile, education reforms that would have increased school resources in low-income communities of color—precisely the same communities that are most targeted by policing—that were mandated by the Illinois State Supreme Court were stalled for decades due to lack of funding. In response, Mariame and abolitionist scholar Erica Meiners laid a foundation for calls to defund police and for #PoliceFreeSchools, writing:

> Because many states spend more on prisons than education, we have to change funding priorities. . . . Why not shift budgets from cops in schools to counselors, from building prisons to opening up additional spaces in free public colleges and universities? Instead of more militarized borders, why not ensure that all youth have access to meaningful, discipline-building co-curricular activities such as music, drama, art, and sports?[106]

In 1999, in response to cuts to education funding and the growth of the prison industrial complex in California, abolitionist scholar Ruth Wilson Gilmore co-founded the California Prison Moratorium Project to advocate against new prison construction.[107] Wilson Gilmore is also a co-founder of Critical Resistance,[108] an organization that grew out of a 1997 conference held in California by "activists challenging the idea that imprisonment and policing are a solution for social, political, and economic problems."[109] Now a national organization, Critical Resistance has shaped thinking and organizing around police and PIC abolition for more than two decades through national and local projects and campaigns. In 2002 it issued a joint statement with INCITE![110] on gender violence and the PIC, articulating demands to divest from policing and invest in community safety: "[W]hen public funding is channeled into policing and prisons, budget cuts for social programs, including women's shelters, welfare, and public housing are the inevitable side effect. These cutbacks leave women less able to escape violent relationships."[111]

Critical Resistance catalyzed a number of local abolitionist organizing projects, including Californians United for a Responsible Budget (CURB), which focuses on reducing state spending on police and prisons. In 2004, CURB co-founded the No New Jails coalition in Los Angeles, which successfully defeated a measure to introduce a new sales tax to hire one thousand cops.[112] Two years earlier, across the country, New York City's Prison Moratorium Project successfully fought to stop the construction of youth jails at a cost of $64 million, calling for investment in schools and youth programming and an end to the "school-to-prison pipeline."[113] Similarly, California's Books Not Bars, a project of Oakland's community-based Ella Baker Center, successfully fought to close California's youth prisons, calling for investments in schools instead.[114] In 2009, Mariame founded Project NIA in Chicago, with the goal of ending youth incarceration through restorative and transformative practices.

Over the past two decades, as police budgets and powers skyrocketed alongside prison expansion and the spread of criminalization,[115] organizers have expanded their focus from curbing prison expenditures to police budgets and the growing scope of policing. The shift has not always been smooth. While a growing number of people agree that we need to drastically reduce the number of people incarcerated in the U.S. and the billions we spend caging them, many stop short at the prospect of shrinking police departments and budgets. Policing is so deeply wedded to safety in our collective imaginations that it is difficult to disentangle them. But as the number of police killings continues to mount, the violence of policing is increasingly laid bare, and attempts at police reform continue to fail, there is a growing consensus that we need a different approach to safety.

While abolitionist struggles have scored some wins, the reality remains that surveillance, policing, criminalization, prisons, and punishment are deeply entrenched in our society. Worse yet, over the past four decades these approaches have increasingly become the sole response to every harm, conflict, and need (real or imagined). This carceral approach to addressing society's problems is what claimed George Floyd, Breonna Taylor, and thousands more Black, Indigenous, disabled, and migrant people's lives, and has driven over 2 million people into cages and placed a total of 6 million under the control of the criminal punishment system, making the U.S. the greatest incarcerator in the world. It also rapaciously consumes an increasing share of collective resources—the very same resources that are urgently needed to fund initiatives that would promote greater safety in our communities.[116]

Drawing on these decades of organizing, the Movement for Black Lives (M4BL), an ecosystem of dozens of Black-led grassroots, state, and national organizations that emerged in the wake of the Ferguson Uprising, made defunding police and investing in Black communities one of the six central planks of its policy platform, the Vision for Black Lives:

> Invest/Divest—We demand investments in the education, health, and safety of Black people, instead of investments in the criminalizing, caging, and harming of Black people. We want investments in Black communities, determined by Black communities, and divestment from exploitative forces including prisons, fossil fuels, police, surveillance, and exploitative corporations.[117]

This divest/invest framework is codified in the BREATHE Act,[118] legislation conceived and drafted by M4BL in 2020. The bill, which Andrea played a role in developing, is a direct challenge to the now-defunct federal

Justice in Policing Act (JPA), proposed in the wake of the police killings of George Floyd and Breonna Taylor. Named after Floyd, the JPA proposed superficial reforms that would not have addressed the root causes of the police violence that killed him. Instead, it would have continued to pour more money into police departments while mandating changes in policy with no means to ensure they were implemented. The BREATHE Act—supported by Congresswomen Ayanna Pressley (D-MA), Rashida Tlaib (D-MI), and thousands of community sponsors—incorporated defund demands from the streets into omnibus legislation that would eliminate federal funding for national, state, and local law enforcement, and create mechanisms to make deep investments in community-based safety strategies, education, health care, housing, and reparations for survivors of the violence of police, jails, prisons, detention, and deportation, while decriminalizing drug, poverty, and prostitution-related offenses. Inspired by the BREATHE Act, Rep. Cori Bush (D-MO) introduced the People's Response Act, which would create a federal funding stream for nonpunitive safety strategies.[119]

Understanding demands to defund and abolish police requires us to know not only where they come from, but also the larger socioeconomic context in which they emerged. Efforts to resist growing investment in police, prisons, and criminalization at the expense of meeting collective needs over the past four decades in the U.S. arose within the larger political context of the evolution of neoliberal economic policies, in service of the ongoing project of racial capitalism.

Getting to the Root:
Racial Capitalism and Neoliberalism

As Wilson Gilmore theorizes, increased investment in police and prisons in the U.S. serves as a mechanism for racial capitalism to save itself from crises of its own creation. For instance, labor rendered superfluous by automation, deindustrialization, and globalization is funneled into police and prisons—white labor as personnel, Black and Brown labor criminalized and caged; surplus land and technology is turned toward increased surveillance and the proliferation of prisons, particularly in rural areas.[120] Divestment from communities similarly serves the interests of racial capitalism: "As racial justice movements succeeded in achieving increased access for Black people, the state simply divested from public schools, hospitals, housing, social benefits and entitlements, while demonizing and projecting individual moral failure onto people who accessed them to survive in the wake of structural economic oppression and exclusion and growing deindustrialization."[121] Building on the work of Marxist geographer David Harvey, Wilson Gilmore names this process "organized abandonment," a concerted divestment from meeting basic needs of the populace while simultaneously promoting criminalization as a response to the fallout.

Organized abandonment is a defining feature of neoliberalism,[122] a term that is widely used but not commonly defined. Generally speaking, it refers to economic and social policies that emerged under the U.S.-sponsored Pinochet dictatorship in Chile, and were popularized under the Reagan administration ("Reaganomics") in the U.S. and Prime Minister Margaret Thatcher ("Thatcherism") in the U.K. They are imposed on nations of the Global South by institutions such as the World Bank and International Monetary Fund as "structural adjustment programs." Neoliberalism "serves as shorthand for shredding social welfare programs, privatization of public institutions and services, elimination of government regulation, and redistribution of resources into the hands of corporations and wealthy elites, all in the name of 'fiscal responsibility.'"[123]

The aftermath of neoliberal policies is bleak: increasingly precarious employment, housing, health care, and care economies for a growing proportion of the population, hitting low-income communities of color and people already struggling to survive the hardest.[124] Then, "Neoliberalism covers up its devastating impacts—declining school enrollment and high unemployment, increased homelessness and participation in criminalized survival economies, increased migration, and a growing population of people whose physical and mental health needs are not met—by labeling them a 'crime problem' caused by individual failure and immorality, often projected onto entire 'dysfunctional' communities and racial groups."[125] Both organized abandonment and criminalization exacerbate existing racial and gender disparities, as the state targets social welfare programs essential to the survival of people experiencing the highest poverty rates in the United States—Native women, Black women, Latinxs, and disabled people—and then criminalizes their efforts to survive by policing underground economies, homelessness, and "welfare fraud." Additionally, many of the responsibilities downloaded by the state onto individuals and communities—such as caring for children, elders, sick, and disabled people—represent gendered labor, placing additional pressures on low-income women of color.[126]

Neoliberalism is a continuation of the long history of structural racial oppression in the U.S. and abroad. It simply represents a current manifestation of racial capitalism, a term initially used to describe apartheid South Africa and universalized by Black Marxist scholar Cedric Robinson as an economic system premised on exploitation of a racialized other.[127] As historian and UCLA professor Robin D.G. Kelley describes, capitalism, racism, and colonialism are co-constitutive, evolving together "to produce a modern world system of 'racial capitalism' dependent on slavery, violence, imperialism, and genocide."[128] Police fabricate and maintain the social order required to sustain this system,[129] serving as the "muscle of racial capitalism," in the words of Alyxandra Goodwin of the Action Center on Race and the Economy (ACRE). The cops, and the prison industrial complex they are part of, are thus essential to what has evolved under neoliberalism into the "carceral state," serving as a vehicle for an iteration of racial capitalism scholar-activist Jackie Wang calls "carceral capitalism."[130]

The carceral state[131] is a web of ideologies and institutions wielding cops, cages, laws, stories, and surveillance to meet the generalized insecurity of racial capitalism. As conditions intensified by neoliberal economic policies have worsened, criminalization, policing, and punishment have increasingly pervaded every aspect of society and governance—all in the interests of protecting the private property and wealth accumulation of a select few.[132] This whole process is, as scholar and writer Arun Kundnani describes, facilitated by cultural promotion and internalization of myths of "individual freedom" and "individual responsibility" that divide individuals into categories of "deserving" and "undeserving" without any regard for the ways in which structural racism and other systemic forms of discrimination and exclusion shape individual choices and life chances.[133] Racialized communities are scapegoated based on projected and perceived moral failings without any systemic analysis of the ongoing impacts of long legacies of colonialism, slavery, segregation, racism, ableism, and patriarchy.[134] As Black feminist abolitionist scholar and former political prisoner Angela Y. Davis points out, this "vast experiment to disappear the major social problems of our time relies on racialized assumptions of criminality"[135] that perpetuate an economic system premised on exploitation of a racialized "other," now framed as inherently "criminal" and therefore completely undeserving of care, support, or social goods. These carceral logics normalize policing and punishment in response to social problems rather than collective care and mutual support.[136] Historian Julilly Kohler-Hausmann points out how these logics "mobilize highly gendered rhetoric" privileging "tough on crime" responses to social problems based on their association with masculine traits rather than their effectiveness, while discrediting "soft" approaches like material aid and social welfare programs by casting them as feminine, effeminate, or maternal, part of a "nanny state."[137]

As authors Kay Whitlock and Nancy Heitzeg elaborate in *Carceral Con: The Deceptive Terrain of Criminal Justice Reform*, the carceral state is "grounded in political production of crime and punishment."[138] The concept of what constitutes "criminality" is not some hard-and-fast category; rather it is constantly shifting to reflect society's anxieties and priorities. A report entitled *The Crisis of Criminalization* co-authored by Andrea and Beth Richie describes criminalization as:

> the social and political process by which society determines which actions or behaviors—and by who—will be punished by the state. At the most basic level, it involves passage and enforcement of criminal laws. While framed as neutral, decisions about what kinds of conduct to punish, how, and how much are very much a choice, guided by existing structures of economic and social inequality based on race, gender, sexuality, disability, and poverty, among others."

The report emphasizes that "criminalization extends beyond laws and policies to more symbolic—and more deeply entrenched—processes of creating categories of people deemed 'criminals,'" using "highly racialized and gendered narratives—whether they are about 'thugs,' 'crack mothers,' 'welfare queens,' or 'bad hombres'. . . to fuel a generalized state of anxiety and fear, and to brand people labeled 'criminal' as threatening, dangerous, and inhuman." Thus, "violence, banishment and exile, denial of protection, and restrictions on freedom, expression, movement, and ultimately existence of people deemed 'criminal' . . . becomes a 'natural' response."[139] Criminalization is also a highly racialized process of determining who is "deserving" of social programs and investment and who is not.[140] And, as organizer and somatics practitioner Prentis Hemphill teaches, it is also about the distribution of trauma, and of opportunities to heal from its consequences rather than be punished for them.[141]

Ultimately, criminalization is a shield behind which neoliberal agendas can advance. Criminalizing people does not solve the problems we face in our communities; it simply recategorizes and attempts to hide them. Yet we're offered palatable messages of "fighting crime" and creating "safer neighborhoods," when, in reality, resources that would meet community needs are diverted to expand policing. Any arguments for change are countered with fearmongering and the specter of increased crime, violence, and harm to those who are deemed "innocent" and "deserving."[142]

These narratives were in full operation in the backlash to the calls to defund police. Neoliberal ideologies—and criminalizing narratives that they require—have been so deeply normalized that they are often taken for granted in debates about policing and safety. As a result, it can be hard to even imagine an alternative way to address community needs like poverty and homelessness beyond individualized policing and punishment. That is why all cops and politicians have to do is raise the specter of rising crime or violence, and the only "logical" response is posited to be to pour more desperately needed resources into police budgets.[143] Yet even the *New York Times*, which continues to publish deeply biased and flawed articles citing law enforcement sources for the proposition that rising crime rates point to the need to increase funding and support to police,[144] conceded at the end of 2021 that "For decades, scholars have acknowledged that local crime rates cannot be predicted by officer strength and police budgets."[145] What we also know is that increasing police budgets takes resources away from income support, mental health care, violence prevention and intervention programs, and infrastructure to meet basic needs and reduce violence across the board. As Davis puts it, "The prison industrial system . . . devours the social wealth needed to address the very problems that have led to spiraling numbers of prisoners."[146] Meanwhile:

> As communities and community institutions like schools, health care facilities, libraries, public spaces are gutted of resources by neoliberal policies, they are flooded with police, policing and punishment reach further into daily interactions like school fights, truancy, and refusal of medical treatment, and the alternatives offered to policing and punishment like shelters and drug treatment programs become sites of policing.[147]

In other words, each fuels the other: neoliberal policies gut the social safety net and loot collective resources for private profit, causing widespread unemployment, poverty, and homelessness. Increasing numbers of people and communities struggling to survive in the fallout of these economic policies are criminalized, requiring more and more police and pushing more and more people into the maw of the criminal punishment system. The costs of criminalization are then used to justify further cuts to social programs and basic infrastructure, and the cycle continues. The end result, as former Chicago mayor Rahm Emanuel put it bluntly during his 2016 mayoral run, is "to increase our investments with more police officers. Every other decision will be made around that priority."[148] This was the future forecast by the California gubernatorial spokesperson in Mike Davis' 1995 article in *The Nation*—in order to sustain the carceral state, funding for police must take priority over everything else.

These are the core political, social, and economic forces and conditions that demands to defund police seek to address. They are met with such virulent opposition from people across the political spectrum because they strike at the heart of a racialized, gendered economic order that protects

wealth and white supremacy. Cops are seeing the threat to their hege-
monic hold on public safety and are becoming more outlandish in their
claims to defend it as police and politicians realize that defund organizers
mean what we are saying, and that we intend to reorganize society around
meeting community needs.

Far more than a budgetary exercise, defunding police means striking
at the root of the forces that have created a society that extracts resources
from Black, Indigenous, migrant, disabled, and low-income populations,
deprives them of basic needs, infrastructure, and shared public goods, and
then criminalizes them for struggling to survive. More than just reducing and ultimately eliminating the resources spent on policing, it means
shrinking the size, scope, equipment, and power of police departments
with a view to dismantling them—and the prison industrial complex they
fuel. It is a step toward divesting financially, practically, ideologically, and
emotionally from policing as a strategy to keep us safe, meet our needs, or
resolve harm or conflict. It is a strategy that brings us closer to the long-
term goal of abolishing policing in all its forms. The goal is not to simply
replace one form of policing with another housed in a different institution, enacted by people wearing different uniforms—it is to create safety
and conditions under which all communities can thrive without the threat
of violence, exile, or punishment. The goal is to strike at the heart of racial
capitalism—and remake society anew.

No More Police

No More Police is a book for people who are engaged in movements to
defund police and abolish the PIC—and for those who want to learn
more about them. It is also an invitation to people fighting interpersonal
and community violence and struggling for racial, gender, reproductive,
health, educational, economic, and migrant justice to consider how policing interferes with their goals, and how defunding and ultimately abolishing police might further them. It is a book rooted in these movements,
written from deep engagement with them, drawing on the knowledge
generated by organizers alongside academic research.

We recognize that readers may not engage with the elements of our case for police abolition in the order we articulate them, and instead may choose to jump to the chapters that address the specific questions they bring, or speak to the type of organizing they are engaged in. While the arguments we make build on each other as we move through the book, we invite you to dive in wherever the issues most pressing to you may be addressed.

We take up the first element of the case—that police don't produce safety, but rather contribute to its absence—in the first two chapters: "Cops Don't Stop Violence" and "We Are Survivors." We argue that, despite being propped up as the only thing standing between us and chaos and mayhem, police do very little to prevent, intervene in, or deter violence and harm from happening in the first place. Research conducted by the *New York Times* in 2020 affirms that point, finding that only 4 percent of police calls are for violent crimes in progress.[149] Far from spending their days stopping violence from happening, cops spend most of their time driving or walking around, looking for people and activity deemed "suspicious," and responding to a range of calls—from taking reports of traffic accidents and conducting "welfare checks" to answering calls from white women threatened by the presence of Black people.[150] In this context, police respond sporadically, and often violently, to community members in Black, Indigenous, migrant, and low-income communities with a plethora of needs and only one number to call: 911. Cops show up to calls for help with an extremely limited set of tools: handcuffs; the power to arrest, threaten, or use force; and license to kill. Even when it comes to calls for help involving domestic violence, sexual assault, robbery, or a home invasion—situations offered up as incontrovertible justifications for cops' existence—in the vast majority of instances, *at best* cops respond after the fact and take a report. On average, police "solve" far fewer than half of homicides or other violent crimes.[151] Even when they do make an arrest, catching and locking up the "bad guys" does not deter the next act of violence, nor is it possible to incapacitate every bad actor indefinitely through incarceration.[152]

It's not just that police are ineffective; they are actively harmful, adding their own violence to the mix—the violence of surveillance, stop and frisk, strip searches and cavity searches, sexual harassment and extortion, harassment, humiliation, degradation, and of course, the beatdowns, the Tasers, the pepper spray and tear gas, the chokings, the killings. Yet the violence of policing doesn't register in conversations about public safety or factor into the price of pursuing policing as the means to achieve it. Police violence is not counted in the crime stats periodically trotted out to justify their existence—even though cops engage daily in actions that fall squarely within the definition of homicide, assault (including sexual assault), home invasions in the form of drug raids, and robbery and theft through asset forfeiture. When their violence is factored into the equation, it becomes clear that safety for a few is achieved at the expense of many, and greater safety would be more achievable without police.

Safety Is Rooted in Abolition

We have been doing this work long enough to anticipate some of the usual questions and concerns that emerge when we state that abolishing polic-ing is necessary to create greater safety. One of the inevitable responses is, *But what about the rapists and the batterers?* Our answer to this question is simple: What about them, indeed. We know that policing and prisons don't stop rape, domestic violence, or child abuse from happening—and in fact, they perpetuate them. They don't offer what survivors say they need, and, in many cases, they place survivors in danger of more violence. For instance, a 2015 survey by the National Domestic Violence Hotline found that 80 percent of survivors are afraid to call the police, 30 percent of survivors felt less safe after calling the police, and 24 percent of survi-vors who called the police were arrested or threatened with arrest.[153] As a result, the vast majority of cases of sexual and domestic violence and child abuse are never reported to police. When they are, the likelihood that police will "solve" the problem or prevent it from recurring is very low, and the likelihood that police will compound the problem and perpetrate additional violence against survivors is high. We also know that the far-ther the survivor is from the idealized victim of violence—white, middle class, cisgender, heterosexual, never used drugs or alcohol, able-bodied, never labeled as mentally "unstable," never criminalized—the truer this is. Very few survivors meet these criteria. As a result, the majority of people who experience violence, including those who seek assistance from police, experience further harm, not greater safety.

We know that police and prisons do not—and cannot—contain all the people who engage in rape, battery, killing, and other forms of violence. Nor should that be our goal—while their actions are heinous, people who perpetrate sexual violence are not some monstrous "other," easily (racially) recognizable and disposable. They are us—members of our families and communities. Eighty percent of survivors know the person who sexually assaulted them.[154] Incarcerating them all would not stop or prevent sexual violence; it would simply move these forms of violence, and the people responsible for them, behind prison walls, where sexual violence is rampant, turning more people into survivors. If we want to *end* violence, including sexual, domestic, racial, homophobic, and transphobic violence, then we have to end police, prisons, and all carceral institutions. These structures breed and perpetuate these same forms of violence while robbing us of the resources needed to prevent and heal from them. As Beth Richie puts it simply, when we try to end violence with violence, "We lose the possibility of freedom from violence."[155]

But there are some Black communities that are calling for more police in the face of high rates of communal and interpersonal violence. We understand these calls from abandoned and oppressed communities as responses to what is perceived as a threat to take away the only resource offered by the state to respond to a multitude of problems—even if most of the time it operates like Russian roulette. Abolition is about creating real solutions to the violence produced by organized abandonment and organized violence through a multitude of resources and services, rather than a single response designed to contain, control, and kill. Economic conditions are the most reliable predictors of violence in our communities, and housing, health care, employment, and living-wage incomes are some of the most reliable prevention tools. But with up to—and sometimes more than— half of city budgets going to police departments, policymakers claim there is no money for these things, even though they are what will actually prevent and shift conditions that produce violence. Police abolition is a process of reallocating resources, funding, and responsibility away from police and toward community-based models of safety, support, and prevention. It is a long-term project that requires both shifting emergency response procedures and getting well ahead of crises by putting in place systems that actually create safer communities and prevent harm.

Well, then, why can't we do both—reduce police budgets and engage in meaningful reform to ensure that the remaining police functions are performed in nondiscriminatory ways that meet the needs and respect the rights of communities? Because this approach misapprehends the core function of police—which is to contain and control, not serve and protect. It also removes the inherent violence of policing from the conversation. As we explore in greater detail in the "Re-Form" chapter, there is no reforming something that is working just as it was designed. Policing at its root is anti-Black, anti-Indigenous, patriarchal, and ableist, and it upholds all other forms of supremacy in service of racial capitalism. Police reforms, while often well-intentioned, misapprehend the purpose of police. There's also the issue of wasted resources and effort. As Naomi Murakawa points out in *Abolition for the People*, police reforms reward and re-entrench policing, consuming a tremendous amount of resources while doing little to prevent police violence from happening in the future.[156] Simply put, reform doesn't work.[157]

But without police, who will we turn to for help? Police abolition is not about making cops vanish overnight without having shifted the conditions that fuel violence. It is about actively shifting responsibility for community safety to people best equipped to respond to and prevent crises. Health care workers, community leaders, violence interrupters, victim/survivor advocates, religious leaders, neighbors, family members, and friends—all of the people who make up the fabric of a community—are in a better position to prevent and respond to crises than armed strangers.

And, it is critical that we proceed with caution with respect to "alternatives" to police. Police killings are not the only grammar of policing; the history and present-day operation of the police state teach us that multiple actors and institutions, including those being proffered as substitutes to police, enact the violence of policing in service of fabricating and maintaining the order racial capitalism requires. In other words, beware the "soft police," as well as the "common sense" narratives of scarcity, competition, deservingness, worthiness, and individual responsibility that drive U.S. social policy. When we start to unpack these, we see the racist, patriarchal, ableist, homophobic, and transphobic notions of "normalcy" that underpin them, and how they are violently policed by cops, medical professionals, social workers, and communities. As we argue in the "No Soft Police" chapter, our vision can't be limited to replacing cops with policing in different forms.

Police abolition is not only about those spectacular moments of police violence that often spark a shifting of consciousness around policing and safety; it is also about confronting the stories we are told about policing and safety that fail to add up. It's about examining the ways police colonize our imaginations, promoting fear that permeates our everyday lives to justify their existence, and making public safety without police unthinkable for so many. It is about challenging the daily devaluation, degradation, and disposal that accompanies criminalization, and the social and economic systems that produce and require it. When fully realized, police abolition dismantles the exploitative systems and practices of power that have shaped the global capitalist system; changes the ways we understand the world and relate to each other; and builds new structures to meet our individual and collective needs as well as prevent, interrupt, and heal from violence and harm.

The project of police abolition faces immense challenges, but it also offers immense possibilities to build a new world free from violence, free from racialization, free from the misery and endless toil directed at endlessly increasing the profits and power of the privileged few. If policing is a process of capitalist order-making, abolition is the creative practice of building new communal and non-coercive institutions at all levels of society. In the "How Do We Get There?" chapter we explore the political commitments, principles, and practices that enable us to unseat carceral logics and reconceptualize public safety.

This book is about both the theory and practice of police abolition—and the thorny questions and pitfalls that lie along the way. We explore those in greater detail in the "Tricks and Tensions" chapter. While abolition requires us to adhere to a clear set of principles and commitments which boil down to dismantling surveillance, policing, punishment, and exile in all circumstances, abolitionists don't all agree on every step of the path forward, or the ultimate shape of the society we are trying to build. How do we collectivize resources for redistribution for the common good without policing, extraction, and exploitation—within the U.S. and on a global scale? How do we engage the carceral state while working to dismantle it, shift resources to communities, and create conditions under which new social and economic relations and forms of governance can emerge to bring us closer to abolitionist futures? In the meantime, how do we break police power and secure accountability and reparations for the violence of policing? We are all in a continuing process of evolution on the road toward the abolitionist horizon.

As we lay out in the "Experiment and Build" chapter, many communities are already practicing how to build greater safety along the way through community conversations, campaigns for #PoliceFreeSchools, mutual aid, transformative justice, and building community safety infrastructures and local and global solidarity economies. In the final chapter, we meditate on the principles of Black feminist abolition that guide this work and illuminate the path forward.

No More Police draws on the lessons of the past two years—and the past two decades—of abolitionist movements toward these goals. It examines the organizing that took place in the spotlight of the 2020 Uprisings as well as the work that proceeds quietly beneath the surface in local campaigns and community-based projects. In just a few short months following George Floyd's murder, ideas about police abolition, previously dismissed as utopian and unrealistic, found their way into the mainstream, and are being debated on many fronts—from movements demanding accountability for cops who kill, to movements to end gender-based and gun violence. At the same time, there has also been an explosion of efforts to dilute, detract, misdirect, silence, and outright attack efforts to defund police on every front.

This book attempts to lay out the clear, compelling case being made in communities across the country and around the world for building safer communities. It is rooted in our experience as Black feminist abolitionists, survivors, and anti-violence advocates who are working directly with organizers on the ground as they develop demands; strategize and build power to achieve them; face setbacks; and grapple with questions of what greater safety for communities could and should look like, and how to get there. This is a book that challenges every one of us to confront the blocks we carry deep within us that prevent us from acting from that moment of reckoning when we questioned the violence of policing. It challenges us to, as Ruth Wilson Gilmore urges us, "change everything" in the name of building safer, more just, and sustainable, thriving communities.

Cops Don't Stop Violence

"If they kill her, call us."[1]

These words, spoken by a Los Angeles police dispatcher to a caller reporting a vicious assault of an undocumented street vendor in 2003, underscore the fact that police do not produce safety. Contrary to police public relations narratives framing cops as quasi-superheroes responding to calls for help and narrowly averting violence, at best, cops respond after violence has already happened. In fact, a *New York Times* investigation based on data collected by police found that only 1 percent to 4 percent of police calls are for "serious violent crime" like homicide, rape, or robbery.[2] When cops do respond to such calls, they find the person responsible for violence a mere one-quarter of the time.[3] Rates of arrest and conviction are even lower.[4] Adding insult to injury, cops often contribute their own violence to the mix.

The dispatcher's dismissal of the call for help described above also demonstrates how police responses to violence are shaped by the interests and

Portions of this chapter are drawn from "Cops Don't Stop Violence: Combating Narratives Used to Defend Police Instead of Defunding Them," by Andrea J. Ritchie and Jared Knowles, Interrupting Criminalization and the Community Resource Hub, communityresourcehub.org/wp-content/uploads/2021/07/0726_PoliceDontStop_C.pdf.

relations of power they serve. In this case, an undocumented Latina trans woman engaged in informal economies was deemed unworthy of protection by a police force whose role is to protect property and "legitimate" businesses, manage a social order premised on violence against racialized women, and police the borders of both the gender binary and the nation to exclude migrant, trans, and gender nonconforming people from the presumed protections of citizenship. The response to the call for help was informed by transphobic and xenophobic narratives that fuel and normalize the violent deaths of trans women. And, it reflects the reality that, far from serving as protectors, police are among the primary perpetrators of violence against many of the groups she is part of: trans women of color, migrants, and people involved in informal economies. In other words, there is no reason for cops to interrupt the violence, as the assailant is simply doing what the police would otherwise do themselves. Sadly, this is far from a historical or isolated incident; it is simply an instructive one. It is incidents like these that drive abolitionist demands—we are abolitionists *because* we care about violence and the people most likely to be targeted by it, and about finding the best ways to stop it.

Policing neither prevents, interrupts, nor offers satisfactory resolution to the vast majority of violence that takes place in our communities. Even though the U.S. spends over $100 billion a year on policing, a figure that has been increasing steadily over the past half century,[5] the U.S. continues to experience some of the highest rates of violence across all industrialized countries. For instance, the *American Journal of Medicine* found that gun-related homicide rates in the U.S. are twenty-five times higher than twenty-two of the world's wealthiest nations.[6] Longitudinal studies indicate that markers of resource deprivation—lack of sufficient income, health care, etc.—are critical factors in heightened violent crime rates.[7] Yet, bottomless police budgets capture a growing share of our collective resources, and programs proven to reduce, prevent, intervene in, and help survivors heal from violence are starved of nutrients.[8] Preventing, interrupting, and healing from violence requires deep investments in meeting communities' economic and social needs, and in community-based violence prevention and interruption programs—not in more violent policing.

In a twisted feat of logic, police trumpet claims that violence is on the rise—evidence of their own failure to prevent it in spite of the billions invested in them—as a reason that they need more cops, more cash, more laws, and, of course, *less* scrutiny and *less* accountability. And they would like to have it both ways: If officially documented rates of violence fall—as they have for the most part over the past four decades—cops claim credit, leveraging the threat of a hypothetical future increase in violence to keep increasing their budgets and power.

Police failure to stop, interrupt, or transform violence is no accident. Policing has never been about preventing violence. It has always been about fabricating and maintaining "order" by using violence—directly and indirectly—to control and contain racialized and gendered populations of people in service of a capitalist economic order.[9] Police—including Border Patrol, immigration, probation, and parole officers, alongside members of the military—are "violence workers," human embodiments of the state's monopoly on violence.[10] Their work implicitly involves the threat of violence at all times, and they do the work of enacting state violence in all its forms, including by enforcing and providing cover for organized abandonment.[11] Police are consistently posited as the only legitimate response to violence,[12] yet in all of these capacities, they actively do violence and withhold protection from violence along axes of power. Cops do not simply enforce laws, they make and use the law—and the power given to them both legally and extralegally—to maintain a raced, gendered, abled, classed, and global social order.[13]

Cultural theorist Stuart Hall wrote extensively about police strategies of perpetual self-justification in the late 1970s: Police manufacture and manipulate data about "violence" and "crime," and conscript the media to produce a narrative of crisis to which policing is the only legitimate response.[14] And that is exactly what happened in 2020. Facing one of the greatest crises of legitimacy in a generation, and on the heels of one of the largest uprisings against police violence in U.S. history, cops and pro-police forces reached for their most reliable weapon to consolidate power: fear. As police killings continued to mount and organizers across the country continued to target bloated police budgets, cops and politicians on the defensive sought to neutralize the threat by raising the specter of violence raging out of control, claiming that a "crime wave" prompted by "the defund movement" was sweeping the nation.

Crime and Violence

The word "crime" is enough to conjure threatening images of violence in the public imagination. Yet crime is not a measure of harm or safety. A crime is simply any activity that violates a criminal law. Not all violence is a crime, and not all crimes involve violence.

In fact, the vast majority of violence is not counted as crime, because a great deal of violence is not criminalized. For instance, the police and military regularly commit violence that is not defined as crime, which allows them to be shielded from accountability. Structural, economic, and environmental violence is generally not incorporated into common conceptions of violence, even though it results in what abolitionist scholar Ruth Wilson Gilmore calls "premature death."[15]

Additionally, most people who experience criminalized violence don't report it.[16] Even when they do report it, cops often don't respond. When they do respond, it doesn't necessarily result in an arrest or criminal conviction—two metrics used to measure police responses to crime. A 2020 study found that "[o]f the crimes we know about, police arrest individuals on average about 10% of the time for major crimes committed, and convict individuals less than 2% of the time."[17]

Conversely, the vast majority of acts defined as crime do not involve violence—including possession of drugs, public order offenses like eating, sleeping, or drinking in public, and regulatory violations like braiding hair or providing childcare without a license. According to the Vera Institute of Justice, a criminal justice policy think tank, less than 5 percent of the 10 million arrests made annually are for what are described as "violent crime."[18]

In other words, crime statistics based on arrests ultimately represent both an overestimate of violence—because not all crime represents violence—and an underestimate of violence, because not all violence is reported or counted as crime. But what is clear is that the vast majority of what cops do has nothing to do with interrupting violence, and claims that "crime is up" do not necessarily mean that any of us are at greater risk of harm. In fact, research shows that many of us greatly overestimate our risk of experiencing violence or crime.[19]

The Construction of Crime

In the end, crime is a constructed category. States can and do decide what actions to label and punish—as crimes or civil violations—and which actions they deem legal.[20] What is labeled as crime is largely the product of political decisions made in service of maintaining existing relations of power. For instance, as Alec Karakatsanis, founder and director of Civil Rights Corps, points out, the state can choose to make shoplifting a crime, but not wage theft, effectively protecting employers who steal from their workers while punishing people who take what they need to survive.[21] According to Karakatsanis, wage theft costs $50 to $100 billion a year. That's five times more than all other property offenses—robbery, burglary, shoplifting, etc.—*combined*.[22] Yet virtually no policing resources are devoted to preventing or stopping wage theft. As Karakatsanis also points out, throwing dice in the street is a crime, but not in a casino, similarly protecting corporate profit.[23]

Decisions about what to criminalize are not random. What states decide to punish—and how—shifts over time based on the political, social, and economic interests of those in power. In an episode on the backlash against the 2020 Uprisings, hosts of the podcast *Citations Needed* trace the rise of policing and disproportionate criminalization of poor people in Europe to industrialization. As workers gained power, the ruling classes mobilized categories of criminalization to undermine those gains. In order to colonize the U.S., the government consolidated its power by confining Indigenous people to "reservations"—essentially open-air prisons—on infertile and desolate land where they struggled to survive. The government then criminalized any efforts they made to leave.[24] Because the U.S. government created criminal categories to authorize its own violence, it was not settler land theft and genocide of the people indigenous to it that became a crime; rather, the U.S. set up Courts of Indian Offenses to criminalize Indigenous social, economic, and religious practices.[25]

Similarly, because controlling enslaved Africans' labor and movements was essential to the maintenance of chattel slavery, the U.S. criminalized refusal of enslavement and running away as both medical conditions and crimes, and regulated movement through "pass laws."[26] Black Codes criminalized certain acts only if performed by Black people.[27] At the same time, political decisions were made to *not* criminalize violence against Black people—such as the rape of Black women that was a systemic aspect of chattel slavery.[28] As historians Sarah Haley and Talitha LeFlouria document extensively, when the institution of slavery was legally abolished in the U.S., the state increasingly criminalized Black women for offenses like vagrancy (for not working in waged labor), theft (for eating leftovers at an employer's house), or disrupting public order (for being loud, or merely present, in public), in an effort to continue to control and capitalize on their sexual, reproductive, and economic labor by forcing them back into domestic servitude through convict leasing.[29]

Because patriarchy requires gender binaries to delineate relations of power, cross-dressing laws were put into place to criminalize wearing articles of clothing associated with a gender other than the one assigned at birth.[30] Enforcement of patriarchal control over white women's sexuality and Black women's labor—along with related anxieties about preserving the "whiteness" of the U.S.—led to the criminalization of prostitution.[31] The social purchase of these racist, gendered fantasies also meant that men were not criminalized for raping their wives or for killing someone they found in bed with their wife.

As is the case today under neoliberal regimes, criminalization has historically focused on violently disappearing signs of social ill and unrest rather than addressing their root causes. Efforts to conceal the disabling human costs of the Civil War—and of racism and poverty—led to the enactment of "ugly" laws, which effectively criminalized the presence of disabled people in public spaces.[32] Conversely, failure to provide universal, free, quality, and accessible health care—which leads to hundreds of thousands of preventable deaths annually—is not criminalized, in the interests of profit.

Criminalization as Power

These are not just old-timey stories; criminalization continues to be deployed as a central mechanism to maintain a neoliberal, racially gendered, social, and economic order. Marijuana was not criminalized until the U.S. decided that migration from Mexico required a mechanism of containment and control. Then, marijuana was criminalized under the pretext that Mexicans brought the drug with them. The drug war continues to serve as a primary justification for violence at, beyond, and within U.S. borders.[33] Former President Richard Nixon infamously declared the "war on drugs" to control Black liberation movements and resistance to the Vietnam War among white youth.[34] Now, in search of revenue, a growing number of states are decriminalizing marijuana. Yet they continue to criminalize Black youth whose use, purchase, or sale of marijuana falls outside a regulatory scheme they are barred from participating in, due to prior criminal convictions flowing from conduct that is no longer criminalized.[35] Criminalization of midwives—who served as critical providers of care to Black and Indigenous communities denied access to formal medical care—beginning in the nineteenth century into the present served to limit access to abortion and concentrate power in male doctors while tying people giving birth to a profitable medical industry.[36] The list goes on. Once you begin to examine how selective criminalization is, you start to see examples everywhere.

Simply put, police, prosecutors, and politicians create and enforce criminal laws to manage relations of power by punishing and controlling specific actions and populations.

Criminalization is fueled by what Black feminist scholar Patricia Hill Collins describes as "controlling narratives,"[37] or, the racialized, gendered, ableist, xenophobic, and anti-poor narratives branding Black, Indigenous, migrant, low-income, disabled, queer, and trans people as inherently "dangerous criminal classes."[38] As a result, even as criminal laws evolve, populations deemed threats are consistently targeted for containment and control.

Beyond the structural oppression embedded in the construction of criminality itself, it is well-known that criminal laws are discriminatorily enforced. For instance, jaywalking, or crossing a street outside of a designated crosswalk—something almost everyone does at one point or another—is technically a crime. In 2017, Sacramento police issued 233 tickets for jaywalking in one police district—nearly triple the number issued in the rest of the city. Almost half were issued to Black people, who made up only 15 percent of residents.[39] Between 2007 and 2011, 88 percent of jaywalking arrests in Champaign, Illinois, were of Black people. In neighboring Urbana, it was over 90 percent.[40] These same disparities exist when it comes to riding a bike on the sidewalk, drunkenly filling the streets and engaging in property damage in celebration of a sports victory or frustration at a defeat, getting into a fight at school, or using cocaine.[41] In other words, criminal laws are used as a pretext to stop, harass, ticket, and arrest the people the cops are already charged with criminalizing.

In 2020, discriminatory enforcement of criminal laws extended to public health orders. The COVID-19 Policing Project tracked publicly reported enforcement of stay-at-home orders, mask mandates, gathering limits, and quarantine orders, finding "racial disparities in rates as well as types of enforcement:" Black, Indigenous, and people of color (BIPOC) were 2.5 times more likely than white people to be policed and punished for violations of COVID-19 orders. Black people were 4.5 times more likely to experience some form of enforcement of public health–related orders and were particularly likely to experience arrest as a form of enforcement.[42] Black women experienced the greatest rates of racial disparities and police violence in the context of pandemic policing. In just one example, Kaleemah Rozier, a young Black mother, was dragged to the filthy floor of a Brooklyn subway station by five cops who piled on top of her in front of her five-year-old child because they didn't like how she was wearing her mask.[43] The project found that pandemic policing replicated and expanded existing policing practices, and "superimposed a new presumption of 'public health disorder' on Black, Brown, Indigenous, migrant, disabled, queer, trans, sex-working, street-vending, and unhoused people whose mere public presence is already framed as dangerous to the public health and 'order.'"[44]

Many people are familiar with—and even invested in challenging or eliminating—such discriminatory policing of minor offenses, but accept the criminalization of violence as a given. Yet, these same discriminatory structures underpin the social response to even the most serious forms of violence. If a U.S. president sends a drone to kill someone in Yemen, the act is not criminalized, but instead celebrated as an act of national heroism. Similarly, cops who consistently claim "self-defense" when they kill, regardless of the circumstances, are routinely given a pass. In a notorious example, one of the cops who killed Amadou Diallo in the vestibule of his own home in the Bronx—claiming he did so because he mistook the wallet Diallo pulled out to comply with cops' demand for ID for a weapon—was acquitted of all charges at trial and then promoted.[45] Meanwhile, as documented by Survived and Punished, an organization Mariame co-founded, survivors of violence are often criminalized for killing in self-defense.[46] Once again, rather than painting an accurate picture of violence, crime rates describe and enforce a stratified relationship to power.

Cops Control Crime Rates

Beyond the fact that crime itself is a political construct, crime rates only reflect violations of the law that: (1) people have reported to police; (2) police choose to report; and (3) have resulted in an arrest.[47] In the summer of 2020, the Research and Evaluation Center at John Jay College of Criminal Justice convened a panel of experts in the fields of criminology, social and behavioral sciences, public health, epidemiology, law, and public policy to study and summarize research on ending violence without police. Their final report confirmed that reliance on crime data based solely on reports to or by police "is wholly insufficient if the goal is to prevent and reduce community violence." They go on to explain:

> For one, most violent acts are not measurable with police data because they are never reported to police. Not only do conventional definitions of violence fail to capture half of all violent acts between neighborhood residents, but they also omit any violent harm resulting from organizational behaviors, social structures, and systematic racial and class oppression. If the goal of violence reduction is to enhance the peace and security of neighborhood residents, efforts to reduce violence should attend to all forms of violence.[48]

In other words, because crime stats don't capture all violence and not all reported crime is violence, crime stats are an unreliable measure of violence and therefore a problematic basis for making policy decisions intended to reduce it.

What is also essential to recognize when looking at crime stats is that cops don't just report crime; they create it. Police enjoy vast discretion around who and what to pay attention to—and how. Every time they decide where to focus their attention, they are making law.[49] Even within what is defined as "crime," cops display selective focus. They generally uphold the status quo and normalize neoliberal economic arrangements by focusing on crimes that penalize poverty and discipline public space—like prohibitions on "disorderly conduct," "drinking in public," and "unreasonable noise."[50] Meanwhile, they largely ignore criminalized activity perpetrated by wealthy white people, such as tax evasion and financial fraud. In short: Enforcement of criminal law ends up facilitating control over systematically under-resourced communities and racialized populations, while protecting wealthy white people from accountability.

By choosing which laws to enforce against whom, which calls to respond to and how, cops decide who and what is out of order, and what actions restoring order requires. For instance, during an LAPD ride-along, Andrea and the cop she was assigned to observed three people urinating in public—an act that was against the law in each case. One, an unhoused Black man with no choice given the lack of public restrooms in the city, was arrested. Another, a white gay man outside a West Hollywood club, was ticketed. The others, a group of giggling white women out for a night on the town, were encouraged to just "go in the bushes" by the cop as he flirted with them. The first two people were perceived as inherently "disorderly," though their punishment varied according to the place they occupied in the hierarchy of power. The cop didn't see the young white women—part of the group for whom social order is explicitly preserved— as "disorderly" at all, even when they engaged in the exact same behavior that had authorized police intervention in the other cases. Cops target Black people hanging out on the corner on the assumption that they are up to no good, stopping and frisking them, demanding their IDs, running their names for warrants, telling them they better not be there when they come back around; white people doing the same are almost invisible to police unless they do something to call attention to themselves. These are but a few examples underscoring how crime rates are better understood as reflections of cops' perceptions of the proper order of things rather than harms people are actually experiencing.

In addition to creating crime data through their actions, cops further shape crime rates by controlling when and how an incident is reported as "crime." Police departments have broad latitude in recording crime statistics. They control the numbers and types of crimes they report to the FBI as well as the general public, and no one is checking their numbers. When cops claim that increased budgets or numbers of cops lead to lower crime rates, they are citing data they themselves produce and control. When cops claim that demands to reduce their budgets are causing an increase in crime, they completely control the "evidence" they offer to support their claims.

There is substantial evidence that police manipulate crime statistics for political purposes. For instance, in 2010, a whistleblower filed a report on the NYPD confirming that the nation's largest police department systematically underreported crimes.[51] John Eterno, who is retired from the NYPD and co-author of *The Crime Numbers Game: Management by Manipulation*, confirmed the existence of the practice: "The (crime) numbers are being gamed, plain and simple, and the numbers are being gamed because the (police district) commanders are under tremendous pressure to make the numbers look good. This is happening all over the city."[52] In 2017, an LAPD captain blew the whistle on her department for doing the same.[53]

Cops manipulate crime data in a number of ways—most commonly by reclassifying crimes or changing the date the crime is reported. They also affect crime rates through the control they have over the charges they bring, enabling them to decide whether to charge someone with a "violent" or "nonviolent" offense, and deciding the severity of the offense.[54] They exercise sole control over what is considered a "credible" crime report and what isn't. When it suits their interests, police departments can reduce crime rates by deeming criminal complaints "unfounded." While the proffered justification is often that a survivor or witness is uncooperative or not credible, there is no way of knowing what has happened, and no recourse. For instance, a ProPublica investigation identified wide variation in the use of the "unfounded" designation in the case of rape reports across many different jurisdictions—and between the number of cases that were internally labeled as unfounded compared to those that were publicly reported as such.[55] According to the report, "[t]he Prince William County Police Department in Virginia, for example, showed no unfounded cases in the government's updated system in 2016. However, internal department records show that it classified nearly 40 percent of all rape cases as unfounded."[56] A review prompted by the investigation led the department to acknowledge that at least 10 percent of these cases were "misclassified."[57] Scholars refer to this process as "statistics-driven policing"[58] and the ensuing crime stats as "dirty data."[59] The ProPublica report concludes that many departments rely heavily on "unfounded" designations, "which can make it appear that they are better at solving rape cases than they actually are."[60]

The fact that cops shape crime data to align with their political interests is not just a technical problem that should trouble researchers; it dramatically affects how all of us should interpret and evaluate crime studies cited by police and pundits. Whether they show crime rates going up or down, crime stats—and the research based on them—are wielded as public relations tools to secure more resources, power, funds, and legitimacy for police.

The way crime data is categorized can also distort our understanding of the danger we actually face. For example, homicide statistics don't just represent shootings but include deaths by other means—such as when someone is killed in a car accident by a reckless driver. Yet when the news reports that homicides are going up, it is easy to think we—or people we care about—are at increased risk of being killed by a stranger. In fact, most people killed intentionally are killed by someone they know.[61] And the risk of dying by homicide is concentrated in the very same communities where abandonment to other forms of violence and deprivation is perpetuated and maintained by the police.[62] A Philadelphia doctor who treats gunshot victims notes that by the time they reach the emergency room, many have already grappled with food insecurity, unstable housing, crumbling schools, and violent crime.[63] Additionally, whether an assault turns fatal, and thus becomes a homicide, depends on factors beyond the incident itself—including proximity to a hospital, access to emergency care, and access to more lethal means of attack. These factors change depending on time and location. For instance, for decades—until local organizers won their fight to get one—there was no trauma center on the South Side of Chicago, making it more likely that shootings would become homicides than in other parts of the city.[64] These contingencies are invisible in crime data, rendering the mere fact of an increase in homicide rates an inaccurate measure of a generalized risk of being murdered. Nevertheless, crime data is routinely mobilized to stoke fear and maintain police funding and power.

Homicide statistics also underestimate the risk of preventable death because they rarely include deaths caused by structural harms. Organized abandonment that manifests, for example, as lack of access to routine health care and healthy foods, unsafe employment, proximity to pollution,[65] or evictions and foreclosures, produces very real increases in risk of premature death that are not reflected in homicide statistics. For instance, by some estimates, evictions directly contributed to more than 11,000 COVID deaths in the U.S. in 2020 that were not counted as homicides[66]—a number certain to increase as eviction moratoriums are lifted while the pandemic rages on.

Homicide rates thus both overestimate the danger of being randomly harmed and underestimate the likelihood that we will experience preventable violence. Regardless, the ups and downs in homicide rates consistently trumpeted by cops as evidence that they are indispensable are not reliable predictors of the risk of being killed.[67]

To be clear, every loss of life, whatever the cause, and no matter how it is or isn't counted, is a profound tragedy for families, loved ones, and communities. Our goal is to stop death by violence *and* deprivation. Our call for abolition is rooted in the fact that police have repeatedly demonstrated that they are not set up to achieve that goal—and worse yet, contribute to preventable death through their own violence and by starving communities of resources that would reduce it.

Cops Don't Stop Violence or Crime

The vast majority of what cops do has nothing to do with preventing or intervening in violence. As noted above, only a tiny fraction of arrests involve "violent crime,"[68] and offenses characterized as serious crimes— like murder, rape, robbery, aggravated assault—very rarely result in arrest and conviction.[69] Though some earlier studies from 1990 to 2001 found that where the number of cops was higher, the number of homicides was lower,[70] subsequent, more rigorous studies found the impact of police numbers on rates of both homicide and violent crime is significantly lower than previously believed.[71] A 2019 study compared police activity as measured by number of arrests instead of the number of cops, and found no relationship between arrest rates and homicide rates.[72] Meanwhile, though the evidence that police stop people from killing each other is weaker than many people previously thought, the evidence that *police kill people* is strong. Police kill over one thousand people a year, a number equivalent to roughly 5 percent of all gun-related homicides.[73]

Not only do numbers of cops or arrests have little to no effect on stopping homicides, more cops doesn't mean less crime. Even with the advantage of being able to manipulate crime data, research shows no relationship between the number of police and crime rates—both from city to city and across the country over time.[74] David Bayley, a preeminent authority on crime and policing, and former dean of criminal justice at University of Albany, wrote in 1994 that "repeated analysis has consistently failed to find any connection between the number of police and crime rates. Second, the primary strategies adopted by modern police have been shown to have little or no effect on crime."[75] Researchers at John Jay College of Criminal Justice came to the same conclusion in 2020: "Few if any studies reporting net positive effects from policing actually show it is specifically the police that reduce crime."[76] Crime rates rise and fall in periodic bursts, but overall have been steadily decreasing over the long term as economic conditions improve, and increasing when they worsen, including during the COVID-19 pandemic. The number of cops, what they do, or how they do it does not affect the equation one way or the other.[77] Researchers in Portland came to the same conclusion in 2021.[78] Police preservationists nevertheless spin this data to maintain and expand their power, interpreting these findings as grounds for throwing more money and resources into policing.

Moreover, studies rarely account for the negative impacts of increased police presence on communities, including increased police killings, sexual harassment and assault, trauma and psychological distress, and criminalization, which may in turn contribute to further escalating violence.[79] Ultimately, police response to violence is simply more violence—through threats, shootings, beatings, sexual assaults, tasings, arrests, and incarceration. More policing *automatically means more violence*.

Still, the question "Who will answer your call when you are in *trouble*?" is the drumbeat marshaled in the face of demands to reduce police budgets. A frequent complaint—particularly in Black communities experiencing organized abandonment, in which police may be the only government service readily available—is that police already don't come fast enough when called for help. Cops can and do manipulate response times to aggravate this problem in the hopes that it will undermine challenges to their power. For instance, organizers in Minneapolis report that police dramatically slowed response times following 2018 budget cuts and the 2020 Uprising.[80] Seattle defund campaigners attempted to foreclose this tactic by mandating that police prioritize calls involving violence in progress.[81] Instead, cops slowed responses to all calls in protest of budget cuts. Meanwhile, cities continued to fail to fund programs that would meet the needs underlying the vast majority of 911 calls.

Studies have also found that efforts to decrease police-response times—in other words, get cops to the scene faster—through changes to staffing and dispatch procedures have largely been ineffective in reducing crime.[82] For one, response times are a red herring. The vast majority of time, police are not responding to crisis calls.[83] And, generally speaking, even in the case of violent crimes, crime victims call someone else first—a friend, relative, or insurance agent—before calling the police; when cops do show up, "there is virtually no chance to make an arrest at the crime scene, no matter how quickly police respond.[84] In other words, even when people call cops for help, no matter how fast they get there, they are primarily documenting what happened after the fact.

After the Fact

Police usually show up after harm has already been done, and do little to prevent violence. Even by their own metrics of "solving crimes" by making arrests, they are failing. According to criminologists, "police still solve only 20–25 percent of reported serious crimes."[85] The rate of unsolved homicides for Black people is even higher at 40 percent compared to 20 percent for white people, 78 percent for Black men compared to 23 percent for white women.[86] For some offenses, the solve rate is even lower, and has been decreasing dramatically. Stolen vehicles, for example, are recovered by police in only 11 percent of car thefts nationwide.[87] And, while TV shows and media have exaggerated the role of forensic evidence through shows like *CSI*, researchers note that the validity of many forensic science techniques that were once accepted—like fingerprinting and DNA evidence—has become questionable in recent years.[88]

The police response to low solve rates is to once again game the numbers by screening out "cases with a very low probability of being solved" in an effort to improve the stats.[89] Or, they'll repeat the refrain that they need *more* resources—for more staffing, more fancy equipment, more "focused" policing, or to "build community trust"—even though the solve rate has stayed the same as police budgets have skyrocketed over decades.

"Data-Driven" Policing

In some cases, police departments' response to research showing that increased police presence and faster response times don't have significant effects on crime rates has been to shift to something called "hot spot policing."[90] This entails concentrating police resources and focusing their activities on specific neighborhoods and locations framed as "hot spots" for crime, and targeting specific groups of people believed to be responsible for the majority of criminalized activity. As with all crime, when it comes to policing, these designations are based on the cops' own statistics and enforcement activities.

"Hot spot" policing is another example of police exercising wide discretion to fabricate and maintain a particular social order. Cops target an area they decide needs to be controlled and contained, generating arrests that are then turned into crime statistics. These, in turn, are used to justify further targeting. It both creates and confirms crime statistics—another self-fulfilling prophecy. As always, they decide which crimes and data they will use. For instance, Wall Street is a "hot spot" for crime if we focus on financial crimes. Fraternity houses are "hot spots" for sexual assault and drug-related offenses. But neither of these is flooded with cops because police generate crime statistics through selective enforcement and then use those statistics to justify their continued presence in the same places they have always targeted. Police might justify their choices with respect to Wall Street by claiming that white-collar crime is not "violent"—but ask the victims of the 2008 foreclosure crisis about the violence of losing your home because someone gambled with your life, or the violence they experienced afterwards when they became unhoused or were forced into less stable housing situations.

Research on "hot spot" policing in Minneapolis found that "increased police presence failed to reduce serious crime."[91] This is not surprising given that it relies on increased police presence and shorter response times—both tactics researchers have found neither deter nor interrupt violence. Subsequent studies have found that hot spot policing has "a modest effect on disorder"—in other words, public order or minor offenses.[92] Given that cops wield power over data by deciding what constitutes "order" and "disorder," and the fact that they are likely to perceive a heavily policed area as more "orderly," this is not surprising. Even where studies have found that aggressive patrols and drug enforcement in small, targeted areas may have an impact on reducing violent behavior,[93] they rely on crime statistics created by police themselves. Many don't have reliable points of comparison,[94] both in terms of comparable neighborhoods and in terms of non-police alternatives.[95] There is also evidence that hot spot approaches simply displace criminalized activity to different geographic locations.[96] And, more importantly, they fail to account for the violent behavior of police, or for their failure to address the root causes of the problems created by organized abandonment in targeted communities.[97] Regardless, even the effects of short, intensive, and selective "crackdowns"—whether it be targeting drunk driving, traffic offenses, or the sex trade—are generally understood to be limited and largely only short-term.[98] As a result, researchers conclude that they are rarely sustainable—particularly given the high personnel costs and other costs associated with arrests. In short, findings show that they "are not long-term solutions."[99] Instead, they create a revolving door of criminalization, pulling people further and further into the system without addressing underlying issues, moving problems from one area to the next, while perpetuating violence through arrest and incarceration.

Rather than concluding that the strategy is limited in its effectiveness in reducing serious harm and comes at a significant cost, particularly compared to directly addressing conditions fueling violence, police preservationists again interpret this data to mean that we should invest in *more* crackdowns and *more* hot spot policing. The police goal is always to contain and control—and to justify the need for their endless growth along the way—not to change or eliminate conditions contributing to violence or criminalized acts.

There is another path to addressing shared concerns about violence: meeting the needs of communities rather than criminalizing, scapegoating, and fomenting fear. Some police scholars are increasingly acknowledging what organizers and community activists have long been saying: the places that are deemed "hot spots" and "problem areas" suitable for "crackdowns" are generally low-income, Black and Brown neighborhoods experiencing organized abandonment in the form of targeted divestment from social services, infrastructure, and public goods. Even the originators and proponents of "problem-oriented policing" acknowledge that "fixing the underlying condition often has a substantial impact,"[100] and that crime prevention lies "mainly outside the realm of policing and emphasizes education, housing, health care, and employment; in other words, create a fair and prosperous society and eliminate the root causes of crime."[101] Yet, cops and their allies are unwilling to support strategies that will put them out of business, even if they know they are more effective. Instead, they insist on *more* money, more cops, more police power, continuing to divert resources from the very things that would address the problems police purport to solve, even while admitting that they can't. If police don't deter, interrupt, or solve crime,[102] why are we investing up to half of city budgets on them?

Defunding Police Will Decrease Violence

"'SKYROCKETING MURDER RATES,' claimed the National Fraternal Order of Police. 'An explosion of violent crime,' said Senate Minority Leader Mitch McConnell. 'Democrat-run cities across the country who cut funding for police have seen increases in crime,' tweeted U.S. Rep. Patrick McHenry, R-N.C."[103]

As calls to defund police and invest in nonpolice safety strategies persist, the opposition is ratcheting up fearmongering crime rhetoric in an effort to take the wind out of the movement's sails. A growing chorus of police chiefs, police fraternal associations, and politicians are claiming that movements to shrink police budgets and power and increase investments in communities are contributing to a surge in violence across the country—even though the amount cut from police budgets across the country in 2020 amounted to less than 1 percent of overall spending on police.[104] The effect has been twofold—increased resistance to any cuts to police budgets and diversion of pandemic relief funds to increase them.

In June of 2021, President Biden paved the way for pouring much-needed pandemic relief funds into police coffers instead of into the pockets of people struggling to survive.[105] His justification was a study showing a 30 percent increase in homicides, a 6 percent increase in aggravated assaults, and an 8 percent increase in gun assaults in 2020 over the previous year in thirty-four U.S. cities. Of course, any increase in violence is heartbreaking—even more so given how many resources have been poured into police over decades in the name of stopping it, instead of into communities to prevent it. Yet Biden doubled down on this failed strategy by recommending that communities use up to $350 billion from the American Rescue Plan Act (ARPA) coronavirus relief package to hire *more* cops—leading jurisdictions nationwide "to use the funds to recruit police, weaponize SWAT teams, and build jails—a move activists are calling a cash grab by law enforcement and its allies."[106] Biden also proposed an *additional* $300 million in the 2022 federal budget for COPS Hiring Program grants to local police departments.

This intervention to bolster police legitimacy while padding their budgets was on brand for Biden, who was the architect of the '94 crime bill that opened up the floodgates for billions of dollars in federal funding to flow to state and local police departments.[107] Neither the president, nor the pundits who picked up the chorus of "a rising crime wave," mentioned that the very same study found that homicide rates remain well below historic rates. In other words, homicide rates have been this high in the past, including during periods when police budgets were unequivocally on the rise.[108]

The president was also selective with his citation: the same study he referenced to stoke fears about homicide rates also found that robbery rates *fell* by 9 percent, and property and drug crime rates—with the exception of motor vehicle theft—all fell significantly during 2020. Residential burglaries also decreased by 24 percent, along with nonresidential burglaries by 7 percent, larceny by 16 percent, and drug offenses by 30 percent.[109] According to previously released FBI data—which reflects data produced by the police themselves—crime was down overall in 2020 by about 6 percent, one of the largest decreases in decades.[110] Those findings were echoed by the Department of Justice, which released similar data in October 2021 confirming—based on reports from crime victims rather than police data—that the total violent victimization rate declined 22 percent from 2019 to 2020.[111]

None of this context stopped politicians and pundits from playing fast and loose with the facts, conflating homicides, "violent crime" (which can include violence against people *or property*), and "crime" in order to claim that all were skyrocketing and would continue to do so unless police budgets are once again increased. At the same time, there is a growing silence about the mounting toll of preventable COVID-19 deaths (not counted in homicide statistics) resulting from government abandonment of vulnerable communities, including disabled, immunocompromised, unhoused, precariously housed, and incarcerated people, health care workers, teachers, and children to the ongoing ravages of the coronavirus pandemic. This illustrates once again how what is defined as "crime" and how we respond to it is a product of social, political, and police decisions.

Undeterred by the facts, and without questioning the underlying figures, the mainstream media whipped up a frenzy of disinformation. They parroted cops who falsely claimed that police departments had been "defunded"—a gross fabrication, as cuts to police budgets in 2020 amounted to less than 1 percent of annual spending on police. This, they argued, was responsible for the supposed crime wave. In fact, the spike in homicides and assaults policymakers and media were pointing to occurred *before* the summer 2020 Uprisings, and subsided in the second half of the year—before any of the minor cuts to police budgets went into effect.[112] What's more, the vast majority of preliminary budget cuts affected vacant positions, which means that budgetary cuts largely did not affect the overall number of cops.

A study of sixty cities found no correlation between the size of protests in the summer of 2020 and any increase in homicides.[113] In fact, as Fordham professor John Pfaff points out, "The rise in homicides has occurred more or less equally in places that adopted reforms and those that rejected them."[114] In other words, the spike in homicides largely took place "on the status quo's watch." Policymakers trying to make the case for funneling more money to the police are "arguing for more of what has mostly failed us this past year."[115] During the period that homicides have been on the rise, police budgets—including in cities experiencing the highest escalations in violence—have stagnated or increased, while investments in meeting community needs and violence prevention have declined. In 2020, cities such as Houston, Nashville, Tulsa, and Fresno experienced a spike in homicides, even as their police budgets increased.[116] In Memphis, $9.8 million in Department of Justice Community Oriented Policing Services (COPS) funding was added on top of the city-funded Memphis Police Department (MPD) budget to support the hiring of fifty additional cops. Yet FBI reports for January through March 2021 compared with the same period in 2020 show that the overall rate of violent crime rose by 26 percent and the murder rate rose by 33 percent there.[117] And yet, police and politicians continue to insist we reward them with still more money. As law professor Aya Gruber concisely puts it: "Policing has an amazing ability to fail up."[118]

What *did* cause the increase in homicides? There are many factors at play and, according to some researchers, as much as 60 percent of variations in homicide rates can be attributed to random fluctuations.[119] Experts, including Patrick Sharkey, a sociologist and criminologist at Princeton, Chuck Wexler, the executive director of the Police Executive Research Forum, and Daniel Webster, director of the Center for Gun Policy and Research at Johns Hopkins University, suggest that the increase in gun violence is more likely due to fallout associated with the pandemic.[120] The year 2020 was one of devastating loss and grief; an unprecedented economic crisis; a looming eviction, foreclosure, and homelessness crisis; an ongoing climate crisis; the closure of community-strengthening spaces and services; and a significant increase in the availability and purchase of guns in 2020 are more likely to be what's driving increases in homicides.[121] Journalist Rachel Cohen addresses this latter point, writing that the FBI's own data suggests that almost 40 million guns were sold in 2020—an increase of 40 percent over the year before. A large chunk of that increase—roughly 20 percent of purchases—is among first-time gun owners.[122] The combination of a pandemic pressure cooker with increased access to guns is a much more plausible explanation for an increase in homicides than cuts to police budgets. But, as Pastor Michael McBride, the executive director of Live Free USA, a violence-interruption program in Oakland, put it, "People do not want to understand the level of distress, grief, trauma and destabilization, both economically and socially, that Black communities have had to endure in this once-in-a generation global pandemic."[123] In fact, the very same report cited by the president to justify increasing the cops' share of the coronavirus relief package concluded: "[T]he pandemic has placed individuals and institutions under tremendous strain, ultimately pushing homicide rates higher. In addition, the pandemic has impeded outreach to at-risk individuals—a key component of most evidence-informed anti-violence strategies."[124]

The relationship between increased socioeconomic pressure on communities—which rose to unprecedented levels in 2020—and increased violence is backed by research. According to the John Jay Research Advisory Group on Preventing and Reducing Community Violence, "Community violence is more prevalent in neighborhoods where residents face severe and chronic financial stress."[125]

So why ignore other potential causes of any increase in violence? Because it doesn't serve the purpose of discrediting demands to shrink police power.

Against this backdrop of selective citation and blatant misinformation, polls measuring people's *beliefs* about whether crime was increasing and what was causing the increase began to be substituted for data actually describing the situations at hand. As the hosts of the *Citations Needed* podcast put it: "Crime waves are really waves of crime reporting."[126] The result is a self-fulfilling prophecy: manufacture a story, measure how successful you are in convincing people that the story is true, and then use the polling data as proof that the story is, in fact, true.[127] Polls, and the media stories they generate, then serve as covers for pro-police politicians, enabling cops to reap the harvest of the misinformation they have sown by demanding a blank check to keep the country from chaos. John Roman, senior fellow at the National Opinion Research Center at the University of Chicago, an independent research institution supporting decision-makers in using data to make policy, says: "If the crime rate is up, we say, 'Well, we need more cops because crime is going up.' If the crime rate goes down, we say, 'Well, we need more cops because what we're doing is working.' It's ludicrous."[128] Nowhere in this rigmarole does anyone actually question the central premise: Do cops actually create safety? Could we address this problem another way? As outlined in the recommendations of the COVID-19 Policing Project, investing funds in direct support and community-based safety strategies toward a just recovery, instead of doubling down on policing, is more likely to produce lasting public safety.[129]

Sadly, using fearmongering as a tool to divert scrutiny from their budgets and practices is a tried-and-true police strategy. In the summer of 2020, police posted billboards outside of Austin, Texas, warning of chaos and lawlessness at the height of the movement to defund the local department. Meanwhile, in Minneapolis, cops kept up a steady drumbeat of claims that dismantling the department would push the city into a dystopian future. Cops are pushing the same narratives in Oakland, San Francisco, New York, Milwaukee, Seattle, and other jurisdictions where organizing to defund the police and invest in true community safety has seen some success. Stoking fear to push "law and order" agendas and pour more and more money into police departments is a tactic that long predates 2020.[130] Lawmakers and the media are simply recycling decades-old talking points about increasing violence and crime in the face of "inadequate" funds for police.

In fact, at its core, policing is about manufacturing—and then promising to assuage—fear to preserve the social order scripted by myths of white supremacy: fear of Indigenous people resisting land theft and genocide, of enslaved Africans rebelling, of an invasion of "foreigners," of workers organizing, of the have-nots coming for the haves, of murder and mayhem, of people taking what's not "theirs" to take. Cops fuel the problem and then offer themselves as the only viable solution. As James Q. Wilson and George Kelling, authors of the magazine article that spawned the "broken windows" policing paradigm, acknowledged: the greatest impact of increasing police foot patrols in neighborhoods is to give people the *impression* of safety by addressing their fears—fears cops themselves have fanned.[131]

Beyond the problematic data around the effects of increased policing on rates of homicide, violence, and crime, there is a deeper crack in the logic of claims that more violence requires more cops: It presumes there are only two options to increase safety. When we discuss things in terms of a singular choice between more cops or fewer cops, we fail to consider other solutions, like increasing investment in the things we need to produce more safety: housing, jobs, education, health care, and community programs.[132] Concerns around defunding or abolishing police inevitably stem from this inability to recognize that there are far more effective options beyond policing. As Rachel Herzing, abolitionist organizer and scholar, put it in a 2020 interview: "What people are getting wrong inside of that is that this is an on-and-off spigot of what currently exists. The way that that sometimes gets articulated is, if there's no cops then there's chaos. . . . There's only one option."[133] In reality, we have many more options beyond simply increasing or decreasing the number of cops or how much money we spend on them. The real choice is between policing and a wide array of other options.

We Can Reduce Violence Without Cops

It's not that we don't know how else to create safety. The fact that we *do* know what makes communities safer, yet policymakers continue to pour more money into police instead, despite decades of evidence indicating that policing is not an effective safety strategy, is egregious. There are other, less costly, less violent, more effective ways to reduce violence. But the relentless pursuit of safety through policing keeps us from enacting them, constrains our imaginations about what is possible, and prevents us from securing the resources to make our visions real.

Conversations around violence and crime posit police as the only possible response, regardless of the question posed. But evidence shows that the best way to reduce violence is to increase access to housing; health care, including mental health care; education; accessible, sustainable, and living-wage jobs; and community care, connection, and programs. It is this knowledge that informs and drives campaigns to defund police and invest in community well-being—because we know that is the only path forward toward safer, more just communities.

As the researchers from the John Jay Research Advisory Group on Preventing and Reducing Community Violence wrote in the summer of 2020, "[A]re there ways to prevent violence without relying on the police? The obvious answer is 'yes.' Policing has never been the primary explanation for obviously varying levels of community safety."[134] They go on to say that their research found that "having *someone* present reduces crime . . . but *not that police must be that someone*."[135] [emphasis added] As history has repeatedly demonstrated, the choice for police to be that "someone" is not a neutral choice. Not only is the fact of police presence a form of violence for targeted communities, but it also increases the likelihood that further violence will occur and establishes criminalization and punishment as the only options for conflict resolution.

There is evidence that organizations focused on meeting community needs and securing structural change have a greater impact on creating safety than increasing numbers of police—even when safety is measured according to the limited metrics of crime data. One study of the three hundred largest cities in the U.S. found that "every 10 additional community nonprofits in a city with 100,000 residents leads to a 12 percent reduction in the homicide rate, a 10 percent reduction in violent crime, and a 7 percent reduction in the property crime rate."[136] Community nonprofits were defined as organizations focused on crime prevention, neighborhood development, substance abuse prevention, job training and workforce development, and recreational and social activities for youth. In other words, adding twenty-four community nonprofits per 100,000 residents led to a 29 percent decline in the murder rate, a 24 percent decline in the violent crime rate, and a 17 percent decline in the property crime rate.[137] Some of the cities that experienced large declines in crime include New York, which added twenty-five nonprofits per 100,000 residents during the study period; Los Angeles, which added thirty-six per 100,000 residents; Chicago, which added forty-seven; and Boston, which added fifty-six.

The authors of the study concluded that "we find strong evidence that establishment of community nonprofits had a substantively meaningful negative effect on murder, violent crime, and property crime."[138] In other words, the 30 percent increase in homicides cited by Biden as reason to increase the police budget could be addressed by increasing investments in community organizations instead. Using ARPA funds as they were intended—to support and strengthen communities and community-based organizations—would likely have a much more profound and lasting effect on reducing homicides than increasing police budgets.

One type of community-driven program that creates greater safety is violence interrupters, also called credible messengers.[139] Violence interrupters are respected community members—many of whom have themselves been criminalized in the past—who conduct daily outreach to their communities. They engage in conflict resolution on the streets, respond to hospitals where gunshot victims are being treated, and connect people to services and resources. Their life experience and ties to the community make them uniquely qualified to de-escalate, prevent, and intervene in potentially violent situations. They're also skilled at responding after the fact to prevent escalation and retaliation. Evaluations of these programs in cities across the country show promising results for one such violence interrupting program—the CURE Violence model—which combines violence interruption strategies rooted in public health and support to individuals.[140] The Health Alliance for Violence Intervention (HAVI) similarly employs a public health model, meeting people who have experienced gun violence in hospitals with the goal of preventing retaliatory violence and ensuring that survivors don't have to return to the same conditions under which they were harmed.[141]

Violence interruption programs have proven to be successful in communities with high rates of violence. For instance, Safe Streets offers services to two areas in Baltimore. They celebrated a full year without a homicide in one area they cover, and marked five hundred days without a homicide in the other. In a single year, the program intervened in almost one thousand conflicts citywide that had the potential to become dangerous. Between June 2020 and June 2021, they resolved over four hundred conflicts in a single neighborhood, 70 percent of which involved someone carrying a gun or known in the community to carry a gun.[142] In Richmond, California, the Operation Peacemaker fellowship program generated a 55 percent reduction in homicides and a 43 percent decrease in assaults.[143] Participants in the program receive a stipend of up to $1,000 a month, as well as individualized mentorship and support.[144]

These programs aren't just effective; they're far less expensive than policing. According to Common Justice, a Brooklyn-based organization that offers restorative justice programs in cases of violence, "Establishing Offices of Neighborhood Safety (ONS) which have violence prevention programs in cities like Milwaukee and Oakland cost $4 and $26 per capita, compared to $502 and $727 per capita spending on their police departments respectively."[145] If we hope to actually address violence in our communities, we need to redirect funds from police, who metastasize harm, to programs with proven records of decreasing it.

While many of the programs described above focus on men, Taller Salud, an organization in Loiza, Puerto Rico, takes an explicitly feminist approach to violence interruption. Beginning with the experiences of women who feared losing their children to violence, through a two-year listening process, the group developed a three-pronged model rooted in community-based definitions of health and involvement of respected members of the community. The first involves creation of individual risk reduction plans with young people who have been exposed to gun violence and in cases of gender-based violence. The plans include an exploration of gender roles and how masculinity is defined in ways that engender and fuel violence. The second involves de-escalation and interruption of conflicts and strengthening the community infrastructure for peace. The third involves community outreach to raise awareness, challenge harmful narratives of masculinity, and develop strategies to challenge the state's failure to provide communities with the necessities. Community members are directly engaged through events, as well as through local institutions and businesses. All three strategies operate in parallel, "with feminism as their center of gravity," and without any involvement of law enforcement. The program is constantly evaluating its practices with community members, while strengthening community ties and a sense of mutual accountability and belonging.[146]

Despite evidence that violence interruption programs are successful in preventing and intervening in violence, they continue to be grossly underfunded, and are often undermined by police who see them as a threat to their monopoly on public safety dollars.[147] At the same time the Biden administration urged local policymakers to funnel in pandemic relief funds to police, it committed a mere $5.3 billion to violence interruption programs. This one-time injection of funds is just a drop in the bucket of the over $100 billion spent on police every year. According to the researchers at John Jay, short-term, one-time funding like this results in "significant challenges for program managers working to secure consistent financial and political support for program operations. The pay and benefits for outreach workers are typically low, despite the high stress and high-risk nature of their jobs."[148]

Based on their survey of the research, John Jay researchers identified additional evidence-based strategies to stop violence that don't involve the police, including increasing green space, improving the quality of housing and buildings in a neighborhood, and increasing public lighting; engaging and supporting youth through employment, mentorship, education, and other supports; drug decriminalization, which has been found to reduce sexual assault, robbery, and burglary (including by police); and mitigating financial stress by offering timely and targeted assistance to provide financial stability and opportunities proven to reduce both violence and involvement in criminalized activity, which is often directly related to poverty.[149] For instance, a study in Philadelphia found a 30 percent reduction in gun violence and a 22 percent reduction in burglaries in communities where vacant lots had been revitalized into green spaces.[150]

Another found a 39 percent reduction in firearm-related violence through remediation of vacant buildings.[151]

Prevention programs, like the one described in a *Washington Post* series on redefining public safety, can have similar impacts. These programs

> equip individuals whose social circumstances put them at elevated risk for violence with the skills and resources they need to avoid, de-escalate and manage violence-prone situations that regularly arise in their lives. These programs sometimes operate in schools, like the Chicago-based "Becoming a Man" program, which provides small-group counseling, skill-building and cognitive behavioral therapy for young men. Randomized controlled trials found that violent-crime arrests declined 45 to 50 percent among program participants, and high school graduation rates increased by 12 to 19 percent.[152]

The takeaway here is that research, conversation, and media coverage around violence, cops, and crime obscures a vast universe of potential interventions that are more effective and less destructive than policing. As Danielle Sered, author of *Until We Reckon* and founder of the Common Justice program in Brooklyn, which diverts people charged with "violent crimes" from prosecution to healing, explains:

> Safety is not produced primarily by force. Safety is produced by resources, by connection, by equity, and by reciprocal accountability among neighbors. The vision of a society that does not rely on policing or on prisons as its primary response to harm is not mostly a vision of less, but a vision of more . . . productive, reliable measures of producing safety: investments in health care, in education, in housing, in living wages, in violence interrupters, and intergenerational interventions that draw on the moral authority of those most respected by their neighbors, in conflict resolution and restorative and transformative justice, and in a social service infrastructure and safety

net that in time will render enforcement not just less dominant, but obsolete.[153]

It's time to recognize that decades of pouring more money, resources, and legitimacy into policing in an attempt to increase safety have failed. We know that police and prisons don't keep us safe or deter violence—and that they contribute tremendous violence to our communities. We need to stop falling for cops' fearmongering and throwing good money after bad in pursuit of a safety that cops are not set up to deliver. Policing is functioning as it is intended: to contain, control, and criminalize Black and Brown communities while creating conditions for capital to flourish. It's time to invest in meeting community needs and building nonpolice community strategies that will lead us toward greater safety. In later chapters, we discuss many more ways to increase safety that groups are experimenting with across the country.

The work will not be easy—in large part because it requires us to confront the many myths around safety and policing that have been aggressively perpetuated throughout history. As Sered and Amanda Alexander, founder of the Detroit Justice Center, wrote in the *Boston Review*:

> When we discuss violence, we must uproot a wide range of myths: the myth that people who are responsible for violence are not also survivors of violence, the myth that prisons reliably produce safety, the myth that individual evil, rather than structural factors, is the primary driver of violence, and more. But perhaps the myth that we must uproot most urgently—if we are to uproot the others and end harm in our communities—is the story that we do not know what to do. In cities and towns across the country, people have produced safety in ways the criminal punishment system has not and cannot. These are solutions people have long needed and deployed, and the moral question of our moment is whether we will invest in them as though every single child's survival is our shared business.[154]

We Are Survivors

We are prison industrial complex (PIC) abolitionists not only because our work and research show us that this is the clearest path to greater safety for our communities; we are also abolitionists because we are both survivors.

Mariame:

On April 19, 1989, a young woman jogging through Central Park in New York City was found badly beaten. She had also been raped.

I was seventeen years old and living in New York City, a senior in high school. My school was across the street from Central Park. I was terrified. Just a few months before, I had been sexually assaulted (not in the park). Now, I was certain that I would be targeted again.

It is difficult to overstate the incessant, sensationalized anti-Black media coverage this case engendered. Within a few days, the police had arrested five teenagers—Antron McCray, Kevin Richardson, Yusef Salaam, Raymond Santana, and Kharey Wise—who described being forced to confess within thirty hours of being taken into custody. The police fanned the flames by claiming that the boys—who were between the ages of fourteen and sixteen—had bragged about committing the crime as part of a night of "wilding," conveying the idea of savage animals preying on defenseless (white) women. Soon the press was describing them as a "wolf pack."

But us Black girls felt vulnerable, too—even though we were certain that had we been the ones victimized, the media would be nowhere in sight, there would be no swell of outrage.

Everyone, it seemed—including Black people in New York City—wanted to see the young men "pay." They were guilty, after all; they had confessed, hadn't they? In the end, the boys were each sentenced to up to twenty years in prison, and they remained incarcerated for a dozen years, until someone else confessed to the rape and their convictions were overturned.

For many, the Central Park Five case was a distant memory until Ava DuVernay's film When They See Us *rekindled interest. But for me, the case has remained a glaring example of the violence of policing since it was seared into my consciousness thirty-two years ago. It was typical: the cops did not stop the rape from occurring, but they did perpetuate violence against "the usual suspects." Elevating a white survivor whose experience fit the racist "stranger danger" narrative, the police and the mainstream media seized on stories as old as slavery to stoke the virulent anti-Black racism that drives criminalization, and, in the process, abandoned the majority of survivors to silence. The collective urge to punish these young Black men regardless of whether they actually did the thing they were accused of— or, more importantly, regardless of whether punishment prevents, heals, or transforms the harm—is the same urge that has fueled the astronomical growth of police and prisons. The Central Park Five case made it clear to me that the criminal punishment system was corrupt, anti-Black, and deeply reactionary—and not actually about protecting survivors like me. I didn't know it at the time, but the case would also inform my later thinking about gendered violence, policing, and prison industrial complex abolition.*

Andrea:

I came to organizing for police abolition both as a survivor and as an advocate for other survivors. I have experienced sexual violence at the hands of a cop, and neither police nor social services have offered me protection from other forms of violence when I needed it. These realities profoundly shaped my understanding that police and policing do not provide safety.

In my twenties, I began to organize with other Black women and women of color around police violence. At the same time, I served on the board of a shelter for domestic violence survivors and unhoused women. It was in this capacity that I was invited to participate in an investigation of police responses to sexual violence in the aftermath of a brutal rape of a woman who, like the Central Park jogger, was white. A court had concluded that her assault was the result—at least in part—of police failure to warn or protect her from a serial rapist, despite the fact that they were aware that she fit the profile of his likely targets.[1] What became clear over the course of the investigation was that police did not prevent sexual violence—even in the serial rapist context sold to us in countless movies and TV shows as the reason police must *exist. And, that cops* perpetrate *sexual violence, primarily against Black, Indigenous, unhoused, disabled, queer, and trans people, who experience the highest rates of sexual violence across the board. The sexual violence perpetrated by police we heard about during the investigation took many forms, including strip searches, sexual degradation, extortion, and violation of people in the sex trades, and in the context of cops' investigation, characterization, and treatment of survivors. I learned that my experience of sexual assault by police was not an isolated incident, but part of the systemic violence of policing.*

I will never forget the day I sat next to a Black Jamaican grandmother, who was the same age then as I am now, as she testified before the Toronto Police Service Commission. She told the commissioners about how the police had sexually assaulted and humiliated her during a domestic violence call she made on behalf of her son's girlfriend. Instead of offering assistance, they began ransacking the house for drugs, violently arrested her, and left her half naked in a cell for hours. Nor will I forget the way the chief of police slammed the table when I testified that our investigation revealed that strip searches and body cavity searches like those she described were common police practice, or the muted responses of the commissioners, or the way the woman who had come there for some semblance of justice folded in on herself as she quietly left the room. That's when I committed to documenting and amplifying stories like hers—and my own—to make the case that police do not protect survivors, and all too often add to the violence we experience.

We are not alone in calling for defunding and abolishing police as survivors of violence. For instance, Amita Swadhin—a survivor of child sexual abuse—also advocates for accountability rather than carceral punishment. Swadhin is the founder of Mirror Memoirs, an oral history project uplifting the narratives, healing, and leadership of LGBTQI survivors of color. In a February 2020 Facebook post, they wrote:

> I believe people who commit rape must be held accountable. Specifically, I believe in survivor-defined accountability (when the terms of accountability do not result in continuing cycles of violence and abuse). I do not believe that punishment, fostering shame, isolation and dehumanization, supports personal transformation. I do not believe in the prison industrial complex. I do not celebrate anyone being incarcerated in the prison system. I am taking a stand for a world without ALL forms of rape, and that means taking a stand against the institutions and cultural norms that promote rape.[2]

Similarly, Aishah Shahidah-Simmons, creator of *NO! The Rape Documentary* and a survivor of both childhood sexual abuse and rape in adulthood who has been fighting sexual violence for over two decades, writes in her introduction to *Love WITH Accountability*, "I am committed to co-creating communal responses to . . . gender-based violence outside of the criminal justice system. I believe people who commit harm in our communities must be held accountable."[3] Hilary Moore, a member of Standing Up for Racial Justice and author of *Beyond Policing*, describes herself as a survivor of violence in the home, community, and by the state, and says she is an abolitionist because she wonders what else is possible.[4] We are just a few among many.

Movements to abolish the PIC are founded, led by, and comprised of survivors of multiple forms of violence—racist violence, gun violence, sexual violence, child abuse, domestic violence, homophobic and transphobic violence, and the many types of violence perpetrated by policing, prisons, borders, the medical industrial complex, and racial capitalism. They are born out of the reality that policing, prisons, and punishment do very little to prevent, interrupt, or heal these kinds of violence—and of the certainty that these carceral systems permit and perpetrate violence every day. These movements are rooted in the fact that far more survivors are seeking solutions to the violence they experience outside of policing and punishment than from them—regardless of whether they are engaged in larger movements to shift our collective response to violence away from police.[5] We call for the abolition of policing because survivors deserve *more* safety and *more* options for healing and transformation—and we recognize that police were never created to provide them.

Cops Don't Protect Survivors

Because the majority of violence is not reported to police,[6] there is no way to know the full extent of it; but there is no question it is rampant. In 2020, there were 4.6 million reported instances of interpersonal violence in the U.S.—notably down from 5.8 million in 2019.[7] Someone is sexually assaulted in the U.S. every 68 seconds.[8] In other words, someone was sexually assaulted in the time it took you to read the last page of this book, and someone will be again by the time you finish reading the next one. Annually, close to half a million people ages twelve and older—80,000 of whom are incarcerated, 60,000 of whom are children, and 18,900 who are members of the military—report that they've experienced a sexual assault.[9] One in 3 women experience sexual violence; 1 in 5 has been raped at least once.[10] One in 4 girls and 1 in 13 boys experience child sexual violence.[11] The numbers are equally devastating when it comes to domestic violence: nearly 1 in 4 women and 1 in 7 men will experience severe physical violence at the hands of an intimate partner.[12] Rates of violence are higher in all categories for Black, Indigenous, disabled, queer, and trans people. Rates of sexual violence are twice as high for Native people, and significantly higher for disabled people.[13]

These numbers are dizzying, as is the fact that we continue to experience these levels of violence despite the over $100 billion (and mounting) we spend annually on policing. This includes roughly $600 million distributed annually through the Violence Against Women Act (VAWA), passed as part of the 1994 crime bill, amounting to over $8 billion between

1995 and 2018.[14] VAWA has served as the primary national strategy to end domestic and sexual violence, primarily by funding law enforcement. According to Leigh Goodmark, a lawyer who has represented victims of domestic violence and studied the legal system's response to intimate partner violence for over a decade, "[A]t its passage in 1994, 62 percent of VAWA money was dedicated to the criminal system; 38 percent funded social services. By 2013, 85 percent of VAWA monies were being funneled into the criminal system."[15] Yet, as Goodmark establishes in *Decriminalizing Domestic Violence*, the criminal system's increased involvement with domestic violence cases over the last forty years has not significantly reduced violence.[16] Simmons similarly emphasizes the failure of increased investment in policing to make a dent in the problem. In a summer 2020 interview, she said: "The assumption is that policing will stop or prevent sexual violence. There is documented evidence that it does not. So why do we rely on the police as the only solution to sexual assault?"[17]

These figures only take into account the violence that is reported. The most recent official data available tells us that *more than half* of violent victimizations are *not* reported to police.[18] Counterintuitively, that is even *more* the case when the survivor is injured.[19] Even when a weapon was involved, only 42 percent of cases resulted in a police report.[20] In other words, as Danielle Sered, author of *Until We Reckon: Violence, Mass Incarceration, and the Road to Repair*, puts it, "More than half the people who survive serious violence prefer *nothing* to everything available to them through law enforcement."[21] This is true even for the kinds of violence people cite as reasons we need police: fewer than half of domestic violence survivors and less than one-quarter of survivors of sexual assault ever call or report to the police—and those numbers are decreasing.[22] In cities where 911 data is publicly available, domestic violence calls make up only 1 to 7 percent of calls.[23] Survivors from communities who experience higher rates of violence are even less likely to report it. For every Black woman who reports a sexual assault, fifteen more do not.[24] More than half of trans people report that they would not call the police for help, and that number increases to two-thirds for Black trans women.[25] Middle Eastern, Black, and multiracial people, as well as trans, disabled, and low-income people, are most likely to feel uncomfortable seeking assistance from police.[26] What that means is that any response to the epidemic of violence in the U.S. that begins with the police *already leaves the majority of survivors behind.*

There are many reasons survivors don't call police—most of them having to do with the way the system operates. The majority of survivors correctly judge that policing, prosecution, and prisons won't bring them or their communities safety in the aftermath of harm.[27] In fact, one survey found that 52 percent of survivors believe that incarceration makes people more violent, not less.[28] Survivors also fear dismissal, mistreatment, violence, or criminalization by police—with good reason.[29] An overwhelming majority (88 percent) of survivors and service providers said police sometimes or often don't believe survivors or take their complaints seriously.[30] More than half reported anti-Black, anti-immigrant, anti-Muslim, and anti-LGBTQ attitudes among police.[31]

Shauntrice Martin, an organizer with BLM Louisville, shared her experience in a June 2021 op-ed calling for a 50 percent cut to the budget of the police department that killed Breonna Taylor:

> I was assaulted on campus at the University of Louisville by someone I knew. As scared as I was, I called 911. The city didn't send a counselor or trauma advocate. Instead, two officers showed up. I could immediately tell they were annoyed. One officer asked if I was "sure," and kept insisting that maybe it was a misunderstanding. I had just been choked and lifted up off the ground while my assailant threatened me, but in the moment when I had to convince two officers that it was more than a misunderstanding, I felt just as helpless.
>
> That was the last time I called the police.[32]

Two-thirds of survivors and service providers said police use force against survivors sometimes or often during domestic violence calls—particularly against survivors from communities already targeted by police. Among survivors of homophobic and transphobic violence who reported it to the police, 33 percent experienced verbal abuse, and 16 percent experienced physical abuse at the hands of police. Overall, women who have histories of intimate partner violence and non-partner sexual violence are more than twice as likely to experience most forms of police violence.[33] That can include the sexual violence by cops Andrea has been documenting since that 1997 hearing before the Toronto Police Commission: research has consistently shown that police target survivors of violence for sexual harassment, extortion, and assault.[34]

Beyond adding their own violence to the mix, cops funnel survivors into other systems and conditions of violence, including criminalization, particularly survivors of color and LGBTQ survivors.[35] Mandatory arrest policies, which require police to arrest someone at the scene of domestic violence calls on the pretext of protecting survivors, have increased arrests of survivors—especially those who are already criminalized.[36] In just one particularly poignant example, Anti Police-Terror Project co-founder Cat Brooks described an incident in which her abusive white husband beat her bloody, and then called the cops as she lay on the floor. When two white cops showed up, they decided that Brooks was the "primary aggressor" even though it was clear Brooks was battered. The even more painful irony is that she was arrested under a law intended to *protect* survivors that her mother, a prominent anti-violence advocate in her community, had fought to pass. Brooks is now a prominent leader in the movement to defund the Oakland police department, working to create and resource community-based responses to violence, including domestic violence, that don't involve the police.[37] Despite their intended aims, mandatory arrest laws are also contributing to criminalization of young survivors, and particularly young women of color, experiencing violence in their families. For instance, in Washington State, Black and Native youth are arrested two to four times more often than white youth under mandatory arrest laws.[38]

Black, Indigenous, migrant, and disabled survivors who defend themselves against violence are also more likely to be criminalized than celebrated for surviving. For instance, as protests against police violence surged through the streets in July 2020, Maddesyn George, a twenty-seven-year-old Native mother and member of the Colville Confederated Tribes was arrested for defending herself against a man who raped her while brandishing a loaded gun. She was sentenced to six and a half years in a federal prison, thousands of miles from her child.[39] The same month, Ky Peterson, a Black trans man incarcerated on a twenty-year sentence for killing someone who raped him, was released after sustained advocacy by anti-violence advocates, including Mariame and members of Survived and Punished, an organization she co-founded to call attention to and organize in defense of criminalized survivors.[40]

Beyond arrests, survivors are punished in other ways when they seek help. For instance, 89 percent of survivors and service providers indicate that police interaction results in contact with the family regulation system ("child welfare"); 61 percent stated it can cause survivors to face criminal charges that could lead to deportation; and 70 percent reported that contact with the police "sometimes" or "often" results in the loss of housing, employment, or welfare benefits.[41]

For many survivors, knowing that a call for help is likely to subject the person who harmed them to the violence of the criminal legal or immigration system is also a barrier to involving the police. Ultimately, many survivors want de-escalation, not criminalization. Mariame found this to be true time and again when she served as a staff person at New York City's Sanctuary for Families—one of the largest domestic violence service providers in the country, and at Between Friends, a Chicago-based domestic violence agency. Survivors who called hotlines didn't want the solutions the organizations were putting forward: arrests, prosecutions, prisons, punishment. Mariame's experience is bolstered by the research. A national study of survivors and service providers found that:

(1) Survivors were looking for options other than punishment for the abuser, options that were not necessarily focused on separation from the abuser;

(2) Survivors feared that once they were involved in the criminal justice system, they would lose control of the process;

(3) Survivors were reluctant to engage the system because they believed that it was complicated, lengthy, and would cause them to suffer more trauma.[42]

Survivors simply want the violence to end. They want safety and healing. They want the person who is hurting them to be transformed into someone who won't hurt them—or anyone else—again. For many survivors, police represent a threat of further violence and retaliation, and of criminalization—either of themselves or of someone they love. They understand that police involvement can lead to economic deprivation, deportation, involvement of the family regulation system, or simply loss of agency over the outcome. As a result, most survivors would rather do nothing about the violence they are experiencing—or take matters into their own hands—than involve a system that puts them at risk for receiving either no response, or a response that increases the violence in their lives.[43] That is a damning indictment of our current approach.

Yet police continue to be promoted as the primary solution to violence, even in the face of evidence that they are unable to meet survivors' needs. Abolitionist disability-justice organizer, attorney, and scholar Talila A. Lewis gives a profoundly poignant example rooted in Lewis' own experience as a survivor of gun violence:

> In January 2007, I was caught in a hail of stray bullets that were the result of a drive-by shooting. Bullet holes peppered my car door and the facade of the apartment building immediately next to me. Fortunately, no one was hurt. Police officers arrested one young man at the scene and a prosecutor brought charges against this young man "to the fullest extent of the law." This episode still haunts me, but not for the reasons that most might assume.[44]

Lewis describes being detained in a cop car following the shooting for hours by cops seeking to coerce Lewis into giving them information Lewis didn't have.[45] "The detective kept trying to convince me that the person was a young Black male of a specific height and build and complexion. I can't tell y'all how many times I told this detective that I did not see anything other than the silhouette through the tinted window," Lewis recounts.[46] Hours later, he said, "Well, if you weren't involved, can you explain why your door has bullet holes?"[47] The cops finally released Lewis—but not before they had visibly questioned Lewis for hours in their car, in the same neighborhood where the shooting had taken place, placing Lewis in fear of retaliation by the people responsible for the shooting. This disregard for Lewis' trauma, safety, or perspective as a survivor of nearly deadly violence extended to the rest of the criminal punishment system:

> I also discovered that my voice and my needs for healing were of no consequence to the state—particularly because my desires were not sufficiently punitive. On the morning after the shooting, the prosecutor called me to gather details. After sharing as much information as I could, I expressed my sincere desire to have a face-to-face conversation with the young person who had been arrested. As a student working three jobs and attending school full-time, who had just begun an internship at the Public Defender Service for the District of Columbia, I thought a conversation might make the world of difference in this person's life and provide closure and healing for me. Upon hearing my request, the prosecutor gruffly stated that "the state would handle it from here," and hung up. The government never contacted me again, never provided further information about this individual or the outcome of this case, and I have no idea what happened to this young person.
>
> Was he even the right person (there was some indication that the police may have arrested the wrong person)? Is he being harmed in a federal prison somewhere? Was he released? If he was released, did he continue a cycle of violence or is he now working to support and mentor other societally marginalized youth? Should I have pressed further to have a conversation? Could that have saved others from being victimized if this young person did in fact continue down a path of violence? Would a conversation have benefited either of us anyway? These are questions that I likely will never be able to answer.
>
> Harsh retribution—which seemingly satisfied the state—actually damaged me, this young man, our families, and every marginalized community to which we belong. Furthermore, some ten years later, I still do not have closure and probably

never will. Our criminal legal system claims to seek justice for victims and survivors of violence, but our voices are not centered unless we are acceptably violent enough to justify the state's pre-ordained violent action; or white, wealthy, or abled enough for our dissent to actually matter.[48]

The result of our exclusive reliance on criminalization to address violence is that an increasing number of survivors—especially migrants, people in the sex trades, and other criminalized populations—have been forced into the shadows while the violence continues unchecked. For instance, groups like Generation FIVE, founded and led by survivors of child sexual abuse, and the Bay Area Transformative Justice Collective (BATJC), which also works with child sexual abuse survivors, have argued that the criminalization of child sexual abuse has not made children safer.[49] Nor has the demonization of people who perpetrate it. Instead, it has pushed child sexual abuse further underground—discouraging disclosure and foreclosing pathways to accountability and repair. This actually increases the risk that people who perpetrate these harms will continue to do so in the future.

The answer does not lie in more training or efforts to improve police response or "build trust" in law enforcement among survivors. Even if the number of survivors who felt comfortable reaching out to police were to increase, by its nature policing is only ever a partial and temporary intervention. Rather than finding solutions to problems within the community and preventing future harm, policing escalates tensions and removes people from communities without transforming them. And rather than addressing the patterns, or the contexts and conditions that produced the violence, it deals only with incidents and individuals after the fact. In the wake of violence, survivors must wait for the police to apprehend one person for one specific thing—to address the violence they experience as though it is separate from cycles of harm, unhealed trauma, loss, conflict, and unmet needs. As Sered says, "Most violence is not just a matter of individual pathology—it is created. Poverty drives violence. Inequity drives violence. Lack of opportunity drives violence. Shame and isolation drive violence . . . violence itself drives violence."[50] That includes the violence of policing and punishment.

Goodmark's research and experience have led her to the clear understanding that increased criminalization of domestic violence has exacerbated harm by increasing economic pressures on communities already facing significant strain—a causal factor for gender-based violence.[51] People who are unemployed or underemployed, or who have experienced trauma,[52] are more likely to commit domestic violence.[53] People who have been criminalized and incarcerated are less likely to be able to access employment, and are therefore more likely to engage in further violence. In other words, when there is external pressure on a community, whether it's the pressure of criminalization, or pressure related to the pandemic, economic downturn, or war, the pressure will be distributed within the community along existing axes of power. If pressure on a community is relieved, and necessary resources are made freely available, violence within the community decreases. Goodmark argues that it would therefore do more good to focus on underlying causes of violence "by funding . . . job creation programs and investing in programs that target the intersection of domestic violence and substance abuse, and in community-based programs that would challenge community norms around violence, teach community members to intervene productively, and shore up community infrastructure."[54] This knowledge—that supporting communities with resources rather than exacerbating conditions that produce violence through criminalization is the most effective strategy for decreasing violence—is precisely what is driving demands to defund and abolish police.

The criminal punishment system also discourages people from admitting to violent behavior and taking accountability for their actions. If they do, they are labeled "guilty," which only further embeds them in cycles of policing and incarceration. Meanwhile, survivors are silenced and denied the things they say they need: validation; to be heard; an apology; repair; to regain control; access to resources for healing and safety without having to engage police; to be safe; to make sure what happened to them doesn't happen to someone else.[55] As Sered points out, the criminal punishment system "delivers almost none of these things to the vast majority of survivors."[56] It's no surprise, then, that a survey found overwhelming levels of support among survivors—exceeding those in the general population—

for greater investments in education, jobs, access to health care, and non-prison responses to violence.[57]

Reliance on policing and punishment doesn't just leave behind most survivors, it fails to reach the majority of people who engage in violence. The vast majority of people who commit sexual assault never see the inside of a courtroom, let alone end up in prison. Out of every 1,000 sexual assaults, only 230 are reported to law enforcement; 46 lead to arrests; 9 get referred to prosecutors; 5 lead to felony convictions; and fewer than 5 lead to incarceration.[58] Bottom line: There are far more people who have committed rape outside of prisons than inside them. The people we are afraid of *already* live among us, not behind prison walls. Many people who commit sexual violence continue to operate with impunity; some even go on to become U.S. presidents, governors, or Supreme Court justices. People who commit sexual violence are not the stranger serial rapist that haunts our imaginations; they are related to us, they are friendly with us, they are known to us. The same is true of people who engage in intimate partner violence. If we tried to lock them all up, the incarcerated population would increase by orders of magnitude without bringing an end to the violence. As abolitionist legal scholar Dean Spade points out:

> Violence, especially sexual violence, is so common that we couldn't possibly lock away every person who engages in it. . . . If we deal with the complexity of how common violence is and let go of a system built on a fantasy of monstrous strangers, we might actually begin to focus on how to prevent violence and heal from it. Banishment and exile, which are the only tools offered by the criminal punishment system and immigration enforcement system, only make sense when we maintain the fantasy that there are evil perpetrators committing crimes, rather than facing the reality that people we love are harming us, and each other, and that we need to go to fundamental root causes to change that.[59]

It was those profoundly anti-Black fantasies of monstrous strangers and evil others—rooted in narratives perpetuated through and beyond slavery—that led to the wrongful imprisonment of the Central Park Five. Meanwhile, Donald Trump, who vociferously called for their incarceration while being repeatedly accused of and admitting to sexual violence over a period of decades, went on to become Commander in Chief.

Ultimately, even according to the problematic terms it has set out for itself, the system has already failed. What people fear about a world *without* police and prisons is already happening in a world *with* police and prisons. Policing is extraordinarily costly to survivors and society in both human and financial terms. Yet we continue to pour more money, resources, and legitimacy into policing in the name of survivors while leaving them even less safe.

This is not something we can fix through better policies and training. The failure of policing to prevent, intervene in, and transform violence is endemic. It cannot be addressed through police public relations campaigns aimed at increased reporting, more training for cops, or more programs promoting collaborations among victim advocates and law enforcement. The answer to the failures of policing, prosecutions, and punishment to prevent or address violence does not lie in continuing to throw more money at it in an effort to increase the numbers of people who are incarcerated. None of these approaches will effectively prevent, intervene in, or heal violence, nor will they address the systemic causes and roots of harm. What they will do is infuse more resources and legitimacy into police and prisons, which are primary sites of racist, gender-based, homophobic, and transphobic violence. And they will keep us from investing in what will actually produce greater safety for survivors.

Cops Perpetrate Violence

The catastrophic failure of policing and punishment to produce safety for the majority of survivors is no accident or glitch in the system. The U.S. was built on, and requires, violence against Black, Indigenous, disabled, migrant, queer, and trans people. As Native scholars have elaborated, theft of the land on which the U.S. was built and genocide of its original inhabitants have gender-based and sexual violence at their core. Rape is, after all, a weapon of war.[60] Likewise, the institution of slavery that drove the U.S. economy was premised on denial of Black people's humanity and violation of every aspect of bodily integrity, including systemic and systematic sexual violence. The enforcement of geographic borders, the borders of the gender binary, and the line between abled and disabled are all enforced and policed through multiple forms of police and state violence.[61] These are not just historical realities; they are present in the ways violence continues to be perpetrated by police and permitted against the same populations. They are present, too, in the ways violence is policed and punished through the criminal legal system that emerged to bolster, reinforce, and perpetuate these systems and relations of power, all while concealing the ravages of neoliberalism, and perpetuating racial capitalism.[62] For these reasons, the carceral U.S. state—in the forms of police, courts, prisons, social workers, and medical providers—cannot adequately recognize, prevent, or redress violence against these populations. Instead, it is charged with perpetuating it. This is what motivates survivor-led calls for the abolition of these systems: we want to build a life-giving society focused on greater safety, particularly for people living at the "dangerous intersections" of race, gender, sexuality, ability, and class under the current white supremacist order.[63]

This requires us to recognize that police are *among* the rapists and abusers. Individual cops commit sexual violence and battery—on and off the clock—with alarming regularity.[64] This should come as no surprise since, by definition, policing is structured by violence. Cops deliberately target criminalized and oppressed groups—always empowered by the badge, the impunity from accountability it offers, as well as the systems of power it protects.[65] These same systems of power produce higher rates of domestic violence among police. According to the National Center for Women and Policing, domestic violence is "two to four times more common among police families than American families in general."[66] In the case of on- and off-duty sexual and domestic violence by cops, researchers agree that reported cases represent only a fraction of the problem. Even fewer survivors report when the perpetrator is a police officer, and action is rarely taken to address the issue.[67]

Abuse perpetrated by individual cops is inextricably bound up with the systemic violence of policing and punishment. Police exercise control over

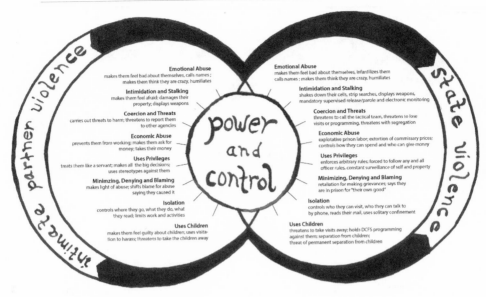

Monica Cosby, designed by Sarah Ross.

communities and individuals in ways that mirror interpersonal domestic and sexual violence—and fuel, facilitate, and exacerbate other forms of violence. Formerly incarcerated survivor and member of Moms United Against Violence and Incarceration Monica Cosby illustrates this point using an image of intersecting power and control wheels. This dynamic is reflected in what Black feminist criminologist and INCITE! and Critical Resistance co-founder Beth Richie describes as the "violence matrix," in which multiple forms and sites of violence—including state violence—fuel and reinforce each other.[68]

Criminalization—no matter whether we are talking about survivors, people who do harm, or people who fall into both categories—perpetuates gender-based violence. For one, the very process of criminalization itself marks people as fair game for sexual violence by police, prison and immigration detention officials, and the public. Black and Indigenous women, queer and trans people, disabled people, people who work in the sex trade, and migrants—groups that are inherently criminalized—report the highest rates of sexual violence in the U.S.[69] Incarceration, disproportionately experienced by the same populations, only increases risk of sexual violence. Sexual violations of incarcerated people—and the loved ones who

The Violence Matrix

	Physical Assault	Sexual Assault	Social Disenfranchisement
Intimate Households	Direct physical assaults by intimate partners or household members, victim retaliation	Sexual aggression by intimate partners or household members	Emotional abuse and manipulation by intimate partners or household members, forced use of drug and alcohol, isolation and economic abuse
Community	Assaults by neighbors, lack of bystander intervention, availability of weapons	Sexual harassment, acquaintance rape, gang rape, trafficking into sex industry, stalking	Degrading comments, hostile neighborhood conditions, hostile or unresponsive school and work environments, residential segregation, lack of social capital, threat of violence
Social Sphere	Stranger assault, state violence (e.g. police), gun control policies	Stranger rape, coerced sterilization, unwanted exposure to pornography	Negative media images, denial of significance of victimization, degrading encounters with public agencies, victim blaming, lack of affordable housing, lack of employment and health care, mistrust of public agencies, poverty

Surrounding the Violence Matrix is the tangled web of structural disadvantages, institutionalized racism, gender domination, class exploitation, heteropatriarchy and other forms of oppression that locks the systemic abuse of Black women in place. Responses need to be developed that take all of the forms of abuse and all of the spheres within which injustice occurs into account.

Beth E. Richie, *Arrested Justice: Black Women, Violence, and America's Prison Nation* (New York: New York University Press, 2021). Do not duplicate without proper citation.

visit them—are routine occurrences in prisons, jails, immigration detention facilities, group homes, and locked hospital wards. In 2015, the latest year for which federal data is available, people incarcerated in prisons and jails made 24,661 allegations of sexual victimization, 58 percent of which involved prison or jail staff. Sexual violence in immigration detention facilities is also rampant and grossly under-reported.[70] Rates of sexual violence are highest for incarcerated women and queer people, and among them, highest for incarcerated trans women.[71] This is why Spade describes police and prisons as "serial rapists." That perspective is echoed by Tourmaline, a Black trans visionary artist, filmmaker, and longtime PIC abolitionist, who calls them "primary perpetrators" of violence against women and queer and trans people of color.

Systems of policing and imprisonment that justify their existence and expansion by claiming to reduce violence—including sexual violence—actually create *more* violence. Police are *sources* of sexual assault, not solutions to it. Police offer neither perpetrators nor survivors any resources toward meaningful healing and transformation. The demonization of people who commit criminalized acts of violence—especially sexual violence—has been used as an excuse for the proliferation of prisons and jails, which are themselves sites of tremendous sexual violence. These are deeply uncomfortable realities for the people who advocate for preserving police and prisons "for the rapists and batterers." If we truly care about ending sexual violence in all its forms, then we cannot look away from the sexual violence perpetrated by the state in the name of "safety;" we need to eliminate police, prisons, immigration, and border patrol.

That does not mean abandoning our communities to violence: ending gender-based violence requires abolition of institutions that perpetrate it—including police—*and* attention to what will *actually* produce safety for Black, Indigenous, disabled, migrant, trans, and queer people—and all survivors of gender-based violence.

Anti-Carceral Movements Against Gender-Based Violence

For the past three decades, as survivors and advocates for survivors in movements to end violence, we've been preoccupied with some version of the following questions: *How can we better prevent violence and protect survivors? How can we interrupt the criminalization and punishment of survivors? How do we transform conditions to minimize the amount of harm in our communities and increase the number of options available to survivors to avoid and escape it? When harm happens, as it inevitably does, who should be empowered to respond and what does justice look like?* These questions are far from new. Black and Indigenous feminists, other feminists of color, and white socialist-feminists have been asking them for decades.

Survivor Roots of Police Abolition

The anti-rape movement of the early 1970s emerged out of radical women's and queer movements suspicious of relying on a white supremacist, patriarchal, homophobic, transphobic state to address their concerns. Early grassroots rape crisis centers did not turn to law enforcement and courts. They explicitly operated outside of the social service paradigm, focusing on mutual aid. Some did so based on a critique of the U.S. state; others based on a culture of care and mutual responsibility. Some neither sought nor accepted state funding, concerned that doing so would make the movement beholden to state interests. Early anti-rape and anti–domestic violence movements were riddled with internal tensions between those who deeply believed that the state needed to be more responsive to violence through the prison industrial complex, and those who insisted that movements work to find non-carceral solutions and remain vigilant about state violence and co-option.

In 1977, feminists from Santa Cruz Women Against Rape (SCWAR) addressed these tensions in an open letter published in the feminist magazine *Off Our Backs*:

> This is an open letter to the anti-rape movement. We, the members of Santa Cruz Women Against Rape, are writing this letter because we are concerned about the direction the anti-rape movement is taking. While we have many concerns . . . we would primarily like to address the issue of the relationship of the anti-rape movement to the criminal justice system. The reasons we are interested in this issue have a lot to do with how we see ourselves as a Women Against Rape group. We are a political group that focuses on the issue of rape and violence against women, and that is working towards the long-range

goal of a radical transformation of the very basis of our society. We do not believe that rape can end within the present capitalist, racist, and sexist structure of our society. The fight against rape must be waged simultaneously with the fight against all other forms of oppression.

When the organized movement against rape first started about five years ago, most of the anti-rape groups were collectives of feminists, who came together because of their anger at the way the police and the courts treated rape victims.

These groups (and ours was among them) were primarily political. We were critics of the police, the courts, and the hospitals, the institutions that traditionally dealt with rape victims. Their awful treatment of women became a topic in the media, largely due to the efforts of the women's movement against rape. In a snowballing fashion, many other anti-rape groups formed. Many of these groups, however, did not consider themselves political, nor even feminist. They considered themselves service groups, who wanted "to help rape victims." They felt that the criminal justice system and the anti-rape movement had a common cause, "to get rapists off the street." Therefore, these groups tended to encourage or cajole women to report rapes to the police.

The more explicitly political groups were frustrated, both by the ineffectiveness and unresponsiveness of the criminal justice system, and because of the increasing rape rate. While many remained critical of the criminal justice system in theory, most groups felt it was important to work on building or improving relationships with the police and other criminal justice agencies. They hoped this would lead to increased prosecution and conviction of rapists. In attempts by anti-rape groups to build good relations with the criminal justice system, criticism of these agencies has been withheld, or dealt with through police channels instead of by applying outside pressure (e.g., through the media, demonstrations, etc.). This tendency to work with the criminal justice system is reinforced by the fact that many groups are supported through government funds. Because of this, there is an inevitable push—if not outright contractual obligation—to persuade women to report rapes to the police.[72]

Despite these clearly articulated concerns, investment in policing and punishment as the predominant response to sexual and domestic violence won the day. While some anti-violence organizers remained committed to a structural analysis of violence that required work toward radical social change, another group coalesced around the carceral state. Beth Richie describes this latter group: "compelled to respond to conservative state tendencies regarding families, gender, and sexuality, they pursued a safer, less antagonistic strategy that they expected would be more acceptable . . . developed a more professional identity as 'specialists' . . . believing they would be better positioned to compete for public support."[73] Meanwhile, she writes elsewhere, "A review of notes from early meetings, coalitions position statements, policy papers, organizational mission statements reveal that there were Black folks who warned—over and over—against overreliance on the state."[74]

The increasing drumbeat for criminalization was part of a larger systemic shift. According to Goodmark, "anti-violence advocates did not advance this carceral agenda in a vacuum. Efforts to increase the criminalization of intimate partner violence paralleled the ascendancy of neoliberalism."[75] The interests of the state in expanding the reach and resources of police coincided with those of anti-violence advocates seeking a collective response to a systemic problem without a systemic critique of the role of the state as a perpetrator of violence. This led to what INCITE! co-founder Mimi Kim describes as "the carceral creep," in which anti-violence movements have been increasingly conscripted to bolster the violence of policing and punishment.[76]

Seizing on and perpetuating the idea that our value as survivors is determined by how much time someone does in a cage for harming us, the anti-rape and anti-domestic violence fields were incredibly successful at passing laws creating new categories of "crimes" to punish sexual and domestic violence. They were eventually joined by mainstream LGBT movements seeking greater visibility and punishment for homophobic and transphobic violence.[77] Since then, mainstream, predominantly white-led anti-violence movements have become deeply invested in policing and punishment as the primary response to sexual, domestic, homophobic, and transphobic violence. As is well documented by the work of many feminist scholars, including Beth Richie's *Arrested Justice: Black Women, Violence, and America's Prison Nation*,[78] and *Abolition. Feminism. Now.*[79] the focus on getting the state to become more responsive to these instances of violence led to a symbiotic relationship between law enforcement and increasingly white, professionalized advocates who are distanced from the communities they serve. This has evolved to a point where, in many places, anti-violence advocates are now literally housed directly inside police precincts, or in offices next to prosecutors.

Increasing collaboration between service providers and the police has left well-meaning therapists, social workers, and advocates with a deep reluctance to challenge the status quo, and it has been destructive for the safety of many survivors of violence. Mariame has firsthand experience of this reality. In the introduction to the Project NIA zine republishing the SCWAR open letter, Mariame wrote:

> When I entered the field, we were far removed from the origins of the modern movement of the early '70s and continued to move further astray. . . . I first read the open letter from Santa Cruz Women Against Rape in the mid-'90s. It was a balm. I was already becoming disenchanted with the funded anti gender-based violence field. The survivors I was working with consistently rejected what we were offering, which were mainly legal solutions.[80]

This is how Mariame came to the position that we need something different. In her words: "I wouldn't know what I know if I didn't do the work. I didn't read it first. I learned it from other survivors." As she wrote in the introduction to the zine, "I am now entering my thirty-first year of working in this area (as an activist, advocate, organizer, or worker) and consider myself an exile of the funded anti-rape and anti-domestic violence fields. From my position of exile, I am committed to reclaiming a model for addressing harm that does not rely on the punishing state as the first resort to mete out so-called 'justice.'"[81]

Andrea came to her commitment to police abolition similarly: by experience. As communications director for a national women's organization in Canada in the early 1990s, she struggled with the group's call for expansion of the criminal code to include stalking as she became more involved in struggles against racialized police violence. As time went on, she learned about case after case in which police not only failed to prevent or interrupt violence, but perpetrated it—beating, raping, killing, and criminalizing survivors seeking help. A decade later, she was further shaped by her law school experiences representing survivors who were denied orders of protection, forced back into unsafe situations through visitation orders, and refused immigration relief under the VAWA despite ample records of calls for help to police who offered none.

Andrea also learned firsthand how destructive the marriage between service providers and law enforcement is for criminalized survivors. Sanctuary for Families, the same agency at which Mariame worked decades before, was a leading opponent of a campaign Andrea co-led to stop police and prosecutors from citing the possession or presence of condoms as evidence of intent to engage in prostitution-related offenses in criminal cases. Despite support from dozens of public health, reproductive rights, HIV, anti-violence, sex worker, LGBTQ, and criminal justice organizations, Sanctuary almost single-handedly stymied the campaign by opposing *any* limitation on police or prosecutors' power to confiscate or use condoms to criminalize—often targeting people who were survivors of multiple forms of violence.[82] They persisted even when confronted with research demonstrating that the practice was jeopardizing the health and safety of people in the sex trades and their communities. They were happy to speak for survivors when it served expansion of police powers and resources, but quickly dismissed and silenced survivors when they sought to limit criminalization and secure their own survival. They have remained vocal and vehement opponents of campaigns to decriminalize prostitution-related offenses led by people in the sex trades, even as criminalization has repeatedly been shown to contribute to increased violence against the people they claim to want to protect, including those who are survivors of sexual violence.[83]

Advancing "feminism" by supporting police, prosecution, and prison-based solutions to violence ("carceral feminism") places survivors squarely in the crosshairs of gender violence by the state and in communities.[84] Carceral feminism allows the state to build up the prison industrial complex in the name of feminism even as it fails to reduce domestic and sexual violence rates in a meaningful way. If it did, surely we would be living in a country nearly free of domestic and sexual violence, given that the U.S. has the highest incarceration rates in the world.

The anti-violence movement's increased investment in criminal punishment has also made it largely unwilling to support criminalized domestic and sexual violence survivors who aren't seen as "perfect victims." This is in part because of their dependence on funding that partners them with law enforcement, and in part because of ongoing and historical racialized narratives about violence. As a result, anti-domestic and sexual violence organizations have refused to participate in organizing campaigns to support criminalized survivors such as Tiawanda Moore, or the survivors of Daniel Holtzclaw, a former member of the Oklahoma police force who sexually assaulted criminalized Black women. Virtually none offer services or supports specifically focused on the needs of survivors of police sexual violence.[85] Deep investment in criminal-punishment approaches to violence often means less organizing to change conditions that *produce* violence—for instance, by supporting free or affordable housing for all.

Carceral feminism's widespread currency has effectively limited survivors' options *and* our collective imaginations on how to interrupt violence—all while giving the state license to impose carceral "solutions" on survivors that place them at greater risk. For example, in 2002, Mariame hosted a speak-out on community violence for high school–aged girls in her Chicago Rogers Park neighborhood.[86] The young women spoke indignantly about the constant street harassment they were subjected to daily: "Why do I have to take the long way home from school?" "Why do I have to get my guy friends to walk me home in order to sidestep the dirty old men who try to grab me by my clothes, hair, backpack, anything really?" two young women demanded. The following summer, Mariame supported eight young women between the ages of sixteen and eighteen in a research project focused on young women's experiences of street harassment,[87] leading to the creation of the Rogers Park Young Women's Action Team (YWAT). Armed with a report of their findings, some of the young women decided to use their research to educate the community about street harassment and mobilize adults in the neighborhood to take concrete steps to help eliminate, or at least lessen, it. About a year after they completed their research, a dozen YWAT members sat with local elected officials and laid out their demands, including improved lighting on two main streets, funding for a poster campaign to encourage local businesses to collaborate with police to enforce loitering laws, youth job programs, and increased police patrols during after-school hours. This last demand was hotly contested among members of the group and was later completely repudiated.

Unsurprisingly, elected officials easily agreed to more policing, including by business owners. Eventually, after many more years of activism and organizing, YWAT succeeded in getting new lighting on two main streets, but the politicians never did deliver on YWAT's demands for more jobs. Instead, they implemented something the young women explicitly told them would *not* create safety. In fact, it made them targets of violence in the neighborhood. During the initial meeting, elected officials asked the girls if placing surveillance cameras in the neighborhood would mitigate some of the street harassment. The girls were unanimous and adamant that they opposed surveillance cameras, explaining that harassers would simply move to other locations, and that they would personally feel uncomfortable in a community where their actions were surveilled. Yet, like Sanctuary for Families, the elected officials imposed carceral solutions in survivors' names, while overriding survivors' concerns for their own safety. Citing the need to protect girls and young women from sexual harassment and assault, they put cameras in various locations in the community. They even went so far as to publicly thank YWAT for their "input" on the matter.

The girls were livid and afraid of how community members would react to the cameras. A few weeks later, those fears materialized: the door and window of their meeting space was tagged with graffiti reading: "Bitches Get Out." One of the young women's partners became a consistent target of police harassment in the neighborhood. Young women going about their daily lives shopping or waiting for public transportation were approached by strangers and asked if they were "the girls who brought the cameras to the neighborhood." Before the camera incident, the young women of YWAT were well-known in Rogers Park. They had appeared on television, in newspapers, and on radio, and held many community events—including town hall meetings. Most of the girls lived and had attended elementary and middle school in the neighborhood. While they were angry about the street harassment, what they hadn't been prior to elected officials imposing cameras on the community in their names was fearful. In the end, the young women decided that they would not be intimidated and that they would continue to organize despite the threats. They learned some important lessons, foremost among them that politicians will always rush to offer more policing as a public safety intervention.

The young women eventually decided as an organization that they would never call for increased policing to address violence. Instead, they practiced a Black feminist politics of care: when a young person needed a place to stay for a few weeks because they had been kicked out of their home, they stayed with Mariame or with someone else in the group. When money was tight at home and a young person needed funds to attend a college visit, YWAT pooled resources to help. YWAT members celebrated birthdays, baby showers, and graduations together. They took care of each other and kept each other safer. The trajectory of their organizing mirrors many survivors' journey toward abolition.

The same is true of recent approaches to anti-Asian violence prompted by racist responses to the pandemic and longstanding policing of Asian communities. Asians and Asian Americans vulnerable to anti-Asian racial and gender violence, including from police, immigration, ICE, detention centers, and deportations, teamed up to create community-based responses that did not involve police. They created community care, healing justice, and community-defense workshops led by women and queer practitioners while also providing mutual aid support for survivors of violence. Yet they were competing with calls for more hate crime legislation, policing, and punishment by Asian groups partnering with conservative and neoliberal politicians. Speaking with *Ms.* magazine, Dr. Connie Wun, director of AAPI Women Lead, a former sex worker, and a survivor, described this tension and frustration: "The rest of us are like: 'What are you doing? We're building community solutions!' They get coverage while everyone else is working with survivors . . . or have been doing this work for a long time to create community-based solutions."[88]

Despite the prevalence of the carceral shift in anti-violence organizing, there are plenty of individuals and organizations who push back. INCITE!—a survivor-led organization—was formed in 2000 in direct response to increased investment in policing and punishment by predominantly white-led mainstream anti-violence organizations.[89] Like SCWAR, instead of seeking more carceral responses to gender-based violence, INCITE!'s work, shaped by Black feminism, was guided by the question "What would it take to end violence against women and trans people of color?" and the answer: "[W]hen we shift the center to survivors of color and our communities, the importance of addressing state and institutional violence becomes evident. This perspective benefits not only survivors of color, but all peoples, because relying on oppressive institutions to end violence in our communities is not an effective strategy for anyone."[90] From this standpoint, rooted in the lived experiences of Black, Indigenous, and migrant women and trans people, INCITE! understood: "It is impossible to seriously address sexual/domestic violence within communities of color without addressing these larger structures of violence, such as militarism, attacks on immigrants' rights and Indian treaty rights, the proliferation of prisons, economic neo-colonialism, and the medical industry."[91]

The *Critical Resistance-INCITE! Statement Against Gender Violence and the Prison Industrial Complex* was published almost two decades before demands to defund police reached a crescendo in the summer of 2020.[92] Emphasizing that the answer to violence is not more policing, punishment, and prisons, the statement called for resources to be redirected toward meeting survivor needs: "When public funding is channeled into policing and prisons, budget cuts for social programs, including women's shelters, welfare and public housing are the inevitable side effect. These cutbacks leave women less able to escape violent relationships."[93] The statement also critiques individualistic approaches to ending violence through reliance on police, shifting "focus from developing ways communities can collectively respond to violence."[94] The statement's closing words highlight the survivor-centered nature of the call for abolition: "We seek to build movements that not only end violence, but that create a society based on radical freedom, mutual accountability, and passionate reciprocity . . . [where] safety and security will not be premised on violence or the threat of violence; it will be based on a collective commitment to guaranteeing the survival and care of all peoples."[95]

For decades now, organizations accountable to communities most impacted by violence have been consistent in their calls for investing in communities rather than policing to increase safety for all. More than four decades since SCWAR sounded the alarm about the anti-violence movement's growing reliance on law enforcement, and two decades after INCITE! and Critical Resistance issued their call, there are signs that we are finally being heard. In 2020, amid the national uprisings against anti-Black state violence, more than fifty mainstream anti-violence organizations across the country responded with a statement entitled "A Moment of Truth":

> We, the undersigned sexual assault and domestic violence state coalitions, call ourselves to account for the ways in which this movement, and particularly the white leadership within this movement, has repeatedly failed Black, Indigenous, and people of color (BIPOC) survivors, leaders, organizations, and movements:
> - We have failed to listen to Black feminist liberationists and other colleagues of color in the movement who cautioned us against the consequences of choosing increased policing, prosecution, and imprisonment as the primary solution to gender-based violence.
> - We have promoted false solutions of reforming systems that are designed to control people, rather than real community-based solutions that support healing and liberation.

- We have invested significantly in the criminal legal system, despite knowing that the vast majority of survivors choose not to engage with it, and that those who do are often re-traumatized by it.
- We have held up calls for "victim safety" to justify imprisonment and ignored the fact that prisons hold some of the densest per-capita populations of trauma survivors in the world.
- We have ignored and dismissed transformative justice approaches to healing, accountability, and repair, approaches created by BIPOC leaders and used successfully in BIPOC communities.[96]

The statement goes on to call for investment in "care, not cops—to shift the work, resourcing, and responsibility of care into local communities" and concludes that "divestment and reallocation [of funds from policing and punishment] must be accompanied by rigorous commitment to and participation in . . . community solutions and supports."[97]

The statement stands in stark contrast to the approach that emerged out of the mainstream #MeToo movement a few years earlier. Riding the tide of outrage following waves of disclosures of sexual violence in Hollywood, corporate C-suites, and the halls of Congress, legal organizations like Time's Up pursued punishment as a primary response. A testament to how deeply ingrained policing is as a response to violence, the focus was on changing laws to increase penalties and extend statutes of limitation for prosecuting rape. If we can't imagine anything else, almost every conversation about harm can quickly become hijacked into expanding systems of surveillance, policing, and punishment that promise something called "justice" and accountability, yet sell out survivors in pursuit of what police and punishment simply can't produce.

For example, in 2018 Mariame co-led a campaign with Survived and Punished NY calling for former New York governor Andrew Cuomo to commute the sentences of incarcerated survivors of violence, many of whom were criminalized for acting in self-defense.[98] At the same time, Time's Up was working with Cuomo to increase penalties for sexual violence in New York, allying itself with a politician who would advance their punishment agenda while failing to protect survivors from the sexual violence of prisons (not to mention someone who perpetrated sexual violence himself).[99] Time's Up also studiously ignored police sexual violence, in spite of Andrea's repeated attempts to put it on their agenda.

For many, the twin national reckonings prompted by #MeToo and #BlackLivesMatter converged in the summer of 2020, expanding and deepening the conversation among survivors, anti-violence advocates, and PIC abolitionists about the role of police. Since the summer of 2020, we have each provided workshops and training for anti-violence organizations and government agencies across the country about the relationship between demands to defund the police and violence prevention, interruption, and response. Their willingness to enter these conversations reflects a growing recognition in some sectors of the anti-violence movement that we will not end rape through criminalization. Yet others continue to resist divestment from policing and punishment despite four decades of evidence that Santa Cruz Women Against Rape were right.

Despite the evidence and growing acknowledgment that police don't stop violence, the perennial response to abolitionist visions remains, *But what about the rapists, the batterers, the child abusers?*

These questions continue to be asked as if abolitionists haven't spent our lives thinking about them, as if they aren't a significant part of what led us to call for abolition in the first place.[100] They are also asked as if it is our sole responsibility to answer them—rather than a collective responsibility to reckon with the reality that policing and prisons have not provided satisfactory answers. They are asked as if the billions we spend on policing each year haven't consistently failed to prevent endemic rates of violence in our communities, and as if policing and prisons are not themselves sites of significant rape, battery, murder, and child abuse. As if criminalized survivors don't describe policing and prisons as extensions of the abuse they experience in their homes and communities. As if a young Black mother trapped in an extremely violent relationship didn't once describe her relationship to police to Andrea in similar terms, saying "I feel like I'm in a domestic violence relationship with the NYPD." As if survivors haven't created defendsurvivors.org, a whole website explaining that "prisons don't stop domestic violence, they *are* domestic violence." As if these aren't the most urgent questions we are trying to answer. As if suggesting that our call for an end to the violence of policing somehow means that we excuse or abandon our communities to violence doesn't compound the harm we've already experienced.

We, too, are desperate to stop violence. We, too, have questions. But unlike those who are willing to continue to delegate responsibility for ending violence to a system that increases it while consistently failing to protect survivors, we are committed to finding new, more effective solutions. We know there is no single system, no "other" police, that we can delegate the problem to. We know that there is just us—and that ending violence requires a multiplicity of responses and systemic change.

While sometimes asked in earnest, these "what about the rapists" questions are often posed disingenuously by people who will never be satisfied with a response, because they fundamentally disagree with our vision. It's time for new and better questions: Why are we leaving more than half of survivors behind? Why are we continuing to invest in responses that *don't* create safety, while starving approaches that *do* of resources? As Jacquie Marroquin, the director of programs at the California Partnership to End Domestic Violence, points out, "community-based responses to crises are already happening, and they're working. We just don't know about it. It's not funded."[101]

We know, and are practicing, better ways to prevent, interrupt, and move toward ending gender-based violence. Survivors of violence have consistently identified the mechanisms that help them prevent, avoid, or escape violence: community, violence prevention programs, non-police first responders, shelters, services, housing, health care, including robust systems of quality, accessible care for disabled people, childcare, immigration status, and living-wage employment. But these sources of safety remain grossly under-recognized, under-resourced, and under-funded. Instead, the vast majority of resources—and legitimacy—go to institutions that don't stop violence at all: police, prisons, immigration enforcement, Border Patrol, and the military. Movements to defund and abolish police are demanding deep investments in community-based safety through true violence prevention and intervention strategies—and by transforming the cultures that make gender-based violence possible in the first place.

Where Do We Go from Here?

For us, the question is: "How do we create safety outside of carceral logics?" Our answer to this question is to abolish systems of policing and punishment; invest in the resources individuals and communities need to be safe and thrive; and build community-based skills, relationships, and infrastructure to prevent, interrupt, respond to, and transform harm. This is where our attention and organizing must focus.

Each of us has a stake in figuring out how we are going to build a system that truly addresses harm. Johonna McCants-Turner, a former member of INCITE!, emphasizes that this means adopting a framework "that doesn't depend on solving violence with another form of violence."[102] The criminal legal system is punitive, oppressive, and ineffective, and dehumanizes us all. If we make sure to keep survivors and marginalized populations at the center of our analysis, there is a very good chance that the new system that we build will be better than the one we have. We can start from where we are: by building healthy relationships that are the foundation of safety. We can also start by asking survivors what they want, need, and deserve. A majority of survivors describe housing, health care, income, and immigration status as things that would enable them to prevent, avoid, escape, and mitigate violence.[103] Housing is the single greatest need identified by victims of intimate partner violence.[104] What we need, then, is housing, income support, prevention and intervention skills—a multiplicity of resources that support survivors in healing and communities in transforming into ecosystems of healthy relationships. These are clear strategies to ensure that so much harm doesn't happen in the first place. They also ensure that, when harm does happen, the tools for repair are readily available.

We are already doing this work and are primarily limited by lack of resources.[105] Successful community-based responses to violence exist. Communities across the U.S. address sexual assault, domestic violence, and child sexual abuse through community-based, non-professionalized, collective responses outside of existing systems of punishment. The Natural Helpers initiative at API Chaya in Seattle, for example, trains and resources the people that survivors are already likely to turn to in their community—faith leaders, health care providers, neighbors, community members—to respond, intervene in, and prevent violence.[106] These responses both challenge policing and adopt frameworks of community accountability and transformative justice as pathways to safety. They include informal conflict de-escalation by neighbors, mediations that interrupt cycles of retaliation, responses that leverage the moral authority of respected people in the community to intervene in patterns of violence before they escalate, and responses that hold those who have done harm accountable. You can learn more about many of these efforts at TransformHarm.org, MillionExperiments.com, and AccountableCommunities .org.

But these solutions are almost never adequately resourced, and their efficacy is often hampered by the involvement of the police. This is why defunding police is a survivor-led anti-violence strategy that stops cops from looting resources that survivors need to prevent, avoid, escape, and heal from violence—and puts more money into violence prevention and interruption, and meeting survivors' needs.[107]

A reorientation to community-based safety strategies is not uncomplicated. While most survivors never contact the police, many also face silence and complicity in the very communities we are proposing to turn to. As Mallika Kaur, founder of the Sikh Family Center, describes:

> I have had strangers step up and provide shelter; friends pack courts during emotional hearings; elders have simple but essential conversations: "I know what's happening, I'll keep checking on her daily, and I will come over if I suspect you've hurt her again." There is a lot of beauty in these responses: They are not only individual interventions; they propel the culture change to prevent domestic violence in the first place. Yet, at the same time, we wrestle with the reality of community members who conspire with the abusive person because of their family ties;

their economic worth; or other shared experience—at times as shamefully simple as "she's complaining about what every wife goes through." We have also grappled with the community members unable to comprehend how even after all the help and support they extended she has not left an abusive situation. And community members who make it impossible (psychologically, emotionally, even physically) for a survivor to seek safety, within the relationship or outside of it.[108]

We know that armed agents of the state cannot produce safety for the vast majority of survivors. The work is to promote the deep shifts in community that are still needed in order to create safety within them. During a conversation about abolition at a 2019 retreat of the In Our Names Network, a national network of organizations, campaigns, and individuals working to end police violence against Black women, girls, trans, and gender nonconforming people Andrea co-founded,[109] Black trans organizer and founder of the Outlaw Project Monica Jones challenged participants by recounting the story of a Black trans woman who had been violently assaulted as community members cheered her assailants on. *If that's the community we're relying on, count me out,* she said, challenging us to recommit ourselves individually and collectively to creating safety for Black trans women as an essential part of our abolitionist struggles. Toni-Michelle Williams, director of the Solutions Not Punishment Collaborative, reminds us that this work requires us to show up physically and financially for Black trans women in our communities and to build infrastructures of safety with Black trans women at the center. Iyanna Dior's brutal videotaped beating in Minneapolis in the weeks following Floyd's murder as conversations about abolishing the MPD were in full swing reinforced the urgent need to live into these commitments.[110] We must, as the CR-INCITE! Statement cautions, avoid romanticized notions of community-based responses to violence outside of policing that "isolate individual acts of violence (either committed by the state or individuals) from their larger contexts" and don't offer adequate protections to survivors.[111] We need, the statement's authors emphasize, strategies that "address how entire communities of all genders are affected in multiple ways by both state violence and interpersonal gender violence."[112] In the words of the authors of *Abolition. Feminism. Now.* "a turn to the 'community' is fraught, sometimes mythic: the community is at once a radical vision, a fugitive possibility, and a struggle—abolition feminism in practice."[113]

The only chance we stand of creating safety for all survivors is by learning from the histories of violence and how they impact individuals and communities on multiple scales. And it is only by listening to the needs articulated by survivors that we stand a chance of creating safety for all.

Re-Form

chokehold bans = please find another way to kill Black people
body cameras = please press record when you kill Black people
repealed privacy laws = the number of Black people you've killed
    must be made public

—Rosamond S. King, "Breathe. As in," *All the Rage* (2021)

I am sick of symbolic things—we are fighting for our lives.

—Fannie Lou Hamer

Following the November 2020 elections, Democratic leadership called former president Barack Obama out from retirement to quell growing public support for shrinking police department budgets and investing in community needs. In an interview on Snapchat's "Good Luck America," Obama admonished protesters and activists: "If you believe, as I do, that we should be able to reform the criminal justice system so that it's not biased and treats everybody fairly, I guess you can use a snappy slogan, like 'defund the police.' But you know, you lost a big audience the minute you say it, which makes it a lot less likely that you're actually going to get the changes you want done."[1]

But the police and criminal punishment system cannot be reformed. Like Fannie Lou Hamer, we are sick of symbolic changes that leave policing's core functions and daily impacts untouched.

Calls for police reform misapprehend the central purpose of police, which inevitably dooms them to failure. As we argue throughout *No More Police*, police exist to enforce existing relations of power and property. Period. They may claim to preserve public safety and protect the vulnerable, but police consistently perpetrate violence while failing to create safety for the vast majority of the population, no matter how much money we throw at them. Their actions reflect their core purposes: to preserve racial capitalism, and to manage and disappear its fallout.

As journalists and organizers Maya Schenwar and Victoria Law put it: "Reform is not the building of something new. It is the re-forming of the system in its own image, using the same raw materials: white supremacy, a history of oppression, and a toolkit whose main contents are confinement, isolation, surveillance, and punishment."[2] We want something new, which requires us to abolish institutions and practices of policing, not simply reshape them.

A commitment to creating safety anew doesn't mean we don't fight for incremental changes, but it does challenge us to make transformational demands that erode the power, resources, and reach of police: defund, decriminalize, and divest from policing. It also challenges us to increase our power to build the world we want through demands for investment in meeting community needs and building strategies that will bring us closer to real safety for all.

As talk of police abolition entered the mainstream in 2020, oppositional calls for reforms grew louder. National and local politicians and policy advocates argued that the way forward was to keep trying to make policing "better," not dispose of it entirely. "Don't defund police, re-fund police," went the reformist refrain—as though the more than $100 billion poured into cop coffers each year somehow deprives police departments of enough money, tools, training, and resources to do their jobs well.

The chorus calling for police reform in the midst and wake of the 2020

Uprisings is made up of a range of voices, including older white liberals; mainline civil rights groups; members of the Black middle class; and new-comers such as Campaign Zero—a group of young Black activists who came together to create social media, data, and policy tools in the context of the Ferguson Uprising.[3] Even Senator Bernie Sanders, who has argued for wholesale reorganization of the U.S. economic system, sidestepped calls to defund police, arguing instead for the "transformation of police departments" into "well-trained, well-educated, and well-paid profession-als."[4] In Minneapolis, where Derek Chauvin killed George Floyd in May 2020, longtime police reformers responded to calls to dismantle the police department and create a new department of public safety by insisting that better rules, stronger oversight, and more accountability for the existing police department are the answer to continuing police violence.[5]

Nationally, reformers argued that police departments could be trans-formed with data, science, and "21st Century" policy recommendations, like those made by the Obama administration's Presidential Task Force on police violence in the wake of the police killing of Mike Brown in 2014.[6] Advocates for police reform coalesced around the federal George Floyd Justice in Policing Act[7] (JPA), as well as state and local legislation that mirrors its provisions.[8] The proposed legislation recycled longstanding proposals: end racial and religious profiling; adopt body and dashboard cameras; limit local departments' access to military-grade weapons; tie police funding to adoption of bans on chokeholds and no-knock war-rants;[9] develop new use of force policies; embrace community policing programs and training; and create more "oversight."[10] The JPA would also have established a National Police Misconduct registry and reduced barri-ers to federal prosecutions and civil lawsuits.[11]

While the federal legislation was being hotly debated in Congress and critiqued by organizers, Campaign Zero introduced a set of eight reforms that essentially functioned as a wedge against defund demands.[12] They claimed, based on contested data,[13] that their #8CantWait reforms would reduce police killings by 72 percent.[14] The #8CantWait proposals included rules prohibiting cops from shooting into moving vehicles, requiring them to announce their intention to kill before shooting, and teaching them a "use of force" continuum—a gradual escalation of force proportional to

(perceived) threat, something that has already been a part of police training for decades. As with the JPA, #8Can'tWait allowed politicians and
celebrities an "out"—they could look like they were backing well-known
young Black leaders calling for change without threatening the existence
or fundamental purpose of policing.

But nothing in the legislation named for him would have prevented
George Floyd's murder, nor changed the conditions that brought him into
contact with the cops who killed him.[15] Millions watched Derek Chauvin,
a cop trained in "implicit bias," de-escalation, and the dangers of putting
pressure on a person's neck, use a "positional restraint"—which is different
than a "chokehold," and therefore permissible under "chokehold" bans—
to snuff out the life of a Black man over a $20 bill.[16] The de-escalation
techniques he was trained on were implemented[17] by a department that
had already faced extensive reform and claimed to have adopted 90 percent of the policies promoted by Obama's Task Force on 21st Century
Policing, as well as at least half of the #8CantWait policies. Many other
departments across the country had already adopted the proposed reforms
while continuing to kill, maim, and harm Black people with impunity.
For instance, the cop who killed Rayshard Brooks two weeks after Floyd's
murder had "undergone 2,000 hours of training, including sessions on
de-escalation tactics, cultural-awareness training, and instruction on use
of deadly force. None of this preparation stopped him."[18]

Neither the JPA's prohibition on "no-knock" warrants nor #8CantWait
policies would have stopped Breonna Taylor's killing: the cops claimed
they knocked before invading her home, and Louisville already has an
"announce before killing" rule. So did Cleveland, yet police killed twelve-
year-old Tamir Rice within seconds of arriving at a playground.[19] The
same is true of North Carolina, where state troopers killed Daniel Harris, a deaf person who didn't hear the sirens of the cop car signaling him
to pull over.[20] In Chicago, adoption of seven of the #8CantWait policies
has not stopped Chicago police from killing Black people at 27.4 times
the rate of white people.[21] To paraphrase Black feminist poet and scholar
Rosamond King whose verse opens this chapter, the JPA and #8CantWait
recommendations boiled down to: *find new ways to kill Black people, make*

a record of it, and make sure everyone knows. The government will pay you to do it.

George Floyd's death pushed many people to look for answers beyond reform, opening unprecedented space for abolitionist critique. Soon after #8CantWait was announced, a group of abolitionists from across the country responded by launching the #8toAbolition countercampaign.[22] Their demands included redistributing police budgets to meet community needs, decriminalizing poverty and survival, disarming police, removing cops from schools, and ensuring safe housing for all. Their goal was not reform, but building "a society without police or prisons, where communities are equipped to provide for their safety and well-being."[23] Abolitionist critiques ultimately eroded support for #8CantWait.[24]

The 2020 Uprisings brought many to the realization that it is time to stop trying to reinvent the wheel. All of us have spent too much time, energy, and resources in pursuit of fruitless "fixes" to reduce the violence and harm of policing. It's time to confront what policing is at its core and move beyond it rather than continuing to try to "re-form" it.

In a testament to the power of this collective shift in consciousness, as calls to defund gained strength, reformers began to appropriate the language of abolitionists while doubling down on policing. Some conceded that police budgets had gotten too big but stopped short of supporting significant cuts. Others agreed that cops should no longer handle mental health crises, round up unhoused people, or address problematic drug use—so that they can focus more time and attention on "real criminals." Some even claimed that they had been on board with "shrinking the police footprint" all along—that now, thanks to the shift in conditions, they were free to "come out" publicly in support of demands to shrink police departments. Campaign Zero, for example, attempted to revive their failed proposals by calling them a program pointing toward abolition.

Likewise, the Center for Policing Equity (CPE), a research and policy organization dedicated to police reform, tried to appear aligned with movement demands by releasing a five-point plan in June 2020. Co-opting abolitionist assertions that "budgets are moral documents," CPE prescribed a "rigorous analysis" of the demand for "public safety" and use of community resources that could "reduce [police] footprint on communities." They went so far as to call for investment in targeted basic income programs.[25] Sounds a bit like demands to defund, right? Except CPE's institutional mission is predicated on ongoing support for police: they work directly with over forty-five police departments across the country.[26] CPE also helped write the JPA, which would have *increased* funding for law enforcement. By positioning CPE's reforms as more "reasonable" and attainable ways to address concerns about police violence than calls to defund, CPE co-founder Phil Goff implicitly undermined abolitionist demands.[27] As with #8CantWait, politicians adopting CPE's approach could appear responsive to protesters' demands and claim alignment with Black-led organizing while preserving policing's core functions. This "cloak of imagined racial solidarity," as Keeanga-Yamahtta Taylor describes it, obscures the role played by groups like CPE acting "as arbiters of political power who willingly operate in a political terrain designed to exploit and oppress" Black people—the realm of policing.[28]

No matter where they came from or what language was used to package them—"reimagining," "fixing," "streamlining," "right-sizing," or "smart policing"—many proposals for change in response to the 2020 Uprisings bore the hallmarks of more fruitless reform. But police reform doesn't work. Demands to defund and abolish policing are based on the lessons of history, emerging from a place of clarity around what policing is and does, and why efforts to change it have failed.

Reform on Repeat

As historian Elizabeth Hinton illustrates in her books *From the War on Poverty to the War on Crime* and *America on Fire*, repeated cycles of police reform have failed for over a century.[29] Every time public outrage reaches a fever pitch, a commission is formed or an investigation is launched, producing recommendations trumpeted as the solutions to police violence while simultaneously bolstering the legitimacy of policing. The New York State Senate's Lexow Committee investigation was one of the first major inquiries into police practices, taking place in 1894, just decades after the first municipal police forces were established.[30] The Committee[31] was established amid widespread reports of extortion and complaints of "clubbing"—violent and routine attacks by "patrolmen armed with nightsticks or blackjacks."[32] In spite of ten thousand pages of testimony given by seven hundred witnesses,[33] no substantive changes were made. In fact, images of NYPD cops beating protesters with batons in the summer of 2020 demonstrate that, more than a century later, clubbing is alive and well.

Further charges of corruption and patronage ushered in the "Reform Era" of policing in the late 1800s and early 1900s. In response, reformers sought to professionalize police by adopting new policies and improving selection, training, and management of police departments.[34] The federal Wickersham Commission was convened in 1929 to study the enforcement of Prohibition. Commissioners offered a scathing indictment of police departments across the country, including evidence of brutal interrogation strategies and widespread financial corruption.[35] Their recommendations? More reform, more professionalization, better leadership and management, more effective recruitment and training, more legislation, and better policies and procedures, more oversight, and greater use of science and technology.[36] Starting to sound familiar? The same solutions are on offer a century later.

Demands for divestment from policing and investment in community safety emerged in the 1960s from incarcerated people and the Black Panther Party,[37] even as reformers continued to call for better police training, more oversight of departments, and better community-police relations. When cops persisted in terrorizing Black, Indigenous, low-income, and migrant communities, rebellions broke out in over seventy cities across the U.S., prompting a wide-ranging investigation by the federal Kerner Commission in 1967. Though the commission made the usual reform recommendations, they also addressed the broader social problems underlying the crisis, calling for investments in job creation and housing as well as an end to segregation.[38] Instead, the federal government made massive investments in policing and criminalization while slashing funding to social programs as neoliberal economic policies took hold.[39]

Consistent with neoliberal narratives that blame individuals for structural conditions, police and policymakers increasingly sought to shift focus away from cops' behavior toward the individuals and communities they policed. Challenges to police legitimacy were met with calls for "building community support for law enforcement" and procedural changes designed to increase public perception of "fairness" in policing. Instead of checking police power, reforms increased police legitimacy by identifying people who don't trust police as the problem, rather than police themselves. Similar calls for procedural changes and "restoring trust in law enforcement" followed the brutal police beating of Rodney King in 1991 in Los Angeles and the subsequent rebellion. Nearly a decade later, the same ineffectual calls were issued in the wake of the 1999 police killing of Amadou Diallo in the Bronx.

The past two decades have brought increased attention to racism in policing—from racial disparities in traffic stops on the New Jersey turnpike;[40] to the New York City Police Department's "stop and frisk" practices; to profiling of Black women at airports,[41] prompting hearings, litigation, and legislative proposals. The U.S. Department of Justice ordered an end to racial profiling by federal law enforcement,[42] sued the state of New Jersey for racial discrimination, and mandated a broad range of reforms.[43] And yet, little has changed: twenty years later, Black drivers on New Jersey's turnpikes are still disproportionately subjected to searches, arrests, and uses of force after traffic stops by state police."[44] Black women continue to experience invasive and humiliating searches at airports,[45] and profiling has significantly expanded in the context of immigration enforcement and the "war on terror."[46] In 2011, over a hundred grassroots, legal, and policy organizations across New York City organized as Communities United for Police Reform (CPR) to demand an end to practices like "stop and frisk."[47] They were successful in making policing a key issue in the 2013 New York City mayoral election. They also secured the most extensive and expansive anti-profiling measure in the country at the time, and a federal court declared the NYPD's stop and frisk practices unconstitutional.[48] But policy changes did not reduce racial disparities in stops, searches, and arrests.[49] Organizers began to more directly target police powers: in the summer of 2020, CPR launched a major campaign to defund the NYPD, calling for at least $1 billion in cuts to the city's $6 billion police budget.[50]

The 1994 crime bill was couched as yet another attempt to "reform" and "improve" policing.[51] The legislation empowered the Department of Justice to investigate local police departments, heralding the advent of "consent decrees"—court-ordered plans to force police reform.[52] Federal intervention and judicial oversight of local police departments were held out as a means of finally rooting out the problematic aspects of policing. Yet consent decrees have also failed to provide sustained relief from police violence.[53]

The first DOJ investigation in 2000 targeted the Pittsburgh Police Department. It was declared a success on all fronts, in spite of the significant costs of implementation:[54] for instance, the development of an "early warning system" intended to catch bad cops cost over a million dollars.[55] A decade later, cops beat an unarmed teenager until his face was swollen and pulled his dreadlocks from his scalp.[56] Pittsburgh police drew further criticism in the years that followed after a shooting paralyzed a Black motorist and protesters filed a class action lawsuit alleging excessive force. These incidents prompted yet another investigation of the Pittsburgh Police Department, this time on the city level.[57] But the city task force's recommendations, which included new use of force policies and better discipline, "closely resembled the changes outlined in the consent decree 23 years earlier."[58] In other words, another ineffectual cycle of reform bringing communities right back to where they started.

We see this same pattern echoed in New Orleans, where particularly egregious police violence emerged in the wake of Hurricane Katrina. One episode in particular prompted widespread outrage and calls for reform: a week after the storm, NOPD cops shot six unarmed people who were crossing the city's Danziger Bridge on foot in an attempt to reach safety and supplies.[59] Two of the people shot were killed and an extensive police coverup followed. Community organizers successfully organized following the incident to compel significant reform, including the establishment of an independent police monitor and a far-reaching consent decree.[60] But these reforms did not lead to reduced police violence or criminalization. Instead, as New Orleans–based abolitionist organizer Lydia Pelot-Hobbs writes, this period of celebrated reform "has seen the enhancement of everyday police power" through additional funding, new technologies, and more aggressive policing at the cost of "disinvestments in life-sustaining infrastructure."[61]

These are but a few examples of the churn of police reform: the same recommendations, which fail in the same ways, are recycled and repurposed in what the *Washington Post* calls a "long line of attempts to cleanse policing in the United States of its persistent afflictions—an ongoing exercise in reform that never ends."[62] The pattern repeated after the police killings of Michael Brown in Ferguson and Eric Garner in New York in 2014: more DOJ investigations, another presidential commission.[63] Abolitionist organizer Rachel Herzing describes this repetitive rehashing:

> Like periods following other rebellions against the violence of policing, 2014 ushered in a rash of newly minted experts offering proposals . . . to reform policing in order to make it less lethal to Black people and to "restore" community trust in police . . . the public was peddled body cameras, implicit-bias training, community oversight bodies, community policing plans packaged in a range of public relations rhetoric.[64]

Not one of these investigations has ended the violence of policing, nor has policing gotten any better at stopping violence in communities. Federal oversight simply offered the conceit of accountability.[65] Where there have been positive outcomes, they could easily have been achieved in other ways. For instance, while arrests on some charges decreased in Ferguson under the consent decree, this same result could have been achieved by decriminalizing things like "walking in the roadway"—the offense Mike Brown was killed over.

Meanwhile, consent decrees have cost millions of dollars—in Ferguson's case, mandating a pay increase for cops. The consent decree imposed after the police killing of Freddie Gray costs Baltimore $1.5 million a year. The tab for Oakland's consent decree, in place since 2003, has already reached $28 million; since 2012, New Orleans and Seattle have spent $55 million and $100 million respectively.[66] Yet the federal government's response to the killings of George Floyd and Breonna Taylor is more of the same: investigations and consent decrees that cost millions of dollars while doing nothing to prevent and intervene in violence.[67]

As Herzing emphasizes, it's not a question of needing different reforms or better implementation: "the failure of these reforms rests more properly on a misunderstanding (or willful ignorance) of what policing is and does."[68]

You Can't Reform Something That Is Doing What It Was Created to Do

Police cannot be reformed because the institution epitomizes the state's dispensation to use violence as it sees fit. As abolitionist scholar Naomi Murakawa summarizes, "Police protect private property, enforce the color line, patrol the gender binary, and hold national borders for everyone except the corporations. No amount of reform can erase these core functions."[69] It's a kind of wishful thinking that a policing system with origins in colonial warfare and genocide, slavery, and anti-Black apartheid could somehow be "magically transformed into a non-anti-Black, non-racial colonial ('racist') system," as Critical Resistance co-founder Dylan Rodriguez emphasizes.[70] The notion of "reform" implies that an institution has strayed from its core responsibilities, that the reins just need to be tightened on individual cops or departments. But there is no "fixing" something that works as intended. Citing operational research theorist Stafford Beer's notion that "the purpose of a system is what it does," writer Teju Cole urges us to stop assuming that the purpose of police is, as they claim, to "serve and protect," with unfortunate acts of police violence a necessary side effect that can be treated. "[T]he outcome," he reminds us, "is the purpose."[71]

Reform will not reduce the violence of policing. Instead, it legitimates it as a solution to the social problems police themselves produce—what Murakawa calls "a crisis of their own making."[72] Reforms have both shielded and fueled ongoing police violence, giving the illusion of change while legitimizing police and funneling more resources and power to them under the pretext of addressing the problem.[73] Reform re-entrenches criminalizing assumptions about Black people through the false narrative that the criminal and legal system are—or can be—neutral and fair, therefore it must be us who are the problem.[74]

In other words: reforms don't just fail to address the damage the system causes, they contribute to further damage. As historian Charlotte Rosen writes, reforms "sap energy from radical visions, do not go far enough, and do not work."[75] Yet, we are asked to believe that *this* time, we can get reform right. We are told that abolition is magical thinking. But what is magical thinking, if not a perpetual belief that failed reforms will eventually work?

More Rules Do Not Mean Less Violence

A central premise of calls for reform is that imposing more rules on cops will make them better at creating safety while reducing the amount of violence they inflict. Where rules fail, the problem is framed as the rule itself, or individual cops and departments, "bad apples" and bad actors, rather than the entire system of policing itself. This, as former NFL quarterback and activist Colin Kaepernick, writing with his *Abolition for the People* co-editors Christopher Petrella and Connie Wun, explains, collapses "a systems-based analysis into individual behaviorist approaches to intervention."[76]

In other words, more rules do not mean less violence.

Police embody and exercise the state's monopoly on the legitimate use of violence.[77] That means that police rules necessarily authorize violence and grant police tremendous discretion to use it. For example, the Minneapolis Police Department's use of force policy, even after it was revamped in the wake of George Floyd's murder, still allows "[t]he amount and type of force that would be considered rational and logical to an 'objective' officer on the scene, supported by facts and circumstances known to an officer at the time force was used."[78] Notice that the policy refers to the amount of force that is "necessary"—defined by a cop's perception of who needs to be put in their place, and how. Illustrating the futility of the new policy, a Minneapolis cop interpreted this to mean that it was necessary to shoot Amir Locke as he lay asleep under a blanket after barging into the apartment he was staying in, on a (supposedly banned) "no-knock" warrant that did not even name Locke.[79]

The doctrine of police discretion argues that the work of law enforcement can only be carried out with preemptive blanket permission to discriminate, use violence, and criminalize as they see fit. As sociologist Brendan McQuade says, "Police must be unencumbered from anything that actually limits their power, capacity, reach, and violence."[80] Likewise, because they cannot possibly respond to every single violation of law, cops also claim discretion to decide who and what presents the greatest threat at any given time, when or whether they should act, and how.

While Department of Justice consent decrees seek to promote "constitutional policing," there is very little in the way of legal limits that can actually be enforced.[81] Most police violence is what *New York Times* columnist Charles Blow describes as "awful, but lawful."[82] Contrary to the story we are told about the law acting as a check on police power, in fact, the law condones, facilitates, and promotes police power. As David Correia and Tyler Wall, authors of *Violent Order: Essays on the Nature of Police*, put it: "[P]olice officers are [the] law's violence workers. It is the violence of police . . . that both makes *and* preserves law."[83] As a result, there is little relief to be found in the law. Instead, the law justifies the broad license for violence afforded to police by appealing to the need for order.[84] For example, the Supreme Court interprets limitations on "unreasonable searches and seizures" and discriminatory state action enshrined in the U.S. Constitution from the point of view of a "reasonable" cop on the scene—essentially opening the door to police to offer virtually any justification for violence.

More often than not, the Court has also narrowly interpreted the Fourteenth Amendment's guarantee of "due process" and "equal protection of the laws" to only prohibit police discrimination that can be proven to be intentional, or conduct that "shocks the conscience."[85] In other words, any pretext other than race, gender, sexuality, or national origin, however small (e.g., a broken taillight), justifies police action.[86] Courts examine claims of constitutional violations from the cop's point of view, unless the use of force is so far out of bounds that it "shocks the conscience." In a society where police violence is normalized, this is an exceptionally high bar. All of this leads to a situation in which, as abolitionist legal scholar Amna Akbar writes, "The rules of policing are not so much 'top-down' (with the law or courts governing the police) but 'bottom-up' (with policing itself driving the law)."[87]

Predictably, courts find a significant amount of police violence to be "reasonable"—a legal fiction that conceals and legitimizes the operation of anti-Blackness, sexism, xenophobia, and Islamophobia in police interactions,[88] along with homophobia, transphobia, ableism, and class bias.[89] Far from serving as a limit to police power, the law actually conceals and enables it. Rather than creating clear boundaries around acceptable and unacceptable police behavior, laws and policies empower police to continue to, according to Akbar, "advance inequality through their distribution of violence and surveillance, death, and debt."[90] "Regulations are also instructions," offering cops a template for how to justify their actions when challenged.[91] Yet, most reformers continue to look to the law for solutions.[92]

What's more, cops simply don't follow rules. They know the rules are not meant for them, and they are right. Citing concerns about the numbers of deaths in police custody, the NYPD changed its policy to completely prohibit the use of chokeholds in 1993. But thousands of chokehold complaints have been filed in the years since—including over two hundred in 2013 alone.[93] In 2014, former NYPD officer Daniel Pantaleo killed Eric Garner with a chokehold.[94] A grand jury then *validated* Pantaleo's discretion in using the banned chokehold. Political economist Mark Neocleous writes that "the act was deemed *acceptable* because the officer judged it to be an act of *necessity*, a reminder that the thing that most often gets classified as an act of political necessity is the discretionary use of violence by agents of the state."[95] Rather than serving as a precise tool to excise violence from policing, the law's reliance on vague terms—"acceptable," "necessary," "reasonable"—all provide cover for the expansive and strategic use of violence.

In 2020, police fraternal associations successfully stopped the New York City Council from passing a law to enshrine the police department's chokehold ban, calling it an "anti-police policy" and claiming it kept them from being able to do their jobs.[96] Neocleous explains that this resistance to regulation by law reflects the police perspective that "to act solely within the law would render them ineffective . . . because to act illegally is what is required to achieve . . . order."[97] Clearly neither Pantaleo, nor the cops who sued to stop the chokehold ban, believe the rules apply to them.

The NYPD chokehold ban is also an example of a deadly game of whack-a-mole, in which laws and policies target *techniques* of violence rather than structures of violence. Banning chokeholds, as Murakawa explains, lets "one particular weapon or tactic absorb the blame, while policing goes on as usual. Same terror, different tools."[98] This perpetual urge to tweak the rules of policing is a trap: it's not the absence of laws or rules that is the problem—it's that what we see *is* the rule.[99] Police are empowered to *make* law and have their decisions validated after the fact by the courts.

Rules are rarely enforced against police except to make an occasional example of individual cops or police departments who are sacrificed in order to reinforce the legitimacy of the institution as a whole and leave the underlying power structures intact.[100] Many commentators argued that Derek Chauvin's conviction of George Floyd's murder proved "the system works;" reformer Al Sharpton went so far as to argue that it signaled that we need to take the lead from police on how to stop their own violence.[101] But the Chauvin conviction did not stop cops from continuing to kill three people a day, on average across the country—including a young Black woman killed by a Cleveland cop as the verdict was being handed down in the Floyd case.[102] It didn't stop Minneapolis police from killing Amir Locke. A single conviction of a single cop won't change the system that produced and enabled him; in fact, it only emboldens it to continue business as usual under the pretext that it can deliver justice.[103]

Yet we continue to be asked to place our hope in more rules: as of June 2021, over two thousand policing-related bills had been introduced nationwide.[104] At what point will we recognize that law and policy are window dressing to cover up the realities of policing? At what point will we acknowledge that the only rules governing policing are those that maintain existing structures and relations of power?

Technology Won't Save Us

Beyond rulemaking, reformers increasingly look to technology for solutions to police violence. But as Princeton professor Ruha Benjamin reminds us, reliance on technology, just like rules, keeps our focus on individual practices rather than on underlying systems that enable them. It makes room for one form of social domination and control to morph into another form or practice.[105]

In the months following the Minneapolis City Council's announcement of its intent to dismantle the city's police department, Camden, New Jersey, was frequently raised as an example of a city that had already successfully done so. Yet, as McQuade wrote in *The Appeal*:

> Camden is not a model for structural change . . . ubiquitous surveillance and aggressive policing lurks underneath the media-friendly optics of community policing and the technocratic luster of "smart, data-driven policing," exemplified by new cameras, ShotSpotter microphones, and license plate scanners, all feeding data to the Real Time Tactical Operational Intelligence Center (RT-TOIC).[106]

Members of the "new" department engaged in the same practices as their predecessors, simply rebranding themselves with new names and aided by new technology. In fact, police contact with communities actually *increased* with cops "citing people for anything and everything."[107] For instance, McQuade reports that "from July through October 2014, the Camden County Police wrote 99 tickets for riding a bicycle without a bell." In the previous year, they had issued one.[108] Citations and tickets increased by almost 100,000 in a single year. In a city of only 73,000 residents, this amounts to an average of 1.7 citations per resident, including toddlers.[109] Complaints about police use of force doubled. Predictably, nothing was done to address them. Meanwhile, the same discrimination that plagues everyday policing is still very much at play: an investigation found that "Black people in Camden are nearly 4.5 times more likely to have force used on them during an arrest than a white person."[110] Dismantling and replacing the department actually led to *more* police contact and violence. It's a consistent theme: as with procedural reforms, technological reforms introduced to reduce harm increase police surveillance and power.

Many reformers have also pinned their hopes on police body cameras, a recommendation that has grown in popularity in the wake of high-profile police killings, including the 2014 death of Michael Brown in Ferguson and the 2016 killing of Charleena Lyles in Seattle.[111] Advocates reasoned that body cameras would create official records that the courts and public could use to determine whether police use of force was "reasonable" without having to rely solely on police accounts. They also argued that the presence of the cameras would improve police behavior. That's not how it has played out. Again, cops don't follow the rules. According to the Stop LAPD Spying Coalition, there is often no footage of violent incidents, because cops turn off or disable body cameras.[112] One report found that body cameras and dashboard cameras were turned off in 60 percent of use of force incidents in New Orleans in the first five months of 2014.[113] In August of that same year, New Orleans cop Lisa Lewis turned off her body camera just before she shot a man in the head following a confrontation.[114] Where footage does exist, police departments have broad discretion in releasing it.[115] In the case of Floyd's murder, the department issued a press release claiming that cops observed "medical distress" after they were "able to get him into handcuffs," but they did not initially produce body camera footage.[116] Their word would likely have remained the story had Darnella Frazier not pressed record on her phone. The department did not release the body camera footage to the public until a court ordered them to do so in August of 2020.[117]

What's more, the devices have done little to improve police behavior. Early studies suggested that the presence of body cameras changed the way police interacted with people. But those have since been debunked by larger, more long-term studies.[118] Anecdotal evidence is also plentiful: the internet is awash with body and dashboard footage of cops brutalizing and killing people with the full knowledge that they are being watched— as Derek Chauvin did as he stared directly into a camera while he suffocated George Floyd to death. Instead, body cameras have increased police departments' capacity for surveillance by putting a camera on every cop.[119]

Meanwhile, cops and corporations profit from it all. Reform proposals reward police and the industries that support them with more money, more power, more discretion, and more legitimacy.[120] As Murakawa writes, "The more police brutalize and kill, the greater their budgets for training, hiring, and hardware."[121] The federal government funneled $43 million into police departments between 2014 and 2016 to purchase body cameras.[122] It's no coincidence that Axon, the company that makes and promotes Tasers—another technological reform that has cost millions while increasing rather than decreasing violence—is the same company that makes and promotes body cameras.[123] And it should come as no surprise that Axon regularly lobbies for police reforms that will increase their profits, and is a regular contributor to police foundations.[124] Cops, too, are capitalizing off reform: organizers are fighting police fraternal association efforts to negotiate contract provisions that reward officers who use body cameras with bonuses.[125] Yes, you read that right. Cops are breaking the rules, and then extorting money to agree to follow them.

Technological "fixes" are not only ineffective, they also operate at cross-purposes to efforts to divest from systems of surveillance, policing, and punishment. Even in the context of defund fights, technology offers a tempting quick fix. In some places, organizers are advocating for red light cameras as less dangerous and discriminatory mechanisms to enforce traffic laws.[126] After all, cameras clock drivers regardless of race, and enforcement looks like a letter in the mail that doesn't beat, sexually harass, or kill people, or create a pretext for a drug search. But they do cost money—$100,000 a camera, plus operation and maintenance costs—and cities recoup those costs through what amounts to a ticket tax. Cameras are placed in the same communities that cops target, and the information they gather creates more possibilities for surveillance.[127]

Calls for "Community Policing"

Crises of police legitimacy consistently produce calls to "improve police-community relations." This logic locates the problem of police failure to produce safety in individuals and community members who refuse to collaborate with police to fight crime, rather than in the inherent violence of policing. In the name of "rebuilding trust" between police and the communities they target, such initiatives flood communities with still *more* cops assigned to "walk the beat," "get to know" people in the community, build "relationships" with community organizations, identify safety concerns, and problem-solve in collaboration with communities to "co-create" public safety. But the reality is that cops, not communities, set the agenda for community policing. That consistently places crime, containment, and control at the top. The goal is not to collectively problem-solve, but to fuel more surveillance and punishment, and to ostracize and evict people from their own communities. As Ferguson activist and legal scholar Justin Hansford explains: "These new police centered 'communities' revolve around events hosted by the police, public forums moderated by the police, and mental health, [and] social services are . . . mediated through the police. Coincidentally, an enlarged social role for the police requires larger budgets and the expansion of benefits for, you guessed it, the police."[128]

The Chicago Alternative Policing Strategy (CAPS), often celebrated as an exemplar of community policing, is a case in point. In 2015, a multiracial group of young Chicagoans attended CAPS meetings and events, producing a "CounterCAPS" report on their findings: "At CAPS meetings, police effectively deputize a small group of residents to engage in surveillance. Their complaints reflect their implicit biases about who to consider 'suspicious.' CAPS meetings legitimize and amplify these biases."[129] In many cases, CAPS meetings are attended by older homeowners concerned about their property values or younger white gentrifiers who are not part of the social fabric of the community.[130] The "community" contemplated by the program did not include unhoused residents or tenants. It also excluded perspectives that do not align with police agendas. Residents often mobilize racist and classist constructions of "crime"—e.g., young people loitering after school; residents of an apartment building behaving "suspiciously"—to demand more police presence, more police power, more police action, and sometimes more prison time. Residents who regularly attended CAPS meetings occasionally showed up in court to demand harsher sentences for the people they called the cops on.[131]

Beyond conscripting segments of communities to policing functions, community policing allows police to abdicate responsibility for violence while consuming public safety resources. For example, Andrea attended a 2019 "community policing" meeting in the predominantly Black Brownsville neighborhood of Brooklyn, which faces some of the highest rates of violence and poverty in the city and has the fewest resources to combat them. Opening the conversation, the NYPD commissioner declared that the department had done "all it could" to address violence in Brownsville and it was now "up to the community" to do something about it. Meanwhile, the NYPD had requested an $18 million budget increase for, among other things, community policing. When Andrea repeatedly asked the commissioner if he would forego the $18 million increase so that the money could go to fund community-driven youth programming and other neighborhood efforts community members were offering up as solutions to violence, he refused to respond. The NYPD got the $18 million, and Brownsville got a new NYPD "community center," granting police even greater access to the populations it targets.[132] Like community policing more generally, the construction of the NYPD "youth center" is yet another strategy to boost cops' legitimacy through projects and tasks not directly related to preventing, intervening in, or resolving violence—such as "social service and general assistance duties" and "educational, recreational, and even counseling services."[133] Cops attempt to distract from the fact that they don't perform the central function we've been told they do—preventing violence and harm—by taking on more and different roles to make themselves appear broadly essential. Far from being a solution to police violence, community policing creates more opportunities for it by infusing cops into neighborhood institutions—expanding and extending police power, and deputizing community members to implement their agenda.

The Lure of Reform

The promises of police reform are seductive. It is easier to tinker with the known than to launch into the unknown. Indeed, each of us has fallen prey to the lure of reform at some point. Mariame was once what she now calls a "police preservationist," encouraging young people to enter into dialogue with cops who were regularly harassing them. Even as an abolitionist attempting to reduce the harms of policing, Andrea has fallen into the trap of trying to pass more laws, enact more policies, and create more rules to limit police power. For instance, she advocated for new and expanded laws prohibiting profiling based on race, gender, sexuality, disability, and housing status; for changes to policies on how police interact with queer, trans, and gender nonconforming people; and for specific provisions in consent decrees. She even testified before the Obama Task Force on 21st Century Policing in an attempt to uplift the experiences of women and LGBTQ people targeted for police violence in the midst of a national conversation that was, once again, poised to erase them.[134] As recently as 2017, she advocated for adoption of some of the Obama task force's recommendations, some of which were based on her testimony. Today, she no longer supports these recommendations.[135] And both of us have called for indictments or prosecutions of individual cops at various junctures. For reasons elaborated on in the "Tricks and Tensions" chapter, we no longer do.

We became abolitionists in part by listening to people on the receiving end of reforms. One of Mariame's mentees responded to her suggestion that he sit down with cops: "I know the cops here very well, and they know me. We know each other too well. That's not the problem."[136] Shira Hassan, the former director of the Young Women's Empowerment Project, which worked with young women and trans people in the sex trades and street economies in Chicago, often told Andrea when she served on the organization's board: "We don't need more laws and rules. Rules never work for us." Participants in "know your rights" trainings sometimes just laughed out loud as Andrea explained the "protections" from police violence offered by laws and policies. We got the message.

Yet the pull to try to reduce harm through more rules is strong. Andrea's efforts, often in concert with other abolitionists, to address police sexual, anti-queer, and anti-trans violence through legal and policy changes have suffered from the constant tension of attempting to reconcile the knowledge that policing *is* and *requires* racialized sexual, gender, homophobic, transphobic violence with the hope of reducing the harms of policing in the immediate term. Her work around increasing awareness and reducing harm of police sexual violence is a case in point: her organizing efforts in the 1990s described in the "We Are Survivors" chapter made it clear to her that policing *is* sexual violence, and sexual violence is a tool of policing and a corollary to criminalization. No policy change will shift that reality. The only way to end police sexual violence is to reduce police contact and power, and ultimately, to end policing. And given how harmful, widespread, and often invisible it is, it feels critical in the meantime to find ways to pinpoint how and where it's happening, prevent it, and increase support to survivors that doesn't just send them back to police. In April 2019, Interrupting Criminalization hosted a day-long convening with organizers and advocates fighting sexual assault and police violence to grapple with the question of whether there is anything short of ending policing that we can do to improve the situation in the short term. We concluded that there are very few things that aren't futile (more rules cops will break) or that don't build the power and legitimacy of policing (more prosecutions and oversight). Almost everything we came up with would require more police training or create more infrastructure to police the police. That would mean investing more resources and legitimacy into systems of policing—and largely responding to the problem after the fact.[137] We concluded that decriminalization and defunding police are our best strategies to reduce and end police sexual violence, and created a toolkit for organizers and sexual assault service providers aimed at increasing support to survivors.[138]

Advocacy for disabled people, who experience disproportionately high levels of police violence, runs into similar problems. Attempting to change how an inherently ableist institution interacts with disabled people often only increases police power over them. Organizer and lawyer Talila A. Lewis has documented the ways in which reforms intended to make police interactions with D/deaf and hard of hearing people safer—model policies, training, placards, registries, identification bands, and cards—have consistently failed to do so.[139] In many cases, they have proven more harmful. "Signing" police with limited ASL proficiency and "deaf and hard of hearing liaison units" have actually led to further criminalization. Lewis also notes that these initiatives siphon off funding that could be "directed into social services [and] community-based resources that help keep Deaf communities healthy and safe and decrease reliance on police."[140] Lewis advocates for solutions that would divest from police and "increase[e] the well-being, resources, opportunities, and power of disabled communities to heal, protect, and provide for themselves (e.g., self-determination)," rather than "help[ing] police register, monitor, surveil, control, or punish disabled people."[141]

Any reform carries within it the seeds of reinscribing, reinforcing, resourcing, and expanding systems of policing, and we are constantly learning about the detrimental impacts of the reforms we pursue. Mariame has supported elected civilian police accountability boards which have the power to hire and fire cops as an interim step towards shrinking the power of police. Yet, as discussed in greater detail in the "Tricks and Tensions" chapter, these boards direct resources, time, attention, and legitimacy to policing and fuel the notion that policing can be "fixed" by just hiring the right people and firing the wrong ones. These reforms also hinge on a fundamentally flawed belief that we can make police something different than they are. Mariame also supported requiring individual cops to carry private liability insurance and assigning police departments financial responsibility for settlements to survivors of police violence and their families. Based on her experience representing both injured workers and survivors of police violence, Andrea argues that both of these reforms are much more likely to be harmful to people harmed by police than they are to change police behavior. Rather than serving as incentives to stop police violence (again, because violence is inherent to what police do), both would create incentives for cops to fight even harder against compensation for survivors and families than they already do through smear campaigns, concealing evidence, and dragging civil litigation out over years and years. This leaves the people we want to protect with even less recourse. Placing people impacted by police violence at the mercy of private insurance companies accountable only to their shareholders and bottom lines (as opposed to public officials, who are at least theoretically accountable to the public) would have the same effect, while increasing private profits.[142] There are many other places to focus our outrage at the high costs of settlements, including by cutting the legal fees and costs cities pay to defend against police brutality suits.[143] We would do far better to work to prevent police violence and to support proposals like Rekia's Law, developed by Chicago's Justice for Families campaign, that would provide for automatic reparations for people killed by police rather than forcing them into lengthy and costly litigation, than to attempt to shift responsibility for compensation for the harm done by police.

In each of these instances, we, too, were seduced by the lure of reform, yet engaging with their impacts on community members in real time reoriented our positions toward the horizon of abolition.

Can't We Do Both?

You might ask, *Why can't we take a "both/and" approach—defund* and *reform?* The Yale Justice Collaboratory, made up of academics from a range of disciplines—many of whom collaborate with police—issued a January 2021 report reflecting this approach: "The group discussed the need to improve existing systems while simultaneously embarking on a project to create and test alternative models."[144] While it might sound "reasonable," a preponderance of evidence and experience makes it clear that there is no "both/and" when it comes to abolition and reform.

It is counterproductive and dangerous to hedge bets and attempt to pursue reform and abolition simultaneously. That's because the former undermines the latter. Reform operates at cross purposes to defunding police because it reinvests money and legitimacy into policing—all in an attempt to recuperate a fundamentally violent institution. In one particularly illustrative example, funders focused on policing issues invested heavily in organizations who drafted and supported the JPA, which would have poured $750 million into local law enforcement agencies to help them train cops on new "rules." That was just $100 million short of the amount organizers managed to extract from police department budgets in 2020 through defund campaigns.[145] Funders then demanded that organizers demonstrate the impact of their defund campaigns—while simultaneously supporting reform efforts that would have effectively thwarted, undermined, and reversed their gains. Similarly, supporting consent decrees places obstacles in the path of efforts to shrink police budgets and increase investments in community safety. In cities like Seattle and Chicago, policymakers opposed defund efforts by pointing to court-ordered requirements for increased training, oversight, public engagement, body cameras, and equipment, citing them as reasons to give police departments *more*, not less, money.[146]

We don't all need to be abolitionists. But we do all need to make a choice—will we continue to invest in attempts to "fix" policing or seek changes that will reduce and eliminate it?

Making Transformative Demands: An Evaluative Framework

The reality that reform will not produce safety doesn't mean that there's nothing to be done until we get rid of the whole system.[147] Quite the contrary. Sometimes abolitionists can become paralyzed by the many potential traps and pitfalls of reform—concerned that pursuing any reforms at all would mean watering down their vision or otherwise embracing cooptation.[148] These tensions quickly surfaced during the 2020 Uprisings, as some abolitionists balked at negotiations with politicians around police department budgets, or calling for anything short of complete abolition. We know abolition won't happen overnight. It is a process that requires us to take, in Herzing's words, "bold steps toward a police free future." As she reminds us, abolition is not "some kind of pure vision that doesn't require strategy or incremental moves." It's the end goal that matters: "Mak[ing] it so the system cannot continue—so it ceases to exist—rather than improving its efficiency."[149]

The key is discerning which steps lead in the right direction: which changes will build, expand, and reinforce the system we seek to abolish, and which will hasten its demise? Or, as Ruth Wilson Gilmore asks, which changes "at the end of the day, unravel rather than widen the net of social control through criminalization"?[150] Theorizing about how to dismantle capitalism in the 1960s, Austrian-French theorist André Gorz proposed that movements should pursue "non-reformist" or "structural" reforms.[151] He defined these as "changes designed to make a practical difference in the short run, while also building toward larger transformations."[152]

Following this line of thinking, in the midst of the Ferguson Uprising Mariame quickly wrote a list of what she considered transformative demands. This list—combined with others developed by fellow abolitionists Dean Spade and Erica Meiners—became the basis of a community discernment process among Chicago activists in 2015 following the release of the video of the murder of Laquan McDonald by Chicago police officer Jason Van Dyke. As a group, they evaluated demands made by organizations across the city and the political spectrum to determine whether each one was recuperative or liberatory. Using the questions as guides, organizers asked themselves whether the proposals being made would restore the legitimacy of policing or lead us toward more justice and freedom.

Key questions that can help us guide this process of discernment include:

- Does the proposal provide material relief or reduce harm to people currently affected by the violence of policing?
- Does relief only reach the *least* marginalized people? Does it leave out people at the margins, such as disabled people, people with criminal records, or undocumented people?
- Does it perpetuate narratives of "deserving" and "undeserving" groups?
- Does it expand or legitimize a system we are trying to dismantle? Does it create window dressing for harmful systems and institutions?
- Does it tinker at the surface without addressing root causes of harm?
- Does it mobilize people most affected by an issue for ongoing struggle? Is it building power?[153]
- Does it seize space in which new social relations can be enacted? Does it create space to experiment and build new ways of addressing need, conflict, harm, violence? Does it engage in community care and produce community safety?
- Does it spread awareness of its ideas? Does it create a participatory or a passive process?

- Does it have elite support? (if it does, it's probably not liberatory).[154]
- Who is working on this initiative? Who isn't? Why?
- Why now?
- Who benefits from this campaign, initiative, reform, form of resistance? Who doesn't, and why?
- What are the logics, languages, and "common sense" that this reform validates or reinforces? Are these logics liberatory or punitive?[155]
- Is this something that we, or others, will need to organize to undo or tear down five years from now? Will it make it easier or harder to fight, experiment, and build new things?

Using these questions, organizers workshopped demands being advanced by different formations across Chicago at the time, including:

- Defund the police in local, state, and federal budgets, and invest those dollars and resources in Black futures.
- Reparations for chattel slavery, Jim Crow, and mass incarceration.
- End all profit from so-called "criminal justice" punishment—both public and private.
- A guaranteed income for all, living wages, a federal jobs program, and freedom from discrimination for all workers.
- The labor of Black transgender and cisgender women (unseen and seen, unpaid and paid) must be valued and supported, not criminalized and marginalized.
- Investments in Black communities that promote economic sustainability and eliminate the displacement of our people.
- Reopen all schools and mental health clinics. Stop replacing housing, health care, and education with prisons.
- End the criminalization of survival. When local and federal government have removed all support systems and social services, fighting to survive is not a crime.

- Decriminalize sex work, drug use and possession, and release all those currently incarcerated on "quality of life" drug, homelessness, and prostitution-related charges.
- Close Homan Square in the city of Chicago and all "black sites" around the world. The "War on Terror" began on U.S. soil in Black and Brown communities.
- Disarm the police, divest from weapons manufacturers, and keep arms out of Black communities worldwide.
- End Stop and Frisk—Stop and Frisk is a racist, classist, sexist, and transphobic practice that targets our communities for harassment and violence. Safety begins when Stop and Frisk ends.[156]
- A participatory city budget in which the public has the power to defund the Chicago Police Department (CPD) and invest those dollars and resources in Black futures by setting a living wage, fully funding health care, social services, public schools, sustainable economic development projects, and Black businesses that support Black communities.
- An immediate end to the criminalization of Black people for minor possession of marijuana and other petty crimes.
- The immediate firing of Officer Dante Servin without a pension for the killing of Rekia Boyd, as well as all other cops who have contributed to the deaths of Black Chicagoans.
- A fully independent civilian police accountability council with hiring, firing, subpoena, and budgeting power. The creation of a Police Accountability Task Force appointed by Mayor Emanuel is insufficient and undemocratic.[157]
- A DOJ investigation and appointment of a special prosecutor for the McDonald case.
- Immediate release of all dashboard camera footage related to any "police-involved shooting."
- Requiring CPD to direct arresting officers to allow arrestees to call legal aid or their lawyer within an hour of being detained and provide contact info for not-for-profit 24/7 legal aid providers at the stations.[158]

- Change police oversight policies at the city and state level, including passage of the Fair Cops Ordinance, which would overhaul current oversight agencies—the Independent Police Review Authority and the Police Board—and provide for independent police oversight and direct accountability to communities.[159]
- No more cops in schools.
- End all juvenile misdemeanor arrests.
- Demilitarize police—end federal grants of military weaponry and equipment to local law enforcement.
- Call for resignation of the Cook County State's Attorney (prosecutor) Anita Alvarez, who participated in a year-long cover-up of the video of McDonald's murder, botched the prosecution of Dante Servin, the cop who killed Rekia Boyd, and prosecuted Tiawanda Moore, a survivor of domestic violence who was sexually assaulted by a cop who responded to her call for help, for recording Internal Affairs Bureau police attempting to dissuade her from filing a complaint.
- Call for resignation of Chicago Mayor Rahm Emanuel, longtime supporter of the Chicago Police Department, who oversaw the closure of over fifty schools and all but one of the city's seven community mental health clinics while steadily increasing and prioritizing the police department budget, and actively participated in the cover-up of the video of McDonald's murder.

Applying the framework questions to the policy proposals, organizers deliberated extensively. The goal was to identify demands that would best meet the criteria of improving material conditions and reducing harms of policing, while building power, participation, and possibilities of practicing new ways of producing safety. Organizers also sought to avoid demands that would fuel harmful narratives or legitimize systems of policing and punishment.

The group defined transformative demands as those that (1) center people and do not presume the existence of police, and (2) hasten the destruction of systems of harm and promote the creation of new systems. They reflect the society we want to build. They landed on four priority demands focused on policing, prefiguring the defund demands that would spread across the country five years later:

- Fully participatory city and county budgets to defund law enforcement and #FundBlackFutures (quality public education, housing, and social services);
- Living wage and guaranteed income;
- Ending the criminalization of survival;
- Call for the resignation of both Alvarez and Emanuel.

The group chose to deprioritize demands that focused on calling for or shaping a DOJ investigation and increased police oversight, arguing that they normalized the need for police; increased rather than decreased funding to police; and failed to take into account the structural realities of policing. They debated whether a demand for the resignation of public officials was transformative or not, and ultimately concluded that it represented a necessary step toward removing people who have engaged in harmful behavior from positions of power, which is essential to abolition.

If we had collectively asked ourselves these questions before demanding more contact between youth and cops, more policies, more laws, more prosecutions, more oversight, more Tasers, more body cameras . . . where might we be today? As we contemplate new mental health crisis responses, diversion programs, and decriminalization efforts, how can we incorporate these guiding questions? What critical assessments do we need to make of each newly proposed reform *before* we commit to a particular path?

For instance, how can we apply these questions and assessments to calls to end qualified immunity for cops? Qualified immunity is a judge-made rule in civil lawsuits, requiring someone harmed by a cop to demonstrate not only that police violated their constitutional rights, but that the right was "clearly established" under law before the person was harmed. For example, if the Supreme Court has ruled that shooting someone in the back as they are running away is unconstitutional, the next cop who does it won't be able to claim qualified immunity—in theory. Whether a right is "clearly established" under the exact circumstances at issue is determined by legal precedent and can be very hard to prove.[160] And if the person is unsuccessful in convincing a judge that it is, their case may not get beyond that point. The facts of the harm done to them may never be heard. Eliminating qualified immunity would improve material conditions for people harmed by police by making it more likely that they would receive compensation for violations of their constitutional rights. At the same time, eliminating qualified immunity would likely leave out people for whom civil suits against cops are not even an option for any number of reasons—because they are undocumented, because too much time has passed, because no lawyer will represent them, because their history of criminalization is too long, etc. Ending qualified immunity would be a reform that tinkers at the edge of the problem of police violence rather than striking at its root causes. While it wouldn't build systems of policing, it would increase their legitimacy by giving the illusion that the courts can adequately remedy police violence. Perhaps most importantly, qualified immunity only comes into play *after* the harm is done, which means it does nothing to stop police violence from happening in the first place. For over fifty years, civil rights attorneys have successfully litigated police violence cases, leading to millions of dollars in settlements or verdicts against police. While these settlements represent critical—though often insufficient—compensation to people who are entitled to repair for the harm they have suffered, civil litigation has not stemmed the tide of police violence. Using the questions outlined above to evaluate calls to repeal qualified immunity, we land on a clear conclusion: the potential impacts of this reform don't justify the amount of energy being devoted to it. In many ways, it is a red herring intended to distract from more transformational demands to divest from policing altogether.

Another good test case is the proposal to create a national decertification registry that would name individual cops and police departments whose certifications have been revoked in any jurisdiction. This proposal was contained in the JPA (and was supported by the forty-fifth president, to the question of "Does it have elite support?"). Funds would be needed to set up and staff the registry, and to handle requests to include individual cops and departments as well as their appeals to be removed from it. By default, the existence of the registry would also provide legitimacy to any cop or department that is *not* on it. Given that placement on the registry would require a finding that a cop broke the rules—usually through a criminal conviction, or at least a complaint sustained by a civilian oversight body—the vast majority of cops who perpetuate harm without consequences won't even be touched by this "solution," because so few are prosecuted and such a small percentage of complaints are sustained. The registry's existence will neither improve material conditions for people harmed by police, nor create new opportunities to organize, grow our movements, or practice a world without police. In fact, just like many of the demands the Chicago organizers chose to avoid, the registry presumes the continued existence of police. Abolitionists can still demand consequences for harm by police. But we look to devise and support actions that would remove cops from being in positions to do further harm *without* perpetuating systems of policing: immediate termination, removal from positions of power, withdrawals of pensions, reparations.

It's not just a matter of assessing reforms against a rubric and choosing which ones to prioritize based on how they score. Herzing emphasizes that anything—policy, legislation, litigation, voting—can be a tool of abolition, depending on how it is used and to what ends.[161] What matters is the operating framework. Transformative change also requires that we constantly assess the impacts, unintended consequences, and potential backlash that proposed changes could prompt. We can't always anticipate every possible impact, outcome, or bump in the road. That's why we need to carefully and closely monitor the implementation of our wins to ensure that they are not gutted or coopted in the process, or inadvertently producing further harm.

We have over a century's worth of evidence demonstrating that attempts to re-form police don't produce different results—whether it's a reduction in police violence or a reduction in violence in communities. The authors of a 2019 study published in *The Lancet* concluded that despite "more recent reform efforts to prevent police violence . . . violence rates and the large racial disparities in fatal police violence have remained largely unchanged or have increased since 1990."[162] As Murakawa points out, at the end of the day, the only people reform works for are the police and those invested in their preservation.[163] Faced with cop-fueled fearmongering about rising rates of violence, some claim that "now is not the time to experiment" with new approaches to safety. Our response is that now is not the time to double down on reforms that have never improved true safety and well-being for our most vulnerable communities.[164] Abolitionists are called dreamers, but it is the promise of reform that works as a fantasy.

Letting go of our relentless and misguided fixation on reform opens up dramatic new possibilities. It also stops us from banging our head on the same walls, coming up against the same result, watching the next video in despair, throwing up our hands in hopelessness. It enables us to build safer futures while reducing the harms of the present, instead of draining our energies trying to squeeze what police are—and always have been—into a different shape. While reform requires us to affirm the current system and surrender our imagination to the carceral state, abolition encourages us to dream new worlds and challenges us to use our best thinking to build a better society.

No Soft Police

Have you ever been policed by an official who wasn't a cop?[1]

Chances are the answer to this question is yes—whether it was someone who held the keys to your education, housing, business license, medical care, income, parental rights, or your freedom. Yet when our organizing focuses exclusively on the more visible violence of police, it can keep us from identifying and addressing the subtle ways that the logics of policing are embedded in social policy and hidden in the day-to-day functions of the state. As Princeton professor Ruha Benjamin explains, focusing on overt police violence conceals "more insidious forms of violence. The less discernible policing becomes, the more pervasive it becomes."[2] When policing is understood as the control and regulation of access to safety, resources, and space to enforce relations of power, we see that police are not the only mechanism of surveillance, control, and punishment,[3] and that force does not require weapons. The state's police power is also located in the social welfare and medical systems offered as "alternatives" to policing. The authority figures who make up the "soft police"—including medical professionals, social workers, and government bureaucrats—engage in policing in their own right, and are often entangled with traditional law enforcement.[4] "Soft policing" by these actors can take many forms, including denying or forcing medical interventions, refusing access to benefits,

Art by Flynn Nicholls for Project NIA.

separating families, or forcing compliance with prescribed behavior. It's critical for us to identify the logics of policing in these day-to-day settings. If we don't, we run the risk of simply replacing more visible state violence with less perceptible—but no less harmful—forms of it.

The impulse to replace every police function with an institutional alternative can actually undermine movements to defund police and invest in community safety. For instance, organizations across the country use slogans like "Counselors, Not Cops," and "Treatment, Not Punishment." While these sentiments might sound innocuous enough, they hinge on the logic of substituting the "soft policing" of medical, social work, and public health–based interventions for police responses to issues like school safety and discipline, mental health crises, houselessness and poverty, involvement in the sex trades, and intracommunal and interpersonal violence. These slogans stand in contrast to abolitionist visions like "Care, Not Cops," "Books, Not Bars," and "Police Free Schools" that open up spaces for us to imagine entirely different possibilities, and to fully explore what collective care and learning could and should look like, rather than simply routing people through different institutions that extend and expand policing.

While these differences in wording might seem trivial, they describe vastly different visions: imagining a future *without policing* is not the same as a future without *police*. One path pushes us closer to the goal of abolition: a society based on mutual care and responsibility, that meets human needs through universal access to collective resources without surveillance, policing, and punishment; the other funnels people into new and expanded arenas of state social control in service of maintaining racial capitalism.

In organizing toward abolitionist futures, we must remember that police are not the state's only mechanism of criminalization and control; many other actors and institutions can and are recruited to the task. To end the violence of policing, we can't stop at eliminating cops, and we need to pay careful attention to what we put in their place.

Social Policy and Police: A Quick History

The term "policing" was first used in the fifteenth century, as capitalism coalesced. Those in power in emerging European nation-states sought to promote commerce and coerce people into wage labor. This was a vastly different economic arrangement than what people had been used to up until this point. Before capitalism became ubiquitous, people lived a life of communal subsistence, which was structured around the smaller-scale production of food (often on shared land known as "the commons"), clothing, and other necessities that would be exchanged or sold within communities.[5] In the context of this shift, "police" was used to describe "policy" enacted, as critical theorists Brendan McQuade and Mark Neocleous write, to "transform commons into private property, dispossess and uproot the people from the land, and rebuild social order through the wage relation." It was part of a process that led to the "systematic colonisation of the world."[6] This massive state project of creating a new social order was called "police science" and it was designed to aid in the accumulation of private wealth.[7] By the beginning of the nineteenth century, "police science" was used to manage the economy by regulating trade and vocation, maintaining public infrastructure and providing public security, and overseeing other "minutiae of social life," including "religion, morals and manners, and the behavior of servants towards their masters."[8]

By century's end, police power had transformed the world; the social order it fabricated—based on individualism, market relations, private property, and wage labor—was normalized to the point where it is considered the "natural" way of life. But this transformation required a dramatic dehumanization and social destabilization. The systemic insecurity it generated by separating people from land bases and communities, making them dependent on a wage, and relegating them to the vagaries of the market produced a politics of "security." In this new system, civil society and the state functioned almost solely to protect an individual's rights and property. The concept of police emerged as agents of enforcement.[9] The emerging police state took on the role of patriarch to manage the problems of the "polis" (the Greek word for city and the root of the words *police* and *policy*) and maintain this new order.[10]

By the 1760s, monarchs played the role of "*pater-familias* of the nation" and deputized "the public police" to manage citizens "like members of a well-governed family," as English judge and politician Sir William Blackstone described it. The public police enforced "the rules of propriety, good neighborhood, and good manners" and maintained social hierarchies."[11] Over time, the meaning of "police" narrowed to law enforcement, and "police science" fragmented into the fields of social policy we recognize today: public health, urban planning, sanitation, social assistance and welfare, workforce development, family regulation, and so on.[12] The goal of police power, no matter which institution wields it, remains as Blackstone described it: to ensure that all of us are "decent, industrious, and inoffensive in their respective stations" through state coercion.[13]

In feudal England, the bailiff or sheriff oversaw peasant labor and debt repayment, beginning the association between police and the protection of property.[14] The duties of the Royal Irish Constabulary—created to maintain British rule in Ireland following an 1798 revolt—included repressing rebellions, and enforcing criminal laws and morals regulations, prefiguring the role of modern police. But they also performed other duties that fell more in line with what we today would call "soft policing": collecting agricultural statistics and population counts, recording evictions and loan frauds. They also enforced what we would now call "public health" policies: the proper handling of dogs, livestock sales, the keeping of pigs, sanitation, and disease control.[15] Similarly, the New York Police Department's earliest responsibilities included everything from street sweeping and boiler inspection; sheltering unhoused people and finding lost children; to enforcing laws controlling the movements of enslaved people.[16]

Today, these functions are spread across a range of government agencies and institutions. Together, they create and administer *social policy*, a collection of rules that govern the management and distribution of resources and enforce social norms. Public schools, health care organizations, and social welfare agencies exercise police power and use coercive means to enforce "social policy." These measures include everything from expulsions and treatment mandates to denial of benefits and family separation. U.S. social policy, bolstered by neoliberal narratives of individual responsibility, controls access to social goods based on structures of "eligibility" rather than entitlement. In other words, rather than presuming that every individual should have what they need to survive and thrive, "eligibility" requirements force people to "prove" that they're deserving of what they need. This system enables the police project of sorting people into categories of "deserving" and "undeserving," and then assigning resources, surveilling, containing, and controlling them to fabricate order, pacify the population, promote "productivity," and maintain existing economic and social systems.

The vast and bureaucratic nature of this system also has the effect of turning structural exclusion into "invisible and normalized aspects of modern administrative life."[17] The combination of the pervasiveness of the system and its normalization produces a kind of manufactured "common sense" that can limit our imaginations and "define the terms of debate over the causes and possible solutions to social problems."[18] Contemporary "common sense" reflects the same concerns of the old "police science": the accumulation and protection of private property; economic regulation and the waged labor system; and the containment, control, exclusion, and exploitation of colonized subjects—including Indigenous, Black, disabled, gender nonconforming people, and migrants.[19] The shrinking availability of social goods under neoliberal economic policies begets more policing, guided by the "common sense" ideology of individual responsibility and self-sufficiency.[20] Social policy normalizes and produces scarcity, and hides the ways policing operates inside seemingly unrelated agencies and institutions. The institutions we think of as advancing social good also work to contain, regulate, and criminalize individuals and populations— all in service of social and economic policy that favors corporations over communities, and individual wealth over collective well-being.[21]

One well-known example of the "common sense" logic at work in social policy is the trope of the "welfare queen." This rhetoric drips with what Black feminist scholar Moya Bailey describes as "misogynoir"—the "uniquely co-constitutive racialized and sexist violence that befalls Black women as a result of their simultaneous and interlocking oppression at the intersection of racial and gender marginalization."[22] The figure of the "welfare queen" emerged in the 1970s, when journalists collapsed three cases of welfare fraud by Black women into a stereotype framing all Black mothers as "a deviant and fraudulent burden on the state who must be punished through heightened surveillance, sterilization, regulation, and punishment by public officials."[23]

The timing of the increased scrutiny of people receiving social assistance was no coincidence; it happened just as civil rights victories expanded access to programs that were previously intended for white widows and pensioners. Ronald Reagan used the "welfare queen" narrative in service

of his neoliberal "Reaganomics" agenda, and President Bill Clinton res-
urrected her in 1996 to justify his punitive overhaul of income support
programs (known as "welfare reform"). "Welfare queens" reportedly give
birth solely to increase their welfare benefits, neglecting and abusing
their children while spending the money on personal extravagances and
refusing to work. These stories of "welfare fraud" paint Black women as
cheating the system with unregulated procreation and refusal of (waged)
labor—both violations of a social policy that is rooted in the preservation
of white supremacy, patriarchy, and racial capitalism.[24]

With an eye to the origins of social policy, we can see the "common
sense" underlying intense policing and regulation of Black women in the
administration of social assistance. We can also see how the "common
sense" of "welfare cheats" organizes U.S. social policy around distribution
of collective resources: strictly policing "undeserving" Black women has
ramifications for *all* people accessing a social good that has become gendered and raced as "Black."[25] Meanwhile, significant state support is consistently funneled to wealthy white people and corporations who receive
subsidies through tax credits and government bailouts. The "common
sense" of this entrenched system also fails to account for the historic and
structural economic and social conditions that cause Black and Native
women and their families—particularly Black and Native queer and trans
women—to experience the highest rates of poverty and lowest wages of
any group in the country.[26]

In practice, this "common sense" made income support programs into
coercive moral regulation regimes, controlling who receives and who is
denied benefits according to family size, relationship status, and drug use.
Time limits on benefits and work requirements push people into the labor
force—often for far less than the already paltry minimum wage.[27] Black
trans filmmaker Tourmaline, a former member of a collective of low-
income queer and trans people called the Welfare Warriors, emphasizes
how strict requirements further burden queer, trans, and gender nonconforming people by tying access to benefits to the "same gendered, ableist,
anti-black, transphobic, homophobic violence" that creates obstacles to
securing housing and employment in the first place.[28] The indignities and
micro-aggressions Tourmaline describes aren't simply due to the personal

biases of workers administering social programs; they are part of a larger police project to push people from social assistance and toward the labor market. Humiliating, degrading, and denying social welfare recipients is one way that social policy acts as social policing.

When administrative rule violations are criminalized as "welfare fraud," the "soft policing" of social benefit agencies funnel people towards more explicit police violence. Police are also physically present in social welfare offices where people seek—and are often denied—benefits, opening these spaces to broader police violence.[29] In a case that went viral in 2018, security officers and cops in a New York City benefits office violently arrested a young Black mother, Jazmine Headley, because she sat on the floor with her child during a long wait in a crowded waiting room. When she refused to stand up, security and police ripped her toddler from her arms and arrested her, forcing her to spend several days in jail before she was reunited with her child.[30]

When we propose pushing people who are currently targeted by cops for poverty-related offenses into social "programs," this is the kind of policing they face. That is why some defund organizers are calling for guaranteed income instead of more of what is currently on offer through "welfare" programs.[31]

Policing of Black women, queer, and trans people through the administration of welfare benefits is just one of many ways that soft policing operates within educational, medical, or other "caring" institutions. Students who fail to respond to traditional education are "tracked" into substandard education,[32] abandoned, or disciplined into what has been dubbed the "school-to-prison pipeline."[33] People who are disabled or neurodivergent are subject to "correction" through medication, coerced treatment, sterilization, or, failing that, incarceration and isolation.[34] People who use prohibited substances are deemed deviant and mandated into treatment or incarceration. People whose gender identity, expression, or marker on their identification doesn't match the gender assigned by the state at birth are disciplined through the denial of gender-affirming medical care, benefits, and access to social spaces—as evidenced by the wave of anti-transgender legislation that is sweeping the U.S.[35] The ways in which the state uses soft policing to discipline along the axes of race, gender, class, and nation are evident in the distribution of benefits, opportunities, trauma, and premature death. They all share a common purpose: to enact social policy that maintains racial capitalism while concealing and managing its true costs through neoliberal social and economic policies.

Soft policing doesn't replace the actual police, who are engaged in the enforcement of social policy through their presence in schools, hospitals, and welfare offices, and in policing youth, disabled and unhoused people, and families. More recently, police were recruited to enforce[36] public health orders during the pandemic, despite their own widespread resistance to mask mandates and COVID vaccination.[37] Community-based organizations are also often sites of intrusion and violence by police and security guards.[38] Social services are tied to law enforcement through mandates that require collaboration with cops and prosecutors, drug testing, criminal background checks, or silence around criminalization of prostitution as a condition for receiving public funding.[39] Additionally, policing is increasingly becoming a required function for the growing number of people and professions providers designated as "mandated reporters"—individuals and institutions that are required to report information to the police.[40]

Someone Else, Somewhere Else[41]

Whether enacted by police or policy, current approaches to social problems share common characteristics: rather than focusing on failed systems that need to be changed, they focus on individuals as subjects to be managed or redeemed, corrected or cast aside, normalized or disciplined. This framework is what drives one of the most common responses to calls to shrink, defund, and ultimately abolish police: *But what will we replace them with?*

Calls for "alternatives" to police are often rooted in this "common sense" presumption that we need to continue to control currently criminalized people and populations by placing them "Somewhere Else." This, in turn, requires having "Someone Else"—if not police—to put them there. At the height of the 2020 Uprisings, this instinct quickly surfaced in an insistence that defund organizers immediately and convincingly answer an avalanche of questions: *If we defund police, who will answer calls about noise complaints? Conflicts? People with unmet mental health needs? Who will get unhoused people off the streets and subways? Who will issue traffic tickets? Who will keep order in schools? What will we do about drug users and dealers? Sex workers? Shoplifters?*

In response, city officials and organizers across the country scrambled to develop proposals for "unarmed responders" and "crisis teams," with varying degrees of separation from, and similarity with, police. For example, cities like Northampton, Massachusetts,[42] Milwaukee, Wisconsin,[43] and Albuquerque, New Mexico,[44] are creating unarmed response teams for calls like noise complaints and abandoned vehicle reports. A number of cities across the country are developing nonpolice mental health crisis response teams modeled after the Crisis Assistance Helping Out On The Streets (CAHOOTS) program in Eugene, Oregon, or the Mental Health First program in Sacramento (discussed in greater detail in the "Experiment and Build" chapter).[45] In Atlanta, people can call 311 and request the Policing Alternatives and Diversion Initiative (PAD) instead of police for concerns related to basic needs, public health, substance use, and mental health.[46] These requests are then passed along to a PAD harm-reduction team that will offer immediate support and connections to housing and other resources. Often, PAD director Moki Macias writes, callers assume the team will remove the person they called about. While some callers genuinely want people to receive any help they need, others simply want individuals out of their sight. Or, they believe that anyone who displays signs of mental distress should be forced into treatment. "And that is the reaction we need to change," Macias says.[47] She points out that what may seem like a mental health issue may actually be the product of something else: homelessness, exposure, hunger, dehydration, pain, violence and fear of violence, structural exclusion—"a human response to the crisis of extreme poverty."[48] She emphasizes that we should "not treat people as problems to be removed from a system that has failed them. Instead, we would seek a change in the conditions."[49]

The question of how to respond to the fallout of organized abandonment and the absence of a robust system of preventative and crisis care is not new. Over the past two decades, "police reform" efforts have included training cops to answer mental health calls and conduct "outreach" to unhoused communities; pairing them with social workers to offer "assistance" to people in the sex trades prior to or during arrests and raids; and granting cops broad discretion in referring people to services instead of making arrests.[50] The "Somewhere Else" logic has also informed the creation of "drug courts," "mental health courts," and programs to divert criminal cases to family or civil court.[51] Even in the context of efforts to shrink the funding and power of police departments, we still see a search for Someone Else to hide the fallout of racial capitalism and neoliberal economic policies Somewhere Else.

Journalists Maya Schenwar and Victoria Law's book *Prison by Any Other Name* demonstrates in granular detail how many of the alternatives to policing "actually rely on forcible confinement, surveillance, and utter control"[52]—whether by the actual police or the "soft police." Ending the *violence* of policing requires us to go deeper, questioning the racist, ableist, sexist, anti-queer, anti-trans, and anti-migrant logics of criminalization that are at the root of social policy and uphold the existing social order. It also requires us to critically examine criminalization in all the forms it takes. We must question whether the behaviors currently deemed "criminal"—e.g., using drugs, drinking, hanging out or sleeping outside, being loud, or trading sex—are inherently harmful or need to be "fixed" in the first place. We must question whether human difference, like neurodivergence, requires regulation and control. And we must question whether harm requires individual or systemic solutions. Not every police function requires a substitute "Someone Else," nor does eliminating police precincts, jails, and prisons require a new "Somewhere Else" for the people currently incarcerated to be scuttled away. Many situations (e.g., houselessness, mental health crises, "loitering," shoplifting) require no "alternative" beyond ensuring that everyone's needs are met. Others require a multitude of responses and systems built around meeting individual and collective safety needs.

As we move to divest from policing and build greater community safety, we must sidestep solutions that fuel soft policing and pursue bigger dreams that demand more fundamental structural changes. We need to unmask social policy for what it is: a police project in service of racial capitalism. We must rebuild the "common sense" of collective care. What follows is an examination of how this might be accomplished within different threads of current movements to divest from police.

From "Counselors, Not Cops" to Police-Free Schools

Police presence in schools dates to the late 1930s, coinciding with conservative anxieties and desire to control the rise of leftist ideologies, including anti-war and pro-labor sentiments.[53] As racial integration of neighborhoods increased, the justifications offered for putting cops in schools included "property protection,"[54] "improving police community relations,"[55] and targeting "dangerous delinquents" and "undesirables" who were accused of "corroding school morale."[56] Police presence was intended to promote "good citizenship" through "Officer Friendly" programs,[57] and quell student organizing against segregation and for quality education.[58] The crime of "disturbing a school" was enacted in the summer of 1967 amid urban rebellions across the country.[59] (Almost fifty years later, this was the same offense used to charge a young Black woman dragged out of her chair by a cop for using a cell phone in class during the 2015 #AssaultAtSpringValley.) The "war on drugs" brought more cops into classrooms through the Drug Abuse Resistance Education (D.A.R.E.) program, which gave police access to 75 percent of classrooms in the country. "Zero tolerance" policies that emerged in the late '80s and early '90s resulted in increased school discipline, expulsion, and arrest for minor offenses.[60] Police presence continued to grow in schools, ostensibly in response to school shootings in predominantly white suburbs. This escalation was made possible by substantial financial and regulatory support from the federal government.[61] In 2015, 70 percent of U.S. students, particularly low-income and students of color, reported the presence of police in their schools.[62] But schools have not become safer. In reality, police criminalize, contain, and control youth of color in school districts increasingly devastated by neoliberal economic policies that have gutted public education and youth programs.[63]

The result? Billions have been spent to police schools instead of supporting students, and there has been a dramatic increase in school-based police violence—including sexual violence—and youth criminalization through student arrests, suspensions, and expulsions.[64] Federal grant programs currently contribute over $1 billion to subsidize more than 7,240 cops in schools—otherwise known as "school resource officers."[65] School discipline, school-based arrests, searches, metal detectors and surveillance cameras, ICE presence in and around schools, corporal punishment, tracking, denial of accommodations to disabled students, and failure to protect girls and LGBTQ students from sexual and homophobic violence in schools are now pervasive. Policing infects every aspect of public education, disproportionately impacting Black, Indigenous, and disabled youth.[66]

Other school personnel also participate in policing—including school nurses and administrators, like the ones at a middle school in Binghamton, New York, who coerced four twelve-year-old Black girls to remove their clothes to search them for drugs because they were "laughing too much."[67] Teachers both police, and—like the one who called the cop in the #AssaultatSpringValley—collaborate with police. The social workers and counselors we call for as an alternative to cops also engage in policing. For instance, in 2020, a social worker at a Florida school called the cops to take a six-year-old Black girl to a hospital for an involuntary mental health evaluation without her mother's consent.[68] Without a critical analysis of the ways in which counselors can also act as cops, we run the risk that calls for "counselors, not cops"[69] could simply shift resources to different forms of policing.[70]

The Dignity in Schools Coalition is a national formation that emerged in resistance to increased policing, decreases in educational funding, and the expansion of the school-to-prison pipeline. In 2021, they reformulated their campaign to "Community Not Cops."[71] In their revised policy agenda, the coalition reiterates its call for complete removal of all police in and around schools—including probation and parole officers, tribal police, and ICE agents. They also clearly state their support for demands to defund police departments and invest in creating safe and welcoming schools for all. The Dignity in Schools platform offers a range of "alternatives" to police that extend beyond school counselors, emphasizing that all school employees should work to create "safe and supportive climates for learning by building relationships with students, getting to the root of problems in the school and surrounding community, and preventing and addressing safety concerns in a way that protects the health, well-being and human rights of students, parents and staff."[72] "Community Not Cops" adopts a more systemic approach instead of one focused on modifying individual behavior. Critical to its implementation will be an eye to whether, and how, policing continues to operate through these interventions if school staff take on the role of "soft police."

The Campaign for #PoliceFreeSchools, coordinated by the Advancement Project and Alliance for Educational Justice, offers an even clearer critique of "soft policing" in schools.[73] #PoliceFreeSchools organizers call for "educators, counselors, restorative and transformative justice practices, and health professionals that support, uplift, and honor, not police and criminalize, children."[74] Finally, the Youth Mandate for Education and Liberation—endorsed by dozens of youth organizations—situates its demands within a larger social policy vision. It calls on all levels of government to "dismantle school policing infrastructure, culture, and practice; end school militarization and surveillance; and build a new liberatory education system."[75] Schools are primary sites for the creation and enactment of social policy through the presence of cops and the operation of "soft policing." Because of that, they can serve as critical laboratories to practice and multiply abolitionist futures, as we explore in greater detail in the "Experiment and Build" chapter.

From "Treatment, Not Punishment" to "Care, Not Cops"

Drug War "Treatment"

Over the past two decades, advocates have sought to address the racially disparate harms of the "war on drugs." They have done so primarily by pushing for reforms that frame drug use as an issue of addiction to be addressed through treatment rather than incarceration.[76] The devil, of course, is in the details. Racialized narratives and a profound shortage of accessible, affirming, and affordable treatment options have the effect of severely limiting who can access treatment.[77] Perhaps even more importantly, drug users and policy experts have offered a fundamental critique of the "treatment, not punishment" framework, pointing out that it substitutes court-mandated, compulsory, or coercive treatment for incarceration.[78] As organizers of a 2019 Drug Policy Alliance conference observed, "many 'treatment' facilities mirror prisons and asylums."[79] In these places, "treatment interventions that fail to prioritize consent," like forced detox and civil commitment, reproduce "the same indignities and consequences commonly associated with criminalization."[80] Ultimately, these programs do the same work of perpetuating "racism, stigmatization, paternalism, ableism, and profit" as the criminal justice system.[81]

At the end of the day, the work of "soft police" often leads right back to criminalization. "Alternative to incarceration" (ATI) programs impose drug testing, treatment, and complete abstinence as standard conditions of participation, despite evidence that abstinence is not always necessary or desirable, and requires more time, grace, and supports than these programs offer.[82] Failure to maintain abstinence is punished. Treatment and testing mandates also interfere with school, employment, and caregiving—often placing people in a position of making impossible choices between, say, picking their child up from school or reporting to a testing facility. Failure to complete the program leads right back to incarceration.[83] Rather than offering an alternative, "treatment, not punishment" ends up continuing, creating, and expanding opportunities for punitive approaches to drug use.

Conditions in drug treatment centers often mirror those in prisons, including emotional, physical, and sexual abuse, forced medication, physical restraints, denial of privacy and confidentiality, isolation, and family separation.[84] Schenwar and Law describe how drug treatment centers operate on "prison-like principles: they confine people under strict watch, hold them to a fixed schedule, and regulate their movements and what they do with their bodies. Outside contact is often bound by a slew of rules and restrictions."[85] And, as is true in jails, prisons, and other places of confinement, trans and gender nonconforming people are often required to attend programs based on the gender they were assigned at birth. Even if not court-mandated, "treatment, not punishment" doesn't, in fact, mean no punishment.

It's also worth unpacking the assumptions built into and perpetuated by a framework like "Treatment, Not Punishment." It inherently presumes that drug use is a problem in need of "treatment." In reality, many people use criminalized drugs without experiencing related problems; in fact, 90 percent of people who use drugs don't meet the criteria for a substance use disorder.[86] The "Treatment, Not Punishment" frame presumes any drug use is problematic—although not for *everyone*.[87] Populations already criminalized—Black and Indigenous people, migrants, low-income people, disabled people, youth—are subject to drug arrests for as little as a blunt, and then forced to choose between treatment and punishment. Wealthy white people, on the other hand, are free to use drugs recreationally without a presumption of addiction. They are rarely criminalized or confronted by the state with a choice between treatment and punishment.[88]

To the extent that drug use *is* genuinely experienced as problematic, "Treatment, Not Punishment" frames it as an individualized condition or moral failure rather than what it is: evidence of a structural crisis. Criminalized drugs are one of few options for self-medication in communities that are subjected to organized abandonment and exposure to trauma—including the trauma of policing. The systemic denial of accessible, nonjudgmental, and noncoercive mental health supports drives the very behavior that is condemned as antisocial. Focusing on drug addiction as an individual "condition" to be cured rather than meeting the needs of people who use drugs as *they* define them, distracts us from the social conditions that shape and drive substance use. That individualistic focus also makes it easier to avoid asking important questions about the social policy that drives the decisions behind which drugs are criminalized, why, how, and in service of what larger agendas.[89]

Mental Health "Treatment"

The demand for "Treatment, Not Punishment," has also been taken up—and similarly critiqued—in response to the incarceration of people labeled as "mentally ill" or "mentally disabled." Jails and prisons warehouse huge numbers of people with unmet mental health needs and/or psychiatric diagnoses. While this fact is often attributed to the deinstitutionalization of psychiatrized and disabled people from state hospitals in the 1950s and 1960s,[90] critical disabilities studies scholar Liat Ben-Moshe corrects the record: it's the result of current conditions.[91] In the absence of a true ecosystem of care, policing and criminalization are the default response to disability and neurodivergence. It's also worth noting that incarceration itself is disabling—thus adding to, rather than reducing, the problem.[92] Any "treatment" provided in jails and prisons is conditioned by the carceral context and often represents another form of punishment, containment, and control. This is also often true of "treatment" imposed in psychiatric hospitals and facilities, nursing facilities, and residential facilities, where criminalized people are regularly incarcerated, restrained, and forcibly medicated unless and until they can prove to a medical official that they are "worthy" of release.[93] In 2019, advocates from the JusticeLA coalition organized to stop the construction of a four-thousand-bed "mental health treatment center" that would have effectively operated as a jail in Los Angeles. A core principle that motivated their action is the understanding that there can be no effective "treatment" in a cage—no matter whether you call it a jail or a "treatment center."[94]

Defaulting to a "Treatment, Not Punishment" approach places disabled people and people with different or unmet mental and emotional health needs at risk of being forced into new sites of violence and coercion rather than consensual spaces that would support their mental health and well-being.[95] The current goal of the "treatment" model is to discipline people into narrow confines of "acceptable" ways of being and acting—a police project enacted by cops, prison guards, and health professionals. Elliott Fukui, an educator with the Fireweed Collective,[96] reminds us that, for disabled people, "our tormentors, jailers, and executioners are your doctors, social workers, security guards, and police officers."[97] That understanding is echoed by Ben-Moshe, who describes psychiatric hospitals, residential institutions for people with intellectual or developmental disabilities, and, "at times, our own homes (or their lack)" as "medicalized carceral spaces," as part of a larger carceral archipelago that includes prisons and jails.[98] This is why, as disability justice scholar Talila A. Lewis argues, abolition "must contend with how disability and ableism interact with carceral-medical systems . . . and be committed to abolishing *all* spaces to which marginalized people are disappeared."[99] Our goal cannot be to simply send disabled people Somewhere Else.

We also need to be wary of replacing one form of policing with another by sending Someone Else to respond when a person is in a mental health crisis. Anywhere between one-third and one-half of people killed by police are—or are perceived to be—in a mental health crisis at the time of their deaths.[100] High-profile cases of fatal and nonfatal police violence against disabled Black and Brown people—like the killing of Walter Wallace by Philadelphia police in 2020[101]—typically prompt a surge of interest in "alternative" mental health crisis response programs. Defund organizers made removing cops from crisis response a high priority in the 2020 Uprisings, and it was the arena in which policymakers were most willing to consider reducing the role of police.

The catch? Involuntary commitment to a hospital or psychiatric facility is often the presumed alternative to arrest and prosecution.[102] As Interrupting Criminalization's report *Defund Police, Invest in Community Care* points out, "When structured with hospitalization in mind, 'alternatives' to police response ensure that medical professionals have the power to forcibly medicate and involuntarily commit people for treatment."[103] Since the dawn of police science, medical professionals have stepped in for (or with) cops to serve as the "soft police."[104] Care should not only never be caged, it should never be coerced—no matter if it happens in a jail, on a street corner, or in a hospital. Coercion is still at play when submitting to treatment is a condition of staying out of a hospital, keeping your kids, your housing, or your benefits. The violence of coerced mental health "treatment" is well documented, and the experience and outcome can be the same as—or worse than—police and prison. As one young Black woman told Andrea, "[A]fter an episode, whether the cops or the EMTs come get me, I often can't tell whether I am in the jail or locked hospital ward. I guess one has slightly nicer sheets." Another Black woman described being confined by "handcuffs or Haldol" (a powerful psychiatric drug) for most of her life.

Medical crisis models are generally rooted in social policy that focuses on "correcting" individual ways of being as a response. But you can't manage a crisis created by social conditions and structural traumas through a narrow, individualistic approach. In addition to crisis response, we need to focus on preventing crises from happening in the first place, which entails restructuring society around the well-being, agency, and self-determination of people with unmet mental health needs, mental health difference, or neurodivergence.

The checklist that accompanies the Interrupting Criminalization report invites careful attention to both the broad goals and details of implementation when envisioning nonpolice mental health crisis responses.[105] What are the overall social policy and political interests served by crisis response programs? Do they represent a new way to manage criminalized and disabled populations instead of addressing the structural conditions produced by organized abandonment? Are they providing a new funding stream for police? Are they deeply rooted in communities, or in the bureaucracy of the "social police"? Do they fully remove police—including "soft police"—from decision-making, and center care and self-determination? Is there room for discretion in deciding who will receive care and who will be criminalized—for instance by limiting nonpolice responses to "nonviolent" situations? Do they create a robust ecosystem of voluntary, low-threshold, accessible, harm-reduction-based preventative and after-care, or do they focus solely on a medical response in moments of preventable crisis? These are among the questions we must ask ourselves as we navigate increased political will and funding to re-examine mental health crisis response.

Sex Work "Treatment"

"Treatment, Not Punishment" is also increasingly offered as an alternative to the criminalization of prostitution and trafficking. Rooted in a presumption that all forms of sex trade are harmful, people who offer sex in exchange for something of value are assumed to be "victims" deserving of "treatment" instead of criminalization. But that's typically only if their experience conforms to highly gendered and racialized narratives of "deserving victims," which excludes the vast majority of people in the trade—particularly Black, trans, and gender nonconforming people. To access "victim" status, people in the sex trade must forsake any claim to agency and commit to immediately end their involvement in sex work.

This framework does not take into account the complexities of the sex trade, in which experiences can change with time and circumstances, and often don't fit into neat little boxes or prevailing narratives.[106] It also fails to account for structural exclusions and labor market conditions that can drive participation in the sex trades and serve as obstacles to alternate sources of livelihood. Once again, "Treatment, Not Punishment" prioritizes individual interventions focused on treatment of trauma—imagined, projected, or real. Unlike conventional therapy, mandated counseling sessions are not confidential: in many programs counselors are encouraged—or even required—to report participants' progress to police, prosecutors, and courts. The knowledge that sharing information with a counselor may lead to adverse consequences clearly infringes on therapeutic possibilities.[107] In programs such as these, "counseling" becomes an extension of policing instead of a substitute for it.

They also serve a social policing function by punishing exercises of economic, bodily, sexual, and reproductive autonomy outside the formal labor market and patriarchal social norms. "Job readiness" classes prepare participants for low-wage jobs in the formal economy, where abuse—including sexual abuse—is rampant. Of course, there is often no job at the end of the "readiness" program—particularly for people with a criminal record. Prostitution-related charges can exclude people from a number of professions, programs, and access to public housing. People sentenced to these programs point out that the problem is not with the font or format of their résumés, but with the absence of accessible, sustainable ways to meet their needs in the first place.

For instance, in New York City, the standard diversion program for people charged with prostitution-related offenses mandates a specific number of "counseling" sessions with an anti-violence agency. Many people involved in the sex trades point out that they don't need counseling to address trauma. Even if they do, it's not their first priority. Their more pressing needs are money to cover rent, put food on the table, and meet their basic needs as well as health care, affordable quality housing, and access to immigration status.[108] None of these needs are met by counseling that is focused on policing their efforts to survive. In fact, community organizer Jenna Torres wrote in *Rewire*:

I didn't need to be treated for sex work. That isn't an illness . . .
the sessions . . . hampered my ability to create a better environment for myself and my children so I wouldn't have to rely on
sex work. . . . They didn't give me what I needed, either . . .
suggesting that I just stop sex work and my life would be magically improved. Stopping sex work for me means not being
able to make money. All the odds were stacked against me.
Nobody was hiring an 18-year-old parent of three young children with a full college schedule.[109]

Even people whose experiences fit predominant narratives of coercion,
violence, trauma, and abuse in the sex trades describe these programs as
substituting one form of coercion for another. Meanwhile, these programs
consistently fail to address the underlying conditions that make people
in the sex trades vulnerable to violence in the first place. And, as with
mandated drug and mental health treatment, failure to participate in
counseling is punished through incarceration, which only leads to further
violence. In one particularly heartbreaking case, when Black trans woman
Layleen Polanco Xtravaganza missed a counseling session mandated by a
prostitution diversion program, she was sent to Rikers jail, where she died
in solitary confinement.[110]

Criminalization Through Treatment

The "Treatment, Not Punishment" paradigm frames treatment and punishment as opposites, when in fact they are on the same spectrum. Not
only is punishment often incorporated into treatment, but treatment often
leads directly back to criminalization and punishment. For instance, medical providers frequently participate in the profiling and criminalization
of pregnant people who use drugs or who experience adverse pregnancy
outcomes that are presumed to be the result of self-managed abortions.[111]
Medical and public health professionals produce evidence and testify in
prosecutions based on self-managed abortion care, HIV criminalization,
drug use and overdose, and self-managed gender-affirming care.[112] They
also offer critical testimony about injuries and fatalities in criminal cases
and police misconduct litigation.[113] Hospital staff call the cops on undoc-

umented migrants and "noncompliant" patients, and providers report people who they suspect of harming their partners or children to the family police.[114] Health care systems refuse treatment or collude with police to punish people in the sex trade.[115] In fact, in Chicago, the Young Women's Empowerment Project received more reports from young people in the sex trades about violence at the hands of police and health care providers than individuals, upending typical narratives about the institutions promoted to "save" them from harms they experience from the people who trade sex with them.[116]

These realities prompted Interrupting Criminalization to launch a project focused on sites and processes of criminalization while accessing—or attempting to access—medical care. In 2019, Andrea partnered with reproductive justice organization SisterSong and the Center for Advancing Innovative Policy (CAIP) to convene organizers, care providers, and public health workers from reproductive justice, migrant, trans, drug policy, and disability justice movements to identify how their constituents experience criminalization in the context of accessing medical care. The group collectively drafted a set of principles for adoption and implementation by public health systems, health care providers, institutions, and associations, under the rubric "Beyond Do No Harm." The principles call on health care providers, medical staff, administrators, and public officials to recognize the inherent harms of criminalization and focus on interrupting the ways in which they facilitate, collaborate with, and condone criminalization—both by serving as "soft police" and by colluding with actual police.

One of the "Beyond Do No Harm" principles calls for removing police and private security from places where people may seek or be mandated to treatment. Police are increasingly found in health care settings: accompanying ambulances, providing "security" in emergency rooms, and conducting investigations.[117] As with police in schools, police presence in health care facilities intensified following the racial integration of hospitals brought about by the civil rights movement.[118] According to San Francisco organizer Fabián Fernandez, hospital "security" policies evolved as groups like the Black Panthers and Young Lords were organizing around health, and the government was launching a "war on crime" and a "war on drugs."[119] Later, as a result of growing collaboration between anti-violence organizations and police, cops were stationed in hospitals to take statements and collect evidence in cases of domestic violence and sexual assault. As with cops in schools, mass shootings have also been offered as justifications for police presence in hospitals.

Far from increasing safety and access to care for patients, growing evidence suggests that "the presence of police officers may increase risk of harm and death for patients."[120] Several police shootings have taken place inside health care facilities, including one in which a patient at UCLA Harbor Hospital was shot and killed by sheriff's deputies in November 2020.[121] In another fatal incident, a woman sought care at a hospital for agonizing pain that prevented her from being able to lie down. Perceiving her as "noncompliant" because she couldn't follow their instructions, hospital staff called a cop to assist. When police allegedly found that the woman had prescription pain pills that did not belong to her, they took her to jail on charges of drug possession. Within two hours of being behind bars, she died of a ruptured ectopic pregnancy.[122] Similarly, Anna Brown, a Black unhoused woman who sought treatment for leg pain at a St. Louis hospital, was removed by cops when she wouldn't leave. She died of blood clots in police custody several hours later.[123]

A San Francisco coalition called DPH Must Divest has been fighting to remove sheriffs from facilities run by the city's department of public health. They have gathered many stories of people seeking care who were met with violence, humiliation, and degradation by the sheriffs stationed at the hospital.[124] Beyond perpetrating fatal and physical violence against people seeking care, police also interfere with care through bedside interrogations and by handcuffing patients. Police presence also agitates traumatized or disoriented patients and increases distrust of health care providers.[125] The negative effects extend to staff as well, as evidenced by the widely seen videotaped arrest of a nurse who refused to collect a blood sample without consent from an unconscious patient in a Utah hospital;[126] the arrest of two Black hospital staff suspected of conducting a drug deal when they were just exchanging keys; or the assault of a Black midwife at a San Francisco hospital when she confronted sheriffs about their mistreatment of a patient.[127] The effects on medical providers are not limited to hospitals: Emergency medical professionals have reported being pressured by cops on the scene to apply physical or chemical restraints to people in mental health crises, in violation of their oaths to "do no harm" and to offer the least restrictive forms of care.[128]

Like #PoliceFreeSchools organizers, groups like DPH Must Divest and Frontline Wellness—a member of the JusticeLA coalition—call for removal of cops from health care facilities. Their "Cops Out of Care" campaigns exist within larger movements to divest from policing and instead invest in community-based safety strategies. They are also doing the work of articulating liberatory visions of care while making immediate demands on institutions and government to improve health care access and experience.[129]

The evidence shows that "Treatment, Not Punishment" approaches expand systems of surveillance and carceral control through "soft policing," create opportunities for unnecessary intervention and coercion in the lives of disabled people,[130] and widen the net of policing for drug using, unhoused, and sex working populations. When access to services is mediated through the criminal punishment system, cops make more contacts and more arrests, and prosecutors and courts expand their reach under the pretext of "helping" people they wouldn't otherwise have a basis for criminalizing.[131] Meanwhile, the privacy and bodily autonomy of criminalized people is further restricted and controlled through mandated psychiatric examinations, drug testing, and nonconfidential "counseling."

Under neoliberal economic regimes, "social police" and private corporations share an interest in expanding "treatment" as an alternative to punishment because it means making a profit. An American Friends Service Committee report describes how "treatment, not punishment" enables the "emerging Treatment Industrial Complex" by "ensnar[ing] more individuals, under increased levels of supervision and surveillance, for increasing lengths of time—in some cases for the rest of the person's life."[132] Indeed, Drug Policy Alliance director Kassandra Frederique notes that, in Oregon, recovery and drug treatment leaders were among the biggest opponents of eliminating drug possession penalties—and thus the basis for mandating people into care. Once again, social control and protecting wealth accumulation are revealed as the core purpose of the "soft police."

Disability Justice and "Treatment"

As abolitionists, we can't stop at questioning the quality of "treatment" provided in jails, prisons, psychiatric hospitals, and other places of incarceration, or practices of coerced or mandated treatment. As with criminalization, we need to examine the presumptions underlying "treatment" and even more euphemistically named "behavioral health interventions." Is "treatment" an appropriate response? Or is it a tool of social policy intended to police and manage a population in service of racial capitalism? Should we instead be thinking of how to meet people's needs as they define them, through voluntary and universal access to care in a multiplicity of forms?

A disability justice[133] analysis offers clear answers to these questions, and raises others about whether drug use, involvement in the sex trades, and nonnormative and neurodivergent ways of being in the world need to be "fixed" at all, whether through incarceration or treatment.[134] As disability justice organization Sins Invalid puts it: "All bodies are unique and essential. All bodies are whole. All bodies have strengths and needs that must be met. We are powerful not despite the complexities of our bodies, but because of them. We move together, with no body left behind."[135] The disability justice framework also recognizes what Ben-Moshe refers to as "raceability" to describe the "impossibility of untangling anti-Black racism from the process of pathologization, ableism, and sanism."[136]

The medical "soft police" who have evolved into what disability justice organizers describe as "the medical industrial complex," are organized around policing the line between "normal" and "not."[137] In fact, they were among the first soldiers of social policy, emerging in the late eighteenth century to implement state medical policy, turning a focus on "the collective health of the population" into policing individuals' health in the interests of economic productivity.[138] "Treatment, Not Punishment" presumes that individuals are the problem to be surveilled, contained, and "fixed," rather than the systems that produce and fail to prevent harm. The "Treatment, Not Punishment" paradigm also privileges some approaches over others, in service of larger social policy imperatives—favoring abstinence over harm reduction and medication over material and peer supports, for instance. For similar reasons, "Treatment, Not Punishment"

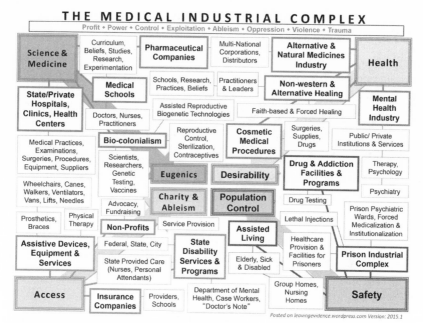

Mia Mingus, Cara Page, and Patty Berne.

encourages suppressing certain states of being, rather than honoring individual agency and what disability justice organizers term "dignity of risk," the right to take chances and make decisions around how to manage their health that non-disabled people enjoy every day.

"Treatment" programs serve as a "Somewhere Else" to put people whose drug use, mental or emotional state, disability, neurodivergence, poverty, or involvement in sexual commerce is deemed troublesome. They serve a disciplining function: people must accept "treatment" as a condition of being released from confinement or "accepted" into society. That process coerces people into striving to achieve racist, patriarchal, anti-trans, and ableist constructs of "normal." And, as mentioned earlier, "treatment" is not equally applied: Some people (usually white and wealthy) are allowed to use drugs, choose a life of leisure subsidized by tax breaks, be "eccentric," and enjoy full sexual and reproductive autonomy.

"Treatment" also fails to address the structural conditions contributing to the "problem" framed as in need of correction. For instance, trans people in drug treatment report that providers tend to focus on their trans identity as the reason for drug use and addiction, ignoring the violence and structural exclusion that shape trans people's daily experiences. By contrast, a disability justice and mad justice framework recognizes the carceral tendencies present in health care and the need to go deeper to address the systemic forces at play if we're actually seeking to support people's health and well-being. As Talila Lewis puts it, disability justice "names, addresses, [and] intervenes in the social, political, medical, legal, familial, economic, etc., conditions that lead to so much of what folks have written off as 'mental health,'" as well as the systems that "medicalize, pathologize, criminalize, and commodify survival, resistance and divergence."[139]

As we contemplate proposals to substitute "treatment" for police, we need to ask ourselves whether the "treatment" offered is what a person needs. Or is it mandated or expected in service of social policy? If they do want and need it, can people freely access treatment without mediation by police or the criminal punishment system? What would it look like to offer people a multiplicity of free and accessible options for care that support individual autonomy and address disabling social conditions? What would demands informed by "Care, Not Cops" look like, in contrast to what flows from "Treatment, Not Punishment"?

A good start would be to demand the decriminalization of all drugs, involvement in the sex trades, and poverty-related offenses, so that individuals who engage in these behaviors are removed from the reach of policing and criminalization. We also need to push for quality universal and accessible health care—including voluntary harm reduction–based services offering a range of options for individual and community care instead of programs that presume coerced medical "treatment."[140] Instead of redirecting police funding to the "Treatment Industrial Complex," resources could be funneled into free, voluntary, accessible care, and healing, as well as to meeting basic needs like housing, income, and food—the absence of which, as Lewis notes, causes, contributes to, and aggravates emotional and mental distress and disruptions. A model of care would ensure that there is funding for every support people need when they experience violence or trauma, without creating legal or regulatory categories that police who can and can't access them. It would mean welcoming the full spectrum of neurodivergence with a range of mental health options, including peer supports available to all who want them. It would mean supporting programs like Mental Health First, a Black-led, community-based, and accountable mental health program that trains community members to answer calls from neighbors to prevent, intervene with, and support people through mental health crises without involving police or involuntary medical treatment.[141] It would also mean unlearning, challenging, and disrupting the ableism that informs mental health interventions. In short, it would mean constructing a society built on a Black feminist politics of care for each of us as we are.

From "Caseworkers, Not Cops" to "Care, Not Cops"

Social programs like welfare and social work–based interventions are also forms of "soft policing," or what Beth Richie and Kayla Martensen call "carceral services" that "replicate the control, surveillance and punishment of the prison nation."[142]

In fact, social work has carceral origins: it evolved alongside industrialization as an attempt to soften the impacts of the social and economic disruptions that resulted from it.[143] Social work also played a critical role in the racist regulation of workforce migration to and within the U.S., working to integrate and assimilate migrants.[144] Social workers advocated for eugenic reproductive practices like forced sterilization, and participated in the genocidal removal of Indigenous children from their homes and communities.[145] Social work's origins as "social police" charged with "correcting" individual deviance through what the authors of *Abolition. Feminism. Now.* call "therapeutic governance" are reflected in present-day practices, such as forcing people into counseling, anger management, parenting, and other "life skills" classes.[146] Rather than addressing root causes and conditions that bring people into contact with police, carceral social services simply replicate and expand the police project.

A group of social workers, including INCITE! co-founder Mimi Kim, use the term *carceral social work* to highlight how coercive and punitive practices are used to manage Black, Indigenous, other people of color, and poor communities across four social work arenas—gender-based violence, child welfare, schools, and health and mental health.[147] According to co-founders of #AbolitionistSocialWork Cameron Rasmussen and Kirk James, carceral social work functions in two interlocking ways—through "the deployment of tactics, within social work, dependent on the same White supremacist and coercive foundations as policing, as well as direct partnership with law enforcement itself."[148] In the summer of 2020, Rasmussen and James critiqued popular defund demands that called for the replacement of cops with caseworkers, noting that social workers more often serve as carceral enforcers than as collaborators toward liberation."[149] As evidence, they cite the head of the National Association of Social Workers (NASW)'s description of the close connections between police and social workers: "'They have our backs as social workers, and we have their backs.'"[150] More recently, anti-carceral social workers challenged an even more obvious manifestation of the intersections of policing and social work in the form of a conference focused on "Police Social Work."[151]

Programs that substitute social workers for cops don't necessarily eliminate police or policing from the equation. In fact, as critics of carceral social work emphasize, "social work ties or abdication to the police further create pipelines to the carceral system within social work systems."[152] Because they are operating under the guise of offering government support rather than policing, there are fewer limits on social workers' reach into the private lives of their clients: they can show up unannounced in people's homes without a warrant, ask questions a cop couldn't ask as a condition of offering benefits, and obtain information that police couldn't otherwise access. Substituting caseworkers for cops can thus extend the tentacles of policing and criminalization further than police could alone.

The potential harms of substituting caseworkers for cops extend beyond the fact that they work hand in hand toward the same ends, potentially increasing policing and police power. Rasmussen and James point out that, like "treatment," social work–based approaches blame the individual: This harmful idea—that society is endangered not by systems and institutions but by individual behavior—has been foundational to the prison industrial complex and much of social work. It is then "not surprising that social work is so readily accepted as a palatable alternative to police."[153]

Family Regulation

The ways in which social workers operate as cops are particularly apparent in the context of "child welfare" systems. People impacted by the system and their advocates commonly refer to "child welfare" as the "family regulation system" or the "family police," highlighting the ways the system parallels, intersects with, and reinforces the criminal punishment system. The following excerpt from Movement for Family Power's groundbreaking report—released in the midst of the 2020 Uprisings against police violence—illustrates how cops and caseworkers collaborate to police Black parents. As the author of the report, Lisa Sangoi, writes, it also captures how a system framed as a "non-adversarial, nonpunitive legal system that supports and preserves families and protects children . . . [exhibits] a laser focus on individual responsibility for alleged parenting failures [and] completely ignores societal ills that often instigate involvement in the first place."[154] The report includes the following case study:

> Ms. L was approached and questioned by Child Protective Services (CPS) a few days after she called the police for help with a domestic disturbance. When CPS asked her if she uses drugs, she truthfully responded that she smokes cannabis [now legal in a number of states] from time to time. This admission and subsequent drug tests led, in part, to a child neglect proceeding against her in which the state failed to present any evidence that Ms. L neglected her child. Nonetheless, the court adjudicated her "neglectful," repeatedly referencing her cannabis use in making this decision, and implemented a "family service plan," a combination of ongoing state surveillance and "service" provisions.
>
> Ms. L's family service plan included the following: parenting classes (though there was no evidence that she was a neglectful parent), anger management classes (though there was no evidence that she had anger management issues),

parenting classes for children with special needs (though she did not have children with special needs), participation in a drug treatment program (though there was no evidence that she had a substance use disorder), submission to drug screenings . . . refraining from drinking alcohol . . . submission to unannounced visits from CPS during which she had to allow full access to the apartment for inspection, and participation in all family court conferences and hearings (regardless of her work schedule).

When Ms. L buckled under the pressure of complying with all these demands and maintaining her job, her children were taken from her and placed in foster care. The state then added to her family service plan individual and family counseling services and supervised visits with her children. Ms. L eventually quit her job in order to comply with the requirements. In spite of her enormous efforts at compliance, Ms. L is facing termination of her parental rights. Her children have rotated through different foster care placements, and the emotional stress of separation from their mother has taken an enormous toll on them.

Ms. L's story is by no means atypical. A significant proportion of child welfare cases involving parental neglect are based on allegations of substance use. And while these cases run the gamut—from allegations of occasional cannabis use to allegations of severe substance use disorders—they all share several common threads. Virtually every case is characterized by gross misinformation on the nature of substance use, involves a punitive legal process that resembles the criminal legal system but lacks even the most basic rights protections, and relies on harsh and non-evidence-based responses to substance use. This is all compounded by the pervasive racial and class disparities in the child welfare system. CPS exercises the same discretion to target "offenders" as police and prosecutors, resulting in a system that, as one leading scholar on race, gender, and the law describes, "systematically demolish[es] black families."[155]

In other words, the family regulation disproportionately targets the same people and communities subject to organized abandonment and criminalization. Sangoi points out that:

> Like people subjected to criminal legal system supervision and control, parents and children ensnared in the foster system are almost all low income, and disproportionately Black, American Indian, and Latinx. They are people from communities hit hard by deindustrialization and skyrocketing unemployment. They use drugs at a similar rate to their richer and whiter counterparts, but they are uniquely the target of foster system intervention.[156]

Beyond differential punishment of drug use, the family regulation system blames, punishes, and separates families for conditions framed as "neglect" that are the product of poverty and structural conditions. Caseworkers act as the "social police," using their powers to individualize social problems, impose individual responsibility in the face of structural exclusions, and to enforce white middle-class heteronormative ableist standards of parenting and living as a condition of social acceptance. As is the case for police, Black, Indigenous, migrant, disabled, low-income, and young people are their common targets. For example, Black lesbians experience high rates of family policing, and some studies have found that lesbian and bisexual parents are over four times more likely to lose custody of their children.[157]

Like other forms of social policing, family policing punishes exercises of autonomy and self-determination in the name of social policy. At a January 2021 rally, two young Black parents described going to the hospital to deliver a baby and coming home without their child. Their newborn was kidnapped by the family police at the behest of medical professionals for "noncompliance" because the parents dared to ask for information and question the need for a blood transfusion for their baby. Caseworkers later came to their home to take away their four-year-old, without any evidence that either is unfit to parent. The rally during which they shared this story was held to mark the placement of a billboard near the headquarters of New York City's Administration of Children's Services, featuring the message, "Some cops are called caseworkers #AbolishNYCACS." The billboard's text, which infuriated administrators, is a reflection of parents' and families' experiences. It also reflects the views of some caseworkers as well. Social workers sometimes train with police, and as one social worker put it bluntly: "Our ultimate goal is the same as the cops."[158]

Joyce McMillan, the rally organizer and founder of an abolitionist organization called JMac For Families,[159] pointed out that stories like these illuminate the fact that caseworkers often have *more* power than cops. They can wield it to remove children without evidence of wrongdoing, shifting the burden of proof onto parents to get them back. While caseworkers do not have arrest powers, they often call in cops to remove children from their homes, even when there has been no violation of criminal law,[160] creating more sites and opportunities for police violence.[161] While most caseworker investigations result in no substantiated findings

Joyce McMillan.

of harm, families are still forced to endure the trauma of invasive interrogations and even the removal of their child from their home.[162]

What does all this have to do with defund demands? For one, as a society, we invest substantially more funds in family regulation and removal of children from their families than on supporting and healing families through nonpunitive systems. Our tax dollars support "child kidnapping," as affected parents call it, and placements "Somewhere Else," such as foster families and group homes, where violence and deprivation of all kinds are well documented. This pattern parallels the ways in which we spend more resources on policing and punishment than on community-based safety strategies. Likewise, in the context of the family regulation system, demands focused on meeting material needs are far more likely to create safety and well-being for families that are currently targeted by both caseworkers *and* cops.

Black feminist legal scholar Dorothy Roberts, who has studied the family regulation system for over two decades, issued an urgent warning to defund organizers at the height of the 2020 Uprisings:

> I am inspired by calls to defund the police. But I am concerned by recommendations to transfer money, resources, and authority from the police to health and human services agencies that handle child protective services (CPS). These proposals ignore how the misnamed "child welfare" system, like the misnamed "criminal justice" system, is designed to regulate and punish black and other marginalized people. . . . Giving child welfare authorities more money and power will result in even more state surveillance and control of Black communities. Rather than divesting one oppressive system to invest in another, we should work toward abolishing all carceral institutions and creating radically different ways of meeting families' needs.[163]

Calls for abolition of the family regulation system are bound to prompt questions about what should happen when abuse and violence *is* happening in families. As in every other arena, our current approach is already failing at addressing this abuse and violence. The family regulation system focuses on "treating" the problem rather than addressing the conditions that contribute to violence and focusing on prevention. As Movement for Family Power puts it, "Social workers mete out consequences instead of providing access to resources."[164] Today, nearly $7 billion in federal funding per year goes to foster care and adoption. Meanwhile, only $546 million goes to child abuse prevention and family preservation.[165] Movement for Family Power argues for defunding both and investing directly in family supports. Most of the financial support available to low-income children flows through the family regulation system instead of directly to families.[166] As Sangoi points out, numerous studies show that "increases in income and the minimum wage, access to childcare, expanding Medicaid, and providing housing, all correlate with decreases in what the foster system defines as 'child maltreatment.'"[167] At this point, you must be recognizing a theme. These very same interventions are at the heart of preventing and addressing every form of violence and neglect we've discussed in this book. Shifting how we invest our collective resources into collective care and support instead of criminalization and punishment is what campaigns to defund and abolish policing are about. That's why calls for "Caseworkers, Not Cops" should yield to calls for "Care, Not Cops."

A Public Health Approach to Policing

Policymakers and public health officials are increasingly calling for a "public health approach" to safety. Some defund organizers are as well. For instance, the 2021 Minneapolis ballot initiative to create a new Department of Community Safety would have mandated that the department adopt such an approach.[168]

Calls for public health–based approaches to violence have their origins in programs that aim to interrupt "gun violence," framing community violence as a contagion that spreads as other diseases do, and requires similar responses.[169] Public health approaches "focus on preventing injury or death by addressing underlying social determinants of health, centering the needs of people most impacted by violence, and providing support for navigating trauma," and are supported by the Centers for Disease Control and Prevention.[170]

In 2018, the American Public Health Association (APHA) adopted a historic resolution declaring police violence a public health issue and demanding a public health approach that "targets the structural inequities that manifest in criminalized behaviors by addressing the social determinants of health," such as access to housing, education, employment, and health care. The resolution confirmed that this approach is "associated with reduced community trauma and interpersonal harm, improved community health and safety."[171] In 2021, the APHA recommended abolishing carceral systems altogether and instead investing in community resources as well as developing "non-carceral measures for accountability, safety, and well-being."

While a public health approach to public safety appears promising, there is still reason to proceed with caution. Public health systems emerged from the "medical police," and a public health framework can all too easily replicate the pitfalls of the "treatment not punishment" and "caseworkers, not cops" approaches. Violence interruption programs that consider gun violence a public health issue still treat individuals as "vectors of violence" and focus on individual "behavioral interventions," rather than addressing systemic economic pressures on communities and cultures of toxic masculinity. Some violence interruption programs also work in collaboration with, or at least with the threat of, police intervention to varying degrees.

Public health systems incorporate surveillance and social control, in some cases making them an extension of policing, rather than an alternative to it. Public health workers have participated in policing since the birth of public health institutions, sorting people as "normal," "healthy," "diseased," and "dangerous," triaging migrants as desirable, diseased, or defective at the nation's borders; enforcing mandatory quarantine and exile of poor people with tuberculosis, typhoid, and other communicable diseases; ordering sterilizations of disabled, Black, and low-income people deemed unworthy of reproducing; experimenting with public health interventions such as syphilis treatment on Black people; and so much more.[172] More recently, public health workers contributed to the vilification and stigmatization of people with HIV/AIDS, further contributing to criminalization through surveillance and prosecution for HIV transmission.[173] We've also seen the connections between public health and policing on full display during the COVID-19 pandemic, with discriminatory and abusive police enforcement of public health orders and the use of electronic monitoring on people in quarantine—while the government simultaneously denies and fails to provide people with what they need to survive.[174] These realities and histories urge us to proceed with caution when calling for the adoption of a public health approach to policing.

Defunding the police cannot mean funding the soft social police. We can't engage in what scholar and writer James Kilgore calls "carceral humanism," which repackages punishment as mandated treatment and normalizes meeting needs through carceral services.[175] Real alternatives meet needs *as needs*; not through policing in one form or another. The paternalistic police power embedded in the "helping professions" must be dismantled, and the work that people in this sector do must support autonomous and community-embedded services. We need to call on educators, health care providers, domestic violence advocates, and social workers to rethink how to be in service to *people* without serving as the social police, and to divest from the social control and anti-Blackness that are found at the origins of so many of these professions.[176] As the Chicago chapter of Social Service Workers United emphasizes, "The history of psychiatric hospitalization, drug treatment, child welfare, and immigration programs and services cannot be divorced from America's history of creating systems to control and harm people of color."[177]

As we move toward a police-free world, it is critical to keep our sights on the goal of ending all forms of surveillance, confinement, containment, and control, including social policy premised on compliance with notions of "normalcy," enacted by the "soft police." We must steer clear of "alternatives" premised on having Someone Else to call or Somewhere Else to put people that simply substitute one form of policing with another. This is what the authors of *Abolition. Feminism. Now.* call the "careful work toward abolition," which requires us to "parse punishment from authentic forms of care, to push back on how the state absorbs the language of community-based demands for affirmation and support and deftly translates these into coercion and repression. . . ."[178]

How Do We Get There?
Toward a Police-Free Future

A growing number of people are recognizing that policing stands in the way of our individual and collective safety: by actively and institutionally perpetrating violence, by failing to offer protection, by diminishing life chances through criminalization, by looting resources from the things we need to generate more genuine and long-term safety for more people, and by sowing fear and capturing our imaginations to prevent anything new from emerging. The question then becomes, what do we build instead? How do we move toward a safer future free of the violence of policing?

We can begin, as many communities have, by focusing on removing police from specific tasks, arenas, and spaces, such as mental health crisis response, traffic enforcement, and schools.[1] We can eliminate the police units, weaponry, and individual cops who are doing the most harm, including "street crime" units, homeless "outreach" units, vice squads, anti-protest units, "party patrols," canine and mounted units, militarized equipment, and surveillance tools. We can prioritize termination of cops with violent track records as we shrink the size, reach, and power of police departments—while simultaneously recognizing that the problem extends beyond individuals.[2] We can divest from police departments and invest in meeting individual and community needs like housing, health care, education, and youth programs, in community-based nonpolice violence prevention, interruption, and transformative justice programs.[3]

But we can't stop there. We need to break the equation of policing with public safety in our imaginations. We must collectively divest not only financially, but ideologically and emotionally, from all forms of policing in order to build genuinely safer futures for all of us. It may seem easier to follow the lure of reform—to continue tinkering with the existing system or replicate policing in our community-based responses—than to build a radically different world. Fear of the unknown keeps many of us frozen in some version of the status quo. But if we are committed to true safety for our communities—the kind of safety that comes from everyone having what they need to live into their fullest human potential—nothing short of wholesale structural social and economic change will lead us there.

That is why the demand to defund police is the floor, not the ceiling. It is a demand in service of a larger vision, not the totality of the vision. Confining our efforts to shrinking police budgets and removing police from a limited set of situations under certain conditions isn't enough. We don't want to keep the system, structures, power, and framework of the prison industrial complex, the structures it upholds, and the violence it perpetuates daily, in place. Our ultimate goal must be abolition of all forms of surveillance, policing, and punishment and the systems that require them if we are to achieve true public safety.

That said, not everyone needs to be an abolitionist to move toward greater safety for our communities. We can travel in the same direction, even if some may choose to take an off-ramp at some point as we move towards the horizon of abolition. But it is critical to recognize that when we pursue reforms that bolster and legitimize systems of policing and punishment or give more power to the "soft police," we are moving in opposite directions and creating obstacles on the path toward greater safety. We must constantly ask ourselves if our efforts to end police violence ultimately legitimize policing and maintain the prison industrial complex (PIC) in its current or new forms, or dismantle systems of surveillance, policing, and punishment and create space for new possibilities for safety to emerge. Whether we understand ourselves to be abolitionists or not, as organizer Angélica Cházaro of Decriminalize Seattle reminds us, our task is to remove obstacles on the path to creating broader and more expansive forms of safety than we currently have.

How do we make sense of the steps on the way to this goal? As we travel down the road to police abolition and collective safety, there are core principles—explored in greater detail throughout the remaining chapters—that can guide our way as we pursue transformative demands toward liberatory goals.

First, as we've outlined in previous chapters, surveillance, policing, criminalization, incarceration, and punishment do not bring us closer to genuine safety because they neither prevent nor interrupt violence. They *are* forms of violence.

Contrary to popular misconceptions, elimination of policing and punishment doesn't mean that there will be no consequences for violence or harm. Instead, abolition focuses on accountability rather than punishment. Punishment is inflicting suffering for the sake of hurting someone, it does not require the person punished to do anything in particular but suffer the punishment; accountability is the voluntary process of stepping into responsibility for causing harm and committing to repair the harm.[4] Whether or not a person steps into accountability, abolition contemplates consequences for acts of violence or harm. Consequences are nonpunitive responses that are necessary to increase safety for both the person harmed and the community. Importantly, these consequences do not deny the dignity and humanity of the person who caused harm, or their potential for transformation. A world without policing is not a world where violence is allowed to proceed unchecked. To the contrary, as discussed in greater detail in the "Experiment and Build" chapter, it is a world that creates greater possibilities for prevention, interruption, healing, and repair of violence by meeting material needs, fostering mutual accountability, and imposing effective consequences when necessary.

Second, as discussed in the "Re-Form" chapter, we cannot seek justice for harm caused by police by legitimizing institutions that we are seeking to dismantle. Safety from the violence of policing cannot be found in the institutions of a carceral state.

Third, eliminating policing requires an end to the systems of racial capitalism that require it.

These abolitionist principles are not just aspirational; they are political commitments we must live by if we are to avoid reproducing violence in new forms. At a fundamental level, they require us to re-examine our conceptions of safety, and how they are shaped by policing in ways that are deeply embedded not only in social policy and state institutions, but in our culture, language, hearts, and minds.

Changing Ideas About Public Safety

Cops dominate conversations about safety. They are perceived as the ultimate authorities on the subject, regardless of whether their claims are based in fact. Defund campaigns invite communities to deeply examine and claim authority around what safety is and requires. For instance, in 2021, Minneapolis mayoral candidate Sheila Nezhad—a leader in local defund campaigns and member of abolitionist organizations Reclaim the Block and MPD150—declared, "I am the public safety candidate in this race. . . . I have spent years working as an organizer and as a policy analyst and budget analyst around community safety strategies and safety beyond policing in Minneapolis, and I have a demonstrated track record."[5] Nezhad correctly positioned her community-based experiences of addressing violence and harm as a form of expertise in creating safety.

Yet, the term "public safety," as it's currently understood, presumes a need for police, the military, or another security force to prevent people from either outside or within communities from causing harm. This reflects a politics of "security," rather than safety. The state produces insecurity through economic and social policies, and then promotes visions of "carceral safety" that can only be achieved through policing, prisons, and banishment.[6] Meanwhile, these very same practices and institutions produce greater unsafety, which is then mobilized to call for yet more police and punishment.[7]

Police play a frontline role in this state protection racket. As authors David Correia and Tyler Wall explain, the "thin blue line" ideology frames cops as all that stands between "civilization" and the unchecked violence and chaos of the "natural order."[8] Cops are deemed indispensable and beyond criticism as an institution because they are framed as an essential

How Do We Get There? Toward a Police-Free Future

181

bulwark against what is imagined as humanity's inherently violent natural state. This is how, Correia and Wall conclude, "order becomes synonymous with police."[9] The trick is that definitions of "civilization" and "order" are premised on what will facilitate and perpetuate racial capitalism. Moreover, Wall reminds us, "this police project is always incomplete, insecure, and unstable:" the "thin blue line" mythology paints safety as always tenuous and society as always at risk of reverting to a natural state of violence, offering up police as the only way to save us from "perpetual crisis" by waging a constant war to preserve and protect humanity against "savagery."[10] In other words, police, the story goes, are what makes society as we know it possible.[11]

Of course, there are racial, gendered, and ableist subtexts to this threatened chaotic violence without police—a reflection of the social and economic order that policing upholds. As currently defined, "public safety" produces separate camps—people who need to be kept safe and the people from whom they must be kept safe. As sociologist Reuben Jonathan Miller puts it, "Public safety, then, is safety for a white public . . . and safety from the presence of black flesh, which has to be chained, mutilated or banished . . . in order for the "We" to feel safe."[12] In other words, anti-Blackness structures our understandings of "public safety"— creating a system where whole groups of people are deemed "not only ineligible for state protection, but as targets of carceral safety's imperative to identify and eliminate threats."[13] "Public safety" also depends upon a sexual and gendered order that is threatened by the presence of trans, gender nonconforming, and LGBTQI people, and by all people rendered "queer" by virtue of their exclusion from socially constructed categories of white femininity and masculinity.[14] "Public safety" is deeply rooted in ableism—positioning disabled bodies and nonnormative behaviors as threats that must be corrected, controlled, or caged.[15] Common conceptions of "public safety" also frame migrants as undeserving "outsiders" who present both an external and internal threat.[16]

What might genuine public safety look like if it were not premised on the necessity of police to maintain existing racialized, gendered, and ableist relations of power, and instead built around ideas like thriving, flourishing, and well-being? As professor of law and sociology Monica

Bell reminds us, communities that are currently thought of as "safer" by the public "are not safer because of policing, but because of the greater front-end resources they enjoy. . . . "[17] Yet our society rarely offers a vision of public safety that doesn't include police, who have so thoroughly colonized and dominated our thinking that we struggle to imagine a world where they don't exist.

Uprooting "Copaganda"

In reality, we haven't always had police. What makes us believe that we always will or that we always will have to?[18] Helping people to divest from the idea that policing was developed to create public safety in the first place, or that it keeps us safe now, is a central aspect of abolitionist work.

Given the stranglehold police exercise over debates around public safety, this is an uphill battle in the best of times. Amid the vicious backlash unleashed by cops, police fraternal associations, and politicians in the wake of the 2020 Uprisings, it's even more difficult. Facing the greatest crisis to their legitimacy in generations, police have reached for their most reliable weapon: fear. They have falsely blamed the movement to divest from policing for increased homicide rates, and constantly dangle the specter of unchecked violence in the face of any challenge to their power. This is an old habit with a long history. During a 2021 discussion of the backlash that defund movements are facing across the country, organizers from Communities of Color United in Austin and Decriminalize Seattle described how police continue to deliberately manufacture crises in their communities, then position themselves as the only ones who can resolve them.[19] These experiences echo the premise of cultural theorist Stuart Hall's *Policing the Crisis*, originally published more than forty years ago in response to a manufactured crisis of muggings in the wake of challenges to police power in the U.K.[20] Police are also constantly reinventing, inserting, and reimagining themselves into new roles in order to preserve their legitimacy. The fact that cops must constantly defend their position suggests that their role in our society is more precarious than it appears. They are, in fact, vulnerable to public pressure and organizing.[21]

Challenging current notions of "public safety" requires us to contend with how deeply the cops, policing, and law enforcement are embedded in our minds as the primary or only source of safety—how it is, as author Patrick Blanchfield put it, that "the police are in our minds as a solution rather than as a problem."[22] It's not simply that we can't imagine a world without police, but that we are disciplined into *not* having that imagination through "copaganda"—propaganda favorable to law enforcement that inundates mainstream media.[23] As author Mark Anthony Neal explains, copaganda has "long been a tool to disrupt legitimate claims of anti-Black violence . . . by reinforcing the ideas that the police are generally fair and hard-working and that 'Black criminals' deserve the brutal treatment they receive."[24] Though the term was coined in the 1950s,[25] the concept isn't new—nor is the media's complicity in propagating copaganda. As early as 1909, Ida B. Wells-Barnett noted the complicity of newspapers in her time in state-sponsored anti-Black violence, describing them as an "accessory" to lynch mobs.[26] Similarly, Mariame frequently refers to contemporary media as "stenographers for the cops" based on their unquestioning repetition of police narratives about violence and safety.

The continued use of the term "officer-involved shooting" is just one example of how media serve as stenographers for the police. For instance, in October 2021, the *Los Angeles Times* described an incident in which a cop killed a woman by stating that she had been "hospitalized after a Simi Valley officer-involved shooting." The article went on to describe how the incident had occurred after "the officers engaged the female, and an officer-involved shooting occurred."[27] This use of the passive voice to describe active acts of police violence has persisted despite the Associated Press revising its style book in the summer of 2020 to discourage news organizations from using it. Jerry Iannelli, a reporter for *The Appeal*, notes that the term "absolves police officers and dehumanizes their (disproportionately Black) victims." He cites a number of examples to illustrate this point, including this one: "The headline 'Bodycam video captures deadly officer-involved shooting in Mantua Township' completely fails to make clear what actually happened: A New Jersey resident called 911 fearing armed trespassers on his property. Police arrived, then killed the caller."[28]

Beyond media narratives, cop shows (for which cops often serve as "consultants"[29]), children's books, cartoons and comics, Lego toys, "Officer Friendly" programs in schools, and other popular cultural artifacts frame cops as heroic, and the people they harm as deserving of their fates.

Everywhere we look, cops are lionized in monuments, memorials, and highway signs. All of this conditions and limits our imaginations. Why does law enforcement need so much advertising? It's hard to think of any other occupation that approaches this degree of public relations effort. Childcare and sanitation workers, for instance, are truly essential to ensuring the functioning of modern society, but there are few television shows portraying them as heroes.[30]

Copaganda does not always come as unambiguously packaged as it does in shows like *Cops, The Thin Blue Line,* or *Law and Order.* For instance, generations of schoolchildren in North America and the U.K. were required to read *Lord of the Flies,* a novel that chronicles how a group of shipwrecked boys descend into violence and chaos in the absence of the structured "order" of society. The book is, among other things, a cautionary tale against a world without policing. Notably, we were not all compelled to learn the true story of six Tongan teens who were trapped on a remote and uninhabited island for fifteen months in the mid-1960s—around the same time *Lord of the Flies* was made into a film. They lived together cooperatively, dividing up labor and generating creative conflict-resolution strategies, such as requiring parties to walk to opposite ends of the island before returning to address the issues at hand with cooler minds.[31] They created a garden, made music, and played sports. In an interview about the experience decades later, one of the survivors credits the culture in which they were raised, where collaboration and spirituality were both valued, and conflict—understood as natural—was always addressed because failing to do so threatened the whole community's survival. He also described learning more from nature, and from the experience of collective survival, than he had in school.[32] The pre-eminence of the fictionalized *Lord of the Flies* narrative over the true story of the Tongan teens is just one example of how the stories we tell, the books we read, and the music we listen to are critical to shaping the worlds we can imagine and create. If we are fed images of dystopian and violent futures without police through stories like *Lord of the Flies,* or films like *Blade Runner* and *The Purge,* then we will fear a police-free society. If we consume images of safety achieved through care and cooperation, we are more likely to reach for them in practice.[33]

How Do We Get There? Toward a Police-Free Future

185

Correia and Wall also point to the insidious way that the ideology of policing is propagated through what they call "copspeak"—a language that defines *how* we talk about violence and safety that limits our ability to understand police as anything other than essential.[34] "Copspeak" describes those targeted by police violence using language like "armed," "gang members," "known to police," "resisting," engaged in "furtive movements." It frames cops' actions as "crime fighting" and "crowd control"; their violence as "positional restraint" and "pain compliance." Copspeak responds to critiques with talk of "rebuilding community trust in law enforcement." Correia and Wall write that this language "comes to us through a register patrolled by police and police reformers . . . when we speak the language of copspeak . . . we see the world as police do."[35] Wall elaborates that "copspeak" reflects "cop knowledge," a way of knowing and understanding the world that places cops at the center.[36] As Correia and Wall put it, the "language of police sanitizes the fact of everyday humiliation and violence enacted by police,"[37] and makes violent realities of policing palatable. Add Correia and Wall, "when we see the world that copspeak and cop knowledge describe to us—one forever threatened by disorder and chaos—we have no choice but to trust" that policing is necessary to safety.[38]

Correia and Wall point out that in order to bring abolitionist dreams into being, "we need a different vocabulary of police, one that is free of the copspeak that constrains every conversation about police."[39] This requires changing the language we use to describe both the problems and the solutions. For instance, as Rachel Herzing often points out, the term "officer"—derived from "official"—presumes reverence and deference, while "cop" (or any number of other words we can use to describe police) doesn't have the same effect. "Over-policing" suggests that we just need to find the *right* amount of policing, when, in fact, *all* policing is violence. Similarly, limiting our vision to "ending mass incarceration" that is "over-policing" suggests that it is simply the number of people who are incarcerated or policed that is the problem, while ignoring the violence that is policing or keeping any human being in a cage. The limited frame of "ending mass incarceration" also fails to address the harms of surveillance and policing that exist beyond cages in the form of probation, parole, and "e-carceration" (the use of electronic monitoring and "house arrest," among other things).[40] "Police brutality" contains the possibility that police can exist without violence, whereas referring to the "violence of policing" makes it clear that they cannot. Even using terms such as "alternatives to police" conditions us to keep prison and police constant in our minds. Adding the word "alternative" in front of a death-making institution only bolsters its core functions, endorsing the "necessity" of this work, and suggesting that it should simply be carried out by a different set of players. By clearly naming policing itself—and the systems it protects and upholds—as the problem, we call attention to the root of the issues we are confronting as well as the limits of many proposed solutions that only end up legitimizing the police.[41]

At bottom, we need to uproot criminalization as a central organizing principle of our society. Criminalization assumes that there will always be individuals whose existence, expressions, productivity, and actions need to be regulated, contained, and controlled, whether that be through criminal law, "treatment," or "behavioral interventions."[42] Of course, individuals who engage in harmful actions, behaviors, and abuses of power must be the subject of prevention, accountability, and healing. But that is not what criminalization is about; criminalization is a social and political process that determines whose actions will be subject to surveillance, policing, and punishment in service of maintaining and reinforcing existing relations of power.[43]

Ultimately, as we discuss in the "No Soft Police" chapter, we need to stop looking for "Someone Else" to call, even if they are not cops in blue uniforms with guns, so that they can take *some* people "Somewhere Else." Instead, we need to start looking for ways to decrease harm by meeting everyone's needs through the universal, accessible, and sustainable distribution of resources, care, and transformative justice. Greater safety is not created through criminalization, no matter what form it takes; carceral responses to harm simply mask the roots of structural and interpersonal violence. Challenging the concept of criminalization itself illuminates the interests and relations of power it serves, as well as its failure to produce safety, and the ways in which it operates through soft policing in "alternatives" to police that replicate patterns and practices of policing in different forms. It requires us to, in the words of Black feminist scholars Alisa Bierria and Jakeya Caruthers "abolish something so deeply rooted that it disciplines meaning itself." [44] Safety is a basic human need, but in order to achieve it, we need to unveil the lies embedded in "copaganda," "copspeak," and "cop knowledge," reclaim narratives around public safety, and create space in our imaginations to build something new. It also requires us to meet people at an emotional level to confront the fears police perpetuate and play on, and to address the very human need for safety.

What Does Safety Mean for You?

Contrary to assumptions that abolitionists don't care about safety, we care a great deal about it. We recognize that safety is a basic human need. We think, talk, and strategize about it constantly in order to bring more of us closer to it. A commitment to creating genuine and lasting safety for all is what drives our desire to remake the world. Our organizing and advocacy toward a world free of policing is rooted in the reality that, for many of us, the cops offer no solution to violence and in fact *are* the killers, rapists, home invaders, and looters, destroyers of lives, families, and communities. *They* are what stands between us and the resources we need to ensure our collective safety and survival.

Ultimately, achieving greater safety requires us to divest financially, ideologically, and emotionally from the violence of policing. That means speaking to and confronting fears arising from the basic human need for safety and survival, which are fueled by propaganda and social policy that offer police and the carceral state as the only possible ways to meet those needs. The idea that policing makes us safe has been so profoundly embedded into our psyches that we can't do this with facts and figures alone. We need to connect with ourselves and each other at an emotional level to disentangle policing from safety in our minds and hearts, as well as in our communities and institutions. And we need to trouble the very notion of safety we have been sold by the carceral state.

As abolitionists, we begin by asking open and generative questions that don't limit our imaginations to policing: *What does safety look like for you and for your communities? What conditions would increase safety for as many people as possible?* We engage individuals and communities on their concrete concerns around what might happen if police no longer exist by asking questions like: *Are you in danger right now? Are you worried about being robbed or assaulted? What have the police done in the past when you or people you love have faced this danger? What do you think the police would do if you faced this danger in the future? If the police were helpful, how were they helpful? If you imagine they would be, what, specifically, do you envision them doing? Could that function be performed by someone who could be helpful without posing a danger to you and other people in your community? Who would be part of strengthening rather than destroying communities? Could this danger be prevented by ensuring your material needs are met or by transforming conditions and cultures of violence? Are you worried about what to do in case you are harmed in the future? What happens if someone commits a mass shooting? Are you worried about your own capacity to keep yourself and each other safe? Are you worried about retribution if you try to intervene to prevent harm?*

So often, our sense of safety and what is needed to achieve it is rooted in hypotheticals, whether that be "stranger danger" or boogeymen in shows and movies like *Criminal Minds* and *Silence of the Lambs*. It is shaped by what Meghan McDowell calls the "affective economy" through which the carceral state provides a structure that teaches people who to hate and fear. It also encourages us to "identify with punishing, containing, or dissociating from those same groups as the primary means to stay safe." As McDowell explains, these "very same racist and xenophobic sentiments" that fall "under the seemingly innocuous banner of public safety" are then used "to rally support for and consent to the expansion of the carceral state."[45]

For the majority of people and communities affected by violence, our sense of safety is often informed by the safety we didn't get—from police, or anyone else—when we did face harm. We hold a wishful hope that next time, cops will get it right. For many communities, police are the only government resource available to meet any and all needs, conflicts, and harms. The notion of removing police raises fear of further abandonment to violence in the absence of any structures or institutions to ensure safety or meet community needs. This is particularly true for people who are at risk of white supremacist and intracommunal violence.

Our sense of safety can also be informed by global conditions. For migrants who came to the U.S. from parts of the world where states had collapsed, prisoners had been released, and violence and chaos reigned, the prospect of defunding and abolishing police and prisons can raise deep concerns. When responding to such concerns, we need to be clear about what fueled societal collapse—the answer is often rooted in colonialism, imperialism, and U.S. intervention in the role of "global cop." We also need to be clear about the conditions abolitionists are working to create. We are not advocating police abolition in a vacuum. Nor are we advocating for abandoning our communities to gender-based, intracommunal, religious, ethnic, or military violence. Quite the contrary. Our goal is to dismantle colonial, imperial, and capitalist structures of violence in the U.S. and beyond, and fill the space with an abundance of resources, programs, and supports to create greater safety for all. We need to hold our communities' fears with care while simultaneously building a shared understanding of violence and harm that includes the violence of police and fellow community members, and of how we might go about creating genuine safety together, in ways that recognize the interconnectedness of our existence, without leaving anyone behind.

Abolition also requires us to unpack the notion of safety itself. While safety is a basic and universal human need, it doesn't have a universal and singular definition. Nor is it a stable category. It shifts in relation to conditions and to other people. No individual or society can be "perfectly safe" at all times and under all conditions. All of us are vulnerable—to the elements, to natural threats like earthquakes or hurricanes, to harm caused by other inhabitants of this planet, to the uncertainty of human existence in a vast universe. Of course, we are not all equally at risk. Our vulnerability to natural disaster, violence, trauma—and our access to opportunities to heal from them—are structured by relations of racial capitalism. Yet, as James Baldwin reminds us:

> Most of us, no matter what we say, are walking in the dark, whistling in the dark. Nobody knows what is going to happen to him from one moment to the next, or how one will bear it. This is irreducible. And it's true of everybody. Now, it is true that the nature of society is to create, among its citizens, an

illusion of safety; but it is also absolutely true that the safety is always necessarily an illusion.[46]

Safety is both illusory and a real concern. This is a difficult line to navigate. As a result, feminist philosopher Amia Srinivasan writes that we need to "take safety seriously as a political issue, while refusing a politics of safety."[47] The carceral politics of safety promoted by the state play on the human vulnerabilities Baldwin describes. The state's carceral safety robs our communities of the conditions and nutrients that would allow greater safety to grow, forcing us into the position of constantly reaching for more security from the very institutions that make us collectively less safe. Police fuel insecurity by constantly reminding us that we are never ever safe, with or without them. They then weaponize this insecurity to enact untold violence, always in the name of producing an impossible and elusive "safety." Their presence represents and announces an absence of safety rather than an embodiment of it.

Ultimately, we need to recognize and break with this obtunded conception of safety, the illusory carceral safety presented as something only the state can produce. That illusion is intended to lull us into passively delegating responsibility for producing safety to police, prosecutors, and prisons, and accepting the violence they perpetrate as the inevitable price of safety. To preserve this conception of safety, the state stokes our fear of one another, discouraging and interfering with our ability to care for each other. We see concrete evidence of this in the ways that police critique de-escalation training, resist efforts to create nonpolice crisis response teams, and actively interfere with violence prevention and interruption initiatives. We're not usually at our best when we're afraid, and we are made even more afraid of each other through the politics of safety.

We also need to let go of the idea that safety is a state of being that can be personally or permanently achieved. Safety isn't a commodity that can be manufactured and sold to us by the carceral state or private corporations. Nor is safety a static state of being. Safety is dependent on social relations and operates relative to conditions: we are more or less safe depending on our relationship to others and our access to the resources we need to survive. In her short film *The Giverny Document*,[48] Ja'Tovia

How Do We Get There? Toward a Police-Free Future

191

Gary asks Black women passing a subway station in Harlem whether they feel safe in their bodies, in their communities, in society. Their answers are equivocal and relative: it depends, they said, on conditions like who they are with, whether their health aide is nearby, where they are, what time of day it is, or if they believe God is with them. If you ask anyone on any given day if they feel more or less safe, their answer will depend on a multitude of things. Did they just get paid and feel less anxious about rent? Did they go outside or did they stay home all day? Did they log on to the internet and find themselves bombarded by copaganda and stories of violent crime, missing white women, and mass shootings? Do they have people to lean on if some calamity befalls them, or will they be left alone to navigate and make sense of it? These conceptions of safety are more nuanced than absolute, more relational than categorical. The more functional and vital question we face is how to create more safety for more people while acknowledging that the concept of safety is contested and its meanings aren't fixed.

Recognizing that safety is changeable and relative actually opens up space for us to better understand our work. Our goal, then, is to shift conditions and relationships in ways that produce greater possibilities of safety for a greater number of people, rather than relying on the state to deliver us to an ever elusive and illusory end point. It allows us to focus on addressing immediate needs for safety while working to abolish death-making institutions. We can create material safety and safety from state violence by divesting from policing and punishment, and we can increase access to greater safety through our relationships.

Abolitionists see safety as a set of resources, relationships, skills, and tools that can be developed, disseminated, and deployed to prevent, interrupt, and heal from harm. We want to increase the number of tools that increase safety for as many people as possible; get rid of the tools that don't actually serve us, like policing and punishment; and undermine the fear driving the politics of safety. As abolitionist mad organizer Elliott Fukui puts it, "[R]elationships are the most important resource we have." Building and strengthening the relationships we need to create collective safety requires us to overcome the fear of and alienation from each other that the state has perpetuated. Collective care is a form of reciprocal community support that Krystle Okafor describes as "how we make each other possible."[49] Ultimately, there will be no safety that we don't make through collective care and the relationships it requires. Our work as abolitionists is therefore to increase our capacity to build relationships and structures of care.

This view of safety presents a challenge, as carceral systems tell us that solutions to violence are simple, straightforward, and absolute. We have been conditioned to see safety in a form only the state can provide. Abolitionists are therefore often expected to offer alternatives based on what currently exists—to take a job away from the police and reassign it to someone else—often a member of the "soft police." Responses to violence that don't rely on police or policing appear to be more complex, exhausting, naïve, or impossible. Or, they are simply illegible to us as "safety." The current approach to "public safety" actually increases risk of premature death, yet we cling to the thing that is failing us. We have to do the work of rejecting the politics of safety, and the carceral and militarized visions of safety, that we have been conditioned to believe are the only path forward.

To this end, thousands of organizers across the country are inviting people to reimagine and reclaim public safety based on their own expertise. They are going door to door, surveying community members online and in person, holding People's Movement Assemblies,[50] and deploying creative tactics to ask people in a variety of ways and settings what safety looks and feels like and stitching their responses into broad and deep visions for safer communities. None of us has all the answers—not even those who want the status quo. Nonetheless, asking each other these questions can point us to different conversations that open up possibilities for more safety for more people.

Shifting core beliefs about public safety often requires more than talking. This can include experiencing or witnessing the full violence of policing. For instance, violent police response to protest can effectively shift perceptions among people who otherwise don't experience the everyday violence of policing as it manifests daily in Black, Indigenous, and Brown communities. Images and experiences of civil rights–era police repression, police violence at anti-apartheid and ACT UP actions, the brutal treatment of protesters during the 1999 WTO protests, two decades of protests at Republican National Conventions, and police violence at Occupy encampments have politicized generations—including many people who continue to lead and participate in abolitionist campaigns and projects. Resistance to violent policing by the South African apartheid state, to occupation of Palestinian territories by the Israeli government, and to the colonial forces seizing Indigenous lands around the world has also shaped many abolitionist organizers. The sight and experience of tanks and tear gas on the streets of Ferguson in 2014 mobilized broad support for what became the Movement for Black Lives. The sight of water hoses deployed on water protectors in below-zero temperatures during the 2016 No Dakota Access Pipeline (NoDAPL) protests at Standing Rock highlighted the role of public and private police violence in protecting corporate and colonial interests. Video of Border Patrol ripping migrant children from their parents' arms and beating Haitian migrants with bullwhips as they attempted to cross the Rio Grande made graphically visible the daily violence of border and immigration enforcement. Each of these instances chipped away at the notion of cops as protectors of democracy and purveyors of safety among a growing number of people.

The historic protests of summer 2020 also significantly eroded the equation of police with safety. The nation once again watched as the police indiscriminately used tear gas against protesters—this time, in the midst of a respiratory pandemic, while trapping them into tight spots where social distancing was impossible. Many cops refused to wear masks while yelling in people's faces, ripping protesters' masks off on the streets to pepper spray them, and putting their lives at risk through arrest and intentionally prolonged incarceration in jails where there were no protections available and COVID-19 spread like wildfire.[51]

The opportunity to see and experience other ways of making safety has also shifted many people's beliefs about policing and state violence. Abandoned by the government to the ravages of the pandemic and the greatest economic crisis in a generation, many more people have had an embodied experience of being cared for and protected by community members through mutual aid and community defense. For instance, when police abandoned communities in Minneapolis to white supremacist violence in the midst of the 2020 Uprisings and deliberately slowed their responses to

911 calls to punish residents, people stepped up to keep each other safe. This cemented the idea that "we keep us safe" with praxis, providing experiences of what safety can look and feel like without—and against—police violence.[52] Groups like the Powderhorn Safety Collective and Little Earth Protectors continue to respond to incidents and patrol neighborhoods, while newer groups, like Relationships Evolving Possibilities, are emerging, offering more people the possibility of experiencing safety without police.

In one poignant example, abolitionist scholar Charmaine Chua describes the fourteen-day occupation of a downtown Minneapolis Sheraton near the burned Third Precinct by organizers and unhoused residents. They used the hotel as a place where people could create and practice the world they were fighting for in the streets. Volunteers ran twenty-four-hour kitchen, laundry, cleaning, and community safety shifts, co-creating a culture of abundance. Chua describes this resident-centered environment:

> [It was] grounded in principles of harm reduction, autonomy, mutual aid, anti-racism, and abolition. No cops were called. Instead, a safety team was on hand to respond. People were free to make choices about engaging in risky behavior, and medics would provide supplies and education to lessen the risk of injury or infection . . . residents set community agreements, signed up for security and cleaning shifts, and helped in the kitchen.[53]

Recognizing that "housing deprivation and incarceration are two sides of the same racial capitalist coin," organizers both practiced and experienced building safety without police through housing and harm reduction–based community safety practices.[54]

Abolishing systems of surveillance, policing, and punishment isn't only about burning police cars and precincts or defunding and dismantling individual police departments; it also requires unearthing and doing away with the ideologies, narratives, and systems that produce and legitimize them. Our objective as abolitionists is not simply to oppose the violence of policing, but to live into our principles, creating a world where prisons, policing, and surveillance are not normalized facets of our society. While none of these experiments represent a singular solution to rooting out the perceived need for policing in our collective imaginations, together, they chip away at its place in our consciousnesses. They make it possible for us to continue to organize and create the conditions that will make even more experiments possible.

Principles for Organizing Toward Police Abolition

Beyond shifting ideas, language, culture, and experiences of public safety, we need to take bold action toward a world without police. The fight is against criminalization, cages, and cops. The fight is also *for* structures that support the kind of relationality we want, that enable and encourage care, belonging, and abundance.

Building a police-free society does not require all of us to do the same things. In fact, it requires a multitude of people performing a multitude of functions oriented toward generating collective safety and well-being. But, for us, organizing toward safer communities beyond policing does require all of us to adopt, adhere to, and be accountable to shared abolitionist values and political commitments:

- We oppose surveillance, policing, or incarceration in any form—including in response to state and white supremacist violence;
- Policing is beyond reform. The changes we work toward must divest resources, power, weaponry, and legitimacy from police, and reinvest those funds and resources into community-accountable institutions[55] and practices that provide real safety;
- Real change comes from material redistribution of resources and access to healing, not simply shifting or renaming systems of policing while maintaining inequalities and relations of power. For example, real change comes from meeting mental health needs through universal, accessible, quality, and voluntary preventative and supportive care for everyone, not renaming violent police and coercive responses to unmet mental health needs

"crisis intervention teams" or diverting people into carceral and punitive mental health systems;

- We need experimentation and innovation towards building safety specific to each community—there is no single "evidence-based" "one-size-fits-all" solution;
- We are committed to disability justice, and to dismantling interlocking systems of oppression rooted in ableism, patriarchy, transphobia, homophobia, racial capitalism, and imperialism;
- We are committed to collective governance and Black feminist practices of collective care that center the safety, needs, visions, and well-being of Black women, queer, and trans communities;[56]
- We practice hope and radical imagination as a discipline.

Over the past two decades, abolitionist organizers have developed practical frameworks that apply these principles. We can use these frameworks to guide our work and bolster our spirits in the face of the inevitable backlash and bumps on the long road ahead. For instance, aworldwithoutpolice.org is a collective of organizers from across the United States and around the world that works to connect people struggling against the everyday violence of the police. They offer *disempower, disarm, disband* as a framework for action. Shiri Pasternak, Kevin Walby, and Abby Stadnyk similarly named an anthology of writings on defund organizing in Canada *Disarm, Defund, Dismantle.*[57] These approaches provide practical, organizational, and theoretical tools for abolitionist organizers. Neutralizing and striking at the power police hold in our society is essential to abolishing the institution. Disarming cops is an idea that carries some appeal—and some *caveats*. People often point to the United Kingdom, and other countries where regular police don't carry guns, as an example of what a disarmed police department might look like. However, as Black people in the U.K. remind us, while the number of people killed or injured by cops may be significantly lower, cops can still do a lot of damage—including deadly damage—with batons, Tasers, and their bare hands (or knee, in Derek Chauvin's case). Even if unarmed, cops can do violence simply by wielding the power of the badge and using the threat of criminalization to extort, criminalize, harass, and abuse. Disarming is necessary, but not sufficient, to the project of police abolition. Disempowering, disbanding, and dismantling systems of policing are essential to the end goal of achieving safety.

A framework many people are familiar with is the *divest/invest* frame articulated by the Movement for Black Lives (M4BL):

> We demand investments in the education, health, and safety of Black people, instead of investments in the criminalizing, caging, and harming of Black people. We want investments in Black communities, determined by Black communities, and divestment from exploitative forces including prisons, fossil fuels, police, surveillance, and exploitative corporations.[58]

M4BL's divest/invest framework informed Black Visions' demands to defund the Minneapolis Police Department, as well as those of many organizations within and beyond the M4BL ecosystem. Mariame elaborates on this frame, noting that "[a]bolitionist organizing insists that we focus on divesting, investing, *and* experimenting. All three are important steps."[59] The "Experiment and Build" chapter of this book explores many such experiments in community safety on the path toward an abolitionist horizon.

The *Dismantle, Change, Build* framework offered by Critical Resistance (CR) remains one of the most powerful ways of understanding the road ahead. In their Abolish Policing Toolkit, CR invites us to ask ourselves: "What specifically are you trying to **dismantle** within the institution of policing, short term and long term? What specifically, in the short and long term, are you trying to **change** in your community's conditions and relationships of power that sustain policing? What specifically do you need to **build** in your community to instead sustain collective health, life, equity and community self-determination?"[60] These questions help us to understand the importance of not only disempowering, disarming, and disbanding death-making institutions, but also changing the ways of thinking, relations of power, and values that produce them. The questions also help guide us in the process of beginning to build life-giving and affirming relationships and structures that will fuel a culture of care and sustain genuine and lasting safety for all.

This doesn't mean that we should overlook the importance of chipping away at the existing system by changing conditions and freeing individuals caught in its web. As emphasized in the "Re-Form" chapter, making transformative demands requires us to constantly ask ourselves whether the changes we seek legitimize systems we are seeking to dismantle, or chip away at their power and make it possible for more people harmed by it to fight back. For instance, Joey Mogul is a lawyer at the People's Law Office and organizer who co-led Chicago's struggle for reparations for survivors of police torture. Mogul often tells a story from an organizing campaign to shut down Marion, a supermax prison in Illinois, during which they were a member of the Committee to End the Marion Lockdown. They would receive letters from prisoners thanking them for fighting to shut the facility down altogether—but also pleading with them to also advocate for the lights to be turned off, given that they were on twenty-four hours a day, causing people to lose all sense of time, day or night, and fueling mental health experiences propelled by their isolation. The story illustrates that we require a systemic analysis as well as a set of demands that targets systems *and* changes current conditions to enable more people directly impacted by criminalization to survive until we are successful. As the authors of *Abolition. Feminism. Now.* put it, organizing in the space "between necessary responses to immediate needs and collective and radical demands for structural and ultimately revolutionary change is a hallmark of abolition feminism."[61]

We see this same approach throughout successful movements in history. Black abolitionists working to end slavery paid ransoms to slave catchers to free community members, despite arguments that doing so would simply feed the system that they were working to tear down. This is also the basis of the Black Panthers' slogan "survival pending revolution," which guided their transition from a party primarily focused on self-defense to one that also created free breakfast programs, medical clinics, and schools. The same is true of the contemporary campaign to #FreeBlackMamas that decarcerated hundreds of Black women and caregivers in time for Mother's Day by paying their bail—and then engaged them in community organizing to chip away at the system that caged them.[62] As abolitionist organizer Rachel Herzing and others remind us, we need to fight on multiple fronts: free as many individual people as we can, reduce

How Do We Get There? Toward a Police-Free Future

199

contact with the criminal punishment system where we can, and empower as many criminalized people as possible to participate in the fight to tear the whole thing down and build the world anew.

Change also means changing ourselves. We can start by organizing communities to stop calling the cops for everything: the neighbor whose music is too loud, the dispute over a parking spot, the trash dumped on their lawn, the neighbor's kid who seems to be on their own more often than not. A 2020 report from the Vera Institute of Justice found that "most of the 240 million annual calls to 911 relate to nonemergency or noncriminal issues, such as noise complaints, parking issues and complaints about unhoused persons."[63] Dontcallthepolice.com was founded in June 2020 by a white social worker who wanted to contribute something concrete to the uprisings. It offers an online list of local resources that she preliminarily investigated to assess their ability to offer help or support for a range of situations, including those that require de-escalation or intervention rather than violence. Similarly, groups like CAT-911 in Southern California, Relationships Evolving Possibilities (REP) in Minneapolis, and Decarcerate Utah in Salt Lake City are creating interactive online directories and apps where people can find information about services that can meet their needs instead of calling cops—and building community response teams to fill the gaps. These resources also include information about how to best access care without being criminalized within larger institutions that may have a policy of collaboration with police.

Breaking reliance on police to respond to every conflict, harm, and need is not simply a matter of making lists of alternative resources available. It also requires organizing people to use them—and to build their own. And it requires strengthening community infrastructure and collective political commitments to each other's safety. For instance, "Harm Free Zones" were envisioned by longtime Black feminist abolitionist and former Critical Resistance national organizing director Kai Lumumba Barrow. They are territories—neighborhoods, buildings, and businesses—where people commit to not calling police for minor things, and to meeting each other's needs for safety. The building blocks for creating Harm Free Zones are existing and emerging structures: tenant and block associations, community organizations and institutions. By building on what already exists to develop abolitionist spaces and practices, this organizing exemplifies what Ruth Wilson Gilmore describes as "the large ways that abolitionists are trying to think . . . concretely . . . about what it is people already do or already know how to do or already should be able to do if they only felt empowered . . . to do it."[64] Harm Free Zones have been practiced by community-based organizations Youth Ministries for Peace and Justice in the Bronx, Sista II Sista[65] and Safe Outside the System[66] in Brooklyn, and Spirit House[67] and Ubuntu in Durham, North Carolina.

Dismantle, Change, Build helps us to understand our job as abolitionists: fighting cops, changing conceptions of safety, directly meeting our communities' needs. According to Ruth Wilson Gilmore, that includes knocking on people's doors and saying "Hello, my name is [ ], and I am here to solve your problems."[68] Gilmore maintains that no matter what problems people identify, they will inevitably be connected to the larger project of abolition—housing, health care, community conflict, climate catastrophe. Everything leads back to the need to radically transform our society away from policing and punishment. It's a point hit home by Charmaine Chua, who explains that "[a]bolitionist praxis . . . orients movements toward meaningful transformations that address the underlying structures that cause people harm, rather than addressing their symptoms."[69] *Dismantle, Change, Build* means we can organize toward the elimination of policing while we attend to our communities' immediate needs for safety.

Building individual and collective investment in abolitionist futures—and the power to create them—requires abolitionist base-building. It means asking people who are directly impacted by the violence of policing what safety looks like to them and building the power to fight for it. It means wresting resources from the state to make it possible. It requires us to study our conditions and our histories, to imagine the future we want, set strategic objectives, and build the structures necessary to get from here to there.[70] It requires an overarching vision that we enact through ongoing struggle, collective experimentation, organizing, and rebellion. It requires us to practice new social relations and practices of governance as we fight. We're dismantling and building at the same time. Abolition is simultaneously elaborating and enacting a vision of a restructured society and eliminating the obstacles to achieving it. It's not a blueprint, but rather another world in the making.

How Do We Get There? Toward a Police-Free Future

201

We don't need all the answers to start down the road toward where we want to go: a world where everyone has safety, food, clean water, shelter, education, health, art, beauty, and rest. As PIC abolitionists, we work to prefigure the world we want by practicing abolition every day. This work involves both organizing for the destruction of death-making institutions and for the creation of life-giving and affirming ones.

Police abolition is not an individual pursuit but a collective project. During a 2020 Rebel Steps podcast interview, the hosts asked Mariame: "What's the world without prisons look like? What is a world without police? Give us the details and give us your imaginary vision." Mariame responded: "How is my personal vision going to be the same as somebody in Iowa's vision of that? We are going to have to build it together, and that means we're going to have to argue over stuff. That means we're going to have to create new norms together for how we treat each other when harm occurs. That's going to take everyone."[71]

Of course, each of us has individual work to do—starting with our approach to the harms we ourselves cause. We have to practice self-accountability,[72] which means constantly asking ourselves what our values are and whether we're living up to them, and when we're not, shifting our behavior so that we are in alignment with our values.

We are both regularly asked for "concrete" examples of what safety without police looks like—as if producing a laundry list of fail-safe examples of where and how such a thing has succeeded before is a precondition to continuing a conversation about police abolition. While both of us can point to numerous individual projects, examples, and experiments (some of which are explored in the "Experiment and Build" chapter, some of which we have been part of), that is not the point. The point is that it is *everyone's* opportunity and responsibility to collectively imagine what creating safety for our communities might look like. Collectively, we need to apply abolitionist principles and frameworks in our neighborhoods and communities. We have the tools we need to begin. Now, we need to roll up our sleeves and do the work of transforming what we imagine into reality.

Tricks and Tensions

When it comes to divesting from policing with an eye to an abolitionist horizon, there is much that can be put into practice right now. Yet there is no blueprint for the abolitionist futures we're imagining and creating—we are building the world anew. There's also no consensus among PIC abolitionists about what shapes these futures should take—or how we get there. The path toward restructuring a society and economy from one built on scarcity, shaped by racial capitalism, and sustained by policing, to one built on abundance, sustainable economies rooted in collective care, and transformative justice requires us to grapple and sit with many unknowns and tensions around the specifics of this transition. As abolitionists, how do we get from where we are to the society we want to create while avoiding the pitfalls along the way?

Central to this question is our relationship to the state. Should defund campaigns fight to move money from police budgets to other state institutions like public housing, education, and health care—even though they also serve as disciplining arms of the carceral state as discussed in the "No Soft Police" chapter—or into community-based institutions and programs that operate outside, or at least without, the state? In other words, how can we extract resources currently devoted to surveillance, policing, and punishment and put them toward meeting community needs and building safety without becoming a cog in a carceral apparatus? What kinds of decision-making processes do we want around how collective resources are generated and spent? How should we govern ourselves and relate to each other? Should we seek control over police departments or work to disband them? Can the state offer justice and repair for the harms of policing and criminalization? In short, what is the role of the state in abolitionist presents and futures?

These were some of the questions tackled at the January 2020 "Building Beyond Policing" gathering hosted by several groups, including Interrupting Criminalization, Critical Resistance, and PolicyLink. Dozens of organizers from across the country came together to assess the state of campaigns for police abolition and find strategic alignment toward building a broader movement. We shared lessons and principles from efforts to "starve the beast" by shrinking the funding, size, power, and reach of police forces, including immigration enforcement and Border Patrol; to break the power of police fraternal associations; to eradicate criminalization; and to build community-based nonpolice responses to conflict, gender-based violence, and other forms of harm. There was general consensus that we need to radically reorganize how we produce and distribute resources, shift whose safety and well-being we prioritize and how, and reconceptualize consequences and accountability for violence and harm without surveillance, policing, or punishment. But critical questions and tensions also emerged in these conversations—and in multiple abolitionist spaces we have been part of prior to, during, and following the 2020 Uprisings. Many of them centered around the role of state power, state institutions, and state regulation in the abolitionist futures our campaigns are building toward.

These questions became even more urgent and relevant when, less than six months after we convened, George Floyd was murdered. Ready or not, we were catapulted into a national conversation about defunding and dismantling police departments, and what is required to build safer communities. In Minneapolis, disagreements emerged almost immediately among organizers—not all of whom are abolitionist—around whether we should be working to defund and eliminate police departments or seeking community control of police. As defund demands continued to spread across the country, so too did questions around organizing strategies in relationship to the state in the present and future—a clear sign that we need to come to greater clarity around the larger political visions, ideologies, and theories guiding our campaigns. After all, our ultimate destination inevitably guides the paths we choose to get there.

Abolitionists continue to grapple with questions around which economic systems and forms of governance will make space for and bring us closer to abolitionist futures. We don't all agree, nor do we have all the answers. That is not only okay, it can be generative, creating necessary space for the robust debates, sharpening our analysis, and inviting experimentation, evaluation, study, and practice that will bring us closer to our vision. Contradictions and tensions are inherent in the work of worldbuilding, and many may remain unresolved. The work of abolition is necessarily always unfinished and in process. Rachel Herzing reminds us that it is essential, however, that we work together to find ways to navigate them that build greater and more authentic and grounded coherence rather than dissention and fragmentation that ultimately disempower us. In the meantime, we continue to navigate immediate strategic questions focused on limiting the state's power to do harm, meeting community needs, and fighting for and practicing more participatory forms of governance.

Dismantling the Carceral State

At their heart, defund campaigns are about budget priorities. And debates around budget priorities are, as abolitionists David Stein and Dan Berger put it, "about what the state can and should be."[1] This begs the question of whether a non-carceral state is possible.

Answering these questions requires us to define what we mean by "the state." Leading abolitionist theorists Ruth Wilson Gilmore and Craig Gilmore describe the state as "a territorially bounded set of relatively specialized institutions that develop and change over time in the gaps and fissures of social conflict, compromise, and cooperation."[2] In other words, the state is a collection of institutions and practices that is shaped by people who inhabit and enact them, as well as by the historical moment, place, and conditions in which they evolve, rather than a fixed structure disconnected from the people who make it up. This perspective is shared by David Graeber and David Wengrow, based on their expansive and exhaustive exploration of human societies, *The Dawn of Everything: A New History of Humanity*,[3] and by many abolitionists.

No matter what shape states take, they represent "a claim to a right to rule on behalf of society at large"[4]—meaning they create and enforce rules and maintain a monopoly on the legitimate use of violence to do so.[5] They also generally have and enforce territorial limits and borders within which state institutions operate and these rules apply.[6] While states may also use control of information and individual charismatic leadership to consolidate power, the threat of violence—police power—is the most ubiquitous and dependable source of state power.[7]

Determining what we believe the state *should* do requires us to understand what a state *does*. According to the Gilmores, the state secures "a society's ability to do different things," "through the exercise of centralized rulemaking and redistribution."[8] Those things can include taxation, military conscription, regulation, criminalization, surveillance, making and facilitating profit, extraction. They can also include building public infrastructure, providing for public education, and offering support in meeting basic needs.[9] These functions are neither fixed nor mutually exclusive—for instance, as discussed throughout *No More Police*, criminalization can and does happen through state provision of public education, public health, and social programs.

Campaigns to defund police and secure resources to meet community needs, including education, housing, income support, health care, and nonpolice mental health crisis responses, among other programs, implicate functions currently performed by the state. This forces us to confront the larger question of whether the state can perform any of these functions *without* the violence of surveillance, police, punishment, coercion, neglect, and abandonment, and if so, which ones. Or does rooting out policing require dismantling states in their entirety and putting in place different systems of governance and resource distribution?

Given that Western settler colonial states emerged for the purpose of wealth accumulation in service of racial capitalism and imperialism, it is challenging to disentangle our ideas about the state from the white supremacy, colonialism, extraction, and exploitation they represent and facilitate. As abolitionist legal scholar and organizer Dean Spade puts it, states as many of us understand them, and the relations of power they uphold, "were created and invented together and they traveled together."[10] Or, as Tyler Wall emphasizes in *Violent Order*, the "[m]odern state and modern police came into being simultaneously, and the most vital institution of the security state is the police."[11] In a capitalist state, Brendan McQuade reminds us, "instead of exercising power, we are administered by power, we are policed."[12] Police and policing, and the social and economic order they manufacture and make possible, are thus so deeply imbricated in our conceptions and experiences of the state that it is difficult for those of us living and struggling in settler colonial carceral capitalist states to imagine the state otherwise.

For instance, Diné (Navajo) scholar Klee Benally understands the state "as centralized political governance" in which "a privileged group makes the decisions for everyone else and upholds those decisions with military and police forces, the judiciary, and prisons."[13] Similarly, Black feminist scholar-activist Robyn Maynard describes the state's relationship to Black and Indigenous life in *Rehearsals for Living*: "we are living and dying in a formation that was not designed for us, but built on top of us, to facilitate the exploitation of lands, labor, but not to facilitate life. And most certainly not Black and Indigenous life. The nation-state requires the dispossession of Indigenous peoples' lands and lives; it requires the destruction of Black peoples' lives, our flesh, our personhood, our timelines of otherwise."[14] She argues that "[t]he nation-state, wherever we find it, is a problem: Black people are still living and dying from the vestiges of colonially-imposed states and the carceral mechanisms installed to support them . . . organizing Black life—and human life—into nation-states forecloses the actualization of freedom for Black peoples."[15] William C. Anderson, author of *The Nation on No Map*, describes the state as "a weapon whose design mandates oppression," emphasizing that "state violence does not occur because the state is working incorrectly, it occurs because this violence is how it maintains power."[16] This perspective understands violence and carceral potential to be inherent in the state form.

Under what abolitionist organizer Jackie Wang describes as "carceral capitalism," "the state is inherently repressive. As an enforcer of contracts, it secures access to land, and represents the interests of the settler propertied class, it has a self-preserving reflex that always results in the crushing of revolution and political dissent."[17] Beyond its repressive functions, Wang describes the carceral state as a "parasitic form of governance" that "extracts from poor and working-class people of color through policing, fee and fine farming, the privatization of public goods, the fining of welfare applicants, and the siphoning of public money into the financial sector."[18] Spade similarly characterizes the state as "a technology of extraction," a structure intended to further racial capitalism by "taking away our means of cooperating to survive with each other and making it so that our survival is mediated through things that generate profit and concentrate wealth."[19] Drawing on his experience studying and representing clients in noncriminal state administrative systems, Spade also argues that privileging "a standardized normal citizenry" through regulation and distribution of public benefits is a fundamental aspect of how the state performs its functions. This process, by necessity, cultivates some life while stigmatizing and abandoning others who are "cast as threats or drains."[20] Through this lens, sorting, managing, and controlling people in ways that differentiate in order to privilege some and criminalize and abandon others is what states do. Again, the question is whether these functions are characteristics of carceral, racial capitalist states, or inherent to all state formations.

Efforts to seize state power and deploy it to different ends appear to lend support to both propositions. Abolitionists cite successful efforts throughout history to shift the processes and priorities of state institutions toward abolitionist ends. For instance, Ruth Wilson Gilmore points to the ways post-colonial states in Guinea-Bissau and Kerala, India, have created increased access to and control over education and the means of production for the common good.[21] In *A World Without Police* Geo Maher describes the autonomous region of Rojava as a sociopolitical formation operating on principles of direct democracy, community autonomy, and feminism, in which the monopoly on state violence is delegated to neighborhood defense committees made up in large part by women.[22] Abolitionists also point to the Reconstruction government in the U.S. as the mechanism through which public education and libraries were institutionalized.

And, many abolitionists, including South African scholars and organizers Kelly Gillespie and Leigh-Ann Naidoo, point out that the past century of post-colonial struggles is replete with examples in which previously colonial subjects were absorbed into the project of state-making while institutions of colonial governments largely remained in place. The carceral state, created under colonial conditions, was then wielded against disempowered and criminalized groups such as migrants, women, people in the sex trades, queer, trans, and disabled people, workers, and to destroy any opposition.[23] As Spade puts it, it is therefore difficult "to imagine . . . having it [turn] out different than it keeps turning out."[24] Based on these histories, Anderson, whose work draws on Black anarchist theory and organizing, comes to the conclusion that "[t]he state is not going to change for us, and we should be wary of efforts to seize state power in hopes of reforming this dangerous weapon into something supposedly better."[25] Or, as Maynard puts it, "Our freedom will not take place as a triumphant entrance into the nation-state."[26]

These arguments hinge on the assumption that the state is a fixed entity that will always reproduce itself into the same shape—one that enshrines and embodies policing. The question as Wang articulates it is "whether the state has an essence, or whether it is a field of contestation open to revision."[27] As reflected in the Gilmores' definition of the state, they see it as a more open-ended and malleable project. Rather than one coherent thing, the Gilmores suggest that the state is simply the sum of its functions and the people who animate them. Similarly, Marxist sociologist and philosopher Nicos Poulantzas famously described "the state as the condensation of a relationship of forces," suggesting that altering the relations between social forces could also transform the state.[28] Graeber and Wengrow's examination of states throughout history would seem to support this proposition.[29] In this light, is there an abolitionist form of "stateness"? What might a state look like if it's unyoked from the system of racial capitalism and explicitly organized around abolitionist priorities? Can we shape the state in a way that's consistent with abolitionist values, transforming it into what Angela Y. Davis and the authors of *Abolition. Feminism. Now.*, building on the work of W.E.B. DuBois, call a present-day "abolition democracy"?[30]

The Gilmores believe such a revision of the state is possible, that its institutional power can be directed toward creating new possibilities for liberatory education, cultural work, meeting material needs at scale, participatory forms of governance, and to build resilience against pandemics and climate catastrophes. For them, it comes down to what the state decides to do with its collectivized resources. Are they put toward development aimed at improving conditions for all? Or, is the aim to generate surplus for the sake of accumulation? Is the rule of law used to police conditions in a way that prioritizes the movement of goods and profit? Or, is it used to advance the interests of collective well-being?[31] "We have to go deeply into the state, in all its aspects," the Gilmores urge, in order to both understand and change it.[32] Under this view, the state as a form of governance is not inextricably linked to violence in service of racial capitalism. Questions remain about whether experiments in remaking states around different priorities can be both anti-capitalist *and* abolitionist, and whether they can be sustained in a global capitalist order in which they have historically been consistently isolated and crushed.

Discerning whether surveillance, policing, punishment, and extraction are inherent to state-based governance is not merely an esoteric pursuit—it has real-life implications for the goals and strategies of abolitionist campaigns. Is our goal to take control of the state—or at least some of its institutions—and turn them to abolitionist ends of meeting collective needs without surveillance, policing, and punishment? Or are such efforts doomed to perpetuate structures that are inherently carceral and oppressive? Wang describes the dilemmas for abolitionist organizing:

> Part of me believes the state will always be repressive and should be overthrown. The pragmatic part of me thinks that if we are stuck with the state, we should demand Medicare for all, social housing, free college, the cancellation of student debt, and so forth. . . . The anarchist part of me thinks we should abolish the family. The pragmatist thinks that cash payments to families could go a long way in ending child poverty.
>
> The pragmatist thinks a federal-jobs guarantee could help a lot of people, the anarchist retorts that we should abolish

work itself. The anarchist part of me believes that mutual aid is necessary for building collective social bonds, for experimenting with new forms of life, and modes of being together, modeled on community and care. The pragmatist replies that not everything can be solved with mutual aid, given the level of investment required to address environmental racism and upgrade our crumbling toxic infrastructure. . . . For me, the ultimate aim is the abolition of the state or the form of the state as it currently exists. At the same time, I support the organized provisioning of public goods, though I reject the surveillance component of the welfare state.[33]

Rather than be immobilized by these contradictions, we ask ourselves what additional possibilities emerge if we move beyond the dichotomy of capturing or dismantling the modern Western state.[34] What if our goal is not to seize the carceral state in an effort to transform it, but to seize power and resources *from* the police state to create conditions under which new economic systems and forms of governance can emerge? Recapturing the resources the state has extracted is a legitimate, and arguably necessary, means of both reducing the misery created by racial capitalism and creating conditions for abolition. Securing direct, collective decision-making power over those resources, whether through participatory budgeting or mutual aid, is a means of practicing new forms of decision-making and governance. Practicing new forms of accountability to collective values and transformative justice rather than ceding power to the state to intervene in instances of conflict, harm, and need can lead us to a better understanding of what individual and collective transformation is required to build abolitionist futures. Understanding the carceral state as a social relation helps us to see, in the words of nineteenth-century social anarchist Gustav Landauer, that it "is a condition, a certain relationship between human beings, a mode of human behavior; we destroy it by contracting other relationships, by behaving differently."[35] Ruth Wilson Gilmore describes this process as rehearsal of new systems and forms of governance beyond the current carceral state.[36]

Speaking as abolitionists organizing in South Africa's post-colonial state, following the failure of the traditional two-stage strategy of seizing the state to transform it,[37] Gillespie and Naidoo invite us to more closely examine the process of transition from a racial capitalist carceral state to new political formations. In the South African context, massive demobilization of revolutionary forces following a negotiated seizure of state power created a vacuum in which multiple violences—of the state, within communities, of global capital—were able to flourish.[38] Drawing on this experience, Gillespie and Naidoo see abolitionist organizing as a way to shape transitions from violent state projects to liberated social conditions. Rather than debating whether state formations can serve as a vehicle for creating these conditions, we might instead ask ourselves "How do we prepare for the life we want to live? What is the work of liberation? What is the psychic work, the relational work, the institutional processes that need to take place in, around, and between us for that liberation to manifest? What kind of schooling or a skilling or readying is necessary to practice self-governance? What do we need to do to make way for liberatory relationships?"[39]

As Grace Lee Boggs urges us in *The Next American Revolution*, "[W]e need to exercise power, not take it," as we transform ourselves to transform the world.[40] There is no single way to go about this—Boggs points to creation of new community institutions "that give us ownership and control over the way we make our living, while helping us to ensure . . . wellbeing of the community and the environment," and organizing that supports the "creation of more *human* human beings and *more democratic* institutions."[41] This work can take place in multiple spaces from multiple vantage points, as explored further in the "Experiment and Build" chapter. The question, then, is what kind of political culture we need to create in order to make these experiments and preparations possible. Trans abolitionist scholar and organizer Eric Stanley offers that one key aspect of this culture is perpetual critique—not as a demobilizing tool, but as one that helps us to guard against our own participation in the creation of the carceral state, and against cooptation, assimilation, and demobilization.[42]

As we explore this path, we can draw on Black and Indigenous ways of thinking and conceptions of governance.[43] For example, Benally offers the Indigenous principle of "mutuality": "Our project is to replace the principle of political authority with the principle of autonomous Indig-enous mutuality . . . the solidarity of mutuality with the earth and all beings."[44] This framework invites us to "buil[d] sustaining and proliferat-ing things like conflict infrastructure, alternative systems, and maintain-ing radical reconnection, and asserting our mutuality outside of the state's control."[45] Anderson offers the concept of intercommunalism advanced by Black Panther Party co-founder Huey P. Newton in a 1971 speech, in which communities collaborate on a global scale to meet basic needs,[46] as one way this principle can be put into practice.

Harsha Walia, author of *Border and Rule* and one of the founders of No One Is Illegal, calls on us to learn from, "affirm and think about the ways in which non-statist forms of governance are actually alive today, even within nation-state structures," particularly Indigenous forms of gover-nance.[47] In *Rehearsals for Living*, Indigenous (Michi Saagiig Nishnaabeg) scholar Leanne Betasamosake Simpson and Maynard similarly offer up Indigenous conceptions of nations in what Robin D.G. Kelley describes in the afterword as a "counter to the colonial/capitalist nation-state."[48] Nations, as distinct from nation-states, are sovereign, self-determining political formations premised on deep reciprocity and collectivity rather than on rules, enforcement, and punishment. Walia reminds us that while Indigenous nations may steward their particular territories, they are held differently than the policing of nation-state borders: not with military and police expelling those "undesirables" who are othered and displaced by racial capitalism, but with questions about consent and power. For example, members of the Wet'suwet'en nation affirm their jurisdiction by asking: What is your intention? How will your visit benefit our com-munity? Are you here on behalf of either industry or the government? If the intention is extractive or harmful, an invitation may be extended to sit with the community to hear the impacts of the intended activity. If the invitation is refused, an individual may be asked to leave the ter-ritory. Importantly, the questions posed are an expansive and explicit counter-force to the very logics of carceral, colonial, and capitalist states.[49] This approach invites us to more deeply explore questions about how we imagine modes of governance focused on self-determination that distinguish between self-defense, defense of collective interests and values, and policing.

Anderson and Black trans abolitionist Che Gossett argue that centuries of denial of Black people's personhood and conditions of effective state-lessness in the U.S. (because the U.S. state has never served our interests) can offer unique perspectives on collectivity for survival.[50] Black feminism similarly invites us to imagine and enact new futures from the perspective of Black women's lived experiences as always outlaws to the carceral settler colonial nation-state, building a politic and ethic of care.[51] Black feminism also roots us in internationalist analyses of these questions—indeed, the success of our experiments requires us to root out racial capitalism at a global scale, not just locally. And, as both Walia and Boggs emphasize, we cannot be content to redistribute resources within nations of the Global North that are obtained through extraction from the Global South. We must attend to redistribution, reciprocity, reparations, and climate justice on a global scale.[52]

Regardless of where we land on the questions briefly explored here, as abolitionists it is essential to expand our imaginations beyond our current conceptions of the state—or, as Gossett puts it, to find a political grammar beyond the state that reflects what we desire.[53]

For us, two things are clear: (1) the carceral, racial capitalist state cannot be reformed or captured and repurposed, and (2) abolition and racial capitalism cannot co-exist.[54] Abolition also requires an end to settler colonial states—to paraphrase Simpson and Maynard, abolition, decolonization, and return of land to original Indigenous stewards (as encapsulated by the slogan #LandBack) are interlocking, transnational projects.[55] While the role of the state in abolitionist futures is in question, abolition in the now invokes a broad strategy to dismantle the carceral state, and to undo settler colonialism, racial capitalism, and imperialism.[56]

The immediate question, then, is: What is the work that needs to be done that will contribute to creating the conditions for something new to emerge? This in turn requires that we grapple with practical questions such as how to organize at the community level at a scale necessary to meet collective needs in a global society in ways that do not replicate the policing functions of the state. As abolitionist organizer Kenyon Farrow points out, shifting away from reliance on the state does not necessarily mean we are "ridding ourselves of the kinds of power dynamics that continue to perpetuate certain types of violence and discrimination and politics of deprivation."[57] Stanley reminds us that the carceral state does not exist outside of us—we're materially and effectively and emotionally reproducing the logic of the state all the time.[58] What liberatory mechanisms of individual and mutual accountability can we imagine and practice within these projects so as not to replicate policing? How might we preserve collective resources for the common good against those who would seek to accumulate them for private gain, or put personal preference above collective goals?[59] How can we create the political conditions that would lead to a complete shift in our modes of governance when our movements are still struggling to force the state to meet our basic needs?[60]

Part of the answer to these questions lies in rebuilding the commons—or, as Brendan McQuade describes it, "commoning" against the carceral state,[61] explored in greater detail below. Part of the answer lies in dual power strategies—what former INCITE! National Collective member Paula X. Rojas describes as "making power" and "taking power."[62] In her foundational essay "Are the Cops in Our Heads and Hearts?," she describes this approach as "thinking beyond the state, and even beyond an alternative version of current institutions, by politicizing every aspect of daily life and alternative forms of dealing with them."[63] Rooted in Indigenous and Black-led struggles in the Global South, dual power strategies—also described as working against the state and outside/without the state—require us to (1) build collective community power to challenge the power and violence of the racial capitalist carceral state, (2) seize and extract resources and concessions from the state that will shift conditions in ways that make it more possible for more collective, participatory, and non-carceral forms of governance to emerge and flourish, and (3) to practice new economic and social relations in our organizing and daily life. In other words, "build from below—not to reach the top but to build strong foundations" for the futures we long for.[64] We explore dual power approaches in greater detail in the "Experiment and Build" chapter.

Rebuilding the Commons

The abolition of policing is about building a new world centered around "the commons"—a term initially used to describe an area of land in the center of medieval towns to be used by all. The commons was a place to graze sheep and plant crops, to meet, to hold weddings and funerals, and to mark the passage of the seasons. Owned by no one, it was used by everyone for collective sustenance and celebration.[65] It has evolved to describe the concept of collective resources for the collective good, while "commoning" has come to describe the process and practice of coming together to cultivate and manage common resources. "Commoning" is about affirming humanity, eliminating inequality and social hierarchies, and promoting shared well-being and greater safety. Police are the antithesis of the commons: their original and continuing role is to police who gets what and when, all towards the purpose of enabling wealth accumulation.[66]

Rebuilding the commons doesn't mean expanding institutions of soft policing in the name of building up "the public sector." Instead, it means abolishing the social order that privatizes and polices the commons so that we can build a new society and forms of governance that will reinstate the commons and grow it sustainably. We're not asking for kinder, gentler cops, or broader or softer lines around who gets what. And we're not demanding more money for public services that are administered in punitive and criminalizing ways. We're demanding the creation and expansion of the commons as part of a Black feminist culture of care rooted in shared resources, infrastructures, and knowledge that will allow communities to self-govern and thrive. The goal is collective flourishing and the acknowledgment of our shared humanity.

How does this translate into actionable demands? Universal accessible, quality womb-to-ancestor health care, education, child and elder care, housing; safe, sustainable, accessible and meaningful ways to contribute to the collective; a universal basic income regardless of whether people choose to work; and everything else needed for life and safety. To make these common entitlements and not "benefits" policed through social policy, they must be universal and, along with land and labor, de-commodified.[67] Recreating the commons also means ensuring de-commodified access to things that make life worth living—the things that are necessary to live fully into our individual and collective human potential, like arts, culture, recreation, and rest. This is about far more than access to goods and services; it's about a new conception of community and social relations.

"Commoning" to meet everyone's material needs requires us to shift from a deficit mindset to one of abundance. It means we must stop constantly looking for the person who is "undeserving," "cheating," taking more than "their share," or "getting over on the system," whose behavior or ways of being must be policed through denial of access to social goods. These frames all come out of policing—labeling someone an "appropriate" target for criminalization, abandonment, or regulation. Instead, we need to create and maintain a sustainable culture in which there is enough for everyone. The degree to which policing interrupts cultures of care was apparent in a (now deleted) tweet posted by the police department in Bloomington, Indiana. The department tweeted that they had noticed people were taking all the books from the town's free library. Despite the fact that this is the explicit intention of a *free* library, the department was agitated. They fixated on a presumption that people were reselling the books on the secondhand book market even though there is no prohibition against doing so. A culture of care makes books available to anyone who needs them, in whatever quantity they need, without question about what they are doing with them, within a broader context of collective care that extends to care for the planet.

Shifting to an abundance mindset can be challenging for many of us—including abolitionists. In Charmaine Chua's recounting of the two-week occupation of the Sheraton in Minneapolis described in greater detail in the "No Soft Police" chapter, she describes the work volunteers had to do to interrupt their own instincts to police, and to instead create a "culture of abundance" within the reclaimed space in which residents were free to take more than one meal or stock up on snacks.[68] Just as we need to unseat the "copaganda," "copspeak," and "cop knowledge" described in the "How Do We Get There?" chapter within ourselves, we also need to interrupt the instincts ingrained by racial capitalism to protect me, mine, and my people at the expense of others. We also need to unseat the instinct to become the "soft police" ourselves, by controlling access to resources in ways that coerce compliance with notions of "normalcy" and "proper citizenship" while still holding people accountable to shared values. At the core of these commitments is a recognition of our deep, collective interdependence. That means taking responsibility for each other's care. It means structuring society in such a way that there is enough to go around, and it doesn't fall to a few individuals to care for others in unsustainable ways.[69]

Cultivating a culture of abundance and meeting communities' material needs will no doubt go a long way toward reducing the likelihood of harm. And, even once all our needs are met, people will still harm each other. We are all still human. However, as Rachel Herzing says, "Eliminating the PIC will expand the context in which we can develop new ways of relating, build protection, and address harm."[70] Policing currently takes up so many resources and so much airtime that it crowds out opportunities for underfunded and unfunded community-based solutions to prevent, intervene in, and help us heal from harm and violence. Defunding police and refunding the commons would generate resources and create space for community programs to grow and practice nonpolice and non-carceral responses to crisis. It will also allow for investment in an ecosystem of preventative and respite care to stop crises from happening in the first place. Reimagining and rebuilding the commons is thus a critical step toward creating futures without policing.

The State in the Meantime

As abolitionist organizers grapple with questions about the nature and role of the state, how do we relate to it in the meantime in ways that make it possible to advance our vision of a future free of policing? Even if we are committed to dismantling the state, we still need to engage with it in order to fight and diminish police power, extract the resources our communities need, and build the capacity to produce safety for ourselves. As Brendan McQuade puts it, "the state is a necessary and an unavoidable site of political struggle."[71] Wang adds, "If we are stuck with the state form for the time being, then we should do everything in our power to move resources away from the military and prison industrial complex, and towards social programs that would enable people to flourish"[72]—while being careful to not legitimize the state's extraction of resources, nor the carceral institutions through which it distributes them. We can start by decreasing the resources devoted to policing, and by purging public institutions—such as public schools, parks, libraries, transit, hospitals, and benefits offices—of police in order to increase their capacity to create conditions under which communities can engage in liberatory practices.

As we do so, we must be wary of the traps inherent in making demands that give the state power over their realization. As an organizer with Communities of Color United in Austin put it: "How much do we depend on the state to liberate us? That's a question we've been pondering and are still pondering as most of our actions have targeted city officials."[73] Organizers are contending with the fact that campaigns to move money and power away from police require a significant amount of interaction with local, county, and state policymakers. They often plunge organizers into the internal workings of municipal and state governments, budgets, and programs, generating more involvement in administrative, bureaucratic, and legislative processes than many groups fighting the violence of police have historically undertaken. While this work seems aligned with the Gilmores' urging to go "deep into the state," it raises questions about how much time and energy organizers want to invest in the day-to-day operations of governments upholding a carceral state. Spade urges us to focus on organizing efforts that both make demands on the state and "will have maximum mobilizing effect and make more people into active participants who have the capacity to co-govern our lives and work."[74] Jamel Campbell-Gooch of Black Nashville Assembly applies this principle specifically to defund campaigns, explaining that they can be a place to build power to liberate resources from the state, and to practice self-governance and liberation at the same time.[75] In other words, we need to go beyond winning concessions of power from the state, "we need to develop capabilities."[76]

In several cities, including Austin, Durham, Oakland, and San Francisco, policymakers responded to calls to defund police by creating municipal task forces to explore cuts to police budgets and examine which police functions could be relocated or eliminated altogether.[77] In New Orleans, organizers fought for and won a city task force focused on creating a non-police mental health crisis response program.[78] In each of these cities, organizers worked with varying degrees of success to ensure that community members directly affected by policing would be included in task-force decision-making, and that current and former law enforcement officers would be excluded. Beyond membership, organizers engaged in struggles around the scope of the task forces' work—such as whether it covered a city or county, whether it would address issues relating to school police or not—their internal processes, compensation for participating community members, and the degree to which task force deliberations should be public. In cities like Austin, Oakland, and Los Angeles, organizers won many of these fights, and task forces were led by abolitionist organizers and made powerful recommendations.[79] In Minneapolis, Reclaim the Block organizer Sheila Nezhad publicly quit the task force created by the mayor to "reform" the Minneapolis Police Department based on members' refusal to make their proceedings public.[80]

In some cases, communities were able to build greater knowledge of state institutions, processes and budgets, and practice new forms of governance with respect to collective resources through participation in municipal task forces. But without any mechanism for community members to enforce them, policymakers and legislators subsequently sought to ignore, block, water down, defuse, and co-opt demands for cuts to police budgets and investment in community-based safety strategies, delay their implementation, or continue to invest in programs enmeshed with policing. Given these experiences, organizers across the country continue to weigh whether it makes sense to engage in state public safety task forces as a meaningful strategy to defund and shrink police departments.[81]

Beyond the carceral state's resistance, successful efforts to divert funds from police department budgets quickly surface another tension: how to move state funds to nonpolice community safety strategies without tying them up with bureaucratic red tape—or worse yet, the cops—in order to access funding. In many cases, state grants and contracts come with burdensome oversight—bordering on surveillance—of grassroots groups' operations. That is precisely why many groups who are engaged in work to promote community-based safety don't accept government funds, leaving open the question about how, and to whom, we can distribute funds extracted from police budgets. Carceral state agencies or large nonprofits with histories of collaboration with police and other carceral state institutions, as well as the inclination and infrastructure in place to manage government funding, then become the most likely candidates to receive diverted funds. Similar questions surfaced in discussions and debates around the BREATHE Act, federal legislation drafted by Movement for Black Lives in 2020 to articulate defund demands at the federal level, and the People's Response Act, inspired by BREATHE and introduced in 2021 by Rep. Cori Bush, a veteran of the Ferguson Uprising.[82] What possibilities and dangers lie in the proposed legislation's creation of government departments within a carceral state with the legitimacy and power to shape and divert resources to "non-carceral" interventions? Some organizers are responding to these dilemmas by seeking power over and changes to the process by which government funds are distributed in an effort to increase access to funding for community-based and accountable organizations while enabling them to continue to operate autonomously from carceral institutions.[83] Others are exploring creative strategies to capture state funding through community foundations and accountable nonprofits who could then redistribute to grassroots organizations without subjecting them to state control. No matter which path we choose, we must consistently ask ourselves, if we must deal with the state for now, how can we avoid unintentionally re-legitimating or even expanding it?

Connected to this question, as we engage in this work, how do we address the ways in which carceral states alternately repress and pacify abolitionist social movements while continually expanding and re-legitimating police power? This dialectic was in full force in the summer of 2020. As ideas around abolition entered the mainstream alongside defund campaigns, repression took brutal forms. The repercussions continue to unfold in pending felony charges and the long-term health effects of tear-gassing, pepper spray, and police violence.[84] A backlash of anti-protest legislation spread across the country, sometimes embedded within legislation designed to prevent cuts to police budgets, making way for future, more brutal repression.[85] Ultimately, a central contradiction of campaigns to defund and abolish police is that we are demanding that a carceral, racial capitalist state disarm itself. We are demanding that it stop performing its central functions: protecting wealth accumulation, white supremacy, and patriarchy; and isolating, targeting, and neutralizing any threats to the order it maintains. That requires us to build power far beyond what is needed to secure temporary cuts to police department budgets, and to understand our campaigns as part of a protracted struggle. We need to fortify ourselves for a fight against a police state.

When organizers persisted with defund demands, and successfully mobilized to extract resources and power from the carceral state, the backlash intensified. While municipal and state legislative bodies have the power to pass budgets, mayors and governors have the power to veto them or block their implementation. In some areas, hard-fought wins were undermined by mayors who refused to follow or undermined legislative directives, and by police chiefs who simply disregarded cuts to overtime and personnel budgets. In many cities, organizers fought to cut municipal funding to police departments only to find that cities and counties had secured federal grants through the Department of Justice Community Oriented Policing Service (COPS) grants and the DOJ's Operation Legend program. These enabled them to hire more police officers or purchase more equipment. Organizers in several cities, including Milwaukee, fought unsuccessfully to secure the refusal or return of these federal grants.[86]

At the federal level, politicians not only considered legislation that would deny federal funds to cities that reduced police department budgets,[87] they allocated hundreds of millions of dollars in 2021 to hiring more cops across the country.[88] The Biden administration encouraged cities and states to spend additional pandemic relief funds on cops—going so far as to include cops as essential workers entitled to individual "hero bonuses" available under the American Rescue Plan Act.[89] While ARPA regulations prohibited using pandemic relief funds to fund bankrupt police pension programs, cities like Milwaukee found a loophole enabling them to do so that the federal government declined to close.[90] Biden also proposed nearly doubling the amount of federal grants to hire more officers, a move challenged by national and local organizers.[91] The sheer number of legislative and executive measures taken to stifle defund demands—and the vehemence behind their enactment, often fueled by police and their allies—made clear both the power of the 2020 Uprisings, the threat they posed to the carceral state, and the power we need to build to withstand the backlash.

As the popularity and public currency of abolitionist demands increased, police, politicians, and pundits also deployed pacification tactics to absorb, adapt to, undermine, and dissipate the threat they pose. Even the most radical demands can be captured—not only by the carceral state, but by its allies in philanthropy, the media, and the academy. This can lead to obviously absurd results, such as creating, promoting and supporting departments focused on building "alternatives to police" *inside* police departments to give the illusion of alignment with movement demands while building the power of police. Sometimes the co-optation is obvious—encapsulated in nonsensical statements such as the one made by Yale Law professor Tracey Meares immediately after claiming to support police abolition: "policing as we know it must be abolished before it can be transformed. One path to that goal is to recenter policing's fundamental nature as a public good. . . . We need to create a kind of policing that we *all* can enjoy."[92] Meares' statement entrenches the presumption that police must exist in some form, even as *part of the* commons. But pacification is often more insidious, including through the assimilation of organizers to the project of state bureaucracy.

Strategies that focus exclusively on shifting budget items are particularly susceptible to co-optation by the state. For instance, some policymakers absorbed demands to defund police by simply moving portions of the police budget or department to other carceral agencies or departments while maintaining the same police power structures, personnel, and practices.[93] Shifting spending from police budgets to other government departments without eliminating police power or practices further conceals the true cost of policing by burying cops' salaries, overtime costs, data, or IT contracts in education, library, construction, general administrative and public works budgets. Tracking and interrupting this shell game requires community members to invest tremendous time and energy into monitoring implementation of municipal and state budgets, which are often obscure and inaccessible. Police budgets, in particular, are intentionally opaque. Departments are rarely required to provide explanations or justifications for their expenditures, and instead receive endless blank checks in the name of "public safety." This raises questions around whether defund campaigns run the risk of effectively turning abolitionist organizers into functionaries of the state, distracting us from the larger project of dismantling current structures of policing and building the community-based safety structures we need.

On the other hand, building skills to analyze and engage with public budgets through trainings, fellowships, and peer learning is one way organizers are skilling up to shift conditions. Honing these skills can also make us better equipped to engage community members in conversations about how we want to redistribute our collective resources, and to practice new forms of governance through participatory budgeting.[94] But ultimately, defund campaigns will only be successful in creating safer communities if we maintain a clear goal of ultimately abolishing both police departments and policing practices. Our critiques of the carceral state—and of the ways in which it operates through "soft policing"—mean we need to move beyond divesting from police departments to wholly eradicating police power from our social relations and institutions and naming the social order we want to create.

Another way the carceral state undermines defund campaigns is by refusing to make the investments necessary to meeting basic community needs and resource community safety strategies at the scale that's necessary to create safer communities. It then weaponizes the fallout of organized abandonment to claim that efforts to divest from policing are jeopardizing public safety. In fact, it's the ongoing and intensifying depletion of resources available to communities under mounting economic pressure that is undermining community safety. No matter what form it takes, greater safety will require deep and expansive investments in our communities that far exceed the size of current police budgets. The billions of dollars distributed through the American Rescue Plan Act (ARPA) and federal infrastructure bill created unprecedented opportunities for counties and municipalities to invest in meeting community needs and in nonpolice responses to conflict and harm. Yet billions in pandemic relief funds instead went to corporations and businesses. Even then, Black- and migrant-owned businesses struggled to access funds. Meanwhile, millions of people suffering food and housing insecurity were offered paltry payments that essentially amounted to a tax refund. The vast majority of people without access to documented employment got no support whatsoever from the state during a protracted—and ongoing—pandemic. Defund organizers worked to direct ARPA funds toward community needs through surveys and participatory decision-making processes. Despite their best efforts, a significant portion of pandemic relief funds intended to help individuals and communities get back on their feet and heal from the devastation of the pandemic was instead funneled into the pockets of police officers and departments, jails, and prisons. ARPA funds were used to effectively reverse any budget cuts made in 2020, and to double down on policing and punishment as the primary response to organized abandonment.[95]

The carceral state's refusal to fully deploy ARPA funds to increase community safety and reduce suffering and immiseration caused by the pandemic illustrated the limitations of making demands focused on budgets without an analysis of power. Instead of making use of an unprecedented opportunity to meet demands for substantial investments in community needs, politicians chose to bolster police departments and build more jails and prisons. Punishing institutions will always have access to public funds because they are the legitimizing and enforcement arm of the carceral state. They will always be a budget priority. Police and other enforcement arms of the state—framed as all that stands between us and unchecked violence—are not subject to the same budgeting principles as social services, which are framed as supporting "undeserving" people. As a result, social services and community programs must constantly prove their effectiveness, and face an uphill battle year after year to maintain budgets relentlessly targeted for cuts under neoliberal economic policies. To the extent that the state does move funds to community programs, it often ensures that police retain power and financial control over them. Abolition requires that we take away the carceral state's power and ability to prioritize policing over all else, and to consistently refuse to resource communities at levels that will produce safety.

A singular focus on city budgets doesn't just leave defund demands open to being co-opted or quashed by the state; it also leaves us open to being overwhelmed by backlash and disappointment when politicians fail to keep their promises as soon as the political winds shift. Campaigns to shrink police budgets and power rode a wave of protest in 2020. But when the wave subsided, organizers found themselves fighting uphill battles to defend and expand their wins when politicians began backtracking. By the fall of 2021, mainstream media declared movements to defund police dead[96]—pointing to the fact that many cities increased police funding and hires in response to fearmongering around rising crime rates.[97] The police state responded to threats to its legitimacy by firmly bolstering its enforcement arm. As the authors of *Abolition. Feminism. Now.* point out, "the haste with which these dominant power structures have mobilized to proclaim the end of #DefundPolice illuminates precisely the power of this demand."[98]

Our task now is to build the power necessary to once again fight back—this time, to wrest not just money from police budgets, but power and resources from the carceral state—including the power they hold to define, absorb, and dilute our demands. The lessons of history teach us that we can count on the fact that policing will continue to reconfigure itself to give the illusion of change while remaining fundamentally the same. That is why it is essential that our demands—and the visions underlying them—remain clear. We must focus our work on dismantling the carceral state and creating conditions for liberatory forms of governance to emerge. A number of tricks, traps, and tensions lie along the way. When assessing whether the policies and ideas that we are pursuing are emancipatory and abolitionist ones, we must ask ourselves whether they are meaningfully "increasing the possibility for freedom."[99]

Police Political Power

As Dan Berger and David Stein assert, "The call to defund is best understood as an effort to revoke the political and economic power of police—and of the larger criminal legal system it upholds."[100] The carceral state is not alone in defending and bolstering its most powerful enforcement arm when its legitimacy is challenged. It is joined by police fraternal associations (PFAs)—also known as police "unions"—who have grown into an independent political power in their own right, occupying a "central place in the constellations of local power."[101] Their endorsement is considered essential to political candidates' success, policymakers act as though no change can move forward without their support, and their opposition is often taken as the final word on all things "public safety." Consistently mobilizing "thin blue line" narratives framing police as essential to staving off violent chaos, they have succeeded in passing "Law Enforcement Officers' Bill of Rights" in over a dozen states and negotiating contract provisions that enable them to deploy violence with impunity.[102] And, it was a PFA that successfully campaigned to enshrine the mandate that Minneapolis maintain a police department of a particular size in the city's charter that defund organizers sought to repeal in 2021.

PFAs have responded to defund campaigns with full-on counterattacks fueled by characteristic vitriol. For instance, in Austin, the local police association mounted a fearmongering billboard campaign in the summer of 2020. In the fall of 2021, they too sponsored a ballot measure that would lock the city into a fixed number of cops based on population size, at the same time organizers were fighting to eliminate a similar requirement in Minneapolis.[103] In Oklahoma, the local police fraternal association blocked cuts to the police department budget with a lawsuit alleging that policymakers did not provide sufficient public notice for the council meeting at which a defund vote took place.[104] In New York City and elsewhere, PFAs held press conferences claiming cuts would result in skyrocketing crime rates. Across the country they targeted, threatened, and doxxed organizers.

Organizers are working to divest power from PFAs using a number of strategies, including pressuring politicians to stop seeking their endorsements or funding, and by exposing those who do.[105] Organizers are also working to constrict the flow of money from politicians and corporations to PFAs,[106] and to expose their corruption and connections to organized white supremacist groups.[107] Defund campaigns are seeking to limit PFAs' ability to negotiate contracts giving cops more impunity, money, and more power—including the power to block defund demands through limitations on layoffs, transfers, and cuts to overtime—in secret. Police contracts can also require minimum staffing levels, lock in raises while other city employees face cuts, or mandate specific working conditions that effectively prevent cuts to personnel, equipment, and benefits. Following the uprisings, policymakers across the country claimed that they couldn't cut police staff or funds because their hands were tied by police contracts. Cops fought for even more power and control over municipalities' ability to cut or move particular units, equipment, functions, or contracts to other departments. They also demanded hiring bonuses and incentives to comply with reforms such as wearing (and turning on) body cameras, getting vaccinated, or simply staying on the job.[108] In cases where cuts were made to overtime budgets, police departments relied on labor laws that require employers to pay overtime accrued to undermine them. In other words, cops simply worked the overtime anyway, and then leveraged state labor laws to force cities to pour money back into their budgets to cover the costs. Unlike the rest of us, cops are free to overdraw their bank accounts by working overtime, and cities are required to replenish them every time.

Confronting organized police power and police contracts raises tensions about how to relate to PFAs in their capacity as police "unions." It's important to note that PFAs are not, in fact, unions acting in service of the interests of working people.[109] They are fraternal associations created to advance cops' interests in securing more resources, power, and impunity. PFAs rarely align themselves with organized labor—in fact they are far more frequently found cracking union organizers' heads and perpetrating violence against union members.[110] Recognizing this, in some places, local labor organizations are distancing themselves from PFAs and aligning themselves with defund organizers. For instance, in the summer of 2020, the Seattle MLK Labor Council recognized the threat police posed to their members and organizing efforts, kicked the Seattle Police Officers' Guild out, and stood with defund organizers in demanding cuts to the police budget.[111] Similarly, the Minneapolis teachers' union supported efforts to remove cops from Minneapolis schools. In Raleigh and Durham, North Carolina, organizers allied with public and private sector unions to fight for reallocation of funds from police departments in order to increase wages for city workers, including social workers and parks employees.[112] While local ruptures between organized labor and PFAs are creating possibilities for new alliances toward safer communities, corporate labor unions are doubling down on their support for associations representing police and prison guards. In the spring of 2021, the AFL-CIO, a national confederation of unions, resisted a concerted campaign to force PFAs out.[113]

These divergent approaches reflect a tension among leftists around how to reduce the power of PFAs. For instance, longtime Black labor organizer and historian Bill Fletcher, who served as a senior staff person at the AFL-CIO, supports expelling PFAs from organized labor. However, he warns against efforts to get rid of them altogether or to limit their power through greater scrutiny of police contract negotiations. Fletcher argues that "[a]ny moves to eliminate police unions will certainly be followed by calls to eliminate other public sector unions, including firefighters, postal workers, and teachers."[114] Similarly, calls to open police contract negotiations to public oversight and participation risk opening the door to right-wing efforts to target public sector union negotiations. However, other labor organizers argue that there are clear distinctions to be made between public sector workers' right to organize and those of PFAs who represent armed cops with the power to kill and criminalize. As Geo Maher, author of *A World Without Police*, puts it bluntly, "No other workers bargain for the right to kill other workers without consequence."[115] These functions, they argue, are precisely what justify public involvement, scrutiny, and accountability around police contracts.[116]

Another tension arises around which contract provisions to target in order to reduce police power. Mainline civil rights groups tend to focus on provisions that would increase data, transparency, and accountability for individual cops.[117] The risk is that such measures drive *more* funding for police infrastructure while failing to strike at the root of police power. It's true that increased access to individual cops' records of complaints, use of force, and discipline *can* help us achieve broader movement goals like identifying the most violent and harmful cops for priority termination in defund campaigns. But focusing only on individual "bad cops" and access to data on police violence should not be the end goal. Similarly, eliminating provisions that allow cops forty-eight to seventy-two hours before being interviewed about fatal shooting incidents and other protections not available to anyone else may change material conditions by making it easier for survivors and families to pursue civil cases. But we must keep an eye on the end goal: systemic change.

Increasingly, defund organizers are focusing on eliminating contractual blocks to defund demands—including limits on layoffs, transfers, and terminations; provisions setting mandatory staffing levels; and attempts to retain control over mental health crisis response or homeless "outreach." For instance, in Louisville, Kentucky, where Breonna Taylor was killed, The 490 Project created a comprehensive toolkit for community members to demand that police contract negotiations be public, that community members be offered a seat at the table, and to remove the "no layoffs" provision in current contracts.[118] Organizers in other cities are also working to eliminate PFAs' power to distribute overtime among their members or to be paid by municipalities to manage police pensions. Our goals with respect to police contracts must be to move past demands focused on documentation and investigation of individual incidents of police violence after the fact, toward the larger goal of reducing police power. For instance, The Prometheus Conspiracy, an organization based in Phoenix, Arizona, offers trainings and technical assistance to groups across the country based on a comprehensive framework for analyzing and dismantling the power of PFAs.[119]

There is also a tension around how to handle the looming fiscal crisis created by police pensions without undermining public sector workers' futures. As the public sector workforce ages, cities are struggling to cover the costs of negotiated pensions and benefits that exceed funds put aside to meet these obligations. Many cities are now seeking to make cuts to public services and direct pandemic relief funds, as well as any funds cut from police departments, to meet their unfunded pension liability rather than investing them into community safety strategies.[120] How do we reconcile a commitment to robust public sector pensions with the reality that police pensions are substantially higher than those of other public sector workers? Right now, municipal obligations to pay retired cops—including those who have done tremendous harm—are getting in the way of investment in public safety.

Ultimately, our goal is to recognize and break organized police power—by taking away their power to hold communities hostage to policing through charter amendments and contract negotiations, repealing legislation that enables police violence with impunity, interrupting the flow of money into their coffers, and challenging their narratives around public safety.

Community Control

In several cities, defund campaigns faced opposition from advocates of community control of police departments. In its most extensive shape, community control involves the creation of elected oversight bodies with the power to hire, fire, and discipline individual cops, and to set departmental policies and budgets. Some proponents of community control see this as a strategy that will offer communities some degree of influence over police departments that will enable them to reduce their harm or even recuperate them; others see it as a mechanism to eventually abolish them; and still others claim that seizing control of the armed wing of the state is the only way that we can build sufficient power to dismantle it.

Abolitionists continue to debate whether community control is a viable strategy to bring us closer to abolition or a fantasy.[121] Is it a call for illusory control within deadly institutions, or for survival pending revolution? How is community control of police similar to, or distinct from, community self-defense and self-determination? In many ways, debates about community control of police recapitulate the larger questions about the state that open this chapter, and about reform discussed in the "Re-Form" chapter.

In Minneapolis, Communities United Against Police Brutality (CUAPB) opposed abolitionist demands to dismantle the Minneapolis Police Department, claiming that creating a new department of Community Safety and Violence Prevention would undermine their efforts to secure greater democratic control over police. CUAPB launched a competing campaign, based on a model developed by the Chicago Alliance Against Racist Police Repression (CAARP), with the goal of amending the city charter to create a Community Police Accountability Council tasked with investigating individual incidents of police violence and setting policy for the department. Organizers have taken up similar calls around the country; some claim to simultaneously support demands to defund, while others recognize the two approaches to be diametrically opposed. For instance, along with demands to divest from policing and invest in community safety, the Movement for Black Lives (M4BL) policy platform demands "direct democratic community control of local, state, and federal law enforcement agencies, ensuring that communities most harmed by destructive policing have the power to hire and fire officers, determine disciplinary action, control budgets and policies, and subpoena relevant agency information."[122] We, along with other members of the M4BL ecosystem, have challenged this provision as being inconsistent with the organization's claim to be working towards abolition.

Proposals for community control of police departments presume the possibility of democratizing the police while failing to recognize the profoundly anti-democratic nature of police, and of the carceral state they serve. If the law affords cops virtually unlimited discretion, if cops ignore rules with impunity, if mayors cannot control their police departments, what makes us think that elected community members—particularly from criminalized and abandoned communities—will be able to? Or, that elections for seats on community control bodies won't be plagued by the same power plays as municipal elections, including infusions of cash from PFAs and a push for candidates—including those from criminalized communities—to sign on to police-friendly "law and order" agendas?[123] Even if all goes according to plan, the reality is that community members—including those from communities directly impacted by policing—frequently find in favor of police, whether they are serving on juries or police oversight bodies. As we've explored in earlier chapters, internalized "copaganda," "cop knowledge," and the "common sense" of social policy are powerful forces that keep us embracing *more* policing—particularly of people we perceive as a threat, even if we are part of communities targeted by policing.[124]

At a more fundamental level, Mariame, along with Rachel Herzing, Beth Richie, Dylan Rodriguez, Melissa Burch, and Shana Agid, point out that community review boards (CRBs) legitimize the role of police and the harm they cause "by suggesting that under the 'right' supervision or control, policing (and police) can be separated from this institutional violence and the historic function of policing."[125] Mariame and her co-authors emphasize that CRBs can't be part of an abolitionist strategy because "oversight of the system does not CHANGE the system. . . . Policing must be abolished in order to end police abuse."[126] Minneapolis defund organizers similarly argue that CRBs "replace the transformative vision of the abolition movement with a bureaucratic "solution" that would turn community leaders into police administrators; it assumes that community boards will support a progressive agenda; and it does not address the underlying causes of crisis, violence, and deprivation in our communities."[127] They urge us to keep an eye on transformative approaches rather than "struggling to take over and redirect the master's tool."[128]

Proponents of community control point to the demand made by the Black Panthers for community control of the institutions and resources that affect our lives. However, the decades since this demand was articulated have taught us a great deal about what is and isn't possible when it comes to "controlling" police—particularly in the context of global racial capitalism. Police in post-colonial African and Caribbean nations have continued to serve the interests of capital, even under the "control" of revolutionary forces. In one striking example from 2012, the South African police—now under the control of the African National Congress, which successfully fought to overthrow apartheid—shot into crowds of protesting miners, killing thirty-four in the Marikana massacre. During a political and cultural exchange with U.S. Black organizers in 2018, South African organizers emphasized that this incident, among many others, illustrated the failures of strategies rooted solely in pursuing Black representation in state bodies. Without striking directly at the heart of the relations of power they protect, namely racial capitalism, police will continue to perform the same functions no matter who is in "control." Young South African organizers writing in the context of the 2020 Uprisings powerfully reiterated these points in a document called *Reimagining Justice in South Africa Beyond Policing.*[129]

Some proponents of community control claim that defund demands reflect a delusion that the state will dismantle its enforcement arm in the face of rational budget demands.[130]As Margaret Kimberley put it in the Black Agenda Report, "Police are supported whether it makes budget sense or not because Black people must be watched, and Black revolt must be kept down. This fundamental role of U.S. police is independent of any budget."[131] She argues that "[c]utting police budgets without establishing public control over their behavior doesn't solve the problem, and invites politicians to shuffle budget numbers around like a three-card monte swindle."[132]

These critiques hinge on a fundamental misunderstanding of defund campaigns. They are not simply about easily co-opted budget demands, they are deeply rooted in our analysis of the role of police, and are directed toward reducing their reach and power.[133] The key is that our focus is on dismantling and building something beyond policing, rather than simply seeking to control it. We understand that achieving this goal requires us to build the power necessary to force concessions from a carceral state, and that this requires more than an ungrounded faith in elected officials. Ironically, community control campaigns depend on the same "rotten democracy" they accuse defund campaigns of foolishly relying on; the Minneapolis proponents of community control of the police department are also seeking passage of a proposed charter amendment, and the success of their strategy depends entirely on elected officials. Their assertion that "the vote is not the road to Black liberation" is therefore in direct contradiction with their own strategy to implement elected community police accountability councils.

In the summer of 2020, Interrupting Criminalization co-hosted a conversation among organizers to clarify the foundations and strands of the competing positions around community control and defund demands and to explore a path forward. The conversation quickly revealed key tensions around the role of the state and strategic differences around how to contend for power with its armed wing, with one group arguing for seizure and control as a means of neutralizing it and ensuring safety, and the other for starving, dismantling, and rendering it irrelevant through community created and controlled non-police safety strategies. Ultimately, the discussion also identified shared longings—for control over safety, for different mechanisms of governance, and for liberation. Activists on all sides share the same desire for "control over the part of social life that is being harmed, in this case, safety," said Jasson Perez, a member of the abolitionist Democratic Socialists of America (DSA) and its Afrosocialists and Socialists of Color Caucus. Aislinn Pulley, co-founder of the Black

Lives Matter Chicago chapter, pointed out that, like defund campaigns, campaigns for community control spark the radical imagination of communities about how we create safety. The central question according to Pulley is "What does it mean to take power?," bringing us back to the strategic questions for abolitionists about our relationship to the state. Does dismantling state and police power require us to seize it first? And, can either of those objectives be achieved through community control of police departments as it is currently being articulated? Or is it a call for illusory control within deadly institutions?

Instead of fighting for control over how force is used, we contend that it's more important to collectively dream and enact new ways to ensure each other's safety *without* relying on force. As former political prisoner and freedom fighter Assata Shakur put it, "Just because you believe in self-defense doesn't mean you let yourself be sucked into defending yourself on the enemy's terms."[134] Perhaps we can find middle ground by working toward community control of safety within our communities—even as we differ on how to wrest power from the carceral state.

Privatization

Community control advocates also argue that defunding municipal police will lead to their immediate replacement with privatized security forces, over which communities have *no* control.[135] For instance, at the height of the uprisings, some local businesses hired private security firms out of fear that the police would be unable to continue to protect their interests; during the resistance to the construction of the Dakota Access Pipeline at Standing Rock, private security hired by the oil company joined forces with state and local police. Community control advocates have pointed to these examples as harbingers of a future in which public police are defunded.

The broader framework of abolition anticipates this concern. Defund campaigns call into question the broader system of order maintenance that carceral states have historically assigned to law enforcement agencies and the "soft police," delegated to private police, or condoned by militias and white supremacist organizations. We oppose and resist policing in all its forms, including firms hired by "business improvement districts" and homeowners' associations; vigilante groups; surveillance technology;[136] and even neighborhood watches, citizens' patrols, and community-based interventions that take on aspects of policing. We don't accept the premise that we have to accept one form of policing in order to avoid another. We fight to proactively block the privatization of police and policing practices on all fronts.

What About Killer Cops?

Throughout the 2020 Uprisings, calls for the arrests of the cops who killed Breonna Taylor rang through the streets, from billboards, and on celebrity social media accounts.[137] As in her case, police who kill or harm are rarely arrested by the departments that employ them, and prosecutions and convictions are even more unlikely.[138] Even when they do happen, prosecutions consume tremendous amounts of resources while leaving a murderous system intact. Not one of them stops the next killing.

Notably, the number of prosecutions and convictions has not increased in spite of consistent uprisings and attention to police violence over the past decade. That's because the law protects cops who kill. Yet the rare conviction is held up as proof that the system holds itself accountable. As discussed in earlier chapters, the state will gladly sacrifice a few cops in unique and spectacular cases in order to preserve the status quo and allow policymakers to peddle the idea that justice has been done. In other words, as Kristian Williams puts it in *Our Enemies in Blue*, "police will be disciplined when their behavior threatens the smooth operation of the institution."[139]

While police preservationists cheered Derek Chauvin's conviction for murder in the second degree as proof the system works to hold bad cops accountable, it represents neither justice nor change. It may offer a measure of solace, but only in comparison to the alternative. No amount of prison time will bring George Floyd back to his loved ones, offer healing or repair, or bring any relief to Black people terrorized daily by cops just like Chauvin. For every conviction of a killer cop, thousands more Black people will be murdered, maimed, raped, criminalized, and dehumanized without consequence. The arrest, conviction, and sentencing of individual cops represent an exception to the rule. The rule is impunity.

Focusing on arrests of cops who harm people leaves the whole system intact. As the popular chant goes, "indict, convict, send the killer cops to jail, *the whole damn system is guilty as hell.*" The answer to why calls for arrests and prosecutions are unlikely to bear fruit, or bring about fundamental change to prevent future killings, can be found in the second half of the chant—which highlights the fundamental flaw in the demand reflected in the first half. Ultimately, a single conviction of a single cop won't change the system that produced and enabled him; in fact, it will embolden it to continue business as usual under the pretext that it can deliver justice.

Not only do prosecutions of killer cops not bring "justice," they don't represent "accountability." Chauvin hasn't taken any responsibility for his actions, and neither have the three cops who stood by as he murdered Mr. Floyd. As PIC abolitionists, we want far more than what the system that killed Breonna Taylor, George Floyd, and thousands more Black people can offer. It is not set up to provide justice for their families and loved ones. Turning away from systems of policing and punishment doesn't mean turning away from accountability. It just means we stop setting the value of a life by how much time another person does in a cage for violating or taking it—particularly when the criminal punishment system has consistently made clear whose lives it will value, and whose lives it will cage.[140]

When agents of the state act violently against an individual, collective responses are both warranted and essential—whether in the form of uprisings, demands against the cops involved, campaigns to defund the police, or calls for compensation, healing, and repair for people harmed or families left behind. But calls for police prosecutions offer an illusion of justice while reinforcing the status quo. That's why they garner widespread support among people invested in upholding it. Arresting individual cops leaves the conditions that make their violence possible unchanged, and injustices multiply in the absence of effective accountability. We want to direct our energies toward collective strategies that are more likely to be successful in delivering healing and transformation and preventing future harms. Families and communities deserve more than heartbreak over and over again each time the system declines to hold itself accountable.

We want a broader and deeper conception of justice for survivors and family members harmed by police violence. In Chicago, Mariame co-led and Andrea supported a successful struggle for reparations for survivors and families of people tortured by former Chicago police commander Jon Burge.[141] The reparations framework of the campaign featured five elements—repair, restoration, acknowledgment, cessation, and non-repetition.[142] Under this framework, survivors and families are entitled to accountability—which could take the form of immediate termination of the cops involved and a ban that would prevent them from holding a position of power that could be abused. But survivors and family members are also entitled to a process through which cops must hear and be accountable to their pain, to know the full value of the life they took, and make amends to their collective satisfaction. They are entitled to repair—to receive compensation for their pain and suffering without having to endure lengthy and costly litigation that will prolong their suffering. They should not have to prove their or their loved ones' innocence or worth to receive this repair. They are also entitled to restoration and healing services. In Chicago, survivors were given an official apology, awarded compensation, and given priority access to jobs and enrollment at city colleges and universities for themselves and their families. The city also committed to including materials on the Burge torture cases and the struggle for justice in the seventh- and eighth-grade public school curriculum—often taught by the survivors themselves. Finally, the city created the Chicago Torture Justice Center—a place where survivors can access healing services. Rather than policing "eligibility" for its programs the center has opened its doors to all people affected by police violence in Chicago.[143] We invite people to learn about more expansive approaches to accountability and repair for police violence through the work of the Chicago Torture Justice Center and Chicago Torture Justice Memorials, and by using the reparations for police violence conversation toolkit Andrea created in partnership with the Chicago Torture Justice Center for the M4BL Reparations Week of Action in June of 2021 available at bit.ly /REPJuneConversationTK.[144]

One thing is certain from our perspective: we must choose responses to police violence that align with abolitionist commitments to oppose *all* forms of surveillance, criminalization, and punishment. As Angela Y. Davis says, we must be "consistent in our analysis." We can't claim the system must be dismantled because it is a danger to Black lives and then turn to it for justice. Longtime abolitionists Rachel Herzing and Isaac Ontiveros reflected on this tension after Oscar Grant was killed by police in 2009, writing that punishing agents of the state acts at counter purposes to our ultimate goals: "Appealing to the same system that engineers and executes repression and genocide of poor people, youth, queer communities, and communities of color for remedies only strengthens that system's hold over us."[145] If we want to prevent the harm of police violence, we cannot turn to a carceral state, we need to dismantle policing.

What Do We Do with All the Cops?

This is an excellent question. We can find some answers in the concept of a "just transition," a framework elaborated with workers in polluting industries that calls for restructuring economies to provide for healthy, sustainable, living-wage work for everyone, and support for workers to transition from deadly industries to life-giving ones.[146] Through a just transition framework, former cops, along with other people employed in other sectors that must be phased out in order to create conditions for thriving communities, would receive support to adjust to the new reality of a police-free world, which may include job-training programs, counseling, support to engage in accountability for harm done, and orientation to new paradigms of safety. As discussed earlier in this chapter, careful attention to the transition from a carceral state to liberated futures is essential to our success.

We can also look to parallel organizing efforts. For instance, many military veterans have become disillusioned with the role they have been forced to play in service of people and institutions who don't serve their interests. Similarly, there are former cops who have come to the conclusion that policing is inherently violent and has nothing to do with the safety and service they signed up to provide. Former Atlanta cop Tom Gissler describes coming to the realization that "when I clock into work, I'm not doing any good, I'm actually doing harm. It dawned on me that the entire system, the entire thing, was just a shitty mafia system."[147] Thomas Owen

Baker, now a criminology PhD, quit his job as a cop when he realized that he was "representing the interests of these rich people upstairs who are making decisions and I was risking my life to clean up their mess on the street and providing them security—but I wasn't fit to eat in the same place as them. I was the help."[148] Like these men, former Border Patrol agent Francisco Cantú now calls for dismantling law enforcement: "The idea of abolishing immigration detention and other cornerstones of border enforcement may sound radical, but it is the only legitimate starting place for negotiation."[149] Many researchers who currently focus on documenting the violence of policing are former cops—including Phil Stinson, one of the primary researchers on police violence, including sexual violence. While there is a history of veterans organizing in support of movements to end state violence like Iraq Veterans Against the War, cops have yet to organize into formations that could recruit cops and former cops disillusioned with the violent system. As the executive director of Veterans for Peace says, "Hopefully these cops and border agents will also find that through activism [and] service, real service, they can get some of their soul back."[150]

While the prospect of working to create a place for the thousands of people currently employed in law enforcement in the futures we are building may seem daunting, abolition is about making way for all of us to reclaim our humanity. The success of our project depends on it.

We recognize that the many tensions and contradictions in abolitionist organizing explored in this chapter will not be solved overnight, and that the future we are trying to build is not yet fully drawn. But we do know this: the carceral state is death-making, policing as we know it today *is violence*, and we desperately need life-affirming institutions built in their stead. This knowledge can ground us as we experiment and build toward a world free of policing.

Experiment and Build

It was 2 a.m. on a Thursday night and the music was blaring again. Chicago apartment building alleys often double as hangout spots where people socialize and, in this case, where teens play loud music. Mariame could feel her shoulders tensing. An insomniac, she wasn't asleep yet and knew one of the neighbors was probably already calling the police. This had been going on for three weeks and the frustration was mounting in her apartment complex. Mariame walked out to her back porch and called out to the teenagers to turn off their music because the cops were likely on their way. In fact, she could already hear the sirens in the distance. She contemplated going downstairs to talk to the group, but she was alone, it was 2 a.m., and she didn't know these particular young people, so she decided against it. The approaching police sirens were soon followed by loud voices, as the young people protested to police that they had a right to be outside after midnight. In fact, at the time, Chicago was one of the many cities across the country with a youth curfew, making it unlawful for people under eighteen to be outside after certain hours. Sometimes the cops simply chased off the teens; sometimes they arrested and loaded them into waiting cars.

A year earlier, in 2009, Mariame had founded Project NIA, a grassroots organization with a vision to end youth criminalization. Their initial focus was to dramatically decrease youth arrests. Project NIA was based in Rogers Park, the same community where Mariame lived, so she decided it was time to find a way to address the noise that did not involve the police—and potential arrests for curfew violations. She began to reach out to her neighbors, and a week later, she convened the first of two meetings at the local parks department community room. By the end of the second meeting, some neighbors agreed to pair up to go to the alley and ask the teens directly to turn down their music. Mariame suggested inviting the young people to lunch instead to discuss the problem. At first, her neighbors expressed nervousness about this idea. What if it exacerbated tensions? What if one of the young people got violent? Mariame offered to reach out to the teens to invite them to lunch in her apartment with only a couple of neighbors so as not to overwhelm the youth. Recognizing that at least two of the young people lived just a couple of blocks away, Mariame started a conversation with one of them when she saw them in the neighborhood a couple of days later. She told them she and her neighbors wanted to find a resolution to the noise problem rather than continuing to rely on the police, and invited them to join her for lunch and to bring their loud music–playing friends.

Five teens and two of Mariame's neighbors came to lunch a few days later. After preliminary introductions, Mariame encouraged everyone to grab some food. As everyone ate, the conversation turned to the loud music. Mariame and her neighbors explained how disruptive the noise was to people's sleep and well-being. They explained that there were small children in the building complex and that the music was disturbing their sleep, too. They asked why the teens chose to play the music so loud at all hours of the night, and what accommodation could be made. The teens listened quietly; after a few minutes one young person explained that they continued to blast music in defiance because they had been "disrespected" by a neighbor who threatened to call the cops a few weeks earlier, without even giving them a chance to turn down the music. Their continued loud music playing was a deliberate act of antagonism. Mariame and her neighbors apologized to the teens for how they had been treated, suggested that it was alright for them to continue to hang out in the alley, and asked them if they would be willing to stop playing music so loud at night. The teenagers agreed to the compromise.

It only took a few meetings for the nightly torment to be resolved. Over the next few years, Mariame and other neighbors became friendly with the teenagers. The neighbors also decided to create a phone tree, improving communication and offering an alternative to police involvement in the complex.

Andrea similarly worked with neighbors in Brooklyn to resolve noise issues—which were many, as her block was home to nightly domino, dice, and card games, weekly income-generating house and street parties, and mas camps (groups of people who come together to make costumes for carnival) leading up to the annual West Indian Day Parade—and to address intra-community conflicts without involving the cops. For example, one day, at the height of the pandemic, a young Black man was furious because his phone had been taken by someone on the block. As he was yelling loudly outside Andrea's window, it became clear that he needed the phone for his business, and that he was stressed and exhausted. He had been up working since 3 a.m., trying to keep himself and his family afloat. He couldn't call the cops even if he had wanted to because his business was criminalized. Several of us listened and affirmed his right to be angry—and to express his anger in ways that Black people are rarely publicly able to do without police intervention. Andrea kept an eye out for the cops with the goal of keeping them at bay in the event they showed up, while neighbors invited the young man to lower his voice to avoid bringing heat to the block while continuing to affirm his frustration. Eventually, someone negotiated with the person who had taken the phone for its return, and everyone went home safely—which could easily not have been the case if the police had gotten involved, or if the community hadn't. This was one of many times a tight-knit, Caribbean working-class community de-escalated fights and rallied whenever cops showed up on the block to cop watch and keep each other safe.

Individuals and community groups across the country are working to build and strengthen community relationships and infrastructure to create safety without cops at the building, block, neighborhood, and city levels. They are doing this through more formal structures like the "Harm Free Zones" discussed in the "How Do We Get There?" chapter, as well as through informal networks centered around buildings, barbershops, and other community institutions. These efforts and experiments illuminate a path toward safer communities based on a principle that generations of community organizers have built upon. adrienne maree brown identifies it as one of the core elements of what she calls "emergent strategy": "How we are at the small scale is how we are at the large scale."[1] For example, disability justice theorist and practitioner Mia Mingus often points out that if we aren't in right relationship at home—as exemplified by little things, like following through on a promise to wash the dishes—we likely struggle to be in right relationship in the broader world. Of course, we understand that there's a big difference between not washing the dishes and actively harming someone. The point is simply that we can start down the path to creating greater safety by paying attention to and shifting the small ways we are in relationship—and accountable—to each other.

Of course, we still need to focus on building power on a broader scale to challenge and dismantle oppressive systems and tackle the larger structural questions around how we collectively govern ourselves, reduce harm, and sustainably meet our needs. But we don't need to have all the answers right now in order to start building the world we want. Neighbors getting together to solve a problem that police wouldn't address without violence are examples of ways we can start today, through daily, small-scale interventions. These daily actions start to chip away at how police shape our understanding of the world and the solutions to the problems we face. They enable us to build the muscles to create greater safety for ourselves and each other, practice cooperation, and engage in collective governance while we tackle larger systemic issues.

Experimenting with building community safety on an individual, neighborhood, workplace, community, or regional level while fighting for structural change is one way to resolve some of the contradictions around the state outlined in the "Tricks and Tensions" chapter. This is what is called a "dual power" strategy, elaborated by organizers in the Global South based on assessments of past struggles to topple and seize colonial and neoliberal states, and in organizing practices emerging from Indigenous, farming, and factory worker communities.[2] Many of us first learned about this approach to revolutionary change from the EZLN (also known as the Zapatistas). After over a decade of quietly organizing, building power, and practicing new forms of governance at the local level, in 1994 the Zapatistas launched an offensive against the Mexican government. The rebellion successfully liberated communities in which over 1.3 million people came together to self-determine new forms of governance.[3] Struggles that were inspired by or emerged contemporaneously to the Zapatista uprising, including the landless workers movement (MST) in Brazil and the unemployed workers' movement in Argentina, "recognize daily life and the creation of liberated communities as political work; support collective, nonhierarchical decision-making; and aim, above all, to build a society grounded in justice and peace for all."[4]

Former INCITE! National Collective member Paula X. Rojas describes this process as "making power" and "taking power"—and as distinct from strategies that focus on capturing the power of a colonial/carceral state.[5] A dual power strategy contemplates organizing simultaneously *outside* and *against* the state.[6] Both fronts of struggle are essential and mutually sustaining. If we focus solely on building small experiments outside the state, our efforts will be vulnerable to attack once they are perceived as a threat to the status quo, or will by necessity only reach a tiny fraction of the population in an effort to avoid being targeted by the state. And, practicing the world we want outside the state is vital to building power from below to limit the power of the carceral state, extract resources from it, and create conditions for more liberated forms of governance to emerge and thrive. Rojas emphasizes that dual power strategies are focused on "the *process* of making power and creating autonomous communities that divest from the state. And as these autonomy movements build, they can become large enough to contest state power."[7] Dual power is not just about "winning a specific political goal, but creating new communities that model the vision for liberation."[8] Importantly, dual power strategies teach us that we can start by practicing the world we want right now, we don't have to wait for some distant future when we are "in charge."

Mijente, a political home for Latinx and Chicanx people who seek racial, economic, gender, and climate justice, describes organizing "sin el estado," or without the state, as a way to "explore other liberatory ways of existing as individuals and communities—right here, and right now."[9] "Sin el estado" organizing "makes power" by meeting basic needs, ensuring survival without the intervention of the state, supplanting harmful institutions and practices, and enabling us to practice new forms of governance and relations.[10] It can include mutual aid, forming childcare collectives and cooperatives, community response teams, and other organizing efforts that enable us to practice collectivity and generatively build and exercise power rather than simply fighting the powers that be. It also imagines new ways of "taking power" that simultaneously offer opportunities to practice new forms of governance, such as participatory budgeting. Mijente emphasizes that "[s]in el estado projects can help individuals and communities get a taste for radical democracy, pro-conflict, confidence-boosting, trust-building new beliefs and behaviors that can help us get the goods and keep them."[11]

Adopting a dual power approach, in which we simultaneously work against the carceral state and outside/without it, opens up space for the kind of organizing and experimentation we need to create safer communities. It frees us from a false sense of urgency created by demands that we produce "evidence-based" "alternatives" with "proven track records" that can be implemented immediately as a precondition to any divestment from current systems of policing and punishment. Police preservationists insist that we can't do away with police until we have all the answers about what will take their place right now, unless we conclusively demonstrate that we can create something that looks like "safety" in the way the carceral state has defined it without policing. But the current system was not built by following a single blueprint handed down by a particular group; it was created over time through the efforts of many. Expecting a "shovel ready" blueprint from abolitionists is therefore inconsistent with how societies have historically evolved. Understanding that we are engaged in a simultaneous process of dismantling the carceral state and practicing the communities we want, rather than a sequential one in which one of these things must precede the other, is central to abolitionist organizing.

There is no cookie-cutter, one-size-fits-all solution to the multiplicity of needs, conflicts, and harms that exist in our individual communities that can immediately be replicated across the country and scaled up to a national level. That is what police falsely claim to be. As Chicago organizer Damon Williams succinctly puts it, "When I see police, I see one hundred other jobs smashed into one thing with a gun."[12] We need to unpack the multiple roles, resources, and relationships that are necessary to meet our individual and collective needs. The most effective approaches are often unique to the communities they arose in, because they are rooted in the particular conditions, relationships, and bonds of trust that exist in specific places or among specific groups of people. We can learn and perhaps draw from elements and experiences of other programs, but they must be adapted to local conditions, and brought to scale at the speed of relationships and trust, with a substantial injection of resources over the long term.[13]

Building greater safety takes time and space—to learn, grow, and change structural conditions to make it more possible. Police have benefited from generations of investments—now over $100 billion a year—and continue to be given the benefit of the doubt, in spite of their consistent failure to produce safety no matter how much money is poured into them. Meanwhile, community-based prevention, intervention, and responses to harm operate with little to no resources. They are shaped by conditions produced by organized abandonment and are given no grace to learn from mistakes and missteps along the way. It should therefore come as no surprise that large-scale and fully formed ecosystems of community care capable of addressing every potential conflict or harm don't yet exist. Safety is—and likely will always be—a work in progress. We need to build toward safer communities based on solid foundations through experimentation and practice, rather than being rushed into re-creating safety on the carceral state's terms. Over time, we can stitch our experiments together into an infrastructure of community safety at a scale that can meet our needs.

Collectively, we must be willing to commit to a spirit of experimentation, build our capacity to try things, embrace failure, and commit to multiple cycles of "practice, fail, learn, repeat." That is the principle behind the millionexperiments.com website and podcast that Interrupting Criminalization launched with Project NIA in 2021. They highlight multiple ways people across the U.S. and around the world are practicing creating greater safety in communities, including through mutual aid projects, community gardens, street fridges, violence prevention and interruption initiatives, community crisis-response models, barbershop conversations, and hotlines for people concerned they might harm someone else. As Ruth Wilson Gilmore reminds us, abolition is a process of repeated rehearsal toward a new future.[14] Rehearsals are just that—practice, not perfection, "abolition unfolding." Reflecting on the title of *Rehearsals for Living*, co-authored with Indigenous (Michi Saagiig Nishnaabeg) feminist Leanne Betasamosake Simpson, Robyn Maynard describes rehearsal as,

> a way of inhabiting our world with intention, as organizers, as theorists, as people in extended communities, based in attunement . . . not only to the unfolding disaster of the present, but to the unfolding experiments in living differently, to the more liberatory ways of organizing human and earthly life that are being seeded, in real time, all around us. And most importantly, it's an invitation to join in . . . and a reminder that liberation is not a destination but an ongoing process, a praxis.[15]

We can focus on advancing the work of creating greater and more liberatory forms of safety by engaging in grounded assessments of our efforts, taking accountability for our failures, and building from lessons learned, rather than undercutting our efforts before they even get off the ground. We need to do the nitty-gritty work of actually creating and building what we need instead of just theorizing and talking about it. We need to overcome our paralyzing fears of trying, experimenting, and getting it wrong that keep us from moving forward even when we might have a good solution. And, in the meantime, we know that meeting material needs will go a long way towards preventing and avoiding harm. We can counter organized abandonment through mutual aid projects, while simultaneously mobilizing to liberate state resources for housing, health care, education, guaranteed income, libraries, parks and green spaces, arts, and youth programming without policing—all essential to creating conditions for community-based safety strategies to flourish.

Importantly, we cannot experiment in isolation—we are not advocating for communal experiments divorced from larger liberatory struggles, nor are we advocating for small-scale experiments within social movements that are inaccessible to broader criminalized communities and do not extend and expand into broader public institutions. This is about building a new society, not reifying the power of individual relationships or networks. That is one reason we explore campaigns for #PoliceFreeSchools as a place where communities can engage in collective experimentation around what safety can look like in public institutions accessible to everyone. Building a world without the violence of policing requires huge social movements, not exclusive clubs. We need to engage all members of our community to shift and expand our understandings and experiences of public safety, weave our experiments together into a broader structural vision for the world we are building, make demands that make that vision more possible, and build movements and power that can turn them into reality.

Redefining and Practicing Safety

As Mariame pointed out in her summer 2020 *New York Times* op-ed, efforts to defund and abolish police are premised on a vision of "a different society, built on cooperation instead of individualism, on mutual aid instead of self-preservation."[16] Organizers across the country are deploying a multitude of tools to help people imagine and enact that vision through community surveys and engagement, participatory budgeting, and People's Movement Assemblies. They are doing the work of meeting each other's needs through mutual aid, and by practicing transformative justice.

Imagining What Safety Looks Like

As discussed in the "How Do We Get There?" chapter, a key component of creating greater safety is challenging the visions of safety we have been fed by the carceral state, and experiencing greater safety through relationships and community. We can start by asking ourselves and each other what safety and freedom look and feel like in our lives—as both of us regularly do in workshops, study guides,[17] and art projects like the Abolition Imagination and COVID safety postcard series.[18] Art and visionary fiction, in particular, play an important role in creating what the authors

of *Abolition. Feminism. Now.* describe as an "abolition feminism aesthetic"
that can unlock imaginations colonized by carcerality.[19] Art can make us
think and feel differently, and to ask ourselves "Why can't we do it this
way?" "Why don't we try this?" and "Why is that not possible?" We can
also ask ourselves these questions in conversation—as abolitionist organizer Benji Hart describes in *Practicing Abolition, Creating Community*,
a zine created for Project NIA and beautifully illustrated by Emma Li.[20]
The African American Roundtable created a zine based on responses to a
prompt in the *Invisible No More Study and Discussion Guide* about what
safer communities might look like that offers another example of what
such an invitation to dream different futures can yield.[21] Black Visions in
Minneapolis,[22] among other organizations, has created self-reflection and
community conversation guides that can serve as tools to help you start
where you are.

Collective imagination exercises can also take the form of community-
based surveys and participatory research projects. For example, during the
2016 youth-led campaign to prevent the construction of a $95 million
police training facility in a Chicago neighborhood where dozens of schools
and clinics were shuttered in a classic case of organized abandonment,
#NoCopAcademy organizers surveyed residents to find out how they
would spend the money instead to build greater safety.[23] They collected
over one thousand community recommendations for investments in public health and safety on the city's West Side. None involved construction of
a new police training facility. Almost half focused on increased spending
on schools and youth programs.[24] Similarly, in 2017, partners in the Liberate MKE campaign in Milwaukee surveyed over one thousand people
about what would create conditions for greater safety. Residents responded
by calling for investments in housing, youth employment, and violence
interruption.[25] In Phoenix, Poder in Action summarized the results of surveys of 10,000 Phoenix residents conducted in 2018 and 2019 in *Phoenix
Futuro*.[26] Over 1,300 Philadelphia residents' responses to similar questions
were summarized by the Movement Alliance Project in *Safety We Can
Feel*.[27] And, in the summer of 2021, the Nashville People's Budget Coalition surveyed over 5,000 residents about their budget priorities as policymakers tried to cite crime rates as a reason to increase, rather than decrease,

police funding.[28] Across the board, the majority of respondents in each of these communities called for investments in public schools, affordable housing, social services, and violence interrupters, rather than in police. These are just a few examples of how community surveys can serve as an important starting point for conversations around what greater safety looks like, and what it would take to create it in communities.[29] Notably, even city-sponsored surveys point us in similar directions—almost 90 percent of 38,000 residents surveyed in Chicago in the summer of 2020 supported divestment from police and investment in community programs.[30] Even where surveys claim low public support for the demands of defund campaigns, when asked about increased investment in housing, jobs, education, and health care and decreased investment in policing and punishment, the majority of respondents support their underlying premise.

When we're reimagining public safety, it is critical to engage and center people who have both experienced and engaged in harm. For instance, with the support of Interrupting Criminalization, the National Council of Incarcerated and Formerly Incarcerated Women and Girls is engaged in a participatory research project with its members as part of their Reimagining Communities campaign. Participants are exploring questions around what would have prevented the harm they experienced and engaged in and what accountability and healing could look like. Based on these conversations, they are imagining and organizing toward the relationships, programs, and institutional responses that would create greater safety for everyone in their communities.

Community events and People's Assemblies can serve as locations where safety dreams can be developed. For instance, in the summer of 2020, the Jackson, Mississippi, People's Assembly—created when former Mayor Chokwe Lumumba was elected to provide a direct mechanism for community accountability and governance—debated what would be possible if police department funds were reinvested in community programs.[31] The Black Nashville Assembly is similarly engaging residents in debates around their visions for safer communities.[32] And, in Minneapolis, a coalition of Minneapolis organizers led by Black Visions held People's Movement Assemblies across the city in 2021 to build a vision of a safer, more just city.[33]

Groups across the country are also using participatory budgeting to gain more direct control over where school, local, and federal funds are spent, and drive investments to meeting material needs and community-based safety strategies.[34] In the midst of the 2020 Uprisings, Decriminalize Seattle was successful in redirecting $30 million from the police to a participatory budgeting process that will take place in 2022. The process will be guided by the Black Brilliance Report, a 1,200-page document[35] summarizing the results of a Black-led research project focused on what will create greater safety in the city. The Black Brilliance Project—launched in 2020—involved over one hundred researchers, including youth, elders, people with experience in the criminal legal system, artists, healers, and "others who have been invited—many for the first time—to engage as researchers in their own communities and lives." Together they worked to answer the following questions based on their lived experiences: What creates true community safety? What creates true community health? What do you need to thrive? This Black-community research project brought thousands of voices across all ethnic and racial backgrounds into the process of envisioning safety, health, and thriving communities. The results focused on five priority investment areas: Housing and Physical Spaces, Mental Health, Youth & Children, Economic Development, and Crisis & Wellness. These will serve as the "buckets" for the participatory budgeting process. The report also lays out recommendations for how the process should unfold, including compensation to community members for participation.[36] Seattle organizers also came together across movements to create the Seattle Solidarity Budget, built on shared values and a refusal to be pitted against each other by city officials.[37] The budget, endorsed by dozens of organizations, calls for a Green New Deal, housing, childcare, and transportation for all, food support and sovereignty, digital equity and internet access, Indigenous sovereignty, and progressive revenue. It also calls for defunding cops and courts by 50 percent while investing in nonpolice responses to crises and harm.

These are but a few of the ways organizers across the country are using multiple strategies to engage communities in the process of reimagining safety and building power and relationships across movements to make abolitionist dreams a reality.

Mutual Aid

Mutual aid is another way to experiment and build toward greater community safety. The devastating conditions of the COVID-19 pandemic, federal abandonment of communities, and climate crises in 2020 brought increased interest in and attention to mutual aid projects. At one point, an online map tracked hundreds of mutual aid projects across the country,[38] as people stepped in to create greater safety for each other through food and medication deliveries, emergency cash assistance, medical, child, and elder care, scheduling vaccination appointments, and more.

Mutual aid enabled people to counter paralyzing fear and catastrophic conditions by plugging in however we could—fundraising for people out of work, fighting for the release of prisoners at risk of infection, learning more about who is isolated in our neighborhoods and making sure they have what they need. Through mutual aid, we don't just collaborate to meet moments of crisis, we practice the world we envision on a small scale, creating abundance in scarcity, mutual care and responsibility in the face of government abandonment, and faith in each other in unprecedented conditions. These are critical building blocks to reimagining safety beyond what the state is currently offering.[39]

In its simplest conceptualization, mutual aid is cooperation for the sake of the common good, rooted in understanding that our survival is tied to that of others.[40] According to Klee Benally, "[M]utual aid is an unbroken tradition across many cycles of colonialism, maintained through traditional teachings."[41] Mutual aid is also deeply rooted in the Black radical tradition of societies of enslaved and formerly enslaved people banding together to buy and preserve each other's freedom, welcome newly liberated people into community, and support each other through the Great Migration. Throughout history it has supported migrants through dislocation, workers through strikes, communities through boycotts, disabled people through denied access to care and community. It formed a central plank of the Black Panthers' "survival pending revolution" framework, best known through free breakfast programs, sickle cell testing, and other medical care. It is an assertion of our own and each other's inherent value in the Black feminist tradition, and an enactment of Black feminist cultures of care.

Mutual aid empowers communities to meet material needs through solidarity, not charity. It rejects saviorism, hierarchy, and authoritarianism. It is distinct from nonprofits, which are set up to put band-aids on social problems, police people through eligibility requirements and program conditions, and pacify revolt against structural conditions by blunting, rather than eliminating, their impacts.[42] As abolitionist legal scholar and organizer Dean Spade puts it, mutual aid is about "people giving each other needed material support, trying to resist the control dynamics, hierarchies, and system-affirming, oppressive arrangements of charity and social services."[43]

As Spade argues in his book *Mutual Aid*, it is more than just "neighbors helping neighbors."[44] It is both a critique and a response. "Mutual aid projects," Spade writes, "expose the reality that people do not have what they need and propose that we can address this injustice together."[45] Mutual aid is a dual power strategy, marrying work outside the state to meet community needs and practice new social relations with political education and organizing to change conditions, challenge power, and dismantle oppressive systems. This was evident in many mutual aid projects responding to the COVID-19 crisis. For instance, in some areas, grocery packing and delivery was combined with political education sessions on gentrification and organizing people to resist evictions. When the New York City mayor closed the subways early in the pandemic, it left many unhoused people without a place to take refuge at night. This forced them into dangerous shelters where COVID-19 ran rampant, or out on the freezing streets. Volunteers handing out clothing and warming supplies formed cop-watch teams and demanded hotel rooms for people being thrown out of subway stations. Similarly, Equity and Transformation (EAT) Chicago handed out COVID-19 "Life Kits" while organizing for a guaranteed income for communities devastated by the pandemic.[46] Black abolitionists who created the People's Grab-n-Go to make food available on the South Side of Chicago expressed hope that mutual aid would make it possible for people to reimagine what their city and country *could* look like. They asked, "What if relationships built through mutual aid led to campaigns to organize tenants for housing rights, make government aid more effective, or minimize the role of the police?"[47]

Ultimately, mutual aid projects are a form of political participation that hinges on recognizing our responsibility to care for one another. As the resource website BigDoorBrigade.com puts it, mutual aid is about "changing political conditions, not just through symbolic acts or putting pressure on their representatives in government, but by actually building new social relations that are more survivable."[48] The mutual aid work we do now can help us prepare for the next weather disaster, earthquake, economic crash, or pandemic. It can also help us create greater safety and prepare and practice for abolition. The more we know the people around us, the more we can practice sharing resources and making decisions together. The more we improve material conditions to create greater possibilities for more people to join liberatory struggles, the safer and more resilient we become.

Mutual aid can prefigure the creation of a new commons—and force the state to resource it. It places organized abandonment, and the neoliberal policies it reflects, in sharper relief, creating pressure on the state to divert resources to meeting community needs. For instance, the Black Panthers' free breakfast programs are credited with essentially shaming the state into creating Head Start and free food programs at schools. As discussed in the "Tricks and Tensions" chapter, there are pros and cons to a carceral state resourcing and potentially absorbing mutual aid programs—state funding for Panther programs operating outside the state enabled them to reach more people while operating more or less autonomously. However, once the state took the programs over, the Panthers' opportunities to organize people through them diminished. In some ways, state absorption of the program served a counterinsurgent function, undermining the power the Panthers were building by engaging people in collectively meeting their needs while offering political education. It also made it easier to isolate, demonize, and criminalize the Panthers by taking over a function they were performing that was widely positively perceived in communities. But in other ways, the creation of Head Start programs reflected the power of mutual aid to push the state to meet the needs mutual aid projects expose. And, the state was able to do so at a scale greater than the Panthers could achieve with the resources they were able to round up from communities, private contributions, and public grants. In any event, the existence of breakfast programs highlighted the devastating impacts of racial capitalism on Black children going to school hungry, the radical possibilities of collective care to meet the need, and the state's failure to fulfill its provisioning function. Mutual aid both manifested critique and produced structural change.

As with any experiment, there are potential pitfalls—like the state, mutual aid programs can create hierarchies of eligibility and "deservingness." They can also reproduce power imbalances and fail to address harm and conflict rather than prefiguring new social relations. Without a solid political foundation, mutual aid projects can operate from a time-bound, individual, charitable approach rather than one focused on systemic change.[49] And, the neoliberal state can simply take advantage of mutual aid programs to avoid responsibility for meeting people's needs—for instance, during the pandemic, organizers in both Minneapolis and D.C. reported that municipal governments simply routed people seeking assistance to mutual aid groups. These failures don't represent reasons to not engage in mutual aid, but rather reasons to do so with care and intention.

No matter how you look at it, mutual aid is critical to survival of organized abandonment, climate injustice, and worsening social and economic conditions around the globe. It is also a key building block to building power outside the state, practicing new forms of governance and new economic systems, and rebuilding the commons. There are many ways to jump into mutual aid efforts—you can start by finding mutual aid projects in your community, or by engaging in mutual aid for incarcerated people.[50] Right now, all of us can move us closer to a safer future without policing by plugging into mutual aid wherever you can.

Transformative Justice

As PIC abolitionists, we embrace transformative justice (TJ) as a vision and framework for action. At its core, TJ is a framework to prevent, interrupt, and redress harm through nonpunitive accountability. It prioritizes relationship-building, developing our skills, and uprooting structural oppression. It seeks to address violence without using more violence. It is not an "alternative to prison" as it is often framed. We're not interested in replacing a rigid set of rules (or laws) with another rigid set of rules applied to every single harm in the same ways. Rather, TJ asserts that policing and incarceration don't address the root causes of violence and harm—making these approaches neither good prevention strategies nor solutions. Transformative justice offers individual, interpersonal, and community-focused practices to address harm that facilitate transformation, accountability, and the beginning of healing rather than punishment. TJ requires that we unseat the political process of criminalization, shifting our focus from "crime" as constructed by a carceral state and punished through enforcement of criminal laws to addressing harm through transformation of social relationships toward solidarity and care. It also requires organizing.

A number of practitioners and thinkers have offered definitions of TJ over the past two decades that illuminate both the breadth of the community of practice and different aspects of transformative justice. They also demonstrate the roots of TJ in survivor-led communities and political formations, and in resistance to all forms of violence—including state violence—while prioritizing increased access to safety for all survivors.

Generation Five, a Bay-Area formation created with the goal of ending child sexual abuse within five generations, articulates the following definition: "Transformative justice (TJ) seeks to provide people who experience violence with immediate safety and long-term healing and reparations while holding people who commit violence accountable within and by their communities."[51]

Transformative justice practitioner Leah Lakshmi Piepzna-Samarasinha elaborates,

> It's any way of dealing with violence, abuse, and harm that doesn't primarily rely on the state (cops, courts, prisons) and that doesn't throw survivors under the bus, created by Black, brown, queer, trans, sex working, poor, working class, immigrant, and more folks because relying on the system has not been an accessible or reliable option. . . . Transformative justice is one way that we are trying to address violence, harm, and abuse in our communities in ways that are generative and do not create more destruction and trauma."[52]

Transformative Justice processes, like mutual aid, are a form of politicized survival work, an "outside the state" strategy that builds power to create the world we want *and* fight the carceral state. TJ is as much about imagining and practicing alternatives as it is dismantling systems that perpetuate violence.

Mia Mingus, a former Generation Five member and founder of the Bay Area Transformative Justice Collective (BATJC), reminds us that

> TJ is not simply the absence of the state and violence, but the *presence* of the values, practices, relationships, and world that we want. It is not only identifying what we don't want, but proactively practicing and putting in place things we want, such as healthy relationships, good communication skills, skills to de-escalate active or "live" harm and violence in the moment, learning how to express our anger in ways that are not destructive, incorporating healing into our everyday lives.[53]

In this way, TJ is distinct from restorative justice practices that focus on addressing harm among individuals *without* addressing the larger conditions that contributed to it. Transformative justice collective Philly Stands Up points out that the framework "recognizes that oppression is at the root of all forms of harm, abuse, and assault," which is why they work "to address and confront those oppressions on all levels and [treat] this concept as an integral part to accountability and healing."[54]

Transformative justice frameworks and practices arose in resistance to the professionalization and depoliticization of anti-violence movements described in the "We Are Survivors" chapter. Feminist scholar Ann Russo writes that TJ "shift[s] the focus and direction of anti-violence efforts from social services and legal advocacy to community-based movement building, from viewing violence as a problem of individual conflict to one rooted in systems of oppression, from agency expertise to community-based knowledge and leadership, and from punishment to accountability."[55]

Each of these definitions emphasizes particular aspects of TJ while illuminating some common principles:

1. TJ was created by Black, Indigenous, LGBTQ, migrant, disabled, sex trading, and low- and no-income people who could not and/or

did not want to rely on cops and carceral social services when they experienced harm.[56]

2. TJ is preventing, intervening in, and transforming violence and harm by focusing on repair, healing, and resources.

3. TJ is not a "program"; TJ is a vision, a framework, and practice.

4. TJ never "partners" with law enforcement; TJ is rooted in abolitionist politics.

5. TJ rejects punishment and embraces nonpunitive accountability.

6. TJ processes are rooted in communities because they are community-based responses to harms.

7. TJ includes community organizing because it includes an analysis and challenge to structural oppressions.

8. TJ is not only about people who have been harmed. It is also concerned with the people who have harmed others and with the broader community that contributed to and was impacted by harm. TJ always strives to be survivor-informed because TJ is a vision and framework that was created and is often led by survivors. TJ rejects simple binaries of perpetrators vs. victims.

People often resist or question TJ because we are so conditioned to seek punishment. Our society has normalized inflicting cruelty or suffering on others in response to harm, violence, or wrongdoing. By this logic, the greater the harm and the more fear a person experiences, the greater their instinct toward punishment. This is one reason why people who otherwise support abolitionist principles have such a hard time letting go of the prosecutions of killer cops, white supremacists, billionaires, and corporate tax evaders, people who commit "white-collar crimes" that devastate the lives of thousands, polluting corporations, people who commit war crimes, and others whose actions they see as particularly heinous and reprehensible. But punishment does nothing to prevent or help people heal from these harms. We cannot effectively teach people not to harm others by harming them. Instead, punishment fuels and legitimizes systems that make the harm possible in the first place while leaving survivors without resources. The practice of punishment itself is harmful and destructive.

Accountability, on the other hand, means taking responsibility for harms, understanding their impact(s), and working to repair them. It is not a singular action or destination; it is an internal process through which we decide to be aligned with a shared set of values, and to be responsible to ourselves and those around us for our choices and their impacts. Accountability is not something that is imposed like a sentence, nor is it an inherent capacity some people have and others don't. Instead, it is an active process that people choose to engage in, voluntarily and on an ongoing basis. As a result, we can't "hold someone accountable." People can only choose to *take* accountability. Communities can create and hold space for people to do so through transformative justice processes. Often, that does not feel satisfying for people. But it's worth remembering that punishment rarely satisfies, either, because it cannot ultimately heal or repair harm. The current criminal punishment system actually discourages people from accepting responsibility and taking action toward repair, because to do so would expose them to harsh punishment.

Danielle Sered, founder of Common Justice and author of *Until We Reckon*, breaks down the differences between accountability and punishment in the chart reproduced below:

Accountability	Punishment
Is something you choose to do	Is imposed by others with power over you
Recognizes and requires your power, including your power to enact repair	Aims to diminish or contain your power, which it presumes can only be harmful
Is fundamentally active: it requires you to address suffering you caused by seeking to transform yourself and to mend and rebuild for others	Is largely passive: it requires you to address suffering you caused simply by suffering yourself with no pathway to provide anything to others
Deepens relationship and connection	Severs relationship and connection
Fosters healing and restoration	Fosters shame and isolation

Transformative justice is only one way forward. Its effectiveness will vary based on who uses it, in what context, and for what kinds of harm. It cannot address all forms of harm. People often offer long lists of people for whom TJ won't work because they will refuse responsibility, accountability, and transformation—including cops, white supremacists, and people who kill, rape, or abuse repeatedly. It is true that accountability cannot be imposed, but that doesn't mean there will be no consequences if someone refuses to take accountability through TJ. Transformative justice envisions nonpunitive consequences that reduce individuals' ability to continue to engage in harmful actions, such as terminating cops and defunding police departments, removing white supremacists from positions of power, and keeping people who repeatedly engage in harmful behavior from doing so in the future. Consequences can be unpleasant and uncomfortable, but they are not intended to hurt people for the sake of hurting them.

People often ask about instances where the state, or its agents, are the ones doing harm—like what about when cops kill, rape, or abuse people? There are reparative frameworks that exist to address state and state-sanctioned violence—such as the Reparations Now! campaign discussed in the "Tricks and Tensions" chapter. As with processes involving community members who do harm, it is critical to focus on not only individual state actors, but the conditions that produced them—which requires us to tackle broader systems of racial capitalism and colonialism facilitated by the carceral state.

Regardless of what forms of harm we are contemplating, it is critical to start from a place of possibility. What if we started by thinking about all the situations and circumstances in which TJ *could* prevent, interrupt, and transform harm, rather than those in which we imagine it can't? We can work with those who *do* want to take accountability and learn how to do that well. We can create a culture where more people will choose to take accountability. We can recognize that people who harm are often survivors of harm themselves. As Sered points out, "No one enters violence by first committing it."[57]

What does that mean for abolitionist work? We can use these insights to continue to develop other frameworks, practices, and structures to address people who refuse to take accountability for harm. Abolitionists are clear that these cannot be prisons, jails, electronic surveillance, punitive fines, and other mechanisms of punishment. Those are the products of a different set of imaginations from a different time. Individually, our imaginations of what a different world can be are limited. But intentionally being in relationship with each other as a part of collective dreaming can help us imagine new forms of justice, and also to imagine ourselves differently.

Collectively, we have enough creativity to figure it out by working to get there. We can move past the question "What do we have now and how can we make it better?" to "What can we imagine for ourselves and the world?" How things are now need not dictate how they are in the future.

People often demand evidence that TJ—currently practiced at an intimate and small scale by communities, collectives, projects, and organizations—can be scaled up into a form that looks like outdated and failed carceral notions of "safety" as defined by the state: a bureaucratic, one-size-fits-all process administered in ways that look familiar and legible to us as a state or quasi-state practice. Practitioners are expected to immediately produce a blueprint for transformative justice everywhere, for every conceivable situation. Yet, as is true with most community-based approaches, these demands are never accompanied by concrete offers of the kinds of funding, resources, or legitimacy that policing has enjoyed for decades. Nevertheless, regardless of how much we invest in TJ processes or practices, they will never—and should never—become a state-run program, nor a blueprint applied everywhere. While the degree of harm in our communities requires us to act with urgency, it cannot push us to acting hastily, lest we simply re-create what already exists in new forms. We know that what we currently have in place is actively causing harm and must be dismantled. What we build in its place will take time to evolve in each community.

Transformative justice is slow work requiring labor from many people and a lot of patience. It is not about happily-ever-afters or forgiveness (except, perhaps, for ourselves when we don't live up to our values). It is a framework for inquiry. It asks vital questions: *How do we respond to violence and harm in a way that doesn't cause more violence and harm? How do we respond to violence and harm in ways that don't rely on the punishing state? How are we actively cultivating the things that will help prevent future violence, like healing and accountability? How do we meet immediate needs in ways that get us closer to the world we want—one that is liberatory and prioritizes collective freedom?*

Transformative justice also requires that we develop a balance of relationship, skills, and structure. If we don't have the trusting relationships, then we need skilled people to help manage conflicts. If we don't have the skills, then we really need a lot of structure. The more we build our relationships, the less structure we'll need.[58] And, above all, transformative justice is rooted in care. If, as Saidiya Hartman teaches us, "care is [an] antidote to violence," then a politics of care must be central to our abolitionist organizing. A practice of abolitionist care underscores that our fates are intertwined, as is our liberation.

We are working on transformative justice now, every day, in communities everywhere in the world. It's not something we are waiting to take on in a nebulous or utopic future.

There are no experts in transformative justice—although there are people with greater skills and experience that we should all strive toward. It is not enough to watch one video and decide that we are equipped to hold a TJ process tomorrow. Like any other set of skills, we need to develop them over time in community. But that doesn't excuse us from trying. Abolitionists who practice TJ are simply willing to put in the work to figure out a better way forward.

As with mutual aid projects, we can each start small—in everyday conversations and actions. Page May, the co-founder of Assata's Daughters based in Chicago, shares the following exchange with a fourth grader:

> At first, he couldn't imagine justice without involving the police. . . . I decided to personalize the question for him. I asked what he would do if I stole something of his—like his favorite toy. What if he knew it was me, but I refused to admit it? I asked him what he would need to happen to feel like "justice was served."
>
> J paused, his smile breaking for the first time. He said he wouldn't call the cops. He said he would pester me, over and over until I admitted what I'd done and apologized. He added that I'd need to replace his toy. I asked if that was enough, since the "crime" was solved and his stuff was returned. He laughed.
>
> He said it wouldn't be enough to just have his stuff back because I'd done more than taken his toy, I'd also broken our friendship. He went on saying he'd go on vacation to turn up with his family and that while he was having a great time and

enjoying himself, I'd have to stay back and watch all of his valuables for him. I'd have to do this, take care of the things he most treasured, every day. And that he'd do this over and over until he trusted me again. He said justice would be complete when he could trust me again."[59]

If a fourth grader can articulate a layered and transformative vision of justice, then it is within everyone's capacity to do the same. We need to practice these new social relations now. With only a subtle shift in thinking, we can creatively solve problems without relying on law enforcement as the first—or even last—resort. For example, a few years ago Mariame's friend emailed her:

> I saw a toddler running down Ashland barefooted and wearing very little clothing. No one was in sight. A month ago, I know that I would have immediately called the police. In light of recent events, I got out of the car and did my own detective work. I was nervous. The child was pre-verbal and I'm not good with small children, plus I didn't know what I was getting myself into. I was painfully conscious, however, that calling the police might bring irreversibly negative consequences for someone—a family, the baby, me.
>
> The good news is that I found another passerby. We wrapped the baby in my sweater and together we went door-to-door until we found the mom, who by that point was hysterical because she realized that her child was missing. Between the neighbors confirming the child's identity and the woman's expression when we walked up with the baby, we were pretty confident the child was hers.

Mariame's friend overcame her nervousness, sought out support, and then problem-solved. In the end, the child was safe. Here, transformative justice looked like collective care: the sweater to keep the baby warm, the pairing up with a passerby, the search for the parent of the baby, and, ultimately, the baby's successful safe return home. Mariame's friend's actions were inspired by the work of Circles and Ciphers, a program Mariame co-founded in Chicago. It's a testament to the fact that, each time we make spaces to dream and practice transformative justice, it can multiply into more everyday practices.

Under a TJ framework, we are all called to labor. All of us can make offerings. We need thousands of tools, not one. We're all collectively responsible for making safer communities. No one person is responsible for coming up with *the* answers; no one person is responsible for the mess we're in. We're all complicit—it's just a matter of degree. In other words: we all have a part to play in transforming our conditions and ourselves. We must practice accountability with those we love, work to uproot all forms of oppression, organize across difference, and build power to challenge the carceral state. It will take all of us to dismantle death-making institutions, change the ways we understand and relate to each other, and build safer and more just communities without them. We're already doing it. We're dismantling, changing, and building all the time, and we can practice wherever we are.

Schools as a Site of Experimentation

In the summer of 2020, over thirty-four U.S. cities voted to eliminate cops from schools—a political victory stemming from the decades-long #PoliceFreeSchools campaigns described in the "No Soft Police" chapter. Imagining and creating police-free schools offers an entry point for conversations about ending policing in all its forms. What we put in place to create safer schools can teach us valuable lessons about *how* we can create greater safety in communities. It can also begin to shift our common sense around whether police need to exist at all.

We can start by immediately eliminating cops from spaces of learning and growth for children and youth.[60] We can work to end the criminalization of youth through arrests, suspension, or discipline for offenses like "disrupting a school," being "ungovernable," or violating dress codes.[61] We can root out other forms of "soft policing" in schools, such as tracking disabled students into substandard education, corporal punishment, bullying, bathroom policing, or educational approaches that are more about preparing subjects for racial capitalism than fostering humans to reach their fullest potential. We can resist efforts to ban teaching students about race, reparations, critical race theory, or gender and sexual diversity.

We can build toward liberatory education. For instance, organizations like Detroit's People in Education create artist residencies and fellowships to facilitate efforts to humanize classrooms and shift relationships between adults and young people in educational environments, while the James and Grace Lee Boggs School is creating conditions for young people to practice transforming themselves to transform the world.[62] And we can ask ourselves how, instead of creating private freedom schools or charter schools that can only be accessed by the few, we can make *all* public schools freedom schools by learning how to maintain public institutions that make up the commons while eliminating their carceral elements?

As evidenced by vociferous and vicious right-wing attempts to bar curricula that address racial and other structural oppressions and histories from schools, burn books, and bar trans students from sports, education is a primary site of political contestation. Reconstruction efforts to create public school systems that would serve an "abolition democracy" illuminate how schools can also be strategic sites for sustained abolitionist intervention in the short and medium term. Schools are already socially embedded into communities, and well-developed ideas of how to further deepen those ties already exist through the community schools framework, which "uses public schools to connect families with community resources and care for the 'whole child.'"[63] Creating safer #PoliceFreeSchools can engage parents, teachers, and administrators, and entire generations of students, in the powerful process of political education and practice. Everyone involved can then take lessons and skills from making abolition real in schools out into the world.

Creating Collective Ecosystems of Care

Beyond schools, communities are coming together to stitch together mutual aid projects, transformative justice practices, and community programs and institutions into broader community infrastructures of care. While processes for doing so vary across communities, they all involve some version of these steps:

1. Assessment of where cops are present in communities and what they are doing: Whose interests are they serving? What harms are

they perpetrating? What is needed there—if anything? Who could be providing what is needed instead?

2. Taking inventory: What already exists that can be woven together into an ecosystem of collective care? Where are there gaps and how can they be filled? What concrete strategies, organizations, or collectives that create safety are already in place? What resources are needed to further that work? What needs to be imagined and built from scratch? Experiments and models from other communities can be helpful in finding what works best in yours and offer important lessons and principles, but it's almost never a question of simply replicating programs developed elsewhere. Each ecosystem of care is unique to the time, place, and people that make it up.

3. Building skills, relationships, and infrastructure: What skills do individuals and communities already have that can be put to use to create safety? What skills and relationships do we need to strengthen and build? What infrastructure needs to be created or funded? Where are the spaces where decisions about safety and accountability are made? What roles might community care coordinators, community safety councils, tenant associations, Harm Free Zone coordinating committees, or labor unions, cooperatives, and workers' associations play in stitching together an ecosystem of care?

Asking and responding to these questions can take place at an organizational level, as it did for Creative Interventions, the Bay Area Transformative Justice Collective, and Seattle's Natural Helpers. All three organizations engaged in a process of documenting and building on community-based responses to interpersonal and family violence rooted in existing relationships—particularly among migrant communities for whom police response often creates more danger, and in cases of child sexual abuse, where reporting to police is infrequent and fraught. These three programs share common characteristics of training and offering resources to people who are most likely to be the first responders to abuse and harm, while simultaneously confronting systemic drivers of violence in our communities.

Similarly, Oakland Power Projects and Rachel Herzing's Build the Block project documented what happened when people called 911 in Oakland and San Francisco, and identified who and what could respond instead.[64] Build the Block also created a neighborhood directory of each household's needs and assets, and took into account the physical layout of the community and where community members spent their time to help shape how they would respond in a crisis.[65] Oakland Power Projects held "know your options" workshops across communities, sharing ways to get help without cops, and how to prepare for instances in which they do show up to maximize safety.[66] The goals of these projects were two-fold: to strengthen the community's ecosystem of care, and to expand people's imaginations beyond the "logic of calling the cops."[67]

Mental Health First emerged in Sacramento to tap into and build skills and infrastructure in Black communities to respond to unmet mental health needs without cops. It has since expanded to Oakland, and "dispatches volunteer medics, mental health specialists, and security to respond in person to people dealing with psychiatric emergencies, substance use, and interpersonal violence."[68] The program emerged from the Anti Police-Terror Project, which has spent years organizing in response to police killings, many of which were the result of a police response to someone in crisis or with unmet mental health or other needs. Led by survivors and community members with medical, de-escalation, and conflict resolution skills, the program operates outside the state (through a direct dispatch line and word of mouth).[69] Mental Health First co-founder Asantewaa Boykin, a psychiatric emergency room nurse, describes their approach: "Our primary goal is just to mitigate the immediate crisis and hopefully help that person come to their own next step. Our framework does not sweep in and tell people what they need or how they need it. We call it self-determined crisis management."[70] It starts by asking "are you safe?" and the entire focus is to get the person to a place where they feel safe rather than to contain or control them.[71]

These are just a few examples of organizations that engaged in an assessment of what already existed in communities to create safety without cops, built programs and practices around them, and fought the state for the space, power, and resources to implement them. In some communities, such as Durham, Oakland, and Austin, this assessment process has been more formalized through public safety task forces.[72] Many more examples of strategies communities are experimenting with and building to create greater safety can be found at MillionExperiments.com, TransformHarm.org, Creative-Interventions.org, defund2refund.org, and defundpolice.org. Of course, these programs do not represent universal solutions. Rather, each can offer glimpses into what building and experimenting toward more liberated conditions might look like outside and against the state, as well as principles and lessons that can guide us.

There are those who will say our communities are not ready for a world without police. It is our job as abolitionists to organize them toward it. We address problems all the time without relying on police, whether as part of an intentional process of building toward abolition, the product of access to an abundance of resources, or because we simply cannot call on the state for a number of reasons. We can identify, re-learn, use, and build on the skills and resources we have, instead of continuing to delegate responsibility for safety to the violence of policing.

There are others who will say that now is not the time to experiment with new approaches because violence is on the rise. But that is precisely why we need to engage in experiments toward building safer communities—because the current approach has consistently failed the vast majority of our communities, consigning us to the twin violence of policing and organized abandonment. We are already living with both uncertainty and the certainty that the violence we face will persist if we don't change course. And there are those who will say that while community-based approaches may work for noise complaints, they are insufficient to meet the challenges posed by gun violence or gender-based violence. But as described throughout *No More Police*, communities are finding ways to meet the most serious forms of violence every single day.

Of course, communities will need dedicated time to build a way forward. In the meantime, we must address the more immediate needs of survivors and people vulnerable to violence. That means building our capacity for mutual aid and for engaging in restorative and transformative justice as we work towards our broader visions. Beth Richie describes abolition feminism in practice as interventions that (1) take the problem of gender violence very seriously and provide support for survivors; (2) use transformative justice approaches and mutual aid to do that; (3) analyze the root causes of violence and develop strategies to change those conditions; (4) build coalition with other social justice groups where those most affected are in leadership; (5) assess campaigns when they fail, regroup, and try again; and (6) recognize and lift up the everyday abolition strategies that people use to take care of themselves and each other without relying on the carceral state. It is not formulaic, but rather a set of practices that are geared toward abolition feminist goals.

Abolition's horizon is long, but it is also already here. "What the world will become," Ruth Wilson Gilmore writes, "already exists in fragments and pieces, in experiments and possibilities."[73] When people tell us there is no possibility of a world without police, we can invite them to experiment, practice, and evolve with us. We can find joy, care, and healing in it. All of us are constantly manifesting potential abolitionist responses, even if we don't call them that. The places we care about most—our homes, schools, and neighborhoods—are precisely where we can nurture and develop them.

Black Feminist Musings

Sometimes we are blessed with being able to choose the time, and the arena, and the manner of our revolution, but more usually we must do battle where we are standing.

—Audre Lorde, *Sister Outsider*[1]

In July 2015, Andrea and Mariame participated in the founding conference of the Movement for Black Lives in Cleveland, Ohio. Over two thousand Black people from across the United States and Canada gathered to discuss state violence, strategize about effective organizing, and simply be together a year into the Ferguson Uprising. Both of us facilitated workshops on police violence and criminalization targeting Black women, trans and gender nonconforming people at the convening. After two days of conversation, strategizing, and community-building, we were getting ready to head home, which, for both of us, was Chicago at that time, where Mariame had lived since 1995 and Andrea had relocated in 2014.

The structure of this chapter is inspired by the Black Feminist Breathing Chorus and collection of Black Feminist Breathing Cards created by Alexis Pauline Gumbs. For more information, please visit: sangodare.podia.com/breathingchorus90.

Mariame had traveled to Cleveland on a bus with a group of young Black organizers affiliated with BYP100, a youth-led organization with chapters across the U.S. As she walked back to the bus with fellow organizers, they encountered a group of people demanding that the police release a twelve- or thirteen-year-old Black boy who was sitting in a bus shelter in handcuffs. Andrea was already on the scene, having run over as soon as she saw a small group of conference participants gathered around the cop cars as she was leaving the conference. Dozens of Black people who had just come together to chart the future of a post-Ferguson Black liberation movement surrounded the bus shelter. A comrade successfully reached the boy's mother on the phone. It was clear that no one was going to leave until she arrived, and the boy was safe.

The cops escalated the standoff when they tried to move the boy towards one of the police cars parked in the street. The steadily growing crowd followed, shouting at the cops to release the boy, telling them that his mother was on her way. Meanwhile, more and more Black people were pouring out of the surrounding buildings from the conference and making their way to the scene.

Suddenly, one cop began indiscriminately spraying the crowd with pepper spray. A couple of other cops joined in, and chaos broke out. The cops didn't care who they were spraying. We were all Black and it didn't matter if we were women, men, gender nonconforming, trans, adult, elder, or child. They sprayed us, as our friend and organizer Page May said, "like we were bugs."

Malik Alim, a young organizer from BYP100 who Mariame knew and who tragically passed away in August 2021, narrated his personal experience of the incident:

> I'd never been maced or pepper sprayed before and the moment between realization and sensation felt like a lifetime, like waiting for the pain receptors to fire after stubbing your toe. I stumbled out of the street and into the grass where a woman from the group I traveled with, we'll call her C, caught me in her arms. I was blinded, but I could hear people screaming. I added my own voice to the ruckus, pleading for water to

rinse the poison from my eyes. Almost immediately, I began to discern some of the yelling voices warning against the use of water and urging able bodies to run to the nearby grocery store for milk. We needed to pour milk into our eyes, to neutralize the poison. As I writhed on the ground in agony, I remember I was wearing contact lenses. I begged C to help me remove them and quickly regretted it. As soon as air hit my pupils, the pain intensified. As I screamed, C quickly explained to me that she was still nursing her young daughter and that she could deliver milk more quickly than the store runners if I let her. I quickly obliged and she administered the cooling substance directly from her breast. I was already crying, but her selfless act of care for me, her fallen comrade, unleashed a reservoir of emotion from deep within me.[2]

When Mariame heard the screams and saw some people falling to the ground, she ran toward the 7-Eleven that was about a block away to purchase milk. When she returned, she noticed that more cops had arrived and that the boy had been moved from the bus shelter into a cop car. The crowd encircled the car to prevent it from moving. Andrea—who had earlier been shoved to the ground by a cop as she and others yelled at police to put away the pepper spray and the Tasers some were starting to unholster—was now huddled in a small group of Black women movement lawyers, negotiating with police to try to stop them from arresting and charging the boy—or anyone else. We were all trying to prevent them from further escalating what was becoming an increasingly tense and dangerous situation. Finally, the boy's mother arrived, and he was released into her custody without charge.

We accomplished our goal: we successfully prevented yet another Black child from being dragged into the maw of the criminal punishment system that day. We did battle where we were standing, with those we were standing with. We put the liberation dreams we had been envisioning and sharpening together over three days at the convening into practice. We insisted that whatever reason cops claimed as justification to cuff and cage a child—failure to pay a transit fare, underage drinking, refusing to get off the bus or comply with their commands, being young and Black—we weren't having it. We won that day when the police returned the boy to his mother. And when we knew we had won, the group broke out into spontaneous cheering and dancing as someone began to chant: "We Gon' Be Alright, We Gon' Be Alright," echoing the lyrics of the Kendrick Lamar song that had rung out the first night of the convening.[3]

"Nobody's free until everybody's free" —*Fannie Lou Hamer*[4]

The incident in Cleveland was a stark reminder to everyone present that all Black people are targets for the violence of the state, and that it will take bold collective action for all of us to get free. As we left a gathering focused on Black liberation, we refused to settle for visions of freedom that did not include a criminalized Black child, his Black mother, and everyone targeted for police violence that day. We engaged in active collective resistance to the violence of policing, we practiced mutual aid and collective care, we refused to allow a mother to be separated from her child by the state, and we demanded a vision of safety that doesn't put children—or anyone—in cages. All of us were needed. All of us had a role to play. All of us were valued. We left nobody behind. We lived into freedom fighter Fannie Lou Hamer's mandate that none of us are free until all of us are free—including everybody in cuffs and cages of any kind.

While initially the target of police action was a Black boy, we recognized, responded to, and resisted all forms of violence against all Black people the incident involved. And we were led, in large part, by Black women, queer, and trans people. Our collective response represented Black feminism in action: Black feminism offers a vision for liberation not just for Black women, but for our entire community, and for all who experience oppression.

We are Black feminist abolitionists. This means we are shaped by Black feminism and abolition feminism—and their intersections. As legendary Black feminist scholar and activist Barbara Smith once stated: "Feminism is the political theory and practice to free all women. . . . Anything less than this is not feminism."[5] For, us, the freedom feminism demands extends to freedom from all forms of violence, including surveillance, policing, punishment, borders, and war. In other words, as the authors of *Abolition. Feminism. Now.* simply state, feminism must be abolitionist, and abolition must be feminist.[6]

Black feminism—from which abolition feminism emerges—is rooted in Black women's lived experiences,[7] in which the violence of the carceral state plays a central role. As Black feminist historian Sarah Haley describes, "the very possibility of black subjects' claim to womanhood was a perceived threat to white supremacy and the carceral state was a key mechanism to crush such a possibility."[8] Black trans feminist scholar and abolitionist Che Gossett elaborates that "[t]he violent figuration of Black people as criminals, thugs and brutal animals . . . is also sexualized and gendered against Black trans, queer, and gender nonconforming people."[9] Black queer and trans feminism deepens our analysis of gendered experiences of anti-Blackness to understand how Blackness is policed and punished as inherently queer and trans;[10] disability justice illuminates the ways in which Black people are policed and punished as inherently disabled.[11] Because Black feminism is concerned about violence in all its forms, wherever it takes place, it must be anti-capitalist and anti-imperialist.[12] And, because Black women, queer, and trans people thus exist at what INCITE! describes as the "dangerous intersections of multiple forms of oppression,"[13] in the words of the Combahee River Collective Smith co-founded, "[O]ur freedom would necessitate the destruction of all the systems of oppression."[14] This is the basis of the declaration that if Black women, trans, and gender nonconforming people are free, then everyone is free. Abolition is essential to achieving its vision.

We came to abolition guided, and deeply informed, by Black feminist theory and practice. Contemporary Black feminist scholars and organizers like Smith, Angela Y. Davis, Beth E. Richie, Ruth Wilson Gilmore, Kai Lumumba Barrow, Rachel Herzing, Tourmaline, Alexis Pauline Gumbs, Kenyon Farrow, Barbara Ransby, and Che Gossett, along with Black feminist leadership of abolitionist organizations like INCITE! and Critical Resistance, have been our touchstones. Hidden histories of Black feminist organizing against the violence of the state, including that of enslaved women resisting criminalization for acting in defense of themselves, Black women in the civil rights movement organizing against police sexual violence, and the multi-movement campaign to free Joan Little after she killed a cop in self-defense as he sexually assaulted her, have all deeply shaped our work. We have learned from Black feminist leaders of anti-colonial and anti-apartheid struggles, and from Black feminists fighting ongoing imperialism, globalization, and climate injustice around the world.

We, in turn, have infused Black abolition feminism in our organizing and advocacy—including into the Vision for Black Lives that emerged from the 2015 founding meeting of M4BL, which both of us contributed to writing, updating, expanding, and deepening to more clearly center Black queer and trans feminism, disability justice, and migrant justice in its demands.[15] Both of us have worked for three decades to bring Black feminist analysis to conversations and organizing around policing, criminalization, and safety. This work has taught us that when we center Black women, queer, and trans people's experiences, we gain a more expansive view of the multiple forms and contexts of policing, a deeper understanding of how far policing reaches into institutions of the carceral state, and a clearer picture of how it manifests in our communities. By rooting our analysis in the lived experiences of Black women, queer, and trans people, we recognize the carceral state as *the* central organizer of racialized gender violence and a primary site and source of unfreedom for Black women.

Abolition feminism and "Black queer and trans and feminist thought provide an arsenal of critique and praxis that allows us to think rigorously . . . about violence,"[16] illuminating how surveillance, policing, and punishment operate along multiple axes of race, gender identity and expression, class, disability, and nation, in multiple settings—home, community, and engagement with the carceral state. Abolition feminism thus enables us to expand the scope of our abolitionist politics to include all arenas in which carcerality operates—including the policing of motherhood, access to care, sexuality, and the sex trade, and the family regulation system. It allows us to see the roots of the carceral state in efforts to control Black women's economic, reproductive, and sexual autonomy in the wake of the legal elimination of slavery.[17] It helps us to understand how the violence of organized abandonment, reflected in staggering rates of poverty, structural exclusion, denial of labor protections, and environmental racism, renders Black women, queer, and trans people more vulnerable to interpersonal and community violence, as well as to the violence inherent in policing, criminalization, and punishment. It points us definitively toward what must be done: as Black feminist scholar Saidiya Hartman puts it, "Incredible vulnerability to violence and to abuse [that] is so definitive of the lives of Black femmes . . . requires abolition, the abolition of the carceral world, the abolition of capitalism. What is required is a remaking of the social order, and nothing short of that is going to make a difference."[18]

Abolition feminism also offers a vision of a world free from all of these forms of violence. As Black feminist abolitionists, we reject the violence of the carceral state in service of racial capitalism; instead, we practice and fight for conditions that will create safer communities and bring us closer to liberation. We understand that carcerality does not attend to the root causes of violence or other social problems. Rather, it simply disposes of individuals who represent these "problems" while leaving underlying conditions of violence untouched. Abolition feminism, in contrast, advances a radical approach to violence—"getting down to and understanding the root cause,"[19] as Ella Baker urges us to—by creating new forms of governance and structures based on support, accountability, and care rather than violence, domination, and control, new economies based on abundance, and prioritizing meeting the needs of all rather than on capitalist logics of scarcity, competition, individualism, profit-making, extraction, and exploitation. Abolition feminism acknowledges that no future will be completely free of harm. However, it does hold that it is possible to build systems and structures that address harm in a manner that facilitates healing and transformation rather than continuing cycles of harm and punishment.

"Black women are inherently valuable"
—Combahee River Collective Statement[20]

Black feminism is an ideology rooted in the simple understanding that Black women are inherently valuable beyond what we produce and reproduce, and that all of us are entitled to dignity, safety, connection, and freedom. It is this commitment to our own and each other's inherent value that leads us to fight for a world in which *all* Black women, queer, and trans people—and by extension all people, and the planet—are made more safe from all forms of violence and policing. Black feminist scholar Hortense Spillers declares that:

> Black feminism, as a repertoire of concepts, practices, and alignments, is progressive in outlook and dedicated to the view that sustainable life systems must be available to everyone; it also stands up for the survival of this planet. . . . If we're going to reach a different place . . . then Black feminist ideas and ideals might be one of the lights leading us there.[21]

Importantly, Black feminism holds that Black women *everywhere* are inherently valuable. It is therefore by necessity a transnational politic keenly attentive to the violence of empire across the globe. From where we sit as two Black women currently living in the United States, we resonate deeply with June Jordan's trenchant question in a January 1984 *Essence* article about the U.S.-backed war against Nicaraguan Sandinistas: "How many of these gentle people have I helped kill just by paying my taxes?"[22] Audre Lorde similarly reminds us, speaking of the suppression of the revolution in Grenada by U.S. invasion in 1981, that our failure to attend to the violences of U.S. imperialism contributes to our sisters' (and siblings') deaths.[23] As people with family and comrades across the world, we want an end to U.S. war-making at home and abroad. While a focus on the U.S. role as global police is beyond the scope of this book, we encourage others to read and engage with the work of scholars and organizers who speak to this.[24]

Black feminism also demands that we pay attention to global implications of our work: our struggle for abolition cannot stop at U.S. borders. As Harsha Walia and Grace Lee Boggs remind us, our efforts to rebuild a world anew in the Global North must attend to the ways in our societies and economies are premised on extraction, destruction, and abandonment of the Global South.[25] It also requires humility, and attention to history. While significant in the U.S. context, the 2020 Uprisings were far from the largest movement in history—statements to that effect erase historic and present-day Black, Indigenous, and people of color–led mass movements around the world.[26] What happens in the U.S. is also not what drives worldwide movements against racial oppression—people are responding to anti-Blackness, racial capitalism, settler colonialism, and imperialism as they manifest where they are.[27] Given the cultural dominance of the U.S. in the world, uprisings against police violence here can breathe air into and bring attention to ongoing and longstanding fights against police violence elsewhere, creating opportunities for global resonance and solidarities. And, it is the responsibility of people living in the U.S. to refrain from claiming those struggles as ours, to learn more about what is driving them, and move beyond statements to authentic solidarity in action.

Moving beyond U.S. exceptionalism also requires us to recognize that our struggles here are deeply shaped and informed by struggles elsewhere—for us, defund demands are rooted in anti-apartheid struggles and divestment campaigns aimed at starving white supremacist carceral states, in boycott, divest, sanctions movements aimed at ending the violent occupation of Palestine, and in anti-colonial movements around the world. Our path forward must be informed by the lessons these struggles offer us about what forms and practices of struggle and governance best create the conditions for liberation.

"Her voice must be heard" —*Anna Julia Cooper*

It is no accident that movements for police and PIC abolition are largely led by Black women, queer, and trans people. Black feminism theorizes and acts from our experiences of violence and unsafety in all aspects of the carceral state. As outlined above and in the "Cops Don't Stop Violence" and "We Are Survivors" chapters, Black women, queer, and trans people's experiences of policing and unsafety in the U.S. point us toward the need for something new. That is why we describe movements to defund and abolish police as survivor-led strategies to create greater safety for all.[28] Our voices must be heard.

Black feminism is also rooted in the resistance to the stories we are told—about ourselves, about each other, about safety. Black feminism requires us to uproot the stories that define, police, erase, suppress, cage, control, and obliterate us in service of existing systems of power. We know these stories all too well—the historical and present-day narratives that criminalize Black women, queer, and trans people, including the survivors who sometimes defend themselves when no one else will because they are framed as having "no selves to defend";[29] the stories that portray Black women as such an inherent threat that we are the group most likely to be killed by police when unarmed; the stories that tell us Black girls as young as five are grown enough to be handcuffed in schools; the stories that sexualize Black women and make us prime targets for predation and denial of protection.[30] Stories that frame Black women as drug users, as couriers, as sex workers, as bad mothers.[31] Stories that tell us that safety is not for us, or can only come from police, at the cost of carceral violence targeting us, our children and families, and communities. Stories that tell us that we must sacrifice group liberation for individual access to safety. These are stories that we are interrupting, disrupting, and retelling through Black feminist abolitionist organizing.

"Turn the light of truth upon them"
—Ida B. Wells-Barnett

Throughout *No More Police*, we attempt to turn the light of truth onto the fact that surveillance, policing, and punishment do not produce safety. In fact, they are obstacles to safety. We have turned a spotlight on the illusions of reform; the dangers of replacing cops with the "soft police"; and the ways in which policing infects our language, our thinking, and our imaginations.

Policing has become a story told and retold over generations, but it wasn't always so. There was a time when the police had yet to be invented. Abolitionist organizers must tell a different story, one that unseats the equation of policing and safety, that helps people unlearn the "common sense" of police and punishment in service of neoliberalism and racial capitalism. As Hartman tells us, "So much of the work of oppression is about policing the imagination."[32] With this in mind, we have also highlighted the imaginaries, frameworks, and principles that can guide us as we chart a path forward, holding up examples of the bold experiments that reveal the ways that people are already practicing abolition and creating safer communities every day. We are writing the stories that enable us to break through the limits on our imaginations, to dream and practice a world in which we are all safer, to make meaning of our lives on our own terms. We are telling new stories about ourselves and about the future we are building.

As organizers, our work is to do at least three things: (1) help people understand the current reality; (2) collectively imagine a future vision of what can be; and (3) diligently labor toward that future. These battles are not only waged in social and political arenas; they are cultural, emotional, and spiritual. As Black feminist abolitionists, we can follow in the tradition of Ida B. Wells-Barnett by documenting and demonstrating the truth: Police do not produce safety because that is not their purpose. The police tell stories that legitimize their existence and validate the political agendas of the powerful; that shape and inform how we see the world through "copaganda," "copspeak," "cop knowledge," and conceptions of safety that posit the carceral state as its only possible source.

A main part of our work, then, is to tell a different story of police and policing, one that disrupts the false narrative of police as benevolent, if occasionally violent, civil servants whose overarching goal is to "serve and protect." This story would lead us to believe that they just need (a seemingly endless) infusion of trust, training, reforms, and resources to figure out how to "do better." By refusing the story of "re-form," and outlining transformational changes as steps toward abolition, we are disputing the story that prisons and policing are inevitable responses to harm. By telling the story that police don't always come in cops' clothing, we are shining a light on the pitfall of replacing one form of policing with another. By showing how we are already creating greater safety without police, we are writing the stories that enable us to break through the limits police stories place on our imaginations, and dream and practice different stories that lead to a world in which we are all safer.

Our abolitionist story is one of collective power rather than coercive power. We want a world where we exercise power together, with each other. We are declaring what must be: a world of abundance and care, without domination and control. We are still writing the stories of what forms our collective power will take, exploring what forms of governance, what economic systems will best hold these abolitionist dreams. Through experimentation, we are discerning what is possible and learning lessons from our failures that will point our compass toward the horizon of abolition.

"We can impose beauty on our future"
—Lorraine Hansberry

Black feminism claims consciousness as a sphere of freedom. Oppression puts a ceiling on our imaginations, rendering many of us unable to think outside of our current structures. As a result, when we talk about abolition, people envision a society that appears exactly like our current one, just without prisons and police—then they understandably freak out. Or, they envision new ways of responding to conflict, harm, and need that resemble policing and punishment in everything but name. Black feminism invites us to liberate our imaginations so that we can conceive of new ways of understanding and creating safety and collective well-being, and to believe that it is possible to make them real through everyday actions toward a world based on "mutual accountability and passionate reciprocity."

"Love is lifeforce"
—June Jordan

Radical care[33] is central to Black feminism. As Black feminist scholar Hortense Spillers put it, "What black feminisms might teach the current social order begins with concernful care for other human beings."[34] Black feminism offers visions of collective practices based in an ethics of care and personal accountability. These practices are rooted in what we have always done: nurtured and cared for ourselves, each other, and our communities, in the interests of survival and liberation. We want to build a future based on non-coercive and consensual care, not punishment. For us, care isn't a feeling; it's an action. Care is not a one-way street; it is an ethic of mutual responsibility. Care is what drives our efforts to fight the violence of the state, secure the resources we need, and build the world we want through mutual aid and transformative justice.

"Despair is a tool of your enemies"
—Audre Lorde

As we completed the manuscript for *No More Police*, organizers were facing a dispiriting moment: mainstream media declaring the death of defund movements, Democratic party repudiation, defeats at the polls, and despair as the pendulum swung away from the heady sense of possibility and a portal into a new world that characterized the 2020 Uprisings. Many organizers, activists, and philanthropists politicized to abolition in the summer of 2020 were demoralized by the swiftness and viciousness of the backlash at all levels—stories of mounting violence and increased homicides; lawsuits by police fraternal associations; felony charges against protesters; threats of recall campaigns and criminal charges for local lawmakers who voted to make modest cuts to police department budgets; state legislation penalizing municipalities that dared to reduce police budgets; ballot initiatives to lock cities into increased numbers of cops; and the fact that huge chunks of federal pandemic relief funding were funneled into police pockets instead of being deployed to ensure our communities' safety and survival now and in the future.

But we must ground ourselves in the fact that abolition is a long game, a marathon. We need to embrace what Angela Y. Davis describes as "abolition feminist temporalities," which recognize that the work we are doing now emerges from work done over centuries, and that the work we do now shapes the future.[35] Che Gossett elaborates on this perspective, writing, "Abolition is untimely, casting off the illusion of capitalist and colonial time as a measure of civilizationist progress. . . . Abolition—as Audre Lorde [describes] . . . revolution . . . is 'not a one-time event' but rather, as Angela Davis contends, 'a constant struggle.'"[36] Black feminists have taught us that it's essential to our survival to hope, to dream, and to continue to act, even in the face of what feel like conditions of impossibility—whether we are in the hold, ripped away from loved ones by slave ships, borders, or cells, or struggling to make a way out of no way. We are often reminded that when Harriet Tubman lived and struggled, dehumanization and enslavement of Black people in the U.S. had been a matter of course for *three centuries*, and the legal end of slavery was still decades away. Similarly, Davis says no one could have predicted in the 1970s when she began abolitionist work that abolition would be part of mainstream conversations in her lifetime.[37] She urges us to continue to meet the backlash by continuing to rehearse toward the world we want.[38] As New York City–based healer Tiffany Lenoi puts it, we can change the present and live the future now.[39]

Many years ago, Mariame heard a nun say, "*Hope is a discipline.*" It's a phrase she has repeated ever since. In August 2021, Mariame closed out Black Feminist Future's Jubilee by reminding all of us that:

> [t]he key to lifelong activism and organizing is to dedicate oneself daily to hope. Hope is a discipline. Hope can be the basis for action. It offers up the foundation for the struggle for liberation. Another world is in fact possible. As we organize, we are always organizing toward a future we will be unlikely to see. It is a future built on the hopes and sacrifices of our ancestors, on whose labor and love we stand. Positive change is difficult. Uprooting oppression is the work of many lifetimes. There are setbacks mixed with some terrific highs. What is most important though, is that we act.
>
> . . .
>
> To transform the conditions of our oppression we can only do what we can today, where we are, in the best way that we know how, in our capacity. As a prison industrial complex abolitionist, I am trying to prefigure the world in which I want to live. I practice abolition every day toward that end. This involves not only organizing for the end of death-dealing and death-making institutions, but the creation of life-giving and affirming ones. As there is no blueprint for abolition, we must spend time imagining, strategizing, and practicing other futures.[40]

"The only way to do it, is to do it"
—Toni Cade Bambara

Black feminism is a not just an ideology; it is a practice of self-definition, self-determination, self-love, and collective survival. We have learned from Black feminists like Toni Cade Bambara that it is essential to practice liberation now in order to pave the way for future liberation. In Cleveland, this is exactly what we did. We were practicing liberation now. Together, we co-created an "elsewhere, within here," [41] a term coined by artist and writer Trinh T. Minh-ha, signifying the feeling of dislocation and displacement in a place that's supposed to be home. We are repurposing the phrase to mean something different: a space of Black fugitivity and prefiguration of abolitionist futures, a practice space for experimentation and the creation of new social relations within oppressive systems and societies. Building the new within the old.

Not only *can* we live in this future; we *must* live in it. Audre Lorde writes: "There is a world in which we all wish to live. That world is not attained lightly. We call it future. If as Black feminists, we do not start talking, thinking, feeling ourselves for its shape, we condemn ourselves and our children to a repetition of corruption and error." [42] Black feminism offers a template for all of our liberations. Let's continue on the path of prefiguring the world in which we want to live—one that invites accountability over punishment, abundance over scarcity, interdependence over selfishness, care over violence, and love over fear.

"I dare myself to dream"
—Joseph Beam

To be a Black feminist is to stay open to possibility. It can be frightening to publicly share our dreams and visions. We are often accused of naïveté or of being unrealistic—or worse, of being enablers of and apologists for violence we or our loved ones have often experienced. But it is our belief that it is the current state of affairs that is unrealistic—and immoral. It is our belief that it is naïve to believe that we can achieve safer, more just communities by continuing to attempt to re-form policing and punishment. While reform requires us to affirm the current system and surrender our imagination to the carceral state, abolition encourages dreaming. It challenges us to use our best thinking to build a better society.[43]

Building new worlds requires creativity and radical imagination. As Black feminist poet, artist, and scholar Eve Ewing teaches us, we must do "the expansive imaginative work of trying to conceive something else."[44] When we embrace abolition, we acknowledge that we want something radically different. We imagine a future that doesn't include death-making institutions. We actively practice addressing harms in ways that facilitate a new vision. We engage in mutual aid. We build. We determine our future together. Black feminism is trans-movement, transnational, transformational.

Art by Amir Khadar.

As Audre Lorde has taught us: we fight where we are currently standing. This book is about unmaking and remaking the current world. Our worldmaking is grounded in Black feminist abolitionist visions and politics. We are seeking a wholesale transformation of the conditions that produce violence. There are no magic or simple solutions; there's only consistent and difficult collective work.

We want a revolution.

"The struggle is eternal, the tribe increases, somebody carries on"
—Ella Baker

If you're still not convinced, we hope that you are at least left with even more questions than when you began. We hope that you've been challenged and unsettled.

If you are persuaded by the case we make in *No More Police*, we hope that you choose to be the somebody who carries on. These are the days to commit to struggle and fight like hell. Keguro Macharia teaches us that at its core, feminism fights oppression and pursues freedom. He often asks on Twitter, "How will you practice freedom today?"[45]

And so we are asking you: *How will you practice Black feminist abolitionist freedom dreams today?*

Acknowledgments

This book draws on the wisdom of organizers too many to name; we risk accidentally leaving some out if we were to even try. We are both deeply indebted to the Black feminist and Black liberation, anti-apartheid, anti-violence, reproductive, economic, and environmental justice movements that raised us and that we remain part of, and to the vision, labor, analytical frameworks, and political homes created by Critical Resistance and INCITE! Feminists of Color Against Violence. We have been and continue to be deeply shaped by visionaries who have served as beloved teachers and touchstones, including Angela Y. Davis, Grace Lee Boggs, Barbara Ransby, Beth Richie, Barbara Smith, and Ruth Wilson Gilmore.

We are profoundly grateful for the communities of organizers we have been part of during and since the 2020 Uprisings, including those who are part of the Cities Initiative, the Community Resource Hub Invest/Divest Learning Communities and Defund Fellowship, the Building Beyond Policing network, the In Our Names Network, the Beyond Do No Harm Coalition, and the informal formations of friends, comrades, and colleagues who came together to support Black Visions and Reclaim the Block in Minneapolis, to wrestle with questions relating to the role of the state and community control in abolitionist futures, and to expand a national infrastructure of transformative justice practitioners.

We deeply appreciate all who gave so generously of their time and energy to review drafts of *No More Police* and to offer rich, thoughtful, and incisive feedback, edits, and suggestions, all of which greatly contributed to and improved the final result, including zakia henderson-brown and Diane Wachtell of The New Press, Onnesha Roychoudhuri, whose skillful developmental and copy editing were a godsend, Amna Akbar, William C. Anderson, Simon Balto, Klee Benally, Rachel Caïdor, Angélica Cházaro, Erin Miles Cloud, Woods Ervin, Kelly Gillespie, Craig Gilmore, Rachel Herzing, David Kaib, Jared Knowles, Victoria Law, Page May, Robyn Maynard, Brendan McQuade, Erica Meiners, Joey Mogul, Kandace Montgomery, Naomi Murakawa, Leigh-Ann Naidoo, Sheila Nezhad, Miski Noor, Tamara Nopper, Cameron Rasmussen, Beth Richie, Lisa Sangoi, Maya Schenwar, Claire Schwartz, Danielle Sered, Micol Siegel, Jacqui Shine, Dean Spade, David Stein, Jackie Wang, and Wesley Ware. The "Cops Don't Stop Violence" chapter is based in part on the report of the same name co-authored by Jared Knowles and Andrea, published by the Community Resource Hub and Interrupting Criminalization in 2021. We are deeply grateful for Brendan McQuade's substantial contributions to the "No Soft Police" chapter. The structure and content of "Black Feminist Musings" was inspired by the Black Feminist Breathing Chorus and cards created by Alexis Pauline Gumbs and Sangodare Akinwole Wallace as part of Mobile Homecoming—learn more at mobilehomecoming.org.

There are no words that can fully encapsulate our gratitude and appreciation to Naimah Thomas, whose gorgeous art graces the cover of *No More Police*—you can support her work at naimahthomasart.com.

Our sincere appreciation to Emily Albarillo, Associate Managing Editor at The New Press, who moved heaven and earth to meet our publication deadline amidst constantly changing conditions, Maury Botton, Senior Managing Editor at The New Press, for working with us to create a cover we love, and Ishan Desai Geller, Assistant Editor at The New Press, and to Jen Ash, Levi Craske, Emi Kane, and Rachael Zafer for their invaluable assistance with endnotes.

Our deepest gratitude to our beloved friends and co-strugglers at Interrupting Criminalization, including Creative Director Eva Nagao, who makes all things possible with ease, joy, and beauty, Administrative Coordinator Erin Glasco, Transformative Justice Fellow Shira Hassan, Beyond Do No Harm Fellow Maria Thomas, and Social Media Coordinator Tiffany Wang. Because we are deeply engaged in this work as we write about it, we are infinitely grateful to all of our comrades and colleagues who extended us endless grace and in many cases took on more labor to enable us to complete this manuscript in between our organizing commitments, including Wes Ware, Jared Knowles, Hiram Rivera, Lauren Williams-Batiste, and Cynthia Conti-Cook. We could not have completed this work without the love, care, and support of our families, friends, and communities (and, of course, the Abolitionist Cat, despite Mariame's antipathy toward her)—again, our beloveds are too numerous to name but appreciated beyond words.

We are each profoundly grateful to the other for the incredibly generative, inspiring, easeful, and collaborative process of writing this book, and for the journeys we have shared over the past two decades.

Last, but certainly not least, we are thankful for all of the young people in our lives who bring us endless joy, tell us jokes and lift our spirits with peals of laughter, offer insights only children can share, serve as readers or quietly work on their own books under our desks as we write, keep us current, and inspire us to fight like hell for the world and police-free future they deserve.

Resources

In addition to the books, articles, reports, and toolkits cited throughout *No More Police*, you can find information about movements to defund and abolish policing and build safer communities at:

- abolitionanddisabilityjustice.com
- abolishdatacrim.org
- defundpolice.org
- creative-interventions.org
- criticalresistance.org/abolish-policing
- dontcallthepolice.com
- mijente.net/freeourfuture
- millionexperiments.com
- movementforfamilypower.org
- policefreeschools.org
- project-nia.org
- transformharm.org

What follows is a non-exhaustive list of resources we and others have created to support organizers working to divest from policing and invest in community safety.

Abolition Imagination Cards, Interrupting Criminalization (2021)
interruptingcriminalization.com/imagination

Abolish Policing, Critical Resistance
criticalresistance.org/abolish-policing

Abortion Criminalization Is Part of the Larger Struggle Against
    Policing and Criminalization, Interrupting Criminalization
    (2021)
interruptingcriminalization.com/decriminalize-abortion

Accountable Communities Videos, Project NIA & BCRW
    (2019–2020)
accountablecommunities.org

Against Punishment Curriculum, Project NIA (2021)
issuu.com/projectnia/docs/against_punishment_curriculum_final

Against Punishment: Incarcerated Comrades Edition, Project NIA
    (2021)
bit.ly/AgainstPunishZine
Supplemental materials: bit.ly/AGPsupplemental

Building the World We Want: A Roadmap to Police-Free Futures
    in Canada (2021), Robyn Maynard, ed.
bit.ly/BWWWCanada

Cops Don't Stop Violence: Combatting Narratives Used to Defend
    Police Instead of Defunding Them, Community Resource Hub
    and Interrupting Criminalization (2021)
interruptingcriminalization.com/cops-dont-stop-violence

Coronavirus Solidarity Poster and Postcard Project, Interrupting
    Criminalization (2020)
interruptingcriminalization.com/postcards

Cosmic Possibilities: An Intergalactic Youth Guide to Abolition,
  Abolitionist Youth Organizing Institute (2021)
bit.ly/CosmicPoss2021

Defund CPD Community Conversation Toolkit (2020)
bit.ly/DefundCPDConversation

Defund CPD Research and Policy Toolkit (2020)
defundpolice.org/wp-content/uploads/2021/03/Defund-CPD
  -Research-Policy-Toolkit.pdf

Defund the Police (video), Project NIA (2021)
bit.ly/DefundVideo
Discussion guide: https://bit.ly/DefundVideoDiscussion

Defund Police, Invest in Community Care: A Guide to Alternative
  Mental Health Crisis Responses, Interrupting Criminalization
  (2021)
interruptingcriminalization.com/non-police-crisis-response-guide
Checklist for Assessing Mental Health Crisis Response Models:
bit.ly/MHCrisisResponseChecklist

Defund Police, Rebuild Our Communities, Dream Defenders
  (2020)
bit.ly/DDDefund

The Demand Is Still #DefundPolice #FundthePeople
  #DefendBlackLives, Interrupting Criminalization (2021)
bit.ly/DefundPoliceUpdate

Disarm, Defund, Dismantle: Police Abolition in Canada, Shiri Pasternak, Kevin Walby and Abby Stadnyk, eds. (Toronto: Between
  the Lines, 2022).

Divesting from Pandemic Policing and Investing in a Just Recovery, Community Resource Hub (2021)
communityresourcehub.org/wp-content/uploads/2021/05
/Unmasked_Update.pdf

Ensuring Federal Stimulus Funds Support Communities, Not Cops, Community Resource Hub (2021)
defundpolice.org/wp-content/uploads/2021/04
/0407_CARES_ARPA_B.pdf

Expanding Our Frame, Deepening Our Demands for Safety and Healing for Black Survivors of Sexual Violence, National Black Women's Justice Institute (2019)
bit.ly/ExpandingOurFrame

In Our Names Network
inournamesnetwork.com

Interrupting Criminalization
interruptingcriminalization.com

Invisible No More Study and Discussion Guide
invisiblenomorebook.com/study-guide

Minneapolis Without Policing, Black Visions (2021)
www.blackvisionsmn.org/mnwithoutpolicing

Navigating DOJ Consent Decrees, Community Resource Hub (2021)
bit.ly/NoMoreConsentDecrees

Navigating Public Safety Task Forces: A Guide from the Ground, Interrupting Criminalization (2021)
interruptingcriminalization.com/task-forces

No Cop Academy Organizing Toolkit (2021)
nocopacademy.com/Toolkit

Our Communities, Our Solutions: An Organizer's Toolkit for
  Developing Campaigns to Abolish Policing, Critical Resistance
  (2020)
bit.ly/CRAbolitionToolkit

Police Abolition 101, Project Nia (2021)
bit.ly/PoliceAbolish2021
Spanish: https://bit.ly/LaAbolicionPolicia

Police Responses to Domestic Violence, Interrupting Criminalization (2020)
bit.ly/PoliceResponsesDV

Power & Control Wheel by Monica Cosby (designed by Sarah Ross)
bit.ly/PowerControlMonica

Practical Abolition video series, Amistad Law Project (2021)
bit.ly/PracticalAbolitionVideos

Preserving Punishment Power: A Grassroots Abolitionist Assessment of New York Reforms (2020)
survivedandpunishedny.org/wp-content/uploads/2020/04/SP
  -Preserving-Punishment-Power-report.pdf

Problems with Community Control of Police and Proposals for
  Alternatives, Beth Richie, Dylan Rodriguez, Mariame Kaba,
  Melissa Burch, Rachel Herzing, and Shana Agid
defundpolice.org/wp-content/uploads/2021/03
  /Problems_w_CRBs_and_Proposals_for_Alternatives-1.pdf

Reformist Reforms vs. Abolitionist Steps in Policing, Critical Resistance

criticalresistance.org/wp-content/uploads/2020/08
 /CR_NoCops_reform_vs_abolition_REV2020.pdf

Reparations for Survivors of Police Violence: Community Conversation Toolkit, Community Resource Hub, Chicago Torture Justice Center, Movement for Black Lives (2021)
bit.ly/REPJuneConversationTK

Resisting Criminalization of Reproductive Autonomy: Policy Do's and Don'ts, Interrupting Criminalization and Center for Advancing Innovative Policy (2019)
interruptingcriminalization.com/resisting-crim

A Revenue Generation Playbook: How to Fully Fund Our Communities, Action Center on Race and the Economy and Community Resource Hub (2021)
bit.ly/RGPlaybook

6Ds Until She's Free, Interrupting Criminalization (2020)
bit.ly/6DsVideo

Shrouded in Silence: What We Know About Police Sexual Violence and What We Can Do About It and Breaking the Silence: Supporting Survivors of Police Sexual Violence—a Curriculum for Sexual Assault Service Providers, Interrupting Criminalization (2021)
interruptingcriminalization.com/breaking-the-silence

Skills, Relationships, Structures Worksheet, Project NIA (2021)
bit.ly/SkillsRelationshipsStructures

Solutions to Violence: Creating Safety Without Prisons or Policing, Common Justice (2021)
commonjustice.org/solutions_to_violence_report

Survived and Punished, Defending Self Defense
survivedandpunished.org/wp-content/uploads/2022/03/DSD
-Report-Mar-21-final.pdf

Tool for Organizers: Mapping the PIC (2022)
bit.ly/MappingThePIC

Unmasked: Impacts of Pandemic Policing, COVID19 Policing
Project, Community Resource Hub (2020)
communityresourcehub.org/wp-content/uploads/2020/12
/Unmasked.pdf

Unraveling Criminalizing Webs, Building Police Free Futures,
Scholar and Feminist Online Special Issue (2019)
sfonline.barnard.edu/unraveling-criminalizing-webs-building
-police-free-futures

We Do This 'Til We Free Us Discussion Guide (2021)
https://bit.ly/WeDoThisFreeUs

What About the Rapists? An Abolitionist FAQ 'Zine, Interrupting
Criminalization (2021)
interruptingcriminalization.com/what-about-the-rapists

What Is Driving the Criminalization of Women and LGBTQ
People? Interrupting Criminalization (2019)
bit.ly/2019ICCrimReport

What's Next: Safer and More Just Communities Without Policing,
Interrupting Criminalization (2020)
interruptingcriminalization.com/whats-next
PDF: bit.ly/WhatsNextIC3

Notes

Foreword

1. Based on Kandace Montgomery and Miski Noor, "We Understand That Abolition Is the Long Game. We're in It for as Long as It Takes," *In These Times*, July 25, 2021, inthesetimes.com/article/minneapolis-defund-police-black-visions-george-floyd and Solana Rice, Miski Noor, and Kandace Montgomery, "The Uprisings: Yesterday, Today, Tomorrow," *The Forge*, May 20, 2021, forgeorganizing.org/article/uprisings-yesterday-today-tomorrow.

Introduction

1. "Update: Unarmed Teen Michael Brown Killed by Ferguson Police," *St. Louis American*, August 10, 2014, www.stlamerican.com/news/local_news/update-unarmed-teen-michael-brown-killed-by-ferguson-police/article_1160a5ba-2050-11e4-aa5c-001a4bcf887a.html.

2. #SayHerName, African American Policy Forum, www.aapf.org/sayhername. *Say Her Name: Resisting Police Brutality Against Black Women*, co-authored by Andrea J. Ritchie and released in May and July 2015, brought further attention to Black women's, girls', and trans people's experiences of policing. The report built on decades of research, analysis, and organizing by Black women and queer and trans people, as documented in *Invisible No More: Police Violence Against Black Women and Women of Color* (Boston: Beacon Press, 2017).

3. GBD 2019 Police Violence US Subnational Collaborators, "Fatal Police Violence by Race and State in the USA, 1980–2019: A Network Meta-Regression," *The Lancet*, thelancet.com/action/showPdf?pii=S0140-6736%2821%2901609-3. *See also* Mike Ludwig, "New Study Shows More Than Half of Police Killings Have Gone Uncounted Since 1980," *Truthout*, October 5, 2021, truthout.org/articles/new-study-shows-more

-than-half-of-police-killings-have-gone-uncounted-since-1980; Tim Arango and Shaila Dewan, "More Than Half of Police Killings Are Mislabeled, New Study Says," *New York Times*, September 30, 2021; Odis Johnson Jr., Keon Gilbert, Habiba Ibrahim, "Race, Gender, and the Contexts of Unarmed Fatal Interactions with Police" (2018), cpb-us-w2 .wpmucdn.com/sites.wustl.edu/dist/b/1205/files/2018/02/Race-Gender-and-Unarmed -1y9md6e.pdf.

4. The Death in Custody Reporting Act was first passed in 2000 and was expanded to require law enforcement agencies to report people killed in the process of arrest in 2014. The federal government's failure to implement the requirements of the act has drawn widespread criticism. *Death in Custody Reporting Act Factsheet*, Bureau of Justice Assistance, bja.ojp.gov/sites/g/files/xyckuh186/files/media/document/DCRA-Factsheet .pdf. *See also* "Jerrold Nadler and Karen Bass to Inspector General Michael Horowitz," January 27, 2020, judiciary.house.gov/uploadedfiles/2020-01-27_letter_to_horowitz -_dcra_failure_to_report_letter_with_rep._bass.pdf; Kenny Lo, "How to Address Concerns About Data on Deaths in Custody," Center for American Progress, May 24, 2021, americanprogress.org/issues/criminal-justice/reports/2021/05/24/499838/address -concerns-data-deaths-custody.

5. Marisa Iati, Steven Rich, and Jennifer Jenkins, "Fatal Police Shootings in 2021 Set Record Since the Post Began Tracking, Despite Public Outcry," *Washington Post*, February 9, 2022. *See also 2021 Police Violence Report*, policeviolencereport.org /policeviolencereport2021.pdf?0.

6. GBD 2019 Police Violence US Subnational Collaborators, "Fatal Police Violence by Race and State in the USA, 1980–2019: A Network Meta-Regression." *See also* Ludwig, "New Study Shows More Than Half of Police Killings Have Gone Uncounted Since 1980"; Arango and Dewan, "More Than Half of Police Killings Are Mislabeled, New Study Says." For example, a *New York Times* article pointed out that George Floyd's death was almost attributed to drug use and underlying medical conditions by both police and the county medical examiner. If it weren't for eyewitness Darnella Frazier's video of his murder, that is likely the story the public would have been told. "How George Floyd Died, and What Happened Next," *New York Times*, November 1, 2021.

7. Matthew Spina, "When a Protector Becomes a Predator," *Buffalo News*, November 22, 2015, s3.amazonaws.com/bncore/projects/abusing-the-law/index.html. *See also* Andrea J. Ritchie, *Shrouded in Silence*, Interrupting Criminalization (2021), bit.ly/PSV-Curriculum; Andrea J. Ritchie, *Invisible No More* (Boston: Beacon Press, 2017).

8. Marisa Iati, Stephen Rich, and Jennifer Jenkins, "Fatal Police Shootings in 2021 Set Record Since The Post Began Tracking, Despite Public Outcry," *Washington Post*, February 9, 2022; John Eligon and Shawn Hubler, "Throughout Trial over George Floyd's Death, Killings by Police Mount," *New York Times*, April 17, 2021.

9. World Health Organization Coronavirus Dashboard, covid19.who.int; Erin K. Stokes, Laura D. Zambrano, Kayla N. Anderson, et al., "Coronavirus Disease 2019 Case Surveillance—United States, January 22–May 30, 2020," *Morbidity and Mortality Weekly Report (MMWR)* 2020; 69:759–765, cdc.gov/mmwr/volumes/69/wr/mm6924e2 .htm.

10. Robyn Maynard and Andrea J. Ritchie, "Black Communities Need Support, Not a Coronavirus Police State," *Vice*, April 9, 2020; *see also* Marc Lamont Hill, *We Still Here: Pandemic, Policing, Protest and Possibility* (Chicago: Haymarket Books, 2020).

11. Steven W. Thrasher, *The Viral Underclass: The Human Toll When Inequity and*

Disease Collide (New York: Celadon Books, 2022); Sebastian D. Romano, Anna J. Blackstock, Ethel V. Taylor, et al., "Trends in Racial and Ethnic Disparities in COVID-19 Hospitalizations, by Region—United States, March–December 2020," *Morbidity and Mortality Weekly Report (MMWR)* 2021;70:560–565, dx.doi.org/10.15585/mmwr .mm7015e2external icon; Jessica Arrazola, Mathew M. Masiello, Sujata Joshi, et al., "COVID-19 Mortality Among American Indian and Alaska Native Persons—14 States, January–June 2020," *Morbidity and Mortality Weekly Report (MMWR)* 2020;69:1853–1856, dx.doi.org/10.15585/mmwr.mm6949a3external icon.

12. Pascal Emmer, et al., "Unmasked: Acts of Pandemic Policing," October 2020, communityresourcehub.org/wp-content/uploads/2020/12/Unmasked.pdf. *See also* Maynard and Ritchie, "Black Communities Need Support, Not a Coronavirus Police State."

13. Naomi Murakawa, "Three Traps of Police Reform," in *Abolition for the People*, Colin Kaepernick, ed. (Kaepernick Publishing, 2021).

14. Larry Buchanan, Quoctrung Bui, and Jugal K. Patel, "Black Lives Matter May Be the Largest Movement in U.S. History," *New York Times*, July 3, 2020.

15. Hannah Jones, "Minneapolis Police Department Budget Cut by $1M to Fund Public Safety Programs Instead," City Pages, December 4, 2018, web.archive.org/web /20200129215226/http://www.citypages.com/news/minneapolis-police-department -budget-cut-by-1m-to-fund-public-safety-programs-instead/501824851.

16. *Enough Is Enough: A 150-Year Performance Review of the Minneapolis Police Department*, MPD150, 2017, mpd150.com/report.

17. "About Black Visions," blackvisionsmn.org/about.

18. "Reclaim the Block," reclaimtheblock.org.

19. Valerie Strauss, "Minneapolis Board of Education Votes to Kick Police Out of Public Schools over George Floyd's Death," *Washington Post*, June 3, 2020.

20. The National Campaign for Police Free Schools, policefreeschools.org.

21. Alicia Lee, "Minneapolis Schools and Parks Cut Ties with Police over George Floyd's Death," CNN, June 4, 2020.

22. Jenna Wortham, "How a New Wave of Black Activists Changed the Conversation," *New York Times*, August 25, 2020.

23. The banner, visible at img.apmcdn.org/5e9be4d516fe415a5002a5b3f110e34f2 adc6719/square/f36517-20200607-mpd01.jpg, read:

1. Decades of police reform efforts have proved that the Minneapolis Police Department cannot be reformed, and MPD will never be accountable for its actions.

2. We are here today to begin the process of ending the Minneapolis Police Department and creating a new transformative model for cultivating safety in our city.

3. We recognize that we don't have all the answers about what a police-free future looks like, but our community does. We're committing to engaging with every willing community member in the City of Minneapolis over the next year to identify what safety looks like for everyone.

4. We'll be taking intermediate steps towards ending the MPD through the budget process and other policy and budget decisions over the coming weeks and months.

24. Wortham, "How a New Wave of Black Activists Changed the Conversation."

25. Wortham, "How a New Wave of Black Activists Changed the Conversation."

26. The 1961 charter amendment was introduced after a measure proposed the previous year threatened cops' independent revenue streams. Supported by the police association, it "would ensure the city had 1.7 officers per 1,000 residents, and that the police department was entitled to $3 annually for every $1,000 of taxable property within the city. This would not only add 150 dues-paying officers to the city (the city was authorized for 672 officers at the time (*Star Tribune*, May 22, 1961), but also secure police funding by placing it into the charter itself. Significant reductions in funding would need to be brought to voters in the form of a charter change." *See also* Anton Schieffer, "A Brief History of Police Politics in the Minneapolis City Charter (1959–1961)," *Wedge Times-Picayune*, July 6, 2020, wedgelive.com/a-brief-history-of-police-politics-in-the-minneapolis-city-charter-1959-1961.

Opponents expressed concerns about the amendment locking the city into an inflexible department size, and whether its passage represented a move toward a "police state." Cops openly and successfully campaigned in favor of their position on the charter change, fearmongering and citing dire staffing shortages, as they would five decades later against efforts to repeal it. Ironically, a campaign to increase funding for libraries through a charter amendment the same year failed. After successfully passing the minimum personnel and funding requirement in 1961, police sought another charter amendment to increase their rate of pay and tie it to wages in the building trades, which was defeated. Meanwhile, "crime continued to rise" in the years following the amendment's passage. *See also* Jason Samuels, "Why 1961 Minneapolis Approved a Police Staffing Minimum in the City Charter That We're Voting in 2021 Whether to Repeal," Medium, October 14, 2021, medium.com/@jasonsamuels/minneapolis-1961-b1c3625c1eca. In 1994, at the height of "tough on crime" rhetoric, the city of San Francisco passed a similar charter amendment that was repealed in July 2020. Since then, the city has increased the number of officers on the force despite community demands to reduce the size of the force. Elizabeth Weill-Greenberg, "San Francisco Voters Abolish Mandatory Staffing Levels for Police," The Appeal, November 4, 2020, theappeal.org/san-francisco-abolish-mandatory-police-staffing-levels.

27. Minneapolis City Charter Amendment Petition Receipt, lims.minneapolismn.gov/Download/FileV2/23681/Petition-Receipt-Summary.pdf.

28. Daily Kos, Minnesota Election Results, elections.ap.org/dailykos/results/2021-11-02/state/MN.

29. For example, see Douglas Hanks, "Groups Want Miami-Dade Police Budget Cut to Boost Services. Mayor: We're Not Chicago," *Miami Herald*, September 7, 2020.

30. Oscar Grant Foundation, "The Shooting of Oscar Grant," oscargrantfoundation.org/shooting-oscar-grant.

31. Defund OPD, defundopd.org.

32. For more information, please visit www.nocopacademy.com.

33. "'Block the Bunker' Activists Vow to Keep Fighting Stalled North Seattle Police Station," *Seattle Times*, September 16, 2016.

34. *Freedom to Thrive: Reimagining Safety and Security in Our Communities*, The Center for Popular Democracy, Law for Black Lives, and Black Youth Project 100, 2017, populardemocracy.org/sites/default/files/Freedom%20To%20Thrive%2C%20Higher%20Res%20Version.pdf.

35. Stephen Semler, "How Much Did the US Spend on Police, Prisons in FY2021?" *Speaking Security Newsletter*, January 20, 2022, stephensemler.substack.com/p/how-much-did-the-us-spend-on-police.

36. *Freedom to Thrive: Reimagining Safety and Security in Our Communities*, The Center for Popular Democracy.

37. Andrea J. Ritchie, "The Demand Is Still #DefundPolice," Interrupting Criminalization, bit.ly/DefundPoliceUpdate. For more details on police budget cuts across the country, see Kristin Musulin and Cailin Crowe, "Calls to 'Defund the Police' Are Upending FY21 Budgets. Here's How," *Smart Cities Dive*, January 26, 2021, smartcitiesdive.com/news/calls-to-defund-the-police-are-upending-fy21-budgets-heres-how/581163.

38. Mariame Kaba, "Yes, We Really Mean Abolish the Police," *New York Times*, June 12, 2020.

39. Andrea J. Ritchie, Mariame Kaba, and Woods Ervin, #DefundPolice #FundthePeople #DefendBlackLives: Concrete Steps Toward Divestment from Policing and Investment in Community Safety, Interrupting Criminalization, June 2020; *see also* Andrea J. Ritchie, "The Demand Is Still #DefundthePolice #FundthePeople #DefendBlackLives," Interrupting Criminalization, January 2021, www.interruptingcriminalization.com/defundpolice-update.

40. Rachel Ramirez, "Obama Says 'Defund the Police' Is a Bad Slogan. This Should Not Come As a Surprise," *Vox*, December 3, 2020, vox.com/2020/12/3/22150452/obama-defund-the-police-snappy-slogan.

41. Matthew Brown, "Democratic Whip James Clyburn: 'Defund the Police' Cost Democrats Seats, Hurt Black Lives Matter Movement," *USA Today*, November 9, 2020; Richard Luscombe, "James Clyburn: 'Defund the Police' Slogan May Have Hurt Democrats at Polls," *The Guardian*, November 8, 2020.

42. Fola Akinnibi, Sarah Holder, and Christopher Cannon, "Cities Say They Want to Defund the Police. Their Budgets Say Otherwise," Bloomberg CityLab, January 12, 2021, bloomberg.com/graphics/2021-city-budget-police-funding.

43. Alex Seitz-Wald, "How Democrats Went from Defund to Refund the Police," NBC News, February 6, 2022, www.nbcnews.com/politics/politics-news/democrats-went-defund-refund-police-rcna14796.

44. Chris Cillizza, "This Was the Single Most Revealing Line in Biden's State of the Union Speech," CNN.com, March 2, 2022.

45. Njeri Mathis Rutledge, "Obama Is Right About 'Defund the Police.' A Terrible Slogan Makes It Hard to Win Change," *USA Today*, December 7, 2020.

46. Kim Parker and Kiley Hurst, "Growing Share of Americans Say They Want More Spending on Police in Their Area," Pew Charitable Trust, October 26, 2021. www.pewresearch.org/fact-tank/2021/10/26/growing-share-of-americans-say-they-want-more-spending-on-police-in-their-area.

47. Data for Progress, unpublished poll results, May 2021, on file with authors.

48. Mychael Schnell, "Poll Finds Only 18 Percent Support 'Defund the Police,'" MSN, March 8, 2021. The poll found that 63 percent of Black voters polled supported allocating portions of police funding to social programs.

49. Keeanga-Yamahtta Taylor, *How We Get Free: Black Feminism and the Combahee River Collective* (Chicago: Haymarket Books, 2017).

50. Garrett Felber, "The Struggle to Abolish the Police Is Not New," *Boston Review*, June 9, 2020, bostonreview.net/race/garrett-felber-struggle-abolish-police-not-new.

51. Leanne Betamosake-Simpson and Robyn Maynard, *Rehearsals for Living* (Chicago: Haymarket Press, 2022); *Building the World We Want: A Roadmap to Police Free Futures in Canada*, Robyn Maynard, ed., 2021, static1.squarespace.com /static/6017561aa0646e0baa91251c/t/60257ae4703af042c3f2dd3e/1613069033514 /NationalDefundingDocument_FINAL+%285%29.pdf; "10 Point Program," The Red Nation, therednation.org/10-point-program.

52. "10 Principles of Disability Justice," Sins Invalid, static1.squarespace.com /static/5bed3674f8370ad8c02efd9a/t/5f1f0783916d8a179c46126d/1595869064521 /10_Principles_of_DJ-2ndEd.pdf. *See also* Talila A. Lewis, "Disability Justice Is an Essential Part of Abolishing Police and Ending Incarceration," in *Abolition for the People*, Colin Kaepernick, ed. (Kaepernick Publishing, 2021); Abigail Abrams, "Black, Disabled, and at Risk: The Overlooked Problem of Police Violence Against Americans with Disabilities," *Time*, June 25, 2020, time.com/5857438/police-violence-black-disabled.

53. Dean Spade, "Rainbow-Washing's True Colors," in *Abolition for the People. See also* Ash Stephens, "Reclaim Pride by Defunding the Police," *The Advocate*, June 12, 2020, advocate.com/commentary/2020/6/12/reclaim-pride-defunding-police; Benji Hart, "Principles of Pride: Police and Prisons Do Not Belong in Our Future," Autostraddle, June 5, 2020, autostraddle.com/principles-of-pride-police-and-prisons-do-not-belong-in -our-future.

54. *See*, e.g., Angela Y. Davis, Gina Dent, Erica Meiners, and Beth E. Richie, *Abolition. Feminism. Now.* (Chicago: Haymarket Press, 2022); Stuart Schrader, "Defund the Global Policeman," NPlusOne, 2020, www.nplusonemag.com/issue-38/politics /defund-the-global-policeman; William I. Robinson, "A Global Police State Is Emerging as World Capitalism Descends into Crisis," *Truthout*, November 28, 2020, truthout .org/articles/a-global-police-state-is-emerging-as-world-capitalism-descends-into-crisis; Arun Kundnani, "What Is Racial Capitalism?" October 23, 2020, kundnani.org/what -is-racial-capitalism; Felber, "The Struggle to Abolish the Police Is Not New"; Harsha Walia, *Border and Rule: Global Migration, Capitalism, and the Rise of Racist Neoliberalism* (Chicago: Haymarket Books, 2019); Marisol Lebrón, *Policing Life and Death: Race, Violence, and Resistance in Puerto Rico* (Chapel Hill: UNC Press, 2019); Robyn Maynard, "Trans-Atlantic Affinities: Post-Ferguson Freedom Dreams and the Global Reverberations of Black (Feminist) Struggle," *Scholar & Feminist Online*, Issue 15.3 (2019), sfonline .barnard.edu/unraveling-criminalizing-webs-building-police-free-futures/trans-atlantic -affinities-post-ferguson-freedom-dreams-and-the-global-reverberations-of-black -feminist-struggle; Stuart Schrader, Badges Without Borders: How Global Counterinsurgency Transformed American Policing (Chapel Hill: UNC Press, 2012); Angélica Cházaro, "The End of Deportation," April 5, 2019, *UCLA Law Review*, forthcoming, ssrn.com/abstract=3415707.

55. Felber, "The Struggle to Abolish the Police Is Not New."

56. Megan Munce, "Gov. Greg Abbott Signs Slate of Legislation to Increase Criminal Penalties for Protestors, Punish Cities That Reduce Police Budgets," *Texas Tribune*, June 1, 2021, texastribune.org/2021/06/01/texas-abbott-defund-police-protest. *See also* "Press Release from the Office of the Texas Governor Greg Abbott," June 1, 2021, gov .texas.gov/news/post/governor-abbott-signs-back-the-blue-legislation; John Pfaff, "The Greatest Threat to Defunding the Police? State Pre-emption," *The Appeal*, April 29, 2021, theappeal.org/defund-the-police-pre-emption; Lauren Dezenski, "Booker Tuber-

ville Spar Over Measure to 'Defund the Police' in Late-Night Vote-a-Rama Drama," CNN, August 11, 2021; Jeff Amy, "Georgia Bill Aims to Block 'Defunding' of Police," Associated Press, February 16, 2021, usnews.com/news/best-states/iowa/articles/2021 -02-16/georgia-bill-aims-to-block-defunding-of-police.

57. Zolan Kanno-Youngs, "Biden Aims to Bolster Police Departments as Homicides Increase," *New York Times*, July 12, 2021.

58. Zeeshan Aleem, MSNBC, September 4, 2021, msnbc.com/opinion/defund-police -dominated-2020-what-happened-n1278506. *See also* Nick Wing, "The New Law Enforcement Spending Spree Is Already Underway," *The Appeal*, March 29, 2022; Brian Dolinar, "It's a Money Grab': Billions in Covid Relief Going to Fund Police and Prisons," *The Appeal*, March 23, 2022; COVID19 Policing Project, *Divesting from Pandemic Policing, Investing In a Just Recovery*, Community Resource Hub, 2021, communityresource hub.org/wp-content/uploads/2021/05/Unmasked_Update.pdf; Community Resource Hub, *Ensuring Federal Stimulus Funds Support Communities, Not Cops*, 2021, community resourcehub.org/wp-content/uploads/2021/04/0407_CARES_ARPA_B.pdf.

59. *See* defundpolice.org.

60. "NYC Budget Justice," Communities United for Police Reform, changethenypd .org/nycbudgetjustice.

61. "Projects," Refund Raleigh, refundraleigh.org/projects.

62. Dream Defenders, dreamdefenders.org; Shauntrice Martin, "LMPD Does Not Keep Us Safe," NewsOne, June 15, 2021, newsone.com/4164834/lmpd-does-not-keep -us-safe.

63. "2021 Report & Demands," Nashville People's Budget Coalition, nashville peoplesbudget.org/2021-report.

64. Our City, Our Future, www.facebook.com/ourcityourfuture; "Defund SLCPD," Decarcerate Utah, decarcerateutah.org/defund-the-police.

65. Decriminalize Seattle, Decriminalizeseattle.com.

66. People's Budget LA, peoplesbudgetla.com.

67. "AART Claims Victory in Omnibus Bill Funding Housing, Not Police," *Milwaukee Courier*, October 22, 2021. *See also* Jon Schuppe, "Police Want a Share of Pandemic Relief Funds. Activists Find That 'Offensive,'" NBC News, June 5, 2021.

68. Megyung Chung, Diana Zúñiga, and Andrea J. Ritchie (with an appendix by Anand Subramian), "Navigating Public Safety Task Forces: A Guide from the Ground," Interrupting Criminalization, 2021, interruptingcriminalization.com/task-forces.

69. Katie Way, "Here's What the Movement to 'Defund the Police' Actually Won," *Vice*, May 24, 2021; ; Ritchie, "The Demand Is Still #DefundPolice."

70. Elvia Díaz, "Minneapolis Killed 'Defund the Police,' and Rightly So. But the Need for Reform Remains," AZ Central, November 4, 2021, azcentral.com/story/opinion /op-ed/elviadiaz/2021/11/04/defund-police-all-but-dead-its-wrong-slogan-anyway /6288224001.

71. Ritchie, "The Demand Is Still #DefundPolice."

72. Dan Berger and David Stein, "What Is and Could Be," in *Abolition for the People*, ed. Kaepernick.

73. Berger and Stein, "What Is and Could Be."

74. "A Revenue Generation Playbook: How to Fully Fund Our Communities,"

Community Resource Hub and Action Center on Race and the Economy, 2021, communityresourcehub.org/wp-content/uploads/2021/05/RGPlaybook.pdf.

75. Ruth Wilson Gilmore, "Prisons and Class Warfare," interview by Clément Petitjean, Historical Materialism, February 19, 2018, historicalmaterialism.org/index .php/interviews/prisons-and-class-warfare.

76. Robyn Maynard, "Toward a Police-Free Future in Canada," *The Breach*, May 25, 2021, breachmedia.ca/toward-a-police-free-future-in-canada. *See also* Robyn Maynard, *Policing Black Lives* (Halifax: Fernwood Publishing, 2017); Maynard and Simpson, *Rehearsals for Living*.

77. Critical Resistance, "Our Communities, Our Solutions: An Organizer's Toolkit for Developing Campaigns to Abolish Policing," October 2020, defundpolice.org/wp -content/uploads/2020/12/national_spaces_budget_toolkit_Our-Communities-Our -Solutions-An.pdf.

78. Liat Ben-Moshe, "The Tension Between Abolition and Reform," in M. Nagel and A.J. Nocella II, eds., *The End of Prisons: Reflections from the Decarceration Movement* (Rodopi Press, 2013).

79. Eric A. Stanley and Nat Smith, eds., *Captive Genders* (Chico, CA: AK Press, 2015), "Introduction."

80. Dan Berger, *The Struggle Within* (Oakland: PM Press/Kersplebedeb, 2014).

81. Ruth Wilson Gilmore, "Prisons and Class Warfare."

82. One Million Experiments, millionexperiments.com. *See also* transformharm.org; Creative Interventions, creative-interventions.org.

83. Neil Agarwal, "Crisis and Liberation Through Space and Time," interview by Mia Karisa Dawson, October 22, 2019, miakd.github.io/2019-10-22-Crisis-and-liberation -through-space-and-time.

84. Erin Miles Cloud, remarks at UCLA Law Review Symposium Conference, January 2022.

85. Ritchie, *Invisible No More*; Kristian Williams, *Our Enemies in Blue: Police and Power in America* (Oakland: AK Press, 2015).

86. Mapping Police Violence, *2021 Police Violence Report*, policeviolencereport.org /policeviolencereport2021.pdf?0.

87. "What Is Driving Mass Criminalization of Women and LGBTQ People," Barnard Center for Research on Women, 2019, view.publitas.com/interrupting-criminalization -byekyy37zyrk/interruptingcriminalization-report/page/1.

88. David Correia and Tyler Wall, *Violent Order: Essays on the Nature of Police* (Chicago: Haymarket Books, 2021).

89. At the time, the organization was called INCITE! Women of Color Against Violence, and later INCITE! Women and Trans People of Color Against Violence and INCITE! Feminists of Color Against Violence. More information at incite-national.org.

90. Ritchie, *Invisible No More*.

91. "Blood at the Root: Unearthing the Stories of State Violence Against Black Women," bloodatrootchicago.wordpress.com.

92. "Policy & Black Lives Teach-In: Threats to Defund, Immigrants, & Climate in the Infrastructure Bill," recorded September 27, 2021, m4bl.org/policy.

93. Andrea J. Ritchie et al., "Reparations Now Toolkit," Movement for Black Lives, 2019, m4bl.org/wp-content/uploads/2021/06/Reparations-Now-Toolkit-FINAL.pdf.

94. Interrupting Criminalization, interruptingcriminalization.org.

95. Center for Black Diaspora, "Black Feminism and Abolition," October 29, 2020, www.youtube.com/watch?v=LSgJmg0K4l0&t=1287s; *see also* Beth E. Richie, "Abolitionist Feminisms with Beth Ritchie, Erica Meiners, and Sonya Clark," February 25, 2021, www.youtube.com/watch?v=GGwaiYDoYB0.

96. Naomi Murakawa, "Three Traps of Police Reform," in *Abolition for the People*, Kaepernick, ed. *See also* Felber, "The Struggle to Abolish the Police Is Not New."

97. "The Black Panther Party Ten-Point Program," *Black Past*, October 15, 1966, blackpast.org/african-american-history/primary-documents-african-american-history /black-panther-party-ten-point-program-1966; Dan Berger and David Stein, "What Is and Could Be," in *Abolition for the People*, Kaepernick, ed.; *see also* Felber, "The Struggle to Abolish the Police Is Not New."

98. Orisanmi Burton, "Eddie Ellis and the Struggle for Black Freedom," Counter-Punch, August 8, 2014, counterpunch.org/2014/08/08/eddie-ellis-and-the-struggle-for -black-freedom.

99. Dan Berger, @dnbrgr, Twitter, December 6, 2018 1:37 p.m., twitter.com/dnbrgr /status/1070749158947008512?s=20&t=OBuVT1z0B1MvqVZkwcjieA.

100. Berger and Stein, in *Abolition for the People*, Kaepernick, ed. *See also* Felber, "The Struggle to Abolish the Police Is Not New."

101. In *Golden Gulag* (University of California Press, 2007), Ruth Wilson Gilmore complicates this analysis, theorizing that California's prison expansion was driven by crises of capitalism and state legitimacy produced by economic, political, and social conditions of the 1980s. In a recent interview, Gilmore elaborated, "The state of California used prison expansion provisionally to fix (to remedy, as well as to set firmly into space) the crises of land, labor, finance capital, and state capacity." *See also* Ruth Wilson Gilmore, "Prisons and Class Warfare"; Ruth Wilson Gilmore and Craig Gilmore, "Restating the Obvious," *Indefensible Space: The Architecture of the National Insecurity State*, Michael Sorkin, ed. (New York: Routledge, 2008).

102. Mike Davis, "Hell Factories in the Field: A Prison-Industrial Complex," *The Nation* 260, no. 7 (February 20, 1995): 229.

103. Davis, "Hell Factories in the Field: A Prison-Industrial Complex."

104. Davis, "Hell Factories in the Field: A Prison-Industrial Complex."

105. Jackie Wang, *Carceral Capitalism* (Pasadena: Semiotext(e), 2018).

106. Mariame Kaba, *We Do This 'Til We Free Us: Abolitionist Organizing and Transforming Justice* (Chicago: Haymarket Books, 2021).

107. Ruth Wilson Gilmore, "Prisons and Class Warfare."

108. Critical Resistance, criticalresistance.org.

109. "History," Critical Resistance, www.criticalresistance.org/about/history.

110. INCITE!, incite-national.org.

111. *INCITE! Women of Color Against Violence and Critical Resistance: Statement on Gender Violence and the Prison Industrial Complex*, incite-national.org/wp-content /uploads/2018/08/incite-cr-statement.pdf.

112. "Milestones," California Prison Moratorium Project, web.archive.org/web /20161026204437/http://www.calipmp.org/milestones.

113. Adrienne Brown, "An Interview with Activists at the Moratorium Project," Grist, June 22, 2005, grist.org/article/brown-prison.

114. "Celebrating the Closure of CA Youth Prisons," Ella Baker Center for Human Rights, ellabakercenter.org/books-not-bars-victory.

115. "Spending and Personnel over Time," defundpolice.org/budgeting-tools/for -spending-and-personnel-over-time.

116. Beth E. Richie and Andrea J. Ritchie, "The Crisis of Criminalization: A Call for a Comprehensive Philanthropic Response," Barnard Center for Research on Women, September 15, 2017, bcrw.barnard.edu/publications/the-crisis-of-criminalization.

117. Movement for Black Lives, "The Vision for Black Lives," "Invest/Divest," m4bl.org /policy-platforms/invest-divest; *see also* "End the War on Black Communities," m4bl.org /policy-platforms/end-the-war-on-black-communities.

118. The Breathe Act, breatheact.org.

119. "The People's Response Act," The Breathe Act, breatheact.org/the-peoples -response-act.

120. Ruth Wilson Gilmore, "Capitalism," Interrupting Criminalization, September 10, 2021; Ruth Wilson Gilmore, *Golden Gulag* (University of California Press, 2007).

121. Andrea J. Ritchie and Black Lives Matter Chicago, "Epicenter: Chicago, Reclaiming a City from Neoliberalism," Political Research Associates, 2019, politicalresearch.org /2019/06/05/epicenter-chicago-reclaiming-a-city-from-neoliberalism.

122. Ruth Wilson Gilmore and Craig Gilmore, "Beyond Bratton," in *Policing the Planet: Why the Policing Crisis Led to Black Lives Matter*, Cristina Heatherton and Jordan T. Camp, eds. (New York: Verso, 2016).

123. Ritchie and Black Lives Matter Chicago, "Epicenter: Chicago, Reclaiming a City from Neoliberalism." *See also* Kay Whitlock and Nancy Heitzeg, *Carceral Con: The Deceptive Terrain of Criminal Justice Reform* (Oakland: University of California Press, 2021); Liat Ben-Moshe, *Decarcerating Disability: Deinstitutionalization and Prison Abolition* (Minneapolis: University of Minnesota Press, 2020); Wang, *Carceral Capitalism*; Ruth Wilson Gilmore and Craig Gilmore, "Beyond Bratton," in *Policing the Planet*, Heatherton and Camp, eds.

124. Ritchie and Black Lives Matter Chicago, "Epicenter: Chicago, Reclaiming a City from Neoliberalism." *See also* Whitlock and Heitzeg, *Carceral Con*; Ben-Moshe, *Decarcerating Disability*; Wang, *Carceral Capitalism*; Ruth Wilson Gilmore and Craig Gilmore, "Beyond Bratton," in *Policing the Planet*, Heatherton and Camp, eds.

125. Ritchie and Black Lives Matter Chicago, "Epicenter: Chicago, Reclaiming a City from Neoliberalism." *See also* Ruth Wilson Gilmore and Craig Gilmore, "Beyond Bratton," in *Policing the Planet*, Heatherton and Camp, eds.

126. Ritchie and Black Lives Matter Chicago, "Epicenter: Chicago, Reclaiming a City from Neoliberalism."

127. Cedric Robinson, *Black Marxism* (Chapel Hill: UNC Press, 1983); *see also* Robin D.G. Kelley, "What Did Cedric Robinson Mean by Racial Capitalism?" *Boston Review*, January 12, 2017, bostonreview.net/race/robin-d-g-kelley-what-did-cedric-robinson -mean-racial-capitalism; Kundnani, "What Is Racial Capitalism?" As defined by Arun Kundnani, at its core, racial capitalism "refers to the mutual dependence of capitalism and racism." Walter Johnson writes that racial capitalism is "a sort of capitalism that relies upon the elaboration, reproduction, and exploitation of notions of racial difference." For Peter Hudson: "Racial capitalism suggests both the simultaneous historical emergence of racism and capitalism in the modern world and their mutual dependence." *See also* Ruth

Wilson Gilmore, "Prisons and Class Warfare"; Gilmore and Gilmore, "Beyond Bratton." *Policing the Planet*, Heatherton and Camp, eds.

128. Kelley, "What Did Cedric Robinson Mean by Racial Capitalism?"

129. Mark Neocleous, *A Critical Theory of Police Power: The Fabrication of Social Order* (Brooklyn: Verso, 2021). *See also* Correia and Wall, *Violent Order*; Stuart Hall et al., *Policing the Crisis: Mugging, the State, and Law and Order* (London: Macmillan, 1978).

130. The term "carceral" simply means of or suggesting jail or prison, or punitive, containing, controlling in nature. Jackie Wang uses the term "carceral capitalism" to describe how the "carceral techniques of the state are shaped by—and work in tandem with—global capitalism." She emphasizes that she does not "posit carcerality as an effect of capitalism, but to think about the carceral continuum alongside and in conjunction with the dynamics of late capitalism." Wang, *Carceral Capitalism*. *See also* Whitlock and Heitzeg, *Carceral Con*, 69, 85.

131. Erica Meiners defines the "carceral state" as "the multiple and intersecting state agencies and institutions (including not-for-profits that do the regulatory work of the state) that have punishing functions and effectively regulate poor communities: child and family services, welfare/workfare agencies, public education, immigration, health and human services, and more." Erica R. Meiners, "Trouble with the Child in the Carceral State," *Social Justice* 41, No. 3, 2015.

132. Gilmore and Gilmore, "Beyond Bratton."

133. Kundnani, "What Is Racial Capitalism?"

134. Ritchie and Black Lives Matter Chicago, "Epicenter: Chicago, Reclaiming a City from Neoliberalism."

135. Angela Davis, "Masked Racism: Reflections on the Prison Industrial Complex," Colorlines, September 10, 1998, colorlines.com/articles/masked-racism-reflections -prison-industrial-complex. *See also* Kundnani, "What Is Racial Capitalism?"

136. Whitlock and Heitzeg, *Carceral Con*. *See also* Ritchie and Black Lives Matter Chicago, "Epicenter: Chicago, Reclaiming a City from Neoliberalism."

137. Paul Rosenberg, "The Deeper History of 'Defund': How the 'Get Tough' Policies of the '70s and '80s Led to Disaster," *Salon*, May 29, 2021.

138. Whitlock and Heitzeg, *Carceral Con*.

139. Richie and Ritchie, *The Crisis of Criminalization*.

140. Ruth Wilson Gilmore, "Organized Abandonment and Organized Violence: Devolution and the Police," Lecture at the Humanities Institute at the University of California Santa Cruz, November 9, 2015, vimeo.com/146450686; Tamara K. Nopper, "Counting Crime: A Lecture on the Politics of Crime Data and Its Uses," July 27, 2021, available at www.youtube.com/watch?v=I0tE96ICNF0. Nopper cites Khalil Gibran Mohammed when discussing how responses to white people accused of crimes differs from Black people, noting that throughout history the former have been seen as deserving of investment and social services to "prevent" their criminal activity, suggesting that people considered their crime as a result of unfortunate circumstances. But racial criminalization associated Black people with crime and thus they were viewed as deserving of harsh punishment rather than more investment to uplift their social circumstances.

141. Prentis Hemphill, webinar, "Healing, Resilience, and Power," April 9, 2020.

142. Ritchie and Black Lives Matter Chicago, "Epicenter: Chicago, Reclaiming a City from Neoliberalism."

143. Matt Vasilogambros, "Rising Gun Deaths Push Cities to Shore Up Police and Services, Pew Research "Stateline," February 10, 2022, www.pewtrusts.org/en/research-and-analysis/blogs/stateline/2022/02/10/rising-gun-deaths-push-cities-to-shore-up-police-and-services.

144. *See* Alec Karakatsanis, @equalityalec, Twitter, January 18, 2022, 2:54 p.m., twitter.com/equalityAlec/status/1483528171374972931?s=20&t=qmgkiO13X6T2UB9EbppNEg.

145. Shaila Dewan, "'Re-Fund the Police'? Why It Might Not Reduce Crime," *New York Times*, November 8, 2021.

146. Angela Davis, "Masked Racism: Reflections on the Prison Industrial Complex," Colorlines, September 10, 1998, colorlines.com/articles/masked-racism-reflections-prison-industrial-complex.

147. Teresa Gowan, "Thinking Neoliberalism, Gender, Justice," *Scholar & Feminist Online* 11.1-11.2 (Fall 2012/Spring 2013).

148. Fran Spielman, "Aldermen Demand at Least 500—and as Many as 1,000—More Cops," *Chicago Sun-Times*, September 7, 2016.

149. Jeff Asher and Ben Horwitz, "How Do the Police Actually Spend Their Time?" *New York Times*, June 19, 2020.

150. Nefertiti Ankra, Zamir Ben-Dan, Julia Jenkins, and Takiya Wheeler, "When White People Call the Cops on Black People, They Lay Bare Classic US Racism," *Truthout*, June 15, 2020, truthout.org/articles/when-white-people-call-the-cops-on-black-people-they-lay-bare-classic-us-racism; Leah Caroll, "A Running List of White Women Calling the Cops on Black People for Ridiculous Reasons," October 12, 2018, www.refinery29.com/en-us/2018/10/213902/white-women-call-cops-on-black-people-for-dumb-reasons; Morgan Jerkins, "Why White Women Keep Calling the Cops on Black People," *Rolling Stone*, July 17, 2018, www.rollingstone.com/politics/politics-features/why-white-women-keep-calling-the-cops-on-black-people-699512.

151. Josie Duffy Rice, "The Abolition Movement," *Vanity Fair*, August 25, 2020.

152. Victoria Law, *"Prisons Make Us Safer" and 20 Other Myths About Mass Incarceration* (Boston: Beacon Press, 2021).

153. National Domestic Violence Hotline, "Who Will Help Me? Domestic Violence Survivors Speak Out About Law Enforcement Responses," Washington, DC (2015), www.thehotline.org/resources/law-enforcement-responses.

154. RAINN, "Perpetrators of Sexual Violence: Statistics," www.rainn.org/statistics/perpetrators-sexual-violence.

155. Angela Y. Davis, Gina Dent, Erica Meiners, Beth E. Richie, and Nia Davis, "Why Policing and Prisons Can't End Gender Violence," *Boston Review*, January 24, 2022.

156. Naomi Murakawa, "Three Traps of Police Reform," in *Abolition for the People*, Kaepernick, ed. *See also* Felber, "The Struggle to Abolish the Police Is Not New."

157. Mike Ludwig, "Amir Locke Murder Shows 'Reforming the Police' Isn't Enough, Activists Say," *Truthout*, February 9, 2022, truthout.org/articles/amir-locke-murder-shows-reforming-the-police-isnt-enough-activists-say; Nathalie Baptiste, "The Violent Sameness of the Police Reform Movement," *HuffPost*, February 8, 2022, www.huffpost.com/entry/police-reform-failed-amir-locke_n_6202b559e4b0500424339c6a; Micah Herskind and Tiffany Roberts, "The Failure of Police Reform," *New York Magazine*, January 31, 2022, nymag.com/intelligencer/2022/01/atlanta-police-reform-failure.html.

Cops Don't Stop Violence

1. Andrea J. Ritchie, *Invisible No More: Police Violence Against Black Women and Women of Color* (Boston: Beacon Press, 2017), 191.

2. Jeff Asher and Ben Horwitz, "How Do the Police Actually Spend Their Time?" *New York Times*, June 19, 2020. While reliance on police data is generally considered a hallmark of "objective" and reliable journalism, in fact, it is reflective of the mainstream media's unquestioning reporting of police narratives, data, and perspectives, rendering them what Mariame calls "stenographers for the police." *See also* Micol Siegel, *Violence Work: State Power and the Limits of Police* (Durham: Duke University Press, 2018).

3. Kenneth Novak et al., *Police & Society*, 7th ed. (New York: Oxford University Press 2017).

4. Shima Baradaran Baughman, "How Effective Are Police? The Problem of Clearance Rates and Criminal Accountability," *Ala. L. R.* 72, 1, 47, (2020): 95.

5. Stephen Semler, "How Much Did the US Spend on Police, Prisons in FY2021?" *Speaking Security Newsletter*, January 20, 2022, stephensemler.substack.com/p/how -much-did-the-us-spend-on-police; Nima Shirazi and Adam Johnson, "Episode 142: The Summer of Anti-BL Backlash & How Concepts of 'Crime' Were Shaped by the Propertied Class," August 4, 2021, in *Citations Needed*, podcasts.apple.com/us/podcast/ep -142-the-summer-of-anti-blm-backlash-and/id1258545975?i=1000531000934. *See also* Black Youth Project 100 (BYP100), The Center for Popular Democracy; Law for Black Lives, *Freedom to Thrive: Reimagining Safety & Security in Our Communities*, July 5, 2017, static1.squarespace.com/static/5500a55ae4b05a69b3350e23/t/595cf69b1b631b031 e0542a5/1499264677929/Freedom+to+Thrive+Web.pdf.

6. Erin Grinshteyn and David Hemenway, "Violent Death Rates: The United States Compared to Other High-Income OECD Countries, 2010," *The American Journal of Medicine* 129, no. 3 (March 2016): 266–273, 10.1016/j.amjmed.2015.10.025.

7. Patricia L. McCall, Kenneth C. Land, and Karen F. Parker, "Heterogeneity in the Rise and Decline of City-Level Homicide Rates, 1976–2005: A Latent Trajectory Analysis," *Social Science Research* 40, no. 1 (2011): 363–378, doi.org/10.1016/j.ssresearch.2010 .09.007.

8. Andrea J. Ritchie, *The Demand Is Still Defund the Police, Fund the People, Defend Black Lives*, Interrupting Criminalization (January 2021), bit.ly/DefundPoliceUpdate. *See also* Black Youth Project 100 (BYP100), The Center for Popular Democracy, and Law for Black Lives, *Freedom to Thrive*.

9. David Correia and Tyler Wall, *Violent Order: Essays on the Nature of Police* (Chicago: Haymarket Books, 2021), 3; Stuart Hall et al., *Policing the Crisis: Mugging, the State, and Law and Order* (London: Macmillan, 1978).

10. Martha K. Huggins, Mika Haritos-Fatouros, and Philip G. Zimbardo, *Violence Workers: Police Torturers and Murderers Reconstruct Brazilian Atrocities* (Berkeley: University of California Press, 2002), 1. *See also* Micol Siegel, *Violence Work*.

11. Huggins et al., *Violence Workers*.

12. Huggins et al., *Violence Workers*.

13. Hall et al., *Policing the Crisis*.

14. Hall et al., *Policing the Crisis*.

15. Ruth Wilson Gilmore, *Golden Gulag* (University of California Press, 2007).

16. Rachel E. Morgan and Alexandra Thompson, "Criminal Victimization, 2020," U.S. Department of Justice, Office of Justice Programs, Bureau of Justice Statistics, October 2021, NCJ 301775, bjs.ojp.gov/library/publications/criminal-victimization -2020. *See also* Andrew Karmen, *Crime Victims: An Introduction to Victimology*, 7th ed. (Belmont, CA: Wadsworth Publishing Company, 2009), 113.

17. Baughman, "How Effective Are Police?," 95.

18. "Arrest Trends," Vera Institute, 2018, arresttrends.vera.org/arrests.

19. Maggie Koerth and Amelia Thomson-DeVeaux, "Many Americans Are Convinced Crime Is Rising in the U.S. They're Wrong," *FiveThirtyEight*, August 2020, fivethirty eight.com/features/many-americans-are-convinced-crime-is-rising-in-the-u-s-theyre -wrong.

20. Andrea J. Ritchie and Beth E. Richie, *The Crisis of Criminalization: A Call for a Comprehensive Philanthropic Response* (Barnard Center for Research on Women, 2017), bcrw.barnard.edu/wp-content/nfs/reports/NFS9-Challenging-Criminalization -Funding-Perspectives.pdf.

21. Alec Karakatsanis, "The Punishment Bureaucracy: How to Think About 'Criminal Justice Reform,'" *Yale Law Journal Forum* 128 (March 2019): 848–935, yalelawjournal.org/pdf/Karakatsanis_vahc6bgb.pdf.

22. Karakatsanis, "The Punishment Bureaucracy."

23. Karakatsanis, "The Punishment Bureaucracy."

24. Ritchie, *Invisible No More*.

25. Ritchie, *Invisible No More*.

26. Talila A. Lewis, "Disability Justice Is an Essential Part of Abolishing Police and Ending Incarceration," in *Abolition for the People*, Colin Kaepernick, ed. (Kaepernick Publishing, 2021). *See also* Ritchie, *Invisible No More*.

27. Ritchie, *Invisible No More*.

28. Ritchie, *Invisible No More*.

29. Sarah Haley, *No Mercy Here: Gender, Punishment, and the Making of Jim Crow Modernity* (Chapel Hill: University of North Carolina Press, 2016). *See also* Talitha LeFlouria, *Chained in Silence: Black Women and Convict Labor in the New South* (Chapel Hill: University of North Carolina Press, 2015).

30. Clare Sears, *Arresting Dress: Cross-Dressing, Law, and Fascination in Nineteenth-Century San Francisco* (Durham: Duke University Press, 2015). *See also* Ritchie, *Invisible No More*.

31. Ritchie, *Invisible No More*.

32. Ritchie, *Invisible No More*.

33. Ritchie, *Invisible No More*.

34. Tom LoBianco, "Report: Aide Says Nixon's War on Drugs Targeted Blacks, Hippies," CNN, March 24, 2016, cnn.com/2016/03/23/politics/john-ehrlichman-richard -nixon-drug-war-blacks-hippie/index.html.

35. "A Tale of Two Countries: Racially Targeted Arrests in the Era of Marijuana Reform," ACLU, April 17, 2020, aclu.org/news/criminal-law-reform/a-tale-of-two -countries-racially-targeted-arrests-in-the-era-of-marijuana-reform; Marijuana Justice Project, "Legalize It Right," www.marijuanajustice.org/legalize-it-right.

36. Jennifer Block, "Criminalization of the American Midwife," *Longreads*, March 2020, longreads.com/2020/03/10/criminalization-of-the-american-midwife.

37. Patricia Hill Collins, *Black Feminist Thought: Knowledge, Consciousness, and the Politics of Empowerment* (New York: Routledge, 2000).

38. Ritchie, *Invisible No More.*

39. Anita Chabria, Nashelly Chavez, and Phillip Reese, "'Racial Profiling'? Jaywalking Tickets Disproportionately Given to Black People in Sacramento," *Sacramento Bee,* April 16, 2017.

40. J. Kelley Lowenstein, "Crunch Time: Black People and Jaywalking in Champaign," *Chicago Tribune,* August 21, 2012.

41. Andrea J. Ritchie, "Black Lives over Broken Windows," *The Public Eye,* July 6, 2016, politicalresearch.org/2016/07/06/black-lives-over-broken-windows-challenging -the-policing-paradigm-rooted-in-right-wing-folk-wisdom.

42. Pascal Emmer, Woods Ervin, Derecka Purnell, Andrea J. Ritchie, and Tiffany Wang, *Unmasked: Impacts of Pandemic Policing,* COVID19 Policing Project at the Community Resource Hub, October 2020, communityresourcehub.org/wp-content/uploads /2020/12/Unmasked.pdf.

43. Emmer et al., *Unmasked.*

44. Emmer et al., *Unmasked.*

45. Geoff Edgers, "Four Police Officers Shot Amadou Diallo 19 Times. A New Photography Project Names Them," *Washington Post,* December 3, 2020.

46. Survived and Punished, www.survivedandpunished.org.

47. Hall et al., *Policing the Crisis.*

48. John Jay College Research Advisory Group on Preventing and Reducing Community Violence, *Reducing Violence Without Police: A Review of Research Evidence* (New York: Research and Evaluation Center, John Jay College of Criminal Justice, City University of New York, 2020).

49. Correia and Wall, *Violent Order. See also* Ritchie, *Invisible No More.*

50. Ritchie, "Black Lives over Broken Windows."

51. Chris Francescani, "NYPD Report Confirms Manipulation of Crime Stats," Reuters, March 9, 2012, reuters.com/article/us-crime-newyork-statistics -idUSBRE82818620120309.

52. Francescani, "NYPD Report Confirms Manipulation of Crime Stats."

53. Matt Hamilton, "LAPD Captain Accuses Department of Twisting Crime Statistics to Make City Seem Safer," *Los Angeles Times,* November 6, 2017. *See also* Baughman, "How Effective Are Police?," 95.

54. Ryan Jacobs, "Just Like in 'The Wire,' Real FBI Crime Stats Are 'Juked,'" *Mother Jones,* June 19, 2012, motherjones.com/crime-justice/2012/06/fbi-crime-stats-fudged -the-wire-nypd.

55. Bernice Yeung et al., "When It Comes to Rape, Just Because a Case Is Cleared Doesn't Mean It's Solved," *ProPublica,* November 15, 2018, propublica.org/article/when -it-comes-to-rape-just-because-a-case-is-cleared-does-not-mean-solved.

56. Yeung et al., "When It Comes to Rape, Just Because a Case Is Cleared Doesn't Mean It's Solved."

57. Yeung et al., "When It Comes to Rape, Just Because a Case Is Cleared Doesn't Mean It's Solved."

58. Yeung et al., "When It Comes to Rape, Just Because a Case Is Cleared Doesn't Mean It's Solved."

59. Rashida Richardson, Jason M. Schultz, and Kate Crawford, "Dirty Data, Bad Predictions: How Civil Rights Violations Impact Police Data, Predictive Policing Systems, and Justice," *NYU L. Rev. Online* 94 (May 2019): 15–55, nyulawreview.org/wp-content /uploads/2019/04/NYULawReview-94-Richardson_etal-FIN.pdf.

60. Yeung et al., "When It Comes to Rape, Just Because a Case Is Cleared Doesn't Mean It's Solved."

61. Erika Eichelberger, "Violence on the Home Front," *Mother Jones*, April 25, 2013, motherjones.com/politics/2013/04/domestic-violence-murder-stats.

62. Lois Beckett and Abené Clayton, "How Bad Is the Rise in US Homicides? Fact Checking the 'Crime Wave' Narrative Police Are Pushing," *The Guardian*, June 30, 2021.

63. Diana Ejaita, "We Can Make Neighborhoods Safer Just by Changing the Physical Environment," *Washington Post*, www.washingtonpost.com/opinions/interactive/2021 /reimagine-safety.

64. Claire Bushey, "How Chicago Activists Organized to Get an Adult Trauma Center," *Popular Resistance*, April 15, 2016, popularresistance.org/how-chicago-activists -organized-to-get-an-adult-trauma-center.

65. "End the War on Black Health and Black Disabled People," M4BL, m4bl.org /policy-platforms/end-the-war-black-health.

66. COVID19 Policing Project, *Divesting from Pandemic Policing and Investing in Just Recovery*, May 2021, communityresourcehub.org/wp-content/uploads/2021/05 /Unmasked_Update.pdf.

67. Richard Rosenfeld and Joel Wallman, "Did De-Policing Cause the Increase in Homicide Rates?" *Criminology & Public Policy* 18 (2019): 51–75, doi.org/10.1111/1745 -9133.12414.

68. "Arrest Trends," Vera Institute.

69. Baughman, "How Effective Are Police?," 95.

70. John L. Worrall and Tomislav V. Kovandzic, "Police Levels and Crime Rates: An Instrumental Variables Approach," *Social Science Research* 39, no. 3 (May 2010): 506–516, doi.org/10.1016/j.ssresearch.2010.02.001.

71. William Spelman, "The Murder Mystery: Police Effectiveness and Homicide," *Journal of Quantitative Criminology* 33 (2017): 859–886.

72. Rosenfeld and Wallman, "Did De-Policing Cause the Increase in Homicide Rates?"

73. "Assault or Homicide," Centers for Disease Control and Prevention, cdc.gov/nchs /fastats/homicide.htm.

74. David Bayley, *Police for the Future* (New York: Oxford University Press, 1994), 3.

75. Bayley, *Police for the Future*.

76. John Jay College Research Advisory Group on Preventing and Reducing Community Violence, *Reducing Violence Without Police: A Review of Research Evidence.* One un-peer-reviewed study found evidence that increasing the number of cops can decrease the number of homicides, particularly among Black populations. Aaron Chalfin, Benjamin Hansen, Emily K. Weisburst, and Morgan C. Williams Jr., "Police Force Size and Civilian Race," NBER Working Paper No. 28202, December 2020. However, the authors acknowledge that this effect is diminished to nonexistent in communities where

there is a significant Black population, and is offset by increased police harassment, arrests, and opportunities for violence through increases in minor arrests. They also acknowledge that other, nonpolice methods to reduce violence exist that do not carry the adverse impacts associated with policing.

77. Novak et al., *Police & Society*, 98. Novak et al. speculate that these results are likely due to inadequate numbers of police across the board. Nevertheless, they conclude that the study results remain relevant to present-day debates around the efficacy of increased numbers of police. *See also* Aya Gruber, "Crime Rates Rise and Fall. The Police Mostly Have Nothing to Do with It," The Garrison Project, October 26, 2021, thegarrisonproject.org/purpose-of-policing.

78. Alex Zielinski, "Portland's Crime Rate Isn't Impacted by Size of Police Force, Data Finds," *Portland Mercury*, November 9, 2021, www.portlandmercury.com/blogtown/2021/11/09/36865079/portlands-crime-rate-isnt-impacted-by-size-of-police-force-data-finds.

79. Alec Karakastanis, "Why 'Crime' Isn't the Question and Police Aren't the Answer," *Current Affairs*, August 10, 2020, currentaffairs.org/2020/08/why-crime-isnt-the-question-and-police-arent-the-answer.

80. Deena Winter, "Minneapolis Cop Says Officers Have Taken 'Hands-Off' Approach to Crime Fighting," *Minnesota Reformer*, October 20, 2021; Lewis Kamb, Daniel Beekman, Manuel Villa, "Seattle 911 Response Times Climbed in Summer 2020. Now, Police and Activists Debate What Comes Next," *Seattle Times*, May 11, 2021; Deena Winter, "Data: A Slower, Less Proactive Minneapolis Police Department Since George Floyd Killing," *Minnesota Reformer*, September 15, 2020, minnesotareformer.com/2020/09/15/data-show-a-slower-less-proactive-minneapolis-police-department-since-george-floyd-killing.

81. Resolution 31962, Seattle City Council, August 10, 2020, seattle.legistar.com/LegislationDetail.aspx?ID=4612654&GUID=6F302CE2-3A7E-4C08-85D3-EA188594CF68.

82. Novak et al., *Police & Society*. *See also* Gruber, "Crime Rates Rise and Fall. The Police Mostly Have Nothing to Do with It."

83. Novak et al., *Police & Society*.

84. Novak et al., *Police & Society*.

85. Novak et al., *Police & Society*; Baughman, "How Effective Are Police?" As noted by legal scholar Shima Baradaran Baughman, a far smaller percentage of "solved" cases lead to arrest and conviction.

86. "Victims: The Murder Accountability Project," murderdata.org/p/victims.html. *See also* Michael Hobbes and Sarah Marshall, *You're Wrong About*: "Murder," July 27, 2020, podcasts.apple.com/us/podcast/murder/id1380008439?i=1000486293801.

87. Hobbes and Marshall, *You're Wrong About*: "Murder."

88. Novak et al., *Police & Society*, 100.

89. Novak et al., *Police & Society*.

90. Novak et al., *Police & Society*.

91. Novak et al., *Police & Society*.

92. Novak et al., *Police & Society*; *see also* Joshua C. Hinkle, David Weisburd, Cody W. Telep, and Kevin Petersen, "Problem-Oriented Policing for Reducing Crime and Disorder: An Updated Systematic Review and Meta-analysis," *Campbell Syst Rev.* 2020;

16:e1089, doi.org/10.1002/cl2.1089, finding significant effects on "crime and disorder," noting that they were heterogenous across communities—while in some communities data showed a reduction in property crimes, in others, the measures involved offenses such as drinking in public. *See also* National Academies of Sciences, Engineering, and Medicine. *Proactive Policing: Effects on Crime and Communities* (Washington, DC: The National Academies Press, 2018), doi.org/10.17226/24928.

93. Novak et al., *Police & Society*; J. MacDonald, J. Fagan, and A. Geller, "The Effects of Local Police Surges on Crime and Arrests in New York City," *PLoS ONE* 11(6) (2016): e0157223, doi.org/10.1371/journal.pone.0157223. ("We found that Operation Impact had a statistically significant but relatively small association with a reduction in total crimes. The formation of impact zones had the largest effect on reducing robbery and burglary offenses. The data, however, do not distinguish a clear mechanism for this effect. The increase in probable cause-related stops after the formation of impact zone had the strongest association with reduced burglary and robbery reports, suggesting that physical presence of more police and enhanced apprehension may have generated a deterrent effect specific to those crimes."); Hinkle, Weisburd, Telep, and Petersen, "Problem-Oriented Policing for Reducing Crime and Disorder."

94. MacDonald et al., "The Effects of Local Police Surges on Crime and Arrests in New York City."

95. Shaila Dewan, "'Re-Fund the Police'? Why It Might Not Reduce Crime," *New York Times*, November 8, 2021; National Academies of Science, *Proactive Policing*.

96. MacDonald et al., "The Effects of Local Police Surges on Crime and Arrests in New York City."

97. Dewan, "Re-Fund the Police?"

98. Novak et al., *Police & Society*. *See also* Gruber, "Crime Rates Rise and Fall. The Police Mostly Have Nothing to Do with It"; National Academies of Science, *Proactive Policing*; MacDonald et al., "The Effects of Local Police Surges on Crime and Arrests in New York City."

99. Novak et al., *Police & Society*. *See also* Gruber, "Crime Rates Rise and Fall. The Police Mostly Have Nothing to Do with It"; National Academies of Science, *Proactive Policing*.

100. Novak et al., *Police & Society*.

101. Novak et al., *Police & Society*.

102. Novak et al., *Police & Society*. *See also* Bayley, *Police for the Future*.

103. David Klepper and Gary Fields, Associated Press, "Homicides Are Up, but GOP Misleads with Claims About Blame," ABC News, June 10, 2021, abcnews.go.com/Politics/wireStory/homicides-gop-misleads-claims-blame-78196565.

104. Another theory that has been floated is that the defund movement has so demoralized police that they are no longer doing their jobs, and quitting *en masse*. The "demoralization" or "de-policing" effect on crime rates has been debunked. Rosenfeld and Wallman, "Did De-Policing Cause the Increase in Homicide Rates?" And while significant numbers of police did quit or take lucrative early retirement deals since 2020, this is part of a larger trend of mass resignation in the context of the pandemic. *See* Derek Thompson, "The Great Resignation Is Accelerating," *The Atlantic*, October 15, 2021. And, as noted above, research shows that increasing police numbers doesn't have a significant impact on reducing violence.

105. The White House, "Fact Sheet: Biden-Harris Administration Announces Comprehensive Strategy to Prevent and Respond to Gun Crime and Ensure Public Safety," June 23, 2021, whitehouse.gov/briefing-room/statements-releases/2021/06/23/fact-sheet-biden-harris-administration-announces-comprehensive-strategy-to-prevent-and-respond-to-gun-crime-and-ensure-public-safety. For further analysis and demands that American Rescue Plan funds not be spent on law enforcement, *see* Community Resource Hub, *Ensuring That Federal Stimulus Funds Support Care Not Cops*, 2021, communityresourcehub.org/wp-content/uploads/2021/04/0407_CARES_ARPA_B.pdf.

106. Michael D. Shear and Zolan Kanno-Youngs, "Walking a Fine Line, Biden Balances Confronting Crime and Supporting Police Reform," *New York Times*, July 12, 2021.

107. David Stein, "The Untold Story: Joe Biden Pushed Ronald Reagan to Ramp Up Incarceration—Not the Other Way Around," *The Intercept*, September 17, 2019.

108. Lois Beckett and Abené Clayton, "How Bad Is the Rise in US Homicides? Fact Checking the 'Crime Wave' Narrative Police Are Pushing," *The Guardian*, June 30, 2021.

109. Richard Rosenfeld, Thomas Abt, and Ernesto Lopez, *Pandemic, Social Unrest, and Crime in U.S. Cities: 2020 Year-End Update* (Washington: Council on Criminal Justice, January 2021).

110. Annie Linskey, Tyler Pager, and Cleve R. Wootson Jr., "Biden Launches an Effort to Head Off Violent Crime—and Political Peril for His Party," *Washington Post*, June 21, 2021.

111. Rachel E. Morgan and Alexandra Thompson, "Criminal Victimization, 2020," U.S. Department of Justice, Office of Justice Programs, Bureau of Justice Statistics, October 2021, NCJ 301775, bjs.ojp.gov/library/publications/criminal-victimization-2020.

112. Rosenfeld, Abt, and Lopez, *Pandemic, Social Unrest, and Crime in U.S. Cities: 2020 Year-End Update*, 6. *See also* Beckett and Clayton, "How Bad Is the Rise in US Homicides?"

113. Beckett and Clayton, "How Bad Is the Rise in US Homicides?"

114. John Pfaff, "Can Criminal Justice Reform Survive a Wave of Violent Crime?" *New Republic*, June 21, 2021. *See also* Kristin Musulin and Cailin Crowe, "Calls to 'Defund the Police' Are Upending FY21 Budgets. Here's How," *Smart Cities Dive*, January 26, 2021, smartcitiesdive.com/news/calls-to-defund-the-police-are-upending-fy21-budgets-heres-how/581163.

115. Pfaff, "Can Criminal Justice Reform Survive a Wave of Violent Crime?"

116. Klepper and Fields, "Homicides Are Up, but GOP Misleads with Claims About Blame." *See also* Kristin Musulin and Cailin Crowe, "Calls to 'Defund the Police' Are Upending FY21 Budgets. Here's How," *Smart Cities Dive*, January 26, 2021, smartcitiesdive.com/news/calls-to-defund-the-police-are-upending-fy21-budgets-heres-how/581163.

117. Klepper and Fields, "Homicides Are Up, but GOP Misleads with Claims About Blame." *See also* Musulin and Crowe, "Calls to 'Defund the Police' Are Upending FY21 Budgets."

118. Gruber, "Crime Rates Rise and Fall. The Police Mostly Have Nothing to Do with It."

119. William Spelman, "The Murder Mystery: Police Effectiveness and Homicide," *Journal of Quantitative Criminology* 33 (2017): 859–886.

120. Rachel M. Cohen, "Fentanyl, Guns, and Murder: Get Ready for a Bloody Summer," *Daily Beast*, June 9, 2021.

121. Cohen, "Fentanyl, Guns, and Murder"; *see* Federal Bureau of Investigation, "NICS Firearm Background Checks: November 30, 1998 -December 31, 2021," www.fbi.gov /file-repository/nics_firearm_checks_-_month_year.pdf/view. The FBI cautions that "[t]hese statistics represent the number of firearm background checks initiated through the NICS. They do not represent the number of firearms sold. Based on varying state laws and purchase scenarios, a one-to-one correlation cannot be made between a firearm background check and a firearm sale." In other words, a background check may be conducted but no purchase may be made. On the other hand, guns may be purchased without a background check in a majority of states. Kennedy Elliott and Robert Gebelhoff, "Gun Policies by State," *Washington Post*, December 9, 2015; Matthew Miller, Wilson Zhang, and Deborah Azrael, "Firearm Purchasing During the COVID-19 Pandemic: Results from the 2021 National Firearms Survey," *Annals of Internal Medicine*, December 21, 2021, www.acpjournals.org/doi/10.7326/M21-3423.

122. Cohen, "Fentanyl, Guns, and Murder." *See also* Beckett and Clayton, "How Bad Is the Rise in US Homicides?"

123. Beckett and Clayton, "How Bad Is the Rise in US Homicides?"

124. Rosenfeld, Abt, and Lopez, *Pandemic, Social Unrest, and Crime in U.S. Cities: 2020 Year-End Update*.

125. John Jay College Research Advisory Group on Preventing and Reducing Community Violence, *Reducing Violence Without Police: A Review of Research Evidence*.

126. *Citations Needed* podcast, "The Summer of Anti-BLM Backlash and How Concepts of 'Crime' Were Shaped by the Propertied Class," episode 142, August 4, 2021, citationsneeded.libsyn.com/ep-142-the-summer-of-anti-blm-backlash-and-how-concepts-of -crime-were-shaped-by-the-propertied-class.

127. Eli Yokley, "Most Voters See Violent Crime as a Major and Increasing Problem, but They're Split on Its Causes and How to Fix It," *Morning Consult*, July 14, 2021, morning-consult.com/2021/07/14/violent-crime-public-safety-polling.

128. Sidney Fussel, "What Disbanding the Police Really Meant in Camden, New Jersey," *Wired*, July 1, 2020.

129. Shear and Kanno-Youngs, "Walking a Fine Line, Biden Balances Confronting Crime and Supporting Police Reform." *See also* D19 Policing Project, *Divesting from Pandemic Policing and Investing in Just Recovery*, May 2021.

130. Paul M. Renfro, "The New 'Crime Wave' Panic and the Long Shadow of John Walsh," *New Republic*, August 13, 2021.

131. Ritchie, "Black Lives over Broken Windows."

132. *See* Chalfin et al., "Police Force Size and Civilian Race."

133. Fabiola Cineas, "What the Public Is Getting Right—and Wrong—About Police Abolition," *Vox*, October 30, 2020, vox.com/21529335/abolish-the-police-movement.

134. John Jay College Research Advisory Group on Preventing and Reducing Community Violence, *Reducing Violence Without Police: A Review of Research Evidence*.

135. John Jay College Research Advisory Group.

136. Patrick Sharkey, Gerard Torrats-Espinosa, and Delaram Takyar, "Community and the Crime Decline: The Causal Effect of Local Nonprofits on Violent Crime," *American Sociological Review* 82, no. 6 (2017): 1214–1240, 1215, doi.org/10.1177 /0003122417736289.

137. Sharkey et al., "Community and the Crime Decline."

138. Sharkey et al., "Community and the Crime Decline."

139. The Justice Collaborative Institute, *The Case for Violence Interruption Programs as An Alternative to Policing*, June 2020, thejusticecollaborative.com/2020/06/new-report -violence-interruption-programs-provide-effective-alternative-to-policing.

140. Common Justice, *Solutions to Violence: Creating Safety Without Prisons or Police*, 2021, resources.commonjustice.org/solutions_to_violence_report; Jeffrey A. Butts et al., "Cure Violence: A Public Health Model to Reduce Gun Violence," *Annual Review of Public Health* 36 (March 2015): 39–53, doi: 10.1146/annurev-publhealth-031914-12250 9.

141. Common Justice, *Solutions to Violence: Creating Safety Without Prisons or Police*; The HAVI, www.thehavi.org.

142. Jessica Anderson and Phillip Jackson, "Safe Streets Celebrates a Year with No Homicides in a South Baltimore Area They Serve, with Hope for Rest of the City," *Baltimore Sun*, June 26, 2021.

143. John Jay College Research Advisory Group on Preventing and Reducing Community Violence, *Reducing Violence Without Police: A Review of Research Evidence*. See *also* Amanda Alexander and Danielle Sered, "Making Communities Safe, Without the Police," *Boston Review*, November 1, 2021, bostonreview.net/law-justice/amanda -alexander-danielle-sered-making-communities-safe-without-police; Common Justice, *Solutions to Violence: Creating Safety Without Prisons or Police*.

144. John Jay College Research Advisory Group on Preventing and Reducing Community Violence, *Reducing Violence Without Police: A Review of Research Evidence*. See *also* Alexander and Sered, "Making Communities Safe, Without the Police"; Common Justice, *Solutions to Violence: Creating Safety Without Prisons or Police*.

145. D'Angelo Cameron, "More Police Is Not the Solution to Gun Violence," *Common Justice*, May 26, 2021, blog.commonjustice.org/blog/gun-violence-policing.

146. Tania Rosario Mendéz, presentation at Community Resource Hub Learning Community, April 2021. For more information on the history and work of Taller Salud, see www.english.tallersalud.com.

147. D'Angelo Cameron, "Violence Prevention Is Infrastructure," *Common Justice*, April 28, 2021, blog.commonjustice.org/blog/infrastructure-american-jobs-plan. *See also* Baynard Woods and Brandon Soderberg, "Credible Messengers," *The Intercept*, July 26, 2020, theintercept.com/2020/07/26/baltimore-safe-streets-public-health-gun-violence -police.

148. John Jay College Research Advisory Group on Preventing and Reducing Community Violence, *Reducing Violence Without Police: A Review of Research Evidence*.

149. John Jay College Research Advisory Group on Preventing and Reducing Community Violence, *Reducing Violence Without Police: A Review of Research Evidence*. We do *not* support the recommendations made in this report focused on increasing surveillance, involuntary demolition of public housing, partnerships between violence interrupters and law enforcement, mandated treatment or enforced sobriety, "workfare" (imposing work

requirements as a condition of receiving social entitlements), or increasing "trust" and legitimacy of systems of policing and punishment. *See also* Alexander and Sered, "Making Communities Safe, Without the Police."

150. Charles C. Branas, Eugenia South, Michelle C. Kondo, Bernadette C. Hohl, Philippe Bourgois, Douglas J. Wiebe, and John M. MacDonald, "Citywide Cluster Randomized Trial to Restore Blighted Vacant Land and Its Effects on Violence, Crime, and Fear," *Proceedings of the National Academy of Sciences* 115 (12) (2018): 2946–2951; doi: 10.1073/pnas.1718503115.

151. Charles C. Branas, Michelle C. Kondo, et al., "Urban Blight Remediation as a Cost-Beneficial Solution to Firearm Violence," *American Journal of Public Health* 106, no. 12 (2016): 2158–2164, doi:10.2105/AJPH.2016.303434.

152. Washington Post Editorial Board, "We Have the Proper Public Safety Tools. Now Hand Them to Community Leaders," March 16, 2021.

153. Danielle Sered, "To Produce Safety, We Must Understand Violence," *Common Justice*, July 8, 2020, blog.commonjustice.org/blog/to_produce_safety_we_must _understand_what_drives_violence; *see also* Washington Post Editorial Board, "We Have the Proper Public Safety Tools."

154. Alexander and Sered, "Making Communities Safe, Without the Police."

We Are Survivors

1. Jane Doe, *The Story of Jane Doe* (Toronto: Random House Canada, 2003).

2. Amita Swadhin (@AmitaSwadhin), "For the Record," Facebook post, February 24, 2020.

3. Aishah Shahidah Simmons, "Dig Up the Roots of Child Sexual Abuse," in *Love WITH Accountability* (Chico, CA: AK Press, 2019). For more information on *NO! The Rape Documentary*, see notherapedocumentary.org.

4. Hilary A. Moore, *Beyond Policing: A Handbook for Community-Led Solutions to the Violence of Policing in Western Europe* (Brussels: Rosa-Luxemburg-Siftung, February 2022), www.rosalux.eu/en/article/2084.beyond-policing.html. Moore introduced herself in this way during the book launch event held on January 31, 2022, attended by co-author Ritchie.

5. Danielle Sered, *Until We Reckon* (New York: The New Press 2019).

6. Rachel E. Morgan and Alexandra Thompson, "Criminal Victimization, 2020," U.S. Department of Justice Bureau of Justice Statistics, October 2021, NCJ 301775, bjs .ojp.gov/library/publications/criminal-victimization-2020.

7. Morgan et al, "Criminal Victimization, 2020."

8. "Scope of the Problem: Statistics," RAINN (Rape, Abuse & Incest National Network), rainn.org/statistics/scope-problem.

9. "Scope of the Problem: Statistics," RAINN.

10. "Preventing Sexual Violence," CDC (Centers for Disease Control and Prevention), www.cdc.gov/violenceprevention/sexualviolence/fastfact.html.

11. "Preventing Child Sexual Abuse," CDC.

12. "Preventing Intimate Partner Violence," CDC (Centers for Disease Control and Prevention), cdc.gov/violenceprevention/intimatepartnerviolence/fastfact.html.

13. "Preventing Sexual Violence," CDC. *See also* Talila A. Lewis, "Disability Justice in the Age of Mass Incarceration" in *Deaf People in the Criminal Justice System: Selected Topics on Advocacy, Incarceration, and Social Justice,* Debra Guthmann et al., eds. (Washington: Gallaudet University Press, 2021); "End the War on Black Women," Movement for Black Lives (M4BL), m4bl.org/policy-platforms/end-the-war-black-women; "End the War on Black Trans Queer, Gender Nonconforming and Intersex People," Movement for Black Lives (M4BL), m4bl.org/policy-platforms/end-the-war-trans.

14. Angela Y. Davis, Gina Dent, Erica Meiners, and Beth E. Richie, *Abolition. Feminism. Now.* (Chicago: Haymarket Press, 2022); Emily Hanson and Lisa Sacco, *The Violence Against Women Act (VAWA) Reauthorization: Issues for Congress,* Congressional Research Service, March 31, 2021, crsreports.congress.gov/product/pdf/R/R46742.

15. Leigh Goodmark, "The Violence Against Women Act Is Unlikely to Reduce Intimate Partner Violence—Here's Why," *The Conversation,* October 17, 2018, theconversation.com/the-violence-against-women-act-is-unlikely-to-reduce-intimate-partner-violence-heres-why-103734. *See also* Jill Theresa Messing, Allison Ward-Lasher, Jonel Thaller, and Meredith Bagwell-Gray, "The State of Intimate Partner Violence Intervention: Progress and Continuing Challenges," *Social Work* 60, 10.1093 (2015).

16. Goodmark, "The Violence Against Women Act Is Unlikely to Reduce Intimate Partner Violence." Goodmark, a law professor at the University of Maryland, analyzed rates of domestic violence and crime statistics and found that "although rates of domestic violence have fallen steadily since the [Violence Against Women Act] legislation was enacted in 1994, the decrease in rates may not be a result of the act. Initially, those declines mirrored decreases in the overall crime rate. And between 2000 and 2010, rates of domestic violence actually fell less than the drop in the overall crime rate—at a time when VAWA was pumping hundreds of millions of dollars into the criminal system."

17. Wilson Wong, "'Defund the Police' Movement Could Offer Sexual Assault Survivors a Different Path for Justice, Experts Say," NBC News, August 2, 2020, nbcnews.com/news/us-news/defund-police-movement-could-offer-sexual-assault-survivors-different-path-n1235478; *Love WITH Accountability: Digging Up the Roots of Child Sexual Abuse,* Aishah Shahidah Simmons, ed. (Chico, CA: AK Press, 2019); *NO! The Rape Documentary* (2006), notherapedocumentary.org.

18. Morgan et al., "Criminal Victimization, 2020"; *see also* Rachel E. Morgan and Barbara A. Oudekerk, "Criminal Victimization, 2018," U.S. Department of Justice Bureau of Justice Statistics, September 2019, NCJ 253043, bjs.ojp.gov/content/pub/pdf/cv18.pdf.

19. Sered, *Until We Reckon. See also* Lynn Langton, Marcus Berzofsky, Christopher Krebs, and Hope Smiley-McDonald, "Victimizations Not Reported to the Police, 2006–2010," U.S. Department of Justice Bureau of Justice Statistics, August 2012, NCJ 238536, bjs.ojp.gov/content/pub/pdf/vnrp0610.pdf.

20. Sered, *Until We Reckon. See also* Langton et al., "Victimizations Not Reported to the Police, 2006–2010."

21. Sered, *Until We Reckon.*

22. Morgan et al., "Criminal Victimization, 2020;" *See also* Morgan and Oudekerk, "Criminal Victimization, 2018."

23. Jeff Asher and Ben Horwitz, "How Do the Police Actually Spend Their Time?" *New York Times,* June 19, 2020; Los Angeles Calls for Service Dashboard, data.lacity.org/ASafe-City/LAPD-Calls-for-Service-2020/84iq-i2r6 (1.5 percent of calls for service in

2020); Seattle Calls for Service Dashboard, www.seattle.gov/police/information-and
-data/calls-forservice-dashboard (4 percent of 911 calls for assaults, 4 percent for domestic incidents in 2019).

24. Andrea J. Ritchie for the National Black Women's Justice Institute, "Expanding Our Frame: Deepening Our Demands for Safety and Healing for Black Survivors of Sexual Violence," February 2019, incite-national.org/wp-content/uploads/2019/07/ritchie -Expanding-Our-Frame-Deepening-our-Demands-for-Safety-and-Healing-for-Black -Survivors-of-Sexual-Violence.pdf. *See also* NOW (National Organization for Women), "Black Women & Sexual Violence," 2018, now.org/wp-content/uploads/2018/02/Black -Women-and-Sexual-Violence-6.pdf.

25. Sandy E. James et al. for the National Center for Transgender Equality, "The Report of the 2015 U.S. Transgender Survey," transequality.org/sites/default/files/docs /usts/USTS-Full-Report-Dec17.pdf.

26. ACLU, "Responses from the Field: Sexual Assault, Domestic Violence, and Policing," October 2015, aclu.org/sites/default/files/field_document/2015.10.20_report_ -_responses_from_the_field.pdf.

27. Sered, *Until We Reckon*.

28. Sered, *Until We Reckon*.

29. Farah Jasmine Griffin, "What Justice Looks Like," *Boston Review*, September 7, 2021, bostonreview.net/arts-society-race/farah-jasmine-griffin-what-justice-looks.

30. ACLU, "Responses from the Field: Sexual Assault, Domestic Violence, and Policing."

31. ACLU, "Responses from the Field: Sexual Assault, Domestic Violence, and Policing."

32. Shauntrice Martin, "LMPD Does Not Keep Us Safe," NewsOne, June 15, 2021, newsone.com/4164834/lmpd-does-not-keep-us-safe.

33. The study's authors noted that "while it is possible that intimate partner and sexual violence victims are more likely to come into contact with police (necessarily leading to increased risk for police violence exposure), we controlled for other factors likely to increase police contact (i.e., histories of mental illness and criminal involvement) and prior research has documented the ways in which survivors have been met with neglectful, harmful, or abusive police responses, including women who had mental illness or substance abuse histories, lower incomes, and women of color." Lisa Fedina, "The Intersection of Interpersonal and State Violence Against Women," *The Gender Policy Report*, genderpolicyreport.umn.edu/the-intersection-of-interpersonal-and-state -violence-against-women. *See also* Lisa Fedina, Bethany L. Backes, Hyun-Jin Jun, Roma Shah, Boyoung Nam, Bruce G. Link, and Jordan E. DeVylder, "Police Violence Among Women in Four U.S. Cities," *Preventive Medicine*, 2018, 106:150–156.

34. Andrea J. Ritchie, *Shrouded in Silence: Police Sexual Violence: What We Know and What We Can Do About It*, Interrupting Criminalization, 2021, interruptingcriminaliza tion.com/breaking-the-silence; Ritchie, *Invisible No More*.

35. Amy Leisenring, "Whoa! They Could've Arrested Me!": Unsuccessful Identity Claims of Women During Police Response to Intimate Partner Violence," *Qualitative Sociology* 34 (2011): 353–370. *See also* Kris Henning, Brian Renauer, and Robert Holdford, "Victim or Offender? Heterogeneity Among Women Arrested for Intimate Partner Violence," *Journal of Family Violence* 21, no. 6 (2006): 351–368.

36. Ritchie, *Invisible No More*; *see also* Leigh Goodmark, *Decriminalizing Domestic Violence* (Oakland: University of California Press, 2018).

37. Cat Brooks, "Cat Brooks Discusses the Obstacles and Complications Behind Ending Domestic Violence," interviewed by NPR's Lulu Garcia-Navarro, October 4, 2021, www.npr.org/2021/10/03/1042802577/cat-brooks-discusses-the-obstacles-and -complications-behind-ending-domestic-viol.

38. Francine T. Sherman and Annie Balck, "Gender Injustice: System-Level Juvenile Justice Reforms for Girls," Law School, Boston College, September 2015, incorrigibles .org/gender-injustice-report.

39. "Maddesyn's Story," Free Maddesyn George, freemaddesyn.com/maddesyns-story. *See also* Madison Pauly, "Two Days Before Rittenhouse Verdict, a Native Woman Was Imprisoned for Killing Her Alleged Rapist," *Mother Jones*, November 19, 2021, mother jones.com/crime-justice/2021/11/rittenhouse-not-guilty-self-defense-maddesyn-george.

40. Survived and Punished, "Free Ky Petersen," survivedandpunished.org/2017/08/15 /free-ky-peterson.

41. ACLU, "Responses from the Field: Sexual Assault, Domestic Violence, and Policing."

42. ACLU, "Responses from the Field: Sexual Assault, Domestic Violence, and Policing."

43. Connie Wun, "Survivors at the Forefront of the Abolitionist Movement," in *Abolition for the People*, Colin Kaepernick, ed. (Kaepernick Publishing, 2021).

44. Talila A. Lewis, "The Birth of Resistance: Courageous Dreams, Powerful Nobodies & Revolutionary Madness," in *Resistance and Hope: Essays by Disabled People*, Alice Wong, ed., Disability Visibility Project, Kindle Edition.

45. Talila A. Lewis, @talilalewis, Twitter thread, September 21, 2016, 4:08 p.m., twitter.com/talilalewis/status/778687325320511488.

46. Lewis, @talilalewis, Twitter thread, September 21, 2016, 4:08 p.m.

47. Lewis, @talilalewis, Twitter thread, September 21, 2016, 4:08 p.m.

48. Lewis, "The Birth of Resistance: Courageous Dreams, Powerful Nobodies & Revolutionary Madness."

49. generation FIVE, *Ending Child Sexual Abuse: A Transformative Justice Handbook*, 2017, www.generationfive.org/wp-content/uploads/2017/06/Transformative-Justice -Handbook.pdf; Bay Area Transformative Justice Collective, batjc.wordpress.com.

50. Sered, *Until We Reckon*.

51. Goodmark, "The Violence Against Women Act Is Unlikely to Reduce Intimate Partner Violence."

52. Casey T. Taft, Laura E. Watkins, Jane Stafford, Amy E. Street, and Candice M. Monson, "Posttraumatic Stress Disorder and Intimate Relationship Problems: A Meta-Analysis," *Journal of Consulting and Clinical Psychology*, February 2011.

53. Goodmark, "The Violence Against Women Act Is Unlikely to Reduce Intimate Partner Violence." *See also* Michael L. Benson and Greer L. Fox, "Concentrated Disadvantage, Economic Distress, and Violence Against Women in Intimate Relationships," 2004, ojp.gov/pdffiles1/nij/199709.pdf.

54. Goodmark, The Violence Against Women Act Is Unlikely to Reduce Intimate Partner Violence."

55. Sered, *Until We Reckon*.

56. Sered, *Until We Reckon*.

57. Sered, *Until We Reckon*.

58. "The Criminal Justice System: Statistics," RAINN (Rape, Abuse & Incest National Network), rainn.org/criminal-justice-system.

59. Dean Spade, remarks at "Invisible No More: Police Violence Against Black Women and Women of Color in Troubled Times" conference, Barnard Center for Research on Women. 2017.

60. Ritchie, *Invisible No More*; Luana Ross, *Inventing the Savage* (Austin, TX: University of Texas Press, 1998).

61. Ritchie, *Invisible No More*; Ross, *Inventing the Savage*.

62. Ritchie, *Invisible No More*; Ross, *Inventing the Savage*.

63. INCITE!, incite-national.org.

64. Ritchie, *Invisible No More*.

65. Andrea J. Ritchie, *Shrouded in Silence: Police Sexual Violence: What We Know and What We Can Do About It*, Interrupting Criminalization, 2021, interruptingcriminalization.com/breaking-the-silence. *See also* Ritchie, *Invisible No More*; Matt Sedensky and Nomaan Merchant, "Investigation Reveals About 1,000 Police Officers Lost Jobs Over Sexual Misconduct," *The Guardian*, November 1, 2015.

66. "Women and Policing," womenandpolicing.com/violenceFS.asp.

67. As the National Center for Women and Policing puts it, "Victims often fear calling the police, because they know the case will be handled by officers who are colleagues and/or friends of their abuser." They "typically fear that the responding officers will side with their abuser and fail to properly investigate or document the crime," or, worse yet, retaliate. National Center for Women and Policing, womenandpolicing.com/violenceFS.asp. *See also* Esther Wang, "Cops Don't Care About Violence Against Women," *Jezebel*, June 11, 2020, jezebel.com/cops-dont-care-about-violence-against-women-1843908761. According to the National Center for Women and Policing, over an eight-year period in the '90s, partners of Los Angeles Police Department officers brought more than 200 cases of domestic violence to the LAPD. The department found fewer than half of those cases worthy of investigation. Of the 91 cases they did investigate, only four officers were convicted on criminal charges. One of those officers only received a fifteen-day suspension. Allegations of domestic violence didn't seem to hurt officers' careers; nearly one-third of those who received these allegations were promoted up the ranks. Not much has changed since then. As the *New York Times* noted in 2013, "In many departments, an officer will automatically be fired for a positive marijuana test, but can stay on the job after abusing or battering a spouse." Sarah Cohen, Rebecca R. Ruiz, and Sarah Childress, "Departments Are Slow to Police Their Own Abusers," *New York Times*, November 23, 2013.

68. Beth E. Richie, *Arrested Justice: Black Women, Violence, and America's Prison Nation* (New York: NYU Press, 2012).

69. Ritchie, *Shrouded in Silence*; *see also* Andrea J. Ritchie, *Invisible No More*.

70. "Widespread Sexual Assault," Freedom for Immigrants, freedomforimmigrants.org/sexual-assault. *See also* "Sexual Abuse in Immigration Detention," ACLU, aclu.org/issues/immigrants-rights/immigrants-rights-and-detention/sexual-abuse-immigration-detention-0.

71. Sandy E. James et al., National Center for Transgender Equality, "The Report of the 2015 U.S. Transgender Survey," transequality.org/sites/default/files/docs/usts/USTS

-Full-Report-Dec17.pdf. *See also* Jason Lyndon et al., "Coming Out of Concrete Closets: A Report on Black & Pink's National LGBTQ Prisoner Survey," October 2015, black andpink.org/wp-content/upLoads/Coming-Out-of-Concrete-Closets.-Black-and-Pink. -October-21-2015.pdf.

72. Robin mc'duff, deanne pernell, and karen saunders, "An Open Letter to the Anti-Rape Movement," Project NIA, 2020, issuu.com/projectnia/docs/letter-to-the-antirape -movement. The original copy of the letter was published in *Off Our Backs* 7, no. 5 (June 1977), 9–10, and can be found at enforcerapelaws.files.wordpress.com/2015/07 /lettertoantirapemovement.pdf.

73. Richie, *Arrested Justice*, 75.

74. Angela Y. Davis, Gina Dent, Erica Meiners, Beth E. Richie, and Nia Davis, "Why Policing and Prisons Can't End Gender Violence," *Boston Review*, January 24, 2022.

75. Goodmark, *Decriminalizing Domestic Violence*.

76. M. Kim, "Dancing the Carceral Creep: The Anti-Domestic Violence Movement and the Paradoxical Pursuit of Criminalization, 1973–1986," *UC Berkeley: Institute for the Study of Societal Issues* (2015), escholarship.org/uc/item/804227k6.

77. Often dubbed "hate crimes." *See* Kay Whitlock and Michael Bronski's *Considering Hate* (Boston: Beacon Press, 2015). *See also* Joey L. Mogul, Andrea J. Ritchie, and Kay Whitlock's *Queer (In)Justice: The Criminalization of LGBT People in the United States* (New York: Penguin Random House, 2012) for a critique of this term and of the move to increase criminal penalties for harms motivated by identity.

78. Kim, *Dancing the Carceral Creep*; Emily Thuma, *All Our Trials: Prisons, Policing, and the Feminist Fight to End Violence* (Chicago: UIC Press, 2019); Anne Russo, *Feminist Accountability: Disrupting Violence and Transforming Power* (New York: NYU Press, 2018); Elizabeth Bernstein, *Brokered Subjects: Sex, Trafficking, and the Politics of Freedom* (Chicago: University of Chicago Press, 2018); and Kristin Bumiller, *In an Abusive State: How Neoliberalism Appropriated the Feminist Movement Against Sexual Violence* (Durham: Duke University Press, 2008).

79. Davis et al., *Abolition. Feminism. Now.*

80. Mc'duff et al., "An Open Letter to the Anti-Rape Movement."

81. Mc'duff et al., "An Open Letter to the Anti-Rape Movement."

82. Ritchie, *Invisible No More*.

83. Kluger, "NY Must Do More for People in Prostitution."

84. Davis et al., *Abolition. Feminism. Now.*; Bernstein, *Brokered Subjects*.

85. Andrea J. Ritchie and Mariame Kaba, *Breaking the Silence: Supporting Survivors of Police Sexual Violence*, Interrupting Criminalization 2021, bit.ly/PSVCurriculum.

86. Mariame Kaba, "Blinders & the Tyranny of Good Intentions: Street Harassment, Stop & Frisk, and Criminalization . . . blog post at usprisonculture.com, August 20, 2013, www.usprisonculture.com/blog/2013/08/20/blinders-the-tyranny-of-good -intentions-street-harassment-stop-frisk-and-criminalization.

87. The youth-led research that YWAT conducted about street harassment was based on questions that the young women themselves wanted to better understand. Some of these questions included: "What do you think makes people harass you?" "Do you think that street harassment is a serious issue?" "Do you feel safe walking through the neighborhood alone?" "Where are you most likely to experience street harassment?" "Do you feel accepted when someone tries to talk to you on the street?"

88. Satya Vaught, "The Ms. Q&A: Dr. Connie Wun on Creating Free Futures and

a World Without Racial and Gender Violence," *Ms.*, May 29, 2021, msmagazine.com /2021/05/29/connie-wun-aapi-women-racial-gender-violence.

89. Davis et al., *Abolition. Feminism. Now.*

90. INCITE!, "Analysis," incite-national.org/analysis.

91. INCITE!, "Analysis," incite-national.org/analysis.

92. Davis et al., *Abolition. Feminism. Now.*

93. INCITE! and Critical Resistance, *Statement on Gender-Based Violence and the Prison-Industrial Complex*, 2002, incite-national.org/incite-critical-resistance-statement.

94. INCITE! and Critical Resistance, *Statement on Gender-Based Violence and the Prison-Industrial Complex.*

95. INCITE! and Critical Resistance, *Statement on Gender-Based Violence and the Prison-Industrial Complex.*

96. "Moment of Truth: Statement in Support of Black Lives," WCSAP (Washington Coalition of Sexual Assault Programs), June 30, 2020, wcsap.org/news/article/2020-06 -30/moment-truth.

97. "Moment of Truth: Statement in Support of Black Lives."

98. Survived and Punished NY, #FreeThemNY, freethemny.com.

99. Diana Colavita, Juli Kempner, Amanda Lawson, Ericka Persson, and Sojourner Rivers, "Cuomo's Gender-Based Violence Includes His Failure to Free Imprisoned Survivors, *Truthout*, March 19, 2021, truthout.org/articles/cuomos-gender-based-violence -includes-his-failure-to-free-imprisoned-survivors; Rachel Kennedy, "Time's Up on New York's Statute of Limitations, *Ms.*, August 14, 2019, msmagazine.com/2019/08/14/times -up-on-new-yorks-statute-of-limitations.

100. Eva Nagao and Mariame Kaba, *What About the Rapists? An Abolitionist FAQ*, Interrupting Criminalization, 2021, static1.squarespace.com/static/5ee39ec764dbd7179 cf1243c/t/6109e65d5a8ce56464ff94eb/1628038750972/WATR+Zine.pdf.

101. Melissa Jeltsen, "Don't Use Domestic Violence Victims to Derail Police Reform," *Huffington Post*, June 5, 2020, www.huffpost.com/entry/domestic-violence-defund -police_n_5eda8fe1c5b692d897d2de13?ped.

102. Wilson Wong, "'Defund the Police' Movement Could Offer Sexual Assault Survivors a Different Path for Justice, Experts Say," NBC News, August 2, 2020.

103. Goodmark, *Decriminalizing Domestic Violence. See also* Sered, *Until We Reckon.*

104. Goodmark, *Decriminalizing Domestic Violence.*

105. Deann Alcantara-Thompson & Sid Jordan, Lifting Up Transformative Approaches to Domestic & Sexual Violence Prevention, Coalition Ending Domestic Violence, September 2021, endgv.org/wp-content/uploads/2021/09/MP_Lifting _Up_Transformative_Frameworks2021.pdf?fbclid=IwAR1GgKJfHWk79wOs0Pi7Y qt3xBYo942oKSE0dA0aRk-W8f_uwLY2jcybzZk.

106. API Chaya, "Organize," www.apichaya.org/organize2.

107. Andrea J. Ritchie, "Police Responses to Domestic Violence: A Fact Sheet," Interrupting Criminalization, static1.squarespace.com/static/5ee39ec764dbd7179cf1243c /t/615d2d8d53ef604bf219fa3f/1633496919504/Police+Responses+to+Domestic+Viole nce_English.pdf. *See also* Alexander and Sered, "Making Communities Safe, Without the Police"; Wun in *Abolition for the People*, Kaepernick, ed.; Corenia Smith and Miski Noor, "Op-Ed: Question 2 Represents a New Beginning for Minneapolis," *Minnesota*

Women's Press, October 29, 2021, womenspress.com/op-ed-question-2-represents-a-new-beginning-for-minneapolis.

108. Mallika Kaur, "Victims Must Not Be Lost in Domestic Violence and Policing Debates," *Ms.*, October 6, 2020, msmagazine.com/2020/10/06/domestic-violence-defund-the-police.

109. In Our Names Network, inournamesnetwork.com

110. EJ Dickson, "A Black Trans Woman Named Iyanna Dior Was Beaten by a Mob in Minneapolis," *Rolling Stone*, June 3, 2020, rollingstone.com/culture/culture-news/iyanna-dior-minneapolis-beating-1009736.

111. INCITE! and Critical Resistance, *Statement on Gender-Based Violence and the Prison-Industrial Complex*.

112. INCITE! and Critical Resistance, *Statement on Gender-Based Violence and the Prison-Industrial Complex*.

113. Davis et al., *Abolition. Feminism. Now.*

Re-Form

1. "Peter Hamby Interviews President Obama," December 2, 2020, youtube.com/watch?v=Yj-eNGfeG0o.

2. Maya Schenwar and Victoria Law, *Prison by Any Other Name* (New York: The New Press, 2020).

3. "Campaign Zero," Wikipedia, www.en.wikipedia.org/wiki/Campaign_Zero.

4. Charlotte Rosen, "Abolition or Bust: Liberal Police Reform as an Engine of Carceral Violence," The Abusable Past, June 25, 2020, radicalhistoryreview.org/abusablepast/abolition-or-bust-liberal-police-reform-as-an-engine-of-carceral-violence.

5. Communities United Against Police Brutality, "What Will It Take to End Police Violence? Recommendations for Reform," communityresourcehub.org/resources/what-will-it-take-to-end-police-violence-recommendations-for-reform. *See also* Nekima Levy Armstrong, "Black Voters Want Better Policing Not Posturing by Progressives," *New York Times*, November 9, 2021.

6. President's Task Force on 21st Century Policing, 2015; Final Report of the President's Task Force on 21st Century Policing (Washington: Office of Community Oriented Policing Services).

7. George Floyd Justice in Policing Act of 2021, H.R. 1280, 117th Congress (2021–2022), congress.gov/117/bills/hr1280/BILLS-117hr1280eh.pdf.

8. Robert Klemko and John Sullivan, *"The Push to Remake Policing Takes Decades, Only to Begin Again,"* Washington Post, June 10, 2021.

9. N'dea Yancey-Bragg, "Justice Department Prohibits Federal Officers from Using Chokeholds, Limits No-Knock Warrants," *USA Today*, September 16, 2021.

10. George Floyd Justice in Policing Act of 2021.

11. George Floyd Justice in Policing Act of 2021.

12. #8cantwait, www.8cantwait.org. *See also* "Recall #8CantWait," OrganizeFor, campaigns.organizefor.org/petitions/recall-8cantwait.

13. Cherrell Brown and Philip V. McHarris, "#8cantwait Is Based on Faulty Data Science," *Medium*, June 5, 2020, medium.com/@8cantwait.faulty/8cantwait-is-based

-on-faulty-data-science-a4e0b85fae40. *See also* Andrew Rogers, "Why 8 Can't Wait? Questions for Campaign Zero on Statistical Validity and Organizational Practicality," *Medium*, June 4, 2020, medium.com/@rogerslandrew/why-8-cant-wait-967fb08c93ea; Olivia Murray, "Why 8 Won't Work: The Failings of the 8 Can't Wait Campaign and the Obstacle Police Reform Efforts Pose to Police Abolition," *Harvard Civil Rights—Civil Liberties Law Review*, June 17, 2020, harvardcrcl.org/why-8-wont-work.

14. The 72 percent figure has since been removed from the #8CantWait site (8cantwait .org) but is memorialized in the pieces critiquing the platform. *See also* Andrew Rogers, "Why 8 Can't Wait? Questions for Campaign Zero on Statistical Validity and Organizational Practicality," *Medium*, June 4, 2020, medium.com/@rogerslandrew/why-8-cant -wait-967fb08c93ea; Murray, "Why 8 Won't Work"; Brown and McHarris, "#8cantwait Is Based on Faulty Data Science."

15. Derecka Purnell, "The George Floyd Act Wouldn't Have Saved George Floyd's Life. That Says It All," *The Guardian*, March 4, 2021.

16. Minneapolis was the subject of a prior Department of Justice intervention to create an "early warning system." Shaila Dewan and Serge F. Kovaleski, "Thousands of Complaints Do Little to Change Police Ways," *New York Times*, June 8, 2020. Yet, Derek Chauvin remained on the force even after twenty-two complaints were made against him over nearly two decades—including one made by a young Black woman named Zoya Code who said that Chauvin knelt on her neck when responding to a domestic violence call in 2017, just as he would kneel on George Floyd's a few years later. Abbie Vansickle and Jamiles Lartey, "'That Could Have Been Me': The People Derek Chauvin Choked Before George Floyd," The Marshall Project, February 2, 2021, themarshallproject .org/2021/02/02/that-could-have-been-me-the-people-derek-chauvin-choked-before -george-floyd. The city also participated in the National Initiative for Building Community Trust and Justice for four years ending in 2018, during which it adopted reforms focused on procedural justice, implicit bias training, and community policing practices. National Initiative for Building Community Trust and Justice, Minneapolis, Minnesota, trustandjustice.org/pilot-sites/info/minneapolis-minnesota. The Initiative is co-led by the Center for Policing Equity and the Yale Justice Collaboratory, among others. *See also* "Minn. Law Enforcement Looking to Adopt 21st Century Policing," *CBS Minnesota*, September 17, 2015, minnesota.cbslocal.com/2015/09/17/minn-law-enforcement -looking-to-adopt-21st-century-policing; Brown and McHarris, "#8cantwait Is Based on Faulty Data Science."

17. Amy Forliti, Steve Karnowski, and Tammy Webber, "Police Official: Chauvin Trained to Avoid Neck Pressure," ABC News, April 6, 2021.

18. Micah Herskind and Tiffany Roberts, "The Failure of Police Reform," *New York Magazine*, January 31, 2022, nymag.com/intelligencer/2022/01/atlanta-police-reform -failure.html.

19. Brown and McHarris, "#8cantwait Is Based on Faulty Data Science."

20. Brown and McHarris, "#8cantwait Is Based on Faulty Data Science."

21. Olivia Murray, "Why 8 Won't Work: The Failings of the 8 Can't Wait Campaign and the Obstacle Police Reform Efforts Pose to Police Abolition," *Harvard Civil Rights—Civil Liberties Law Review*, June 17, 2020, harvardcrcl.org/why-8-wont -work.

22. #8toAbolition describe themselves as "a geographically dispersed, loose formation of abolitionists across the U.S.," including "people who are Black, Latinx, Asian,

Arab, Muslim, white, trans, queer, migrant, disabled, sex working, caregiving, and working-class." Contributors to 8 to Abolition include: Mon Mohapatra, Leila Raven, Nnennaya Amuchie, Reina Sultan, K. Agbebiyi, Sarah T. Hamid, Micah Herskind, Derecka Purnell, Eli Dru, and Rachel Kuo.

23. #8toAbolition, 8toabolition.com.

24. Ernest Owens, "The Rise and Rupture of Campaign Zero," *New York Magazine*, January 31, 2022.

25. "Our Principles," Center for Policing Equity, policingequity.org/what-we -do/our-principles. *See also* "A RoadMap for Exploring New Models of Funding Public Safety," Center for Policing Equity, policingequity.org/images/pdfs-doc /RoadMap_for_Exploring_New_Models_of_Funding_Public_Safety.pdf.

26. "Impact," Center for Policing Equity, policingequity.org/what-we-do/local -impact.

27. Melvin L. Oliver, Andrea J. Ritchie, john a. powell, and Phillip Atiba Goff at "Racial Justice in Our Time: A Conversation with Activist Scholars," Pitzer College, September 10, 2020, pitzer.edu/racial-justice-initiative/racial-justice-in-our-time -a-conversation-with-activist-scholars.

28. Keeanga-Yamahtta Taylor, *From #BlackLivesMatter to Black Liberation* (Chicago: Haymarket Books, 2016).

29. Elizabeth Hinton, *From the War on Poverty to the War on Crime* (Cambridge: Harvard University Press, 2017). *See also* Elizabeth Hinton, *America on Fire* (New York: Liveright, 2021).

30. Slave patrols, progenitors of U.S. police forces, were formed much earlier, beginning in the late seventeenth century. *See* Andrea J. Ritchie, *Invisible No More*; Kristian Williams, *Our Enemies in Blue: Police and Power in America* (Oakland: AK Press, 2015).

31. Daniel Czitrom, *New York Exposed: The Gilded Age Police Scandal That Launched the Progressive Era* (Oxford: Oxford University Press, 2016).

32. Marilynn Johnson, *Street Justice: A History of Police Violence in New York City* (Boston: Beacon Press, 2003).

33. Johnson, *Street Justice*.

34. Kenneth Novak et al., *Police & Society*, 7th ed. (New York: Oxford University Press, 2017).

35. Johnson, *Street Justice*; *See also* Saidiya Hartman, *Wayward Lives, Beautiful Experiments* (New York: W.W. Norton & Company, 2019); Cheryl D. Hicks, *Talk with You Like a Woman* (Chapel Hill: The University of North Carolina Press, 2010); Cynthia Blair, *I've Gotta Make My Livin'* (Chicago: The University of Chicago Press, 2010).

36. Johnson, *Street Justice*.

37. Dan Berger and David Stein, "What Is and Could Be," in *Abolition for the People*, Colin Kaepernick, ed. (Kaepernick Publishing, 2021). *See also* Garrett Felber, "The Struggle to Abolish the Police Is Not New," *Boston Review*, June 9, 2020, bostonreview .net/race/garrett-felber-struggle-abolish-police-not-new.

38. Elizabeth Hinton, *America on Fire: The Untold History of Police Violence and Black Rebellion Since the 1960s* (New York: Liveright, 2021). *See also* "Police Conduct and Patrol Practices" in *Report of The National Advisory Commission on Civil Disorders*, 1968, www.eisenhowerfoundation.org/docs/Kerner%20Commission%20Report.pdf.

39. Elizabeth Hinton, *From the War on Poverty to the War on Crime: The Making of Mass Incarceration in America* (Cambridge, MA: Harvard University Press, 2017).*See also* Hinton, *America on Fire.*

40. Klemko and Sullivan, "The Push to Remake Policing Takes Decades, Only to Begin Again."

41. Andrea J. Ritchie, *Invisible No More* (Boston: Beacon Press, 2017).

42. U.S. Department of Justice, "Fact Sheet on Racial Profiling," June 17, 2003, justice .gov/archive/opa/pr/2003/June/racial_profiling_fact_sheet.pdf.

43. New Jersey Office of the Attorney General, "State Police Racial Profiling Consent Decree Dissolved. Federal Judge Acts on Joint Petition by State and U.S. Justice Department," September 21, 2009, nj.gov/oag/newsreleases09/pr20090921a.html.

44. Klemko and Sullivan, "The Push to Remake Policing Takes Decades, Only to Begin Again."

45. Susan Ferriss, "In Horrifying Detail, Women Accuse U.S. Customs Officers of Invasive Body Searches," *Washington Post*, August 19, 2018.

46. Ritchie, *Invisible No More.*

47. Communities United for Police Reform, changethenypd.org.

48. *David Floyd et al. v. The City of New York*, 08 Civ. 1034 (SAS), Document 373, filed August 12, 2013, ccrjustice.org/sites/default/files/assets/Floyd-Liability-Opinion -8-12-13.pdf. *See also* ccrjustice.org/home/what-we-do/our-cases/floyd-et-al-v-city-new -york-et-al; *David Floyd et al. v. The City of New York*, 08 Civ. 1034 (SAS), Document 372, filed August 12, 2013, ccrjustice.org/sites/default/files/assets/Floyd-Remedy -Opinion-8-12-13.pdf; Center for Constitutional Rights, Summary of Remedial Opinion and Order in *Floyd, et al. v. City of New York*, 08-cv-1034 (SAS)," ccrjustice.org/sites /default/files/attach/2015/09/Floyd-Remedy-Decision-Summary-8-12-13.pdf.

49. Center for Constitutional Rights, "New Stop-and-Frisk Report: NYPD Racial Bias Persists," October 28, 2020, commondreams.org/newswire/2020/10/28/new-stop -and-frisk-report-nypd-racial-bias-persists.

50. "NYC Budget Justice," Communities United for Police Reform, changethenypd .org/nycbudgetjustice.

51. Violent Crime Control and Law Enforcement Act of 1994, H.R. 3355, 103rd Congress (1993–1994). *See also* Deanna Hoskins, Andrea C. James, and Kumar Rao, "The '94 Crime Bill 25 Years Later: It's Time for a Reckoning," *Truthout*, September 30, 2019, colorlines.com/articles/94-crime-bill-25-years-later-its-time-reckoning-op-ed; "94 Crime Bill," The People's Coalition for Safety and Freedom, safetyandfreedom.org/the -94-crime-bill.

52. Wesley C. Ware and Andrea J. Ritchie for the Community Resource Hub, "Navigating DOJ Consent Decrees in the Context of Campaigns to Defund the Police," June 2021, communityresourcehub.org/wp-content/uploads/2021/06/0602_DOJ_B.pdf.

53. Ware and Ritchie, "Navigating DOJ Consent Decrees in the Context of Campaigns to Defund the Police."

54. Robert C. Davis, Christopher W. Ortiz, Nicole J. Henderson, Joel Miller, and Michelle K. Massie, *Turning Necessity into Virtue: Pittsburgh's Experience with a Federal Consent Decree*, Vera Institute, September 2002, vera.org/downloads/Publications /turning-necessities-into-virtue-pittsburghs-experience-with-a-federal-consent-decree /legacy_downloads/Pittsburgh_consent_decree.pdf; vera.org/downloads/Publications

/can-federal-intervention-bring-lasting-improvement-in-local-policing-the-pittsburgh
-consent-decree/legacy_downloads/277_530.pdf.

55. Davis et al., *Turning Necessity into Virtue*.

56. Klemko and Sullivan, "The Push to Remake Policing Takes Decades, Only to Begin Again."

57. Klemko and Sullivan, "The Push to Remake Policing Takes Decades, Only to Begin Again."

58. Klemko and Sullivan, "The Push to Remake Policing Takes Decades, Only to Begin Again."

59. Jordan Flaherty, *Floodlines: Community and Resistance from Katrina to the Jena Six* (Chicago: Haymarket, 2010); A.C. Thompson, "Six More Charged in New Orleans Danziger Bridge Shootings," *ProPublica*, July 13, 2010.

60. Lydia Pelot-Hobbs, "Accept Nothing Less Than Police Abolition," *Boston Review*, June 24, 2020, bostonreview.net/law-justice/lydia-pelot-hobbs-accept-nothing-less -police-abolition.

61. Pelot-Hobbs, "Accept Nothing Less Than Police Abolition."

62. Klemko and Sullivan, "The Push to Remake Policing Takes Decades, Only to Begin Again."

63. U.S. Department of Justice, "Final Report of the President's Task Force on 21st Century Policing," NCJ 248928, May 2015, ojp.gov/ncjrs/virtual-library/abstracts/final -report-presidents-task-force-21st-century-policing.

64. Rachel Herzing, "The Fantasy of Police," in David Correia and Tyler Wall, eds., *Violent Order*.

65. Herzing, "The Fantasy of Police."

66. Wesley C. Ware and Andrea J. Ritchie for the Community Resource Hub, "Navigating DOJ Consent Decrees in the Context of Campaigns to Defund the Police."

67. U.S. Department of Justice, "Attorney General Merrick B. Garland Announces Investigation of the City of Minneapolis, Minnesota, and the Minneapolis Police Department," April 21, 2021, justice.gov/opa/pr/attorney-general-merrick-b-garland -announces-investigation-city-minneapolis-minnesota-and. *See also* "U.S. Department of Justice, Department of Justice Announces Investigation of the Louisville/Jefferson County Metro Government and Louisville Metro Police Department," April 26, 2021, justice.gov/opa/pr/department-justice-announces-investigation-louisvillejefferson -county-metro-government-and.

68. Herzing, "The Fantasy of Police."

69. Naomi Murakawa, "Three Traps of Police Reform," in *Abolition for the People*, Kaepernick, ed.

70. Dylan Rodriguez, "Police Reform as Counterinsurgency," in *Abolition for the People*, Kaepernick, ed.

71. Teju Cole, Facebook, March 19, 2021, facebook.com/permalink.php?story_fbid =10158930820587199&id=200401352198&_rdc=1&_rdr.

72. Murakawa, "Three Traps of Police Reform." *See also* Amna Akbar, "An Abolitionist Horizon for (Police) Reform, *California Law Review* 108, no. 6 (December 2020), californialawreview.org/print/abolitionist-horizon-police-reform.

73. Murakawa, "Three Traps of Police Reform."

74. Charlotte Rosen, "Abolition or Bust: Liberal Police Reform as an Engine of Carceral Violence," *Radical History Review*, June 25, 2020, radicalhistoryreview.org /abusablepast/abolition-or-bust-liberal-police-reform-as-an-engine-of-carceral-violence.

75. Rosen, "Abolition or Bust: Liberal Police Reform as an Engine of Carceral Violence."

76. Colin Kaepernick, *Abolition for the People*, "Introduction."

77. Correia and Wall, *Violent Order*, "Introduction."

78. Minneapolis Police Department, "The Minneapolis Police Department Policy and Procedure Manual," last updated October 8, 2021, published February 25, 2019, 235, 237, 240, minneapolismn.gov/media/-www-content-assets/documents/MPD-Policy -and-Procedure-Manual.pdf.

79. Mike Ludwig, "Amir Locke Murder Shows 'Reforming the Police' Isn't Enough, Activists Say," *Truthout*, February 9, 2022, truthout.org/articles/amir-locke-murder -shows-reforming-the-police-isnt-enough-activists-say; Nathalie Baptiste, "The Violent Sameness of the Police Reform Movement," *HuffPost*, February 8, 2022, www.huffpost .com/entry/police-reform-failed-amir-locke_n_6202b559e4b0500424339c6a.

80. Brendan McQuade, "The Prose of Pacification: Critical Theory, Police Power and Abolition Socialism," *Social Justice* 47, no. 3/4 (2020): 57. *See also* Brendan McQuade, *Pacifying the Homeland: Intelligence Fusion and Mass Supervision* (Oakland: University of California Press, 2019), 9–15, 25–40.

81. U.S. Department of Justice, "Community Relations Services Toolkit for Policing: Policing 101," justice.gov/file/1376626/download.

82. Charles Blow, "Awful but Lawful," *New York Times*, April 7, 2021.

83. Correia and Wall, *Violent Order*, "Introduction."

84. Correia and Wall, *Violent Order*, "Introduction"; *see also* Barry Friedman and Maria Ponomarenko, "To Rein In Abuse by the Police, Lawmakers Must Do What the Supreme Court Will Not," *New York Times*, October 27, 2021.

85. U.S. Constitution, amend. XIV, constitution.congress.gov/constitution /amendment-14. *See also* Jennifer Laurin, Michael Avery, David Rudovsky, and Karen Blum, *Police Misconduct Law and Litigation*, 3rd ed. (Thompson-Reuters, 2017).

86. *Whren v. United States*, 517 U.S. 806 (1996).

87. Akbar, "An Abolitionist Horizon for (Police) Reform."

88. Devon W. Carbado, "From Stopping Black People to Killing Black People: The Fourth Amendment Pathways to Police Violence," *California Law Review* 105, no. 125 (2016). *See also* Ritchie, *Invisible No More*.

89. Ritchie, *Invisible No More*.

90. Akbar, "An Abolitionist Horizon for (Police) Reform."

91. Murakawa, "Three Traps of Police Reform."

92. Dylan Rodriguez writes that the logic of "reformism," "the ideological and political position that fixates on reform as the primary if not exclusive engine of social change/justice," "sees the law as the only legitimate form of protest, collective cultural/political expression, and/or direct intervention on systemically violent conditions." Dylan Rodriguez, "Police Reform as Counterinsurgency," in *Abolition for the People*, Kaepernick, ed. This is logic of the prison industrial complex, which "affirms that any attempts at reforms of the criminal legal system must be found within the confines of the system itself," rather than looking beyond it. Whitlock and Heitzeg, *Carceral Con*, 46.

93. Conor Friedersdorf, "Eric Garner and the NYPD's History of Deadly Chokeholds: The Context for Another Officer-Involved Homicide," *The Atlantic*, December 4, 2014.

94. Friedersdorf, "Eric Garner and the NYPD's History of Deadly Chokeholds."

95. Mark Neocleous, *A Critical Theory of Police Power: The Fabrication of Social Order* (Brooklyn: Verso, 2021).

96. Ali Watkins and Ashley Southall, "N.Y.C.'s Police Chokehold Ban Is Struck Down by Court," *New York Times*, June 23, 2021. The Eric Garner Anti-Chokehold Act makes strangulation causing death by a police officer a felony, nyassembly.gov/leg/?default _fld=&leg_video=&bn=A06144&term=2019&Summary=Y&Actions=Y.

97. Neocleous, *A Critical Theory of Police Power*.

98. Murakawa, "Three Traps of Police Reform."

99. Murakawa, "Three Traps of Police Reform."

100. Mariame Kaba and Andrea J. Ritchie, "A World Where George Floyd and Ma'Khia Bryant Would Still Be Here Is a World Without Police," A Year in Social Justice, One Digital, newsone.com/4143261/george-floyd-makhia-bryant-abolition-police.

101. Al Sharpton, "Derek Chauvin's Trial Shows Police Reform Needs to Come from Cops," MSNBC.com, April 8, 2021, msnbc.com/opinion/how-derek-chauvin-s-trial -shows-things-can-fact-change-n1263431.

102. Kaba and Ritchie, "A World Where George Floyd and Ma'Khia Bryant Would Still Be Here Is a World Without Police." *See also* Simon Balto, "This Much Is Clear: Derek Chauvin's Trial Won't Change Policing in America," *The Guardian*, April 15, 2021.

103. Kaba and Ritchie, "A World Where George Floyd and Ma'Khia Bryant Would Still Be Here Is a World Without Police." *See also* Balto, "This Much Is Clear: Derek Chauvin's Trial Won't Change Policing in America."

104. Klemko and Sullivan, "The Push to Remake Policing Takes Decades, Only to Begin Again." According to defundpolice.org, as of November 2021, 152 of these pieces of legislation advanced goals of divesting from policing and investing in community-based safety strategies. However, these were clearly in the minority.

105. Ruha Benjamin, Plenary, "Our Tech Futures: A Convening on Tech Surveillance and Accountability," Just Futures Law Conference, June 1, 2021, fb.watch/9dwGBp0Ov0.

106. Brendan McQuade, "The Camden Police Department Is Not a Model for Policing in the Post-George Floyd Era," *The Appeal*, June 12, 2020, theappeal.org/camden-police -george-floyd.

107. McQuade, "The Camden Police Department Is Not a Model for Policing in the Post-George Floyd Era"; *see also* Whitlock and Heitzeg, *Carceral Con.*

108. McQuade, "The Camden Police Department Is Not a Model for Policing in the Post-George Floyd Era."

109. McQuade, "The Camden Police Department Is Not a Model for Policing in the Post-George Floyd Era."

110. McQuade, "The Camden Police Department Is Not a Model for Policing in the Post-George Floyd Era."

111. Andrea J. Ritchie, "A Deadly Three Minutes: The Web of Police Violence That Killed Charleena Lyles," *Rewire*, June 22, 2017, rewirenewsgroup.com/article/2017/06 /22/deadly-3-minutes-charleena-lyles. *See also* "The Fatal Police Shooting of Charleena Lyles Cries Out for Body Cameras. But 7 Years On, We Still Don't Have Them," *Seattle Times*, June 21, 2017.

112. Stop LAPD Spying Coalition, "Body Cameras Have Not Helped Enforce Accountability Among Various Police Departments," January 2015, stoplapdspying.org/wp-content/uploads/2015/03/Body-Camera-Fact-Sheet-Jan-2015-1.pdf. *See also* Stop LAPD Spying Coalition, "Body-Worn Cameras: An Empty Reform to Expand the Surveillance State," April 2015, stoplapdspying.org/wp-content/uploads/2015/04/Stop-LAPD-Spying-Coalition-Report-on-Use-of-Body-Cameras-by-Law-Enforcement-April-2015.pdf.

113. Stop LAPD Spying Coalition, "Body Cameras Have Not Helped Enforce Accountability Among Various Police Departments." *See also* Stop LAPD Spying Coalition, "Body-Worn Cameras: An Empty Reform to Expand the Surveillance State."

114. Stop LAPD Spying Coalition, "Body Cameras Have Not Helped Enforce Accountability Among Various Police Departments." The 60 percent statistic comes from a 2014 story by Connie Fossi-Garcia and Dan Lieberman for Fusion, "Investigation of 5 Cities Finds Body Cameras Usually Help Police," December 2014, fusion.tv/story/31986/investigation-of-5-cities-finds-body-cameras-usually-help-police.

115. Stop LAPD Spying Coalition, "Body Cameras Have Not Helped Enforce Accountability Among Various Police Departments."

116. "How George Floyd Died, and What Happened Next," *New York Times*, November 1, 2021.

117. Brakkton Booker, "Body Camera Video of George Floyd and Police Offers New Details of Deadly Encounter," NPR, August 14, 2020.

118. Candice Norwood, "Body Cameras Are Seen as Key to Police Reform. But Do They Increase Accountability?" PBS, June 25, 2020, pbs.org/newshour/politics/body-cameras-are-seen-as-key-to-police-reform-but-do-they-increase-accountability. *See also* Nell Greenfieldboyce, "Body Cam Study Shows No Effect on Police Use of Force or Citizen Complaints," *All Things Considered*, NPR, October 20, 2017.

119. Stop LAPD Spying Coalition, "Body-Worn Cameras: An Empty Reform to Expand the Surveillance State."

120. Murakawa, "Three Traps of Police Reform."

121. Murakawa, "Three Traps of Police Reform."

122. Murakawa, "Three Traps of Police Reform."

123. Rory Kramer and Brianna Remster, "The Slow Violence of Contemporary Policing," SocArXiv, July 27, 2021, doi:10.31235/osf.io/zuych. *See also* Ritchie, *Invisible No More*; Andrea J. Ritchie and Joey L. Mogul, "In the Shadows of the War on Terror: Persistent Police Torture of People of Color in the United States," *Race, Racism and the Law*, April 14, 2019.

124. Ruha Benjamin, Plenary, "Our Tech Futures: A Convening on Tech Surveillance and Accountability," Just Futures Law Conference, June 1, 2021, fb.watch/9dwGBp0Ov0; Color of Change, *Police Foundations: A Corporate-Sponsored Threat to Democracy and Black Lives*, 2021, policefoundations.org/wp-content/uploads/2021/10/Color-Of-Change-Report-Police-Foundations-A-Corporate-Sponsored-Threat-to-Democracy-Black-Lives.pdf.

125. *See, e.g.*, Tina Moore and Danika Fears, "City to Pay NYPD Cops More to Wear Body Cameras," *New York Post*, December 26, 2016; Sharon Coolidge, "Cincinnati Police Union Wants More Pay for Officers to Wear Body Cameras," *USA Today*, August 19, 2016.

126. Brandon Blackburn-Dwyer, "How Technology Will Lead to Better (and Safer) Policing," *Global Citizen*, July 8, 2016, globalcitizen.org/en/content/police-technology -stop-shootings.

127. Emily Hopkins and Melissa Sanchez, "Chicago's 'Race-Neutral' Traffic Cameras Ticket Black and Latino Drivers the Most," *ProPublica*, January 11, 2022, www .propublica.org/article/chicagos-race-neutral-traffic-cameras-ticket-black-and-latino -drivers-the-most; Andrea J. Ritchie, "Epicenter: Chicago, Reclaiming a City from Neoliberalism," Political Research Associates, 2019, politicalresearch.org/2019/06/05 /epicenter-chicago-reclaiming-a-city-from-neoliberalism.

128. Justin Hansford, "Community Policing Reconsidered," in *Policing the Planet: Why the Policing Crisis Led to Black Lives Matter*, Jordan T. Camp and Christina Heatherton, eds. (Brooklyn: Verso, 2016).

129. We Charge Genocide, "Counter-CAPS Report: The Community Engagement Arm of the Police State," 2015, wechargegenocide.org/wp-content/uploads/2015/10 /CAPSreport-final.pdf.

130. "Studies have shown that police will solicit the opinions of business owners and church leaders and disproportionately seek out whites, later presenting the opinions of this narrow slice of the population as the community voice." Hansford, "Community Policing Reconsidered."

131. "A World Without Prisons: A Conversation with Mariame Kaba," *Lumpen* magazine, April 7, 2016.

132. Andrea Leonhart, "NYPD to Open Its First Community Center in East New York," *BK Reader*, August 9, 2019, bkreader.com/2019/08/09/nypd-to-open-its-first -community-center-in-east-new-york.

133. Novak et al., *Police & Society*.

134. Communities United for Police Reform, Testimony for President's Task Force on 21st Century Policing: Public Listening Session on Policy & Oversight, "LGBT People's Experiences of Policing," "Women of Color's Experiences of Policing," changethenypd .org/testimony-presidents-task-force-21st-century-policing-public-listening-session -policy-oversight.

135. Andrea J. Ritchie, "As We #SayHerName, 7 Policy Paths to Stop Police Violence Against Black Girls and Women," *Colorlines*, May 19, 2016.

136. Mariame Kaba, "The System Isn't Broken," *The New Inquiry*, June 2015, reprinted in *We Do This 'Til We Free Us* (Chicago: Haymarket Books, 2020).

137. With respect to prosecutions for police sexual violence, *see* Andrea J. Ritchie, "States Are Trying to Tackle Police Sexual Violence, but the Solutions Fall Dangerously Short," *Think Progress*, May 10, 2018, archive.thinkprogress.org/states-police-sexual -violence-solutions-fall-short-7cb18a268253.

138. Ritchie and Kaba, *Breaking the Silence: Supporting Survivors of Police Sexual Violence.*

139. Talila A. Lewis, "Disability Justice in the Age of Mass Incarceration," in *Deaf People in the Criminal Justice System: Selected Topics on Advocacy, Incarceration, and Social Justice*, Debra Guthmann et al., eds. (Washington: Gallaudet University Press, 2021), 229–303.

140. Lewis, "Disability Justice in the Age of Mass Incarceration."

141. Lewis, "Disability Justice in the Age of Mass Incarceration."

142. Andrea J. Ritchie and Maurice B-P Weeks, "In Calling to Defund Police, Don't Fixate on Costs of Police Settlements," *Truthout*, September 12, 2020.

143. Ritchie and Weeks, "In Calling to Defund Police, Don't Fixate on Costs of Police Settlements."

144. Policing Project at NYU School of Law and The Justice Collaboratory at Yale Law School, "Reimagining Public Safety: First Convening Report," January 2021, law.yale.edu/sites/default/files/area/center/justice/rps_session_i_report.pdf.

145. Andrea J. Ritchie, "The Demand Is Still #DefundthePolice #FundthePeople #DefendBlackLives," Interrupting Criminalization, January 2021, interruptingcriminalization.com/defundpolice-update.

146. Wesley C. Ware and Andrea J. Ritchie for the Community Resource Hub, "Navigating DOJ Consent Decrees in the Context of Campaigns to Defund the Police."

147. John Duda, "Towards the Horizon of Abolition: A Conversation with Mariame Kaba," *Next System Project*, November 9, 2017, thenextsystem.org/learn/stories/towards-horizon-abolition-conversation-mariame-kaba.

148. Mark Engler and Paul Engler, "Making Our Demands Both Practical and Visionary," August 3, 2021, forgeorganizing.org/article/making-our-demands-both-practical-and-visionary.

149. Rachel Herzing, "Big Dreams and Bold Steps Toward a Police-Free Future," *Truthout*, September 16, 2015, truthout.org/articles/big-dreams-and-bold-steps-toward-a-police-free-future.

150. Ruth Wilson Gilmore, *Golden Gulag* (University of California Press, 2007).

151. Angela Y. Davis, Gina Dent, Erica Meiners, and Beth E. Richie, *Abolition. Feminism. Now.* (Chicago: Haymarket Press, 2022).

152. Mark Engler and Paul Engler, "Making Our Demands Both Practical and Visionary."

153. Dean Spade, CLAGS Kessler Award Lecture, 2016, youtube.com/watch?v=VNKTX6RqTlM.

154. Peter Gelderloos, *The Failure of Non-Violence: How Nonviolence Protects the State* (Left Bank Books, 2015).

155. "Meditations on Abolitionist Practices, Reformist Moments, with Rachel Herzing and Erica R. Meiners," in *The Long Term: Resisting Life Sentences, Working Toward Freedom*, Alice Kim, Erica R. Meiners, Audrey Petty, Jill Petty, Beth E. Richie, and Sarah Ross, eds. (Chicago: Haymarket Books, 2018), 201.

156. #STOPTHECOPS and #FUNDBLACKFUTURES demands issued at an action targeting the 2015 International Association of Chiefs of Police conference in Chicago.

157. "BYP100 Feature: Official Statement from the BYP100 on the Firing of CPD Police Superintendent," BYP100, December 7, 2015, blackyouthproject.com/byp-100-feature-official-statement-from-the-byp100-on-the-firing-of-cpd-police-superintendent; demands made by Black youth and allies at an action targeting the annual conference of the International Association of Chiefs of Police held in Chicago in 2015.

158. First Defense Legal Aid, www.first-defense.org.

159. The Community Renewal Society, a faith-based coalition in Chicago.

160. Friedman and Ponomarenko, "To Rein In Abuse by the Police, Lawmakers Must Do What the Supreme Court Will Not."

161. Rachel Herzing, "Advice to New Abolitionists," 2020, criticalresistance.org/advice -to-new-abolitionists.

162. GBD 2019 Police Violence US Subnational Collaborators, "Fatal Police Violence By Race and State in the USA, 1980–2019: A Network Meta-regression," *The Lancet*, thelancet.com/action/showPdf?pii=S0140-6736%2821%2901609-3. *See also* Mike Ludwig, "New Study Shows More Than Half of Police Killings Have Gone Uncounted Since 1980," *Truthout*, October 5, 2021, truthout.org/articles/new-study-shows-more -than-half-of-police-killings-have-gone-uncounted-since-1980; Tim Arango and Shaila Dewan, "More Than Half of Police Killings Are Mislabeled, New Study Says," *New York Times*, September 30, 2021.

163. Murakawa, "Three Traps of Police Reform."

164. Brown and McHarris, "#8cantwait Is Based on Faulty Data Science."

No Soft Police

1. Project NIA, "Against Soft Police," drive.google.com/file/d/1kkciRKHkU5 x5jNLXphExqZZgrYepUdbh/view?usp=sharing.

2. Ruha Benjamin, "Opening Plenary, Our Tech Futures Conference," June 1–2, 2021, Just Futures Law, ourtechfutures.com/resources.

3. Mark Neocleous, *A Critical Theory of Police Power: The Fabrication of Social Order* (Brooklyn: Verso, 2021), 22.

4. Neocleous, *A Critical Theory of Police Power.*

5. Jill Lepore, "The Invention of the Police," *New Yorker*, July 13, 2020, newyorker .com/magazine/2020/07/20/the-invention-of-the-police. *See also* Brendan McQuade and Mark Neocleous, "Beware Medical Police," *Radical Philosophy* 2, no. 8 (2020): 3.

6. McQuade and Neocleous, "Beware Medical Police." *See also* Jackie Wang, *Carceral Capitalism* (Pasadena: Semiotext(e), 2018).

7. McQuade and Neocleous, "Beware Medical Police." *See also* Wang, *Carceral Capitalism.*

8. Neocleous, *A Critical Theory of Police Power. See also* George S. Rigakos et al., *A General Police System: Political Economy and Security in the Age of Enlightenment* (Ottawa: Red Quill Books, 2009).

9. Karl Marx, "On the Jewish Question" in *The Marx-Engels Reader*, Robert Tucker, ed. Robert Tucker (New York: Norton & Company, 1978), 26–46. *See also* Wang, *Carceral Capitalism*, citing President Lyndon Johnson's 1965 speech in what Wang describes as "the eve of mass incarceration": "Experience and wisdom dictates that one of the most legitimate functions of government is the preservation of law and order."

10. Markus Dubber, *The Police Power: Patriarchy and the Foundations of American Government* (New York: Columbia University Press, 2005).

11. Lepore, "The Invention of the Police."

12. Neocleous, *A Critical Theory of Police Power.*

13. Lepore, "The Invention of the Police."

14. McQuade and Neocleous, "Beware Medical Police."

15. McQuade and Neocleous, "Beware Medical Police."

16. *What's Next: Safer and More Just Communities Without Policing*, Mariame Kaba,

ed., Interrupting Criminalization: Research in Action, Project Nia, 2020, static1 .squarespace.com/static/5ee39ec764dbd7179cf1243c/t/5f85c390635cac03f35913d5 /1602601934251/What%27s+Next+Report+.pdf. *See also* Lepore, "The Invention of the Police"; McQuade and Neocleous, "Beware Medical Police"; Kristian Williams, *Our Enemies in Blue: Police and Power in America* (Oakland AK Press, 2015).

17. R. Delgado and J. Stefancic, *Critical Race Theory: An Introduction* (New York: New York University Press, 2001).

18. Paul Rosenberg, "The Deeper History of 'Defund': How the 'Get Tough' Policies of the '70s and '80s Led to Disaster," *Salon*, May 29, 2021.

19. Brendan McQuade, "The Prose of Pacification: Critical Theory, Police Power and Abolition Socialism," *Social Justice* 47, no. 3/4 (2020): 57; *See also* Brendan McQuade, *Pacifying the Homeland: Intelligence Fusion and Mass Supervision* (Oakland: University of California Press, 2019), 9–15, 25–40.

20. Andrea J. Ritchie and Black Lives Matter Chicago, "Epicenter: Chicago, Reclaiming a City from Neoliberalism," Political Research Associates, 2019, politicalresearch .org/2019/06/05/epicenter-chicago-reclaiming-a-city-from-neoliberalism. *See also* Ruth Wilson Gilmore and Craig Gilmore, "Beyond Bratton," in *Policing the Planet*, Jordan Camp and Christina Heatherton and Camp, eds. (Brooklyn, Verso Press, 2016); Wang, *Carceral Capitalism*.

21. Frances Fox Piven and Richard Cloward, *Regulating the Poor: The Functions of Public Welfare*, 2nd ed. (Vintage Books, 1993).

22. Moya Bailey, *Misogynoir Transformed: Black Women's Digital Resistance* (New York: New York University Press, 2021).

23. Ritchie, *Invisible No More*. *See also* Kaaryn Gustafson, *Cheating Welfare: Public Assistance and the Criminalization of Poverty* (New York: New York University Press, 2011); Dorothy Roberts, *Killing the Black Body: Race, Reproduction, and the Meaning of Liberty* (New York: Vintage Books, 2000).

24. Andrea Ritchie, *Invisible No More: Police Violence Against Black Women and Women of Color* (Boston: Beacon Press, 2017).

25. Wang, *Carceral Capitalism*.

26. "End the War on Black Women," Movement for Black Lives (M4BL), m4bl.org /policy-platforms/end-the-war-black-women. *See also* "End the War on Black Trans Queer, Gender Nonconforming and Intersex People," Movement for Black Lives (M4BL), m4bl.org/policy-platforms/end-the-war-trans.

27. Gustafson, *Cheating Welfare: Public Assistance and the Criminalization of Poverty*.

28. Tourmaline, "From Combahee to Stonewall to Say Her Name" presentation, "Invisible No More: Resisting Police Violence Against Black Women and Women of Color in Troubled Times," New York, NY, November 3–4, 2017. *See also* Ritchie, *Invisible No More*; Welfare Warriors Research Collaborative, *A Fabulous Attitude: Low-Income LGBTGNC People Surviving & Thriving on Love, Shelter & Knowledge* (New York, 2010).

29. Ritchie, *Invisible No More*.

30. Anne Branigan, "Jazmine Headley, Violently Arrested for Sitting on the Floor of a Human Resources Building, Sues New York City," *The Root*, August 9, 2019, theroot .com/jazmine-headley-violently-arrested-for-sitting-on-the-1837107825.

31. Pascal Sabino, "Can $500 a Month Keep Formerly Incarcerated People from Reoffending? West Side Study Will Test Guaranteed Income," *BlockClubChicago*, Octo-

ber 27, 2021, blockclubchicago.org/2021/10/27/west-side-guaranteed-basic-income-500
-monthly-formerly-incarcerated-people. *See also* "Pilot Program to Give $500 a Month to
Some Low-Income National City & San Diego Residents, No Strings Attached," NBC
News, April 8, 2021, nbcsandiego.com/news/local/pilot-progam-to-give-500-a-month
-to-low-income-national-city-san-diego-residents-no-strings-attached/2571879; Abigail
Johnson Hess, "Meet the Mayors Pushing for Guaranteed Income in 30 Cities Across the
Country," CNBC.com, January 19, 2021, cnbc.com/2021/01/19/the-mayors-piloting
-guaranteed-income-programs-across-the-us.html.

32. Daniel J. Losen, "Silent Segregation in Our Nation's Schools," *Harvard Civil
Rights-Civil Liberties Law Review* 34, no. 2 (Summer 1999): 517–545, harvardcrcl.org
/wp-content/uploads/sites/10/2015/07/Silent-Segregation-in-Our-Nations-Schools.pdf,
See also Subini Ancy Annamma, *The Pedagogy of Pathologization: Dis/abled Girls of Color
in the School-Prison Nexus* (New York: Routledge, 2017).

33. Monique W. Morris, *Pushout: The Criminalization of Black Girls in Schools* (New
York: The New Press, 2015).

34. Talila A. Lewis, "Disability Justice in the Age of Mass Incarceration," in *Deaf
People in the Criminal Justice System: Selected Topics on Advocacy, Incarceration, and Social
Justice*, Debra Guthmann et al., eds. (Washington: Gallaudet University Press, 2021),
229–303. *See also* "Reckoning with the History of Eugenics," Brian Lehrer interview
with Jack Tchen and Cara Page, *The Brian Lehrer Show*, September 27, 2021, podcast
audio, www.wnyc.org/story/reckoning-history-eugenics; Liat Ben-Moshe, *Decarcerating
Disability: Deinstitutionalization and Prison Abolition* (Minneapolis: University of Min-
nesota Press, 2020); Natasha Lennard, "The Long, Disgraceful History of American
Attacks on Brown and Black Women's Reproductive Systems," *The Intercept*, Septem-
ber 17, 2020, theintercept.com/2020/09/17/forced-sterilization-ice-us-history; Project
South, "Black Feminist Voices: Roundtable Discussion on the Legacies of Sterilization
& Resistance," November 12, 2020, webinar, vimeo.com/480034664; "Health, Healing
Justice & Liberation Statement," projectsouth.org/healing-justice-statement/?eType=Em
ailBlastContent&eId=1e542cb0-0fd4-47b3-9905-0051f8c0c62a; Movement for Black
Lives (M4BL) et al., "Reparations Now Toolkit," 2019, m4bl.org/wp-content/uploads
/2021/06/Reparations-Now-Toolkit-FINAL.pdf; s.e. smith, "Disabled People Are Still
Being Forcibly Sterilized—So Why Isn't Anyone Talking About It?" *Rewire News Group*,
November 17, 2014, rewirenewsgroup.com/article/2014/11/17/disabled-people-still
-forcibly-sterilized-isnt-anyone-talking; Lisa Ko, "Unwanted Sterilization and Eugenics
Programs in the United States," PBS, January 29, 2016, pbs.org/independentlens/blog
/unwanted-sterilization-and-eugenics-programs-in-the-united-states; Eugene Volokh,
"Sterilization of the 'Intellectually Disabled,'" *Washington Post*, April 18, 2014.

35. Melissa Gira Grant, "Republicans Are Already Trying to Pass as Many Anti-Trans
Bills as Possible in 2022," *The New Republic*, February 10, 2022, newrepublic.com
/article/165334/republicans-anti-trans-bathroom-sports-bills-north-dakota-kristi-noem;
Evan Urquhart, "The New Wave of Anti-Trans Legislation Sure Looks a Lot Like Eugenics," *Slate*, March 3, 2021, slate.com/human-interest/2021/03/anti-trans-legislation
-eugenics-sports-puberty.html. *See also* Democracy Now!, "Trans Day of Visibility:
Activists Chase Strangio and Raquel Willis Demand Action on Anti-Trans Laws," 15:44,
March 31, 2021, linktv.org/shows/democracy-now/clip/trans-day-of-visibility-activists
-chase-strangio-and-raquel-willis-demand-action-on-anti-trans-laws; "End Transphobia
at the Human Resources Administration Now!," Sylvia Rivera Law Project, srlp.org
/end-transphobia-at-the-human-resources-administration-now. *See also* "We Won't Be

Erased: The Audre Lorde Project's Statement on the Health and Human Services' Proposed Definition of Sex," The Audre Lorde Project, alp.org/media/statements/we-wont -be-erased-audre-lorde-projects-statement-health-and-human-services-proposed; "Victory in Fight for Access to Benefits for Trans Communities!" Sylvia Rivera Law Project, srlp.org/hrawin.

36. Trevor Hoppe, *Punishing Disease: HIV and the Criminalization of Sickness* (Oakland: University of California Press, 2018). *See also* Mogul et al., *Queer (In)justice: The Criminalization of LGBT People in the United States*; Laura Flanders, "Kenyon Farrow on COVID-19: Racial Justice and Lessons from the AIDS Crisis," *The Laura Flanders Show*, 7:59, March 18, 2020, linktv.org/shows/laura-flanders-show/clip/kenyon -farrow-on-covid-19-racial-justice-and-lessons-from-the-aids-crisis.

37. Zusha Elinson, "Police Officers Resist Getting Vaccinated for Covid-19, Now Their No. 1 Killer," *Wall Street Journal*, September 24, 2021, wsj.com/articles/police -departments-strive-to-persuade-officers-to-get-covid-19-vaccine-11632488400. *See also* Kevin Rector, "LAPD Officers Are Supposed to Wear Masks. They Keep Getting Caught Without Them," *Los Angeles Times*, August 12, 2021; Pascal Emmer et al., *Unmasked: Impacts of Pandemic Policing*, October 2020, communityresourcehub.org/wp -content/uploads/2020/12/Unmasked.pdf; COVID19 Policing Project, *Divesting from Pandemic Policing and Investing in Just Recovery*, May 2021, communityresourcehub.org /wp-content/uploads/2021/05/Unmasked_Update.pdf.

38. Lara Brooks and Mariame Kaba, *Whose Security Is It Anyway?: A Toolkit to Address Institutional Violence in Nonprofit Organizations*, September 2017, oregoncam- puscompact.org/uploads/1/3/0/4/13042698/whose_security_toolkit_2017__lara _brooks_and_mariame_kaba_.pdf.

39. "Anti-Prostitution Loyalty Oath (APLO)," CHANGE, June 2020, srhrforall.org /download/fact-sheet-anti-prostitution-loyalty-oath-aplo/?wpdmdl=2361&refresh=61 91659ef2e6b1636918686.

40. Jessica Mindlin, "Understanding Your Role: Notice & Mandatory Reporting Made Easy," presentation, National Network to End Domestic Violence, Scottsdale, Arizona, September 27, 2009, doj.state.or.us/wp-content/uploads/2017/03/nnedv_ mandatory_reporting.pdf.

41. This framework first emerged in conversation between Mariame and Maya Schenwar and Victoria Law, authors of *Prison by Any Other Name* (The New Press, 2021).

42. Jackson Cote, "What If You Called 911 and Someone Other Than the Police Showed Up? Northampton Explores Creating New Unarmed Response Department," *Masslive*, March 30, 2021, masslive.com/police-fire/2021/03/what-if-you-called-911 -and-someone-other-than-the-police-showed-up-northampton-explores-creating-new -unarmed-response-department.html.

43. Isiah Holmes, "City Task Force Considers Unarmed First Responders," *Urban Milwaukee*, July 8, 2021, urbanmilwaukee.com/2021/07/08/city-task-force-considers -unarmed-first-responders.

44. Ted Alcorn, "Albuquerque's Vision for Nonpolice First Responders Comes Down to Earth," *New Mexico in Depth*, January 17, 2021, nmindepth.com/2021/01/17 /albuquerques-vision-for-non-police-first-responders-comes-down-to-earth.

45. Mimi E. Kim et al., "Defund the Police—Invest in Community Care," Interrupting Criminalization, May 2021, interruptingcriminalization.com/non-police-crisis -response-guide.

46. Moki Macias, "We Need to Rethink Mental Health Care—and the Assumptions We Have About What Support Means," *Washington Post*, May 6, 2021.

47. Macias, "We Need to Rethink Mental Health Care—and the Assumptions We Have About What Support Means."

48. Macias, "We Need to Rethink Mental Health Care—and the Assumptions We Have About What Support Means."

49. Macias, "We Need to Rethink Mental Health Care—and the Assumptions We Have About What Support Means."

50. "LEAD National Support Bureau," The LEAD National Support Bureau, www.leadbureau.org.

51. Schenwar and Law, *Prison by Any Other Name*.

52. Schenwar and Law, *Prison by Any Other Name*.

53. "Resources," Police Free Schools, policefreeschools.org/resources. *See also* the Advancement Project and the Alliance for Educational Justice, *We Came to Learn: A Call to Action for Police-Free Schools*, 2018, advancementproject.org/wecametolearn.

54. "Resources," Police Free Schools; the Advancement Project and the Alliance for Educational Justice, *We Came to Learn*.

55. "Resources," Police Free Schools.

56. "Resources," Police Free Schools.

57. "Resources," Police Free Schools.

58. "Resources," Police Free Schools.

59. "Resources," Police Free Schools.

60. "Resources," Police Free Schools. *See also* Ritchie, *Invisible No More*; Morris, *Pushout*.

61. "Resources," Police Free Schools. *See also* Ritchie, *Invisible No More*.

62. "Resources," Police Free Schools.

63. "Resources," Police Free Schools.

64. Kate Hamaji and Kate Terenzi, *Arrested Learning: A Survey of Youth Experiences of Police and Security at School*, May 2021, static1.squarespace.com/static/601b54abb7de8229ddb416d1/t/606c9982a8f63426e7b83c40/1617729927701/Police-Free+Schools+Final+V4+%281%29.pdf. *See also* policefreeschools.org/map; Ritchie, *Invisible No More*; Annamma, *The Pedagogy of Pathologization: Dis/abled Girls of Color in the School-Prison Nexus*; the Advancement Project and the Alliance for Educational Justice, *We Came to Learn*; Morris, *Pushout*; "End the War on Black Youth," Movement for Black Lives (M4BL), m4bl.org/policy-platforms/end-the-war-on-black-youth.

65. Youth Mandate, *Youth Mandate for Education and Liberation*, 2021, static1.squarespace.com/static/601b54abb7de8229ddb416d1/t/6074d127aaf374451dc27ea9/1618268463975/Youth+Mandate+for+Education+and+Liberation.pdf.

66. Youth Mandate, *Youth Mandate for Education and Liberation*. "Black students were only 15.5 percent of all students, but accounted for nearly 35 percent of school-related arrests, according to the most recently available data. Furthermore, while students with disabilities were about 12 percent of all students, they accounted for 27.5 percent of the students referred to law enforcement or arrested in school." *See also* Kate Hamaji and Kate Terenzi, *Arrested Learning: A Survey of Youth Experiences of Police and Security at School*, May 2021, static1.squarespace.com/static

/601b54abb7de8229ddb416d1/t/606c9982a8f63426e7b83c40/1617729927701/Police-Free+Schools+Final+V4+%281%29.pdf; Ritchie, *Invisible No More*; Annamma, *The Pedagogy of Pathologization*; the Advancement Project and the Alliance for Educational Justice, *We Came to Learn*; Morris, *Pushout*; "End the War on Black Youth," Movement for Black Lives (M4BL), m4bl.org/policy-platforms/end-the-war-on-black-youth.

67. Michael Gold, "After Report of 4 Girls Strip-Searched at School, Cuomo Calls for Inquiry," *New York Times*, January 30, 2019.

68. Rae Rosario Stevenson and Joan M. Blakey, "Social Work in the Shadow of Death: Divesting from Anti-Blackness and Social Control," *Advances in Social Work* 21, no. 2/3 (2021). *See also* Madeline Holcombe, "A 6-Year-Old Was Held Without Parental Consent Under a Law That Allows for Involuntary Examination of Minors," CNN, February 17, 2020.

69. *See, e.g.*, Ayanna Pressley, "H.R.4011—Counseling Not Criminalization in Schools Act," Congress, June 17, 2021, congress.gov/bill/117th-congress/house-bill/4011.

70. Youth Mandate, *Youth Mandate for Education and Liberation*.

71. Dignity in Schools Project, "Community Not Cops," dignityinschools.org/take-action/community-not-cops. Project NIA, an organization Mariame founded and directs, is a member of the Dignity Not Schools Coalition and signatory to the "Communities, Not Cops" policy agenda.

72. Dignity in Schools Project, "Community Not Cops."

73. Police Free Schools, "Police Free Schools," policefreeschools.org.

74. Police Free Schools, "About Us," policefreeschools.org/about.

75. Youth Mandate, *Youth Mandate for Education and Liberation*.

76. Justice Policy Institute, "Substance Abuse Treatment and Public Safety," January 2008, justicepolicy.org/wp-content/uploads/justicepolicy/documents/08_01_rep_drugtx_ac-ps.pdf. *See also* Drug Policy Alliance, "Race and the Drug War," drugpolicy.org/issues/race-and-drug-war.

77. Joyce McMillan, "How the Media Portrays Black and White Drug Users Differently," *Salon*, May 27, 2018, salon.com/2018/05/27/how-the-media-portrays-black-and-white-drug-users-differently; Rebecca Tiger, "Race, Class, and the Framing of Drug Epidemics," *Contexts,* December 18, 2018, contexts.org/articles/race-class-drugs. For example, there are very few drug treatment programs available to pregnant or parenting people, and very few are affirming and accessible to queer, trans, and gender nonconforming people. Many programs refuse people with a "dual diagnosis" of "substance abuse disorder" and other mental disabilities, and few are fully accessible. Migrants without authorization may be reluctant to access publicly funded drug treatment programs for fear of detection by immigration authorities, or of being deemed ineligible to adjust their immigration status because use of public programs may subject them to exclusion under the "public charge" rule, which denies entry to migrants deemed likely to become a burden to the state.

78. Drug Policy Alliance, "Coercive Treatment—Moving Beyond 'For Your Own Good,'" drugpolicy.org/event/coercive-treatment-moving-beyond-your-own-good. *See also* Schenwar and Law, *Prison by Any Other Name*.

79. Drug Policy Alliance, "Coercive Treatment—Moving Beyond 'For Your Own Good'"; Drug Policy Alliance, "Involuntary Treatment," drugpolicy.org/issues/involuntary-treatment.

80. Drug Policy Alliance, "Coercive Treatment—Moving Beyond 'For Your Own Good'"; Drug Policy Alliance, "Involuntary Treatment."

81. Drug Policy Alliance, "Coercive Treatment—Moving Beyond 'For Your Own Good'"; Drug Policy Alliance, "Involuntary Treatment."

82. Gabrielle Glaser, "The Irrationality of Alcoholics Anonymous," *The Atlantic*, April 2015, theatlantic.com/magazine/archive/2015/04/the-irrationality-of-alcoholics -anonymous/386255.

83. Schenwar and Law, *Prison by Any Other Name*.

84. Schenwar and Law, *Prison by Any Other Name*; Andrea J. Ritchie, "Expanding Our Frame: Deepening Our Demands for Safety and Healing for Black Survivors of Sexual Violence," February 2019, incite-national.org/wp-content/uploads/2019/07/ritchie -Expanding-Our-Frame-Deepening-our-Demands-for-Safety-and-Healing-for-Black -Survivors-of-Sexual-Violence.pdf.

85. Schenwar and Law, *Prison by Any Other Name*.

86. Drug Policy Alliance, "Substance Use Disorder Treatment," drugpolicy.org/issues /SUD-treatment.

87. Clay Skipper, "What If Drugs Aren't as Bad as We've Been Told?" *GQ*, February 16, 2021, gq.com/story/imagining-a-world-where-all-drugs-are-legal-carl-hart.

88. Drug Policy Alliance, "Race and the Drug War," drugpolicy.org/issues/race-and -drug-war; *see also* Skipper, "What If Drugs Aren't as Bad as We've Been Told?"

89. Drug Policy Alliance, "Race and the Drug War," drugpolicy.org/issues/race-and -drug-war; *see also* Skipper, "What If Drugs Aren't as Bad as We've Been Told?"

90. Laura M. Maruschak, Jennifer Bronson, and Mariel Alper, "Disabilities Reported by Prisoners," U.S. Department of Justice, Bureau of Justice Statistics, March 2021, bjs.ojp.gov/content/pub/pdf/drpspi16st.pdf; *see also* Jennifer Sarret, "US Prisons Hold More Than 550,000 People with Intellectual Disabilities—They Face Exploitation, Harsh Treatment," *The Conversation*, May 7, 2021, theconversation.com/us-prisons-hold -more-than-550-000-people-with-intellectual-disabilities-they-face-exploitation-harsh -treatment-158407; Jennifer Bronson, Laura M. Maruschak, and Marcus Berzofsky, "Disabilities Among Prison and Jail Inmates, 2011–12," U.S. Department of Justice, Bureau of Justice Statistics, December 2015, bjs.ojp.gov/content/pub/pdf/dpji1112 .pdf; Talila A. Lewis, "Disability Justice in the Age of Mass Incarceration," in *Deaf People in the Criminal Justice System: Selected Topics on Advocacy, Incarceration, and Social Justice*, eds. Debra Guthmann et al. (Washington: Gallaudet University Press, 2021); Ben-Moshe, *Decarcerating Disability*.

91. Ben-Moshe, *Decarcerating Disability*.

92. Liat Ben-Moshe, Chris Chapman, and Allison C. Carey, eds., *Disability Incarcerated: Imprisonment and Disability in the United States and Canada* (New York: Palgrave Macmillan, 2014). *See also* Lewis, "Disability Justice in the Age of Mass Incarceration"; Ben-Moshe, *Decarcerating Disabilty;* James Kilgore, "Repackaging Mass Incarceration," *Counterpunch*, June 6, 2014, counterpunch.org/2014/06/06/repackaging-mass -incarceration; Schenwar and Law, *Prison by Any Other Name*, 67–70, 101.

93. Lewis, "Disability Justice in the Age of Mass Incarceration." *See also* Ben-Moshe, *Decarcerating Disability*; Ben-Moshe, Chapman, and C. Carey, eds., *Disability Incarcerated*; Sins Invalid, *Skin, Tooth, and Bone: The Basis of Movement Is Our People* (Primedia eLaunch LCC, 2019); Ritchie, *Invisible No More*; Schenwar and Law, *Prison by Any Other Name*.

94. Francisco Aviles Pino, "Los Angeles County Votes to Stop Construction of New Jail-Like Facility, Adding Momentum to National Abolition Movement," *The Intercept*, August 22, 2019, theintercept.com/2019/08/22/los-angeles-county-mental-health-facility-abolition. *See also* Mark Anthony Clayton-Johnson, Shamsher Samra, and Jeremy Levenson, "Allying Public Health and Abolition: Lessons from the Campaign Against Jail Construction in Los Angeles," *American Journal of Public Health* iii, no. 4 (April 1, 2021): 574–576, ajph.aphapublications.org/doi/full/10.2105/AJPH.2020.306065.

95. Ben-Moshe, *Decarcerating Disability*. *See also* Lewis, "Disability Justice in the Age of Mass Incarceration"; Sins Invalid, *Skin, Tooth, and Bone*; Ritchie, *Invisible No More*; Schenwar and Law, *Prison by Any Other Name*.

96. The Fireweed Collective is a mental health education and mutual aid project that understands "mental health struggles not as faulty brains, but in the context that we live in a faulty world that is not healthy for us," "Our History," Fireweed Collective, fireweed collective.org/our-history.

97. Elliott Fukui, "An Open Letter to the Psychiatrists, Doctors, Nurses, Social Workers, Therapists and Cops Who Detain Disabled and Neurodivergent People," Mad Queer Organizing Strategies, March 2, 2021, madqueer.org/reflections/an-invlusive -abolitinism.

98. Ben-Moshe, *Decarcerating Disability*.

99. Talila A. Lewis, "Disability Justice Is an Essential Part of Abolishing Police and Prisons," in *Abolition for the People*, Kaepernick, ed..

100. Lewis, "Disability Justice in the Age of Mass Incarceration." *See also* Sins Invalid, *Skin, Tooth, and Bone*; Ritchie, *Invisible No More*.

101. Jon Hurdle, Campbell Robertson, and Richard A. Oppel Jr., "Days from Election, Police Killing of Black Man Roils Philadelphia, *New York Times*, October 29, 2021.

102. Mimi E. Kim et al., "Defund the Police—Invest in Community Care," *Interrupting Criminalization*, May 2021, interruptingcriminalization.com/non-police-crisis -response-guide.

103. Kim et al., "Defund the Police—Invest in Community Care."

104. McQuade and Neocleous, "Beware Medical Police."

105. Kim et al., "Defund the Police—Invest in Community Care."

106. For example, the majority of people in the sex trades are not coerced into involvement by another person. Mutual aid and harm reduction practices employed by people in the sex trade, such as sharing accommodations, credit cards, and income; providing security, childcare, or web hosting services for each other; working together and referring each other safe(r) clients, are criminalized under statutes prohibiting solicitation and promotion of prostitution, "keeping a place of prostitution" (i.e. a "brothel"), and benefiting from income earned through the sex trade. Criminalization of people in the sex trade and people and activities surrounding them further isolates sex workers, leaving them more vulnerable to violence, not less.

107. *See, e.g.,* the popular LEAD program (Law Enforcement Assisted Diversion), "About LEAD," The LEAD National Support Bureau, leadbureau.org/about-lead; Nina Luo, *Decriminalizing Survival: Policy Platform and Polling on the Decriminalization of Sex Work*, Data For Progress, 2019, filesforprogress.org/memos/decriminalizing-sex-work .pdf.

108. Nina Luo, *Decriminalizing Survival*. See also Survived and Punished, *Preserving Punishment Power: A Grassroots Abolitionist Assessment of New York Reforms* (2020), survivedandpunishedny.org/wp-content/uploads/2020/04/SP-Preserving-Punishment-Power-report.pdf; Jenna Torres, "How New York City's Treatment of Sex Workers Continues to Harm Us," *Rewire News Group*, September 22, 2015, rewirenewsgroup.com/article/2015/09/22/new-york-citys-treatment-sex-workers-continues-harm-us; Red Umbrella Project, *Criminal, Victim, or Worker? The Effects of New York's Human Trafficking Intervention Courts Prostitution-Related Offenses*, October 2014, nswp.org/sites/nswp.org/files/RedUP-NYHTIC-FINALweb.pdf; Meredith Dank et al., *Surviving the Streets of New York: Experiences of LGBTQ Youth, YMSM, and YWSW Engaged in Survival Sex* (The Urban Institute, 2015), urban.org/sites/default/files/publication/42186/2000119-Surviving-the-Streets-of-New-York.pdf; Young Women's Empowerment Project, *Bad Encounter Line*, 2012, ywepchicago.files.wordpress.com/2011/06/bad-encounter-line-report-20121.pdf; Young Women's Empowerment Project, *Girls Do What They Have to Do to Survive: Illuminating Methods Used by Girls in the Sex Trade and Street Economy to Fight Back and Heal*, 2009, ywepchicago.files.wordpress.com/2011/06/girls-do-what-they-have-to-do-to-survive-a-study-of-resilience-and-resistance.pdf.

109. Torres, "How New York City's Treatment of Sex Workers Continues to Harm Us."

110. Nina Luo, *Decriminalizing Survival: Policy Platform and Polling on the Decriminalization of Sex Work*, Data For Progress, 2019, filesforprogress.org/memos/decriminalizing-sex-work.pdf. *See also* Casey Quinlan, "Layleen Cubilette-Polanco Died at Rikers Island. Her Family Wants Justice," *ThinkProgress*, August 13, 2019, archive.thinkprogress.org/family-of-trans-woman-who-died-at-new-yorks-rikers-island-files-suit-e07436e43095.

111. "Abortion Criminalization Is Part of the Larger Struggle Against Policing and Criminalization," Maria Thomas, ed., Interrupting Criminalization (2021), interruptingcriminalization.com/decriminalize-abortion.

112. "Abortion Criminalization Is Part of the Larger Struggle Against Policing and Criminalization," Thomas, ed.

113. "Abortion Criminalization Is Part of the Larger Struggle Against Policing and Criminalization," Thomas, ed.

114. "Abortion Criminalization Is Part of the Larger Struggle Against Policing and Criminalization," Thomas, ed.

115. "Abortion Criminalization Is Part of the Larger Struggle Against Policing and Criminalization," Thomas, ed.

116. Young Women's Empowerment Project, *Bad Encounter Line. See also* Young Women's Empowerment Project, *Girls Do What They Have to Do to Survive*.

117. Molly Taft, "Cops Are Illegally Detaining and Hurting Mental Health Patients," *Vice*, January 21, 2020, vice.com/en/article/akwv9b/cops-are-illegally-detaining-and-hurting-mental-health-patients.

118. DPHMustDivest, "FAQ," dphmustdivest.com/faqm citing Russel L. Colling, *Hospital and Health Care Security* (Boston: Butterworth-Heineman, 2001).

119. "Cops Out of Care," a webinar series, Interrupting Criminalization, www.interruptingcriminalization.com/cops-out-of-care.

120. Leah A. Jacobs et al., "Defund the Police: Moving Towards an Anti-Carceral Social Work" (Pittsburgh: University of Pittsburgh, 2020); *see also* d-scholarship.pitt.edu/39769/1/JPHS_Defund%20the%20Police_092520_dscholarship.pdf; Ji Seon Song,

"Policing the Emergency Room," *Harvard Law Review*, June 10, 2021, harvardlawreview .org/2021/06/policing-the-emergency-room.

121. Richard Winton, "Patient Shot by Sheriff's Deputy Inside Harbor UCLA Hospital Dies," *Los Angeles Times*, November 17, 2020.

122. Jeanne Flavin and Lynne Paltrow, "'Do No Harm' Like You Mean It: Hospital Workers' Role in the Policing of Pregnant Women," *Scholar & Feminist Online* 15, no. 3 (2019), sfonline.barnard.edu/unraveling-criminalizing-webs-building-police -free-futures/do-no-harm-like-you-mean-it-hospital-workers-role-in-the-policing-of -pregnant-women.

123. Matt Pierce, "Homeless Woman's Death in Police Custody Stirs Anger in St. Louis," *Los Angeles Times*, March 29, 2012.

124. DPH Must Divest, dphmustdivest.com/stories.

125. Jennifer Tsai, "Get Armed Police out of Emergency Rooms," *Scientific American*, July 14, 2020, scientificamerican.com/article/get-armed-police-out-of-emergency -rooms. *See also* Breanna Cooper, "'It Makes Our Jobs Harder': Police in Emergency Rooms," *Indianapolis Recorder*, May 20, 2021, indianapolisrecorder.com/it-makes-our -jobs-harder-police-in-emergency-rooms; Medha Makhlouf, "Compounding Vulnerability: Hospital Emergency Rooms as Sites of Race- and Class-Based Police Surveillance," *Journal of Things We Like (Lots)*, November 15, 2021, health.jotwell.com/compounding -vulnerability-hospital-emergency-rooms-as-sites-of-race-and-class-based-police -surveillance; Interrupting Criminalization, *Shrouded in Silence: Police Sexual Violence: What We Know and What We Can Do About It*, April 2021, static1.squarespace.com /static/5ee39ec764dbd7179cf1243c/t/609b0bb8fc3271012c4a93c5/1620773852750 /Shrouded+in+Silence.pdf.

126. Flavin and Paltrow, "'Do No Harm' Like You Mean It: Hospital Workers' Role in the Policing of Pregnant Women."

127. DPH Must Divest, dphmustdivest.com/stories.

128. Andy Mannix, "At Urging of Minneapolis Police, Hennepin EMS Workers Subdued Dozens with a Powerful Sedative," *Star Tribune*, June 15, 2018, startribune.com/at -urging-of-police-hennepin-emts-subdued-dozens-with-powerful-sedative/485607381. *See also* Jacob Vaughn, "Don't Wanna Be Sedated," *Dallas Observer*, July 24, 2020, dallasobserver.com/news/police-and-emts-use-of-anesthetics-to-control-suspects-debated -11927060.

129. DPH Must Divest, dphmustdivest.com/alternatives.

130. Linda Steele, *Disability, Criminal Justice and Law: Reconsidering Court Diversion* (New York: Routledge, 2020). Ben-Moshe calls this "carceral ableism": "the praxis and belief that people with disabilities need special or extra protections, in ways that often expand and legitimate their further marginalization and incarceration." Ben-Moshe, *Decarcerating Disability*.

131. Schenwar and Law, *Prison by Any Other Name*.

132. Schenwar and Law, *Prison by Any Other Name*.

133. "10 Principles of Disability Justice," Sins Invalid, www.sinsinvalid.org/blog/10 -principles-of-disability-justice. *See also* Abolition and Disability Justice, abolitionand-disabilityjustice.com; Alice Wong, *Disability Visibility* (New York: Knopf Doubleday, 2020); Leah Lakshmi Piepzna-Samarasinha, *Care Work: Dreaming Disability Justice* (Vancouver: Arsenal Pulp Press, 2018).

134. Ben-Moshe, *Decarcerating Disability*.

135. Sins Invalid, *Skin, Tooth, and Bone*.

136. Ben-Moshe, *Decarcerating Disability*; Talila A. Lewis, "Disability Justice Is an Essential Part of Abolishing Police and Prisons," in *Abolition for the People*, Kaepernick, ed.

137. Susan Raffo, Anjali Taneja, and Cara Page, "Healing Histories Project: Disrupting the Medical Industrial Complex," carapage.co/the-medical-industrial-complex -mic. Page, Mia Mingus, and Patti Berne describe the medical industrial complex as: "a system about profit, first and foremost, rather than 'health,' wellbeing and care. Its roots run deep and its history and present are connected to everything including eugenics, capitalism, colonization, slavery, immigration, war, prisons, and reproductive oppression. It is not just a major piece of the history of ableism, but all systems of oppression." Mia Mingus, "Medical Industrial Complex Visual," *Leaving Evidence*, Wordpress, February 6, 2015, leavingevidence.wordpress.com/2015/02/06/medical-industrial -complex-visual. Policing in the context of the medical industrial complex has taken the form of:

> continued targeting of disabled bodies as something to fix . . . experimentation on black bodies, . . . pathologized treatment of and violent attempts to cure queer and trans communities . . . humiliating, lacking or flat-out denial of services to poor communities . . . forced sterilization and dangerous contraceptives trafficked to young women of color . . . forced medicalization used in prisons . . . demonization and erasing of indigenous healing and practices . . . the never-ending battle to control populations through controlling birth, birthing, and those who give birth in this country, to the countless doctors and practitioners who have raped and sexually assaulted their patients . . . the systematic targeting of oppressed communities under the guise of care, health and safety.

Mingus, "Medical Industrial Complex Visual."

138. McQuade and Neocleous, "Beware Medical Police"; Neocleous, *A Critical Theory of Police Power*.

139. Lewis, "Disability Justice Is an Essential Part of Abolishing Police and Prisons."

140. Kassandra Frederique, "To Truly Reimagine Safety, We Must End the War on Drugs," *Washington Post*, March 16, 2021; Movement for Black Lives, End the War on Black Health and Black Disabled People, *Vision for Black Lives*, m4bl.org /policy-platforms/end-the-war-black-health. *See also* Mimi E. Kim et al., "Defund the Police—Invest in Community Care," Interrupting Criminalization, May 2021, inter ruptingcriminalization.com/non-police-crisis-response-guide.

141. Kim et al., "Defund the Police—Invest in Community Care."

142. Beth E. Richie and Kayla M. Martensen, "Resisting Carcerality, Embracing Abolition: Implications for Feminist Social Work Practice," *Affilia: Journal of Women and Social Work* 35, no. 1 (2020): 12–16, journals.sagepub.com/doi/abs/10.1177 /0886109919897576?journalCode=affa.

143. Jacobs et al., "Defund the Police: Moving Towards an Anti-Carceral Social Work." *See also* Rae Rosario Stevenson and Joan M. Blakey, "Social Work in the Shadow of Death: Divesting From Anti-Blackness and Social Control," *Advances in Social Work* 21, no. 2/3 (2021).

144. Jacobs et al., "Defund the Police: Moving Towards an Anti-Carceral Social Work."

See also Stevenson and Blakey, "Social Work in the Shadow of Death: Divesting from Anti-Blackness and Social Control."

145. Jacobs et al., "Defund the Police: Moving Towards an Anti-Carceral Social Work." *See also* Stevenson and Blakey, "Social Work in the Shadow of Death: Divesting from Anti-Blackness and Social Control."

146. Angela Y. Davis, Gina Dent, Erica Meiners, and Beth E. Richie, *Abolition. Feminism. Now.* (Chicago: Haymarket Press, 2022).

147. Jacobs et al., "Defund the Police: Moving Towards an Anti-Carceral Social Work."

148. Cameron Rasmussen and Kirk "Jae" James, "Trading Cops for Social Workers Isn't the Solution to Police Violence," *Truthout*, July 17, 2020, truthout.org/articles/trading -cops-for-social-workers-isnt-the-solution-to-police-violence.

149. Rasmussen and James, "Trading Cops for Social Workers Isn't the Solution to Police Violence."

150. Rasmussen and James, "Trading Cops for Social Workers Isn't the Solution to Police Violence."

151. Caitlyn Becker, "We Social Workers Should Remember Our Values and Stop Policing," *Filter Magazine*, October 19, 2021, filtermag.org/social-workers-stop-policing.

152. Jacobs et al., "Defund the Police: Moving Towards an Anti-Carceral Social Work."

153. Rasmussen and James, "Trading Cops for Social Workers Isn't the Solution to Police Violence."

154. Lisa Sangoi, "'Whatever They Do, I'm Her Comfort, I'm Her Protector.' How the Foster System Has Become Ground Zero for the U.S. Drug War," Movement for Family Power, June 2020, static1.squarespace.com/static/5be5ed0fd274cb7c8a5d0cba /t/5eead939ca509d4e36a89277/1592449422870/MFP+Drug+War+Foster+System+Re port.pdf.

155. Sangoi, "Whatever They Do, I'm Her Comfort, I'm Her Protector."

156. Sangoi, "Whatever They Do, I'm Her Comfort, I'm Her Protector."

157. Nancy D. Polikoff, Jesse McGleughlin, and Urvashi Vaid, "A Discussion Paper on LGBT Parents in the Child Welfare System," October 2018 (on file with authors). *See also* Kathi L.H. Harp and Carrie B. Oser, "Factors Associated with Two Types of Child Custody Loss Among a Sample of African American Mothers: A Novel Approach," *Social Science Research* 60 (2016): 283–296.

158. Schenwar and Law, *Prison by Any Other Name*.

159. JMac for Families, www.jmacforfamilies.com.

160. Schenwar and Law, *Prison by Any Other Name*.

161. Schenwar and Law; Ritchie, *Invisible No More*.

162. Schenwar and Law, *Prison by Any Other Name*.

163. Dorothy Roberts, "Abolishing Policing Also Means Abolishing Family Regulation," *Abolition Journal*, July 4, 2020, abolitionjournal.org/abolishing-policing-also -means-abolishing-family-regulation.

164. Sangoi, "Whatever They Do, I'm Her Comfort, I'm Her Protector."

165. Sangoi, "Whatever They Do, I'm Her Comfort, I'm Her Protector."

166. Sangoi, "Whatever They Do, I'm Her Comfort, I'm Her Protector."

167. Sangoi, "Whatever They Do, I'm Her Comfort, I'm Her Protector."

168. Alexander and Sered, "Making Communities Safe, Without the Police."

169. National Network of Hospital-Based Violence Intervention Programs, "Hospital-Based Violence Intervention: Practices and Policies to End the Cycle of Violence," static1 .squarespace.com/static/5d6f61730a2b610001135b79/t/5d83c0d9056f4d4cbdb9acd9 /1568915699707/NNHVIP+White+Paper.pdf. *See also* "The Public Health Approach to Violence Prevention," Centers for Disease Control and Prevention, cdc.gov /violenceprevention/about/publichealthapproach.html; The Annie E. Casey Foundation, *Improving Community Safety Through Public Health Strategies: Lessons from Atlanta and Milwaukee* (Baltimore, Maryland, 2021), assets.aecf.org/m/resourcedoc /aecf-improvingcommunitysafety-2021.pdf; "Addressing Law Enforcement Violence as a Public Health Issue," American Public Health Association, apha.org/policies -and-advocacy/public-health-policy-statements/policy-database/2019/01/29/law -enforcement-violence.

170. Alexander and Sered, "Making Communities Safe, Without the Police." *See also* "The Public Health Approach to Violence Prevention," Centers for Disease Control and Prevention.

171. American Public Health Association, "Advancing Public Health Interventions to Address the Harms of the Carceral System."

172. Cara Page, Susan Raffo, and Anjali Teneda, "Healing Histories Project: Disrupting the Medical Industrial Complex," carapage.co/the-medical-industrial-complex-mic.

173. Trevor Hoppe, *Punishing Disease: HIV and the Criminalization of Sickness* (Oakland: University of California Press, 2018).

174. Pascal Emmer et al., "Unmasked: Acts of Pandemic Policing," October 2020, communityresourcehub.org/wp-content/uploads/2020/12/Unmasked.pdf.

175. Kilgore, "Repackaging Mass Incarceration."

176. Rae Rosario Stevenson and Joan M. Blakey, "Social Work in the Shadow of Death: Divesting From Anti-Blackness and Social Control," *Advances in Social Work* 21, no. 2/3 (2021).

177. Stevenson and Blakey, "Social Work in the Shadow of Death: Divesting from Anti-Blackness and Social Control."

178. Davis et al., *Abolition. Feminism. Now.*

How Do We Get There? Toward a Police-Free Future

1. Angela Y. Davis, Gina Dent, Erica Meiners, and Beth E. Richie, *Abolition. Feminism. Now.* (Chicago: Haymarket Press, 2022).

2. Andrea J. Ritchie, *The Demand Is Still Defund the Police, Fund the People, Defend Black Lives*, Interrupting Criminalization (January 2021), bit.ly/DefundPoliceUpdate. *See also* "Defund the Police," defundpolice.org.

3. Ritchie, *The Demand Is Still Defund the Police*; "Defund the Police," defundpolice .org.

4. Ritchie, *The Demand Is Still Defund the Police*; "Defund the Police," defundpolice .org.

5. Danielle Sered, *Until We Reckon* (New York: The New Press 2019).

6. Brandon Bell, "Minneapolis Set to Vote on Dissolving Police Department,"

Truthout, October 30, 2021, truthout.org/articles/minneapolis-set-to-vote-on-dissolving
-police-department.

7. Meghan G. McDowell, "Insurgent Safety: Theorizing Alternatives to State
Protection," *Theoretical Criminology* 23, no. 1 (2019): 45–46, doi.org/10.1177
/1362480617713984.

8. Stuart Hall et al., *Policing the Crisis: Mugging, the State, and Law and Order*
(London: Macmillan, 1978). See also David Correia and Tyler Wall, *Violent Order: Essays
on the Nature of Police* (Chicago: Haymarket Books, 2021); Brendan McQuade and Mark
Neocleous, "Beware Medical Police," *Radical Philosophy* 2.08 (2020): 3; David Graeber
and David Wengrow, *The Dawn of Everything: A New History of Humanity* (London:
Allen Lane, 2021).

9. Correia and Wall, *Violent Order*, 3–9. The notion of police as a "thin blue line"
between violent chaos and civilization takes many forms, including the television show of
the same name promoted by then LAPD Chief Darryl Gates in 1952 as part of a program
of recuperating legitimacy for the police department. Simon Balto, *Occupied Territory:
Policing Black Chicago from Red Summer to Black Power* (Chapel Hill: The University of
North Carolina Press, 2019). It is also reflected in the imagery of a U.S. flag with a thin
blue line running through it that has become increasingly popular among police preservationists and white supremacists in the wake of the 2020 Uprisings. David Graeber and
David Wengrow's *The Dawn of Everything: A New History of Humanity* challenges this
conventional narrative of human history of evolution, which posits that without states as
we currently know them and the police that make them possible, humans lived lives of
violence, ruthless competition, and deprivation.

10. Correia and Wall, *Violent Order*.

11. Correia and Wall, *Violent Order*.

12. Correia and Wall, *Violent Order*.

13. Unpublished comments, on file with authors.

14. Meghan G. McDowell, "Insurgent Safety: Theorizing Alternatives to State Protection," *Theoretical Criminology* 23, no. 1 (2019): 47, doi.org/10.1177/1362480617713984.

15. Andrea J. Ritchie, *Invisible No More: Police Violence Against Black Women and
Women of Color* (Boston: Beacon Press, 2017). *See also* C. Riley Snorton, *Black on Both
Sides: A Racial History of Trans Identity* (Minneapolis: University of Minnesota Press,
2017); "Cruising in the End Times: An Interview with Che Gossett," Verso, December 18, 2016, versobooks.com/blogs/3016-cruising-in-the-end-times-an-interview-with
-che-gossett; Joey L. Mogul, Andrea J. Ritchie, and Kay Whitlock, *Queer (In)Justice: The
Criminalization of LGBT People in the United States* (Boston: Beacon Press, 2017).

16. Lewis, "Disability Justice Is an Essential Part of Abolishing Police and Prisons," in
Abolition for the People, Colin Kaepernick, ed. (Kaepernick Publishing, 2021). *See also* Susan
Raffo, Anjali Taneja, and Cara Page, "Healing Histories Project: Disrupting the Medical Industrial Complex," carapage.co/the-medical-industrial-complex-mic; Ben-Moshe,
Decarcerating Disability; "10 Principles of Disability Justice," Sins Invalid, static1
.squarespace.com/static/5bed3674f8370ad8c02efd9a/t/5f1f0783916d8a179c46126d
/1595869064521/10_Principles_of_DJ-2ndEd.pdf; Abolition and Disability Justice,
abolitionanddisabilityjustice.com; Wong, *Disability Visibility*.

17. Angélica Cházaro, "The End of Deportation," UCLA Law Review, forthcoming,
ssrn.com/abstract=3415707. *See also* Ritchie, *Invisible No More*.

18. Unpublished comments, on file with authors.

19. Mariame Kaba, "To Stop Police Violence, We Need Better Questions—and Bigger

Demands," *Medium*, September 25, 2020, gen.medium.com/to-stop-police-violence-we-need-better-questions-and-bigger-demands-23132fc38e8a.

20. Hall et al., *Policing the Crisis*.

21. Hall et al., *Policing the Crisis*.

22. Kaba, "To Stop Police Violence, We Need Better Questions—and Bigger Demands."

23. "From Racial Capitalism to Prison Abolitionism: a BISR Teach-In (Day One)," Brooklyn Institute for Social Research, June 26, 2020, www.youtube.com/watch?v=Yg0erOhKL3s&t=15s.

24. Mark Anthony Neal, "The Myth of the Good Cop," in *Abolition for the People*, Kaepernick, ed., (Kaepernick Publishing, 2021).

25. It seems that one of the earliest uses of the term was in an ad for Lucky Strikes called "Thinklish" consisting of cartoons captioned by made-up combined words, one of which was "copaganda" under a cartoon captioned "Police Publicity." Advertisement on file with authors.

26. Ida B. Wells, "Lynching Our National Crime," Black Past, blackpast.org/african-american-history/1909-ida-b-wells-awful-slaughter.

27. Gregory Yee, "Woman Hospitalized After Being Shot by Simi Valley Police," *Los Angeles Times*, October 5, 2021.

28. Jerry Iannelli, "Why the Media Won't Stop Using 'Officer-Involve Shootings,'" *The Appeal*, October 12, 2021, theappeal.org/officer-involved-shooting-media-bias.

29. Adrian Horton, "'The Uprisings Opened Up the Door': The TV Cop Shows Confronting a Harmful Legacy," *The Guardian*, April 24, 2021, www.theguardian.com/us-news/2021/apr/24/tv-police-cop-shows-hollywood-legacy.

30. Iannelli, "Why the Media Won't Stop Using 'Officer-Involved Shootings.'"

31. Clay Risen, "Peter Warner, 90, Seafarer Who Discovered Shipwrecked Boys, Dies," *New York Times*, April 22, 2021. *See also* Julian Morgans, "I Spent 15 Months Shipwrecked on An Uninhabited Island," *Vice*, March 30, 2021, vice.com/en/article/4adky9/shipwrecked-on-uninhabited-desert-island; Julian Morgans, "S3E5—Shipwrecked on an Island," *Extremes*, March 30, 2020, open.spotify.com/episode/0pLjRHihvnhkFIhcDrfDts.

32. Morgans, "S3E5—Shipwrecked on an Island."

33. *See, e.g.*, Graeber and Wengrow, *The Dawn of Everything*.

34. David Correia and Tyler Wall, *Police: A Field Guide* (London; Brooklyn: Verso, 2018).

35. Correia and Wall, *Police: A Field Guide*.

36. Correia and Wall, *Violent Order*.

37. Correia and Wall, *Police: A Field Guide*.

38. Correia and Wall, *Police: A Field Guide*.

39. Correia and Wall, *Police: A Field Guide*.

40. "Challenging E-Carceration," challengingecarceration.org/what-is-e-carceration.

41. Davis et al. name developing new vocabularies such as "prison-industrial complex," and "abolition," pointing to new theoretical strategies was one of the explicit goals of Critical Resistance. *Abolition. Feminism. Now.* (Chicago: Haymarket Press, 2022).

42. Hall et al., *Policing the Crisis*.

43. Beth E. Richie and Andrea J. Ritchie, "The Crisis of Criminalization: A Call for a Comprehensive Philanthropic Response," Barnard Center for Research on Women, September 15, 2017, bcrw.barnard.edu/publications/the-crisis-of-criminalization.

44. "Introduction," in *Abolition Feminisms, Volume 2: Feminist Ruptures Against the Carceral State*, Alisa Bierria and Jakeya Carruthers, eds. (Chicago: Haymarket Books, 2022).

45. Meghan G. McDowell, "Insurgent Safety: Theorizing Alternatives to State Protection," *Theoretical Criminology* 23, no. 1 (2019): 45–46, doi.org/10.1177 /1362480617713984.

46. James Baldwin, *James Baldwin: The Last Interview and Other Conversations* (Brooklyn: Melville House, 2014).

47. Amia Srinivasan, "The Politics of Safety," *Financial Times*, August 13, 2021.

48. Ja'Tovia Gary, "The Giverny Document (2019)," jatovia.com/the-giverny -document-2019#1.

49. Krystle Okafor, "What Is 'Collective Care' Today?" (2020), 1–13, cdn.filepicker.io /api/file/ZWwFn4pvSIqNJldXzHLa?&fit=max.

50. Project South, "The Peoples Movement Assemblies Offer Spaces for Us to Practice Community Governance and to Coordinate Together Across Multiple Strategies and Multiple Geographies," projectsouth.org/global-movement-building/peoples-movement -assemblies.

51. Pascal Emmer et al., *Unmasked: Impacts of Pandemic Policing*, October 2020, com-munityresourcehub.org/wp-content/uploads/2020/12/Unmasked.pdf.

52. Mike Ludwig, "Minneapolis Neighborhoods Defend Against Police and White Supremacists," *Truthout*, June 1, 2020, truthout.org/articles/minneapolis-neighborhoods -defend-against-police-and-white-supremacists. *See also* Sarah Holder, Rachael Dottle, and Marie Patino, "Police Response Slowed. The Community Stepped In," *Bloomberg*, October 30, 2020, bloomberg.com/news/features/2020-10-30/what-slower-911 -responses-meant-for-minneapolis.

53. Charmaine Chua, "Abolition Is a Constant Struggle: Five Lessons from Minne-apolis," *Theory & Event* 23, no. 4 Supplement (October 2020): S-127-S-147, muse.jhu .edu/article/775394.

54. Chua, "Abolition Is a Constant Struggle: Five Lessons from Minneapolis."

55. Nashville People's Budget Coalition, "Nashville People's Budget Coalition," nash-villepeoplesbudget.org.

56. These principles are drawn in part from Interrupting Criminalization's *What's Next: Toward a Police Free Future*, Mariame Kaba, ed. (Interrupting Criminalization, 2020), interruptingcriminalization.com.

57. *Disarm, Defund, Dismantle: Police Abolition in Canada*, Shiri Pasternak, Kevin Walby, and Abby Stadnyk, eds. (Toronto: Between the Lines, 2022).

58. Movement for Black Lives, *Vision for Black Lives*, "Invest/Divest," m4bl.org/policy -platforms/invest-divest.

59. Kaba, "To Stop Police Violence, We Need Better Questions—and Bigger Demands."

60. Critical Resistance, "Our Communities, Our Solutions: An Organizer's Toolkit to Develop Demands to Abolish Policing," 2020, criticalresistance.org/abolish-policing -toolkit.

61. Davis et al., *Abolition. Feminism. Now.*

62. National Bail Out, "History of Black Mama's Bail Out," nationalbailout.org /history.

63. Katrina Feldkamp and S. Rebecca Neusteter, "The Little Known, Racist History of the 911 Emergency Call System," *In These Times,* January 26, 2021, inthesetimes.com /article/911-emergency-service-racist-history-civil-rights. *See also* S. Rebecca Neusteter et al., *Understanding Police Enforcement: A Multicity 911 Analysis* (Vera Institute of Justice, 2020), vera.org/downloads/publications/understanding-police-enforcement-911 -analysis.pdf.

64. "Ruth Wilson Gilmore Makes the Case for Abolition," Chenjerai Kumanyika interview with Ruth Wilson Gilmore, *The Intercept,* June 10, 2020, theintercept.com /2020/06/10/ruth-wilson-gilmore-makes-the-case-for-abolition.

65. Sista II Sista, "Sistas Making Moves: Collective Leadership for Personal Transformation and Justice," in *Color of Violence: The INCITE! Anthology* (Boston: South End Press, 2006).

66. Ejeris Dixon, "Building Community Safety: Practical Steps Toward Liberatory Transformation," in *Beyond Survival: Strategies and Stories from the Transformative Justice Movement*, Ejeris Dixon and Leah Lakshmi Piepzna-Samarasinha (Chico, CA: AK Press, 2020). Andrea was a member of the Safe Outside the System Collective from 2007 to 2009.

67. Spirit House, "The Harm Free Zone," www.spirithouse-nc.org/harm-free-zone.

68. Ruth Wilson Gilmore, "Capitalism," Interrupting Criminalization, September 10, 2021.

69. Chua, "Abolition Is a Constant Struggle: Five Lessons from Minneapolis."

70. Left Roots, Roundtables for Radicals; Fahd Ahmed.

71. "Join the Abolitionist Movement," *Rebel Steps Podcast,* June 23, 2020, rebelsteps .com/episodes/abolition-with-mariame-kaba.

72. Shannon Perez-Darby and Mia Mingus, "What Is Self-Accountability?" *BCRW Videos,* 3:56, October 26, 2018, vimeo.com/291929245?embedded=true&source=vid eo_title&owner=1739030.

Tricks and Tensions

1. David Stein and Dan Berger, "What Is and What Could Be: The Policies of Abolition," in Colin Kaepernick, ed., *Abolition for the People* (Kaepernick Publishing 2021).

2. Ruth Wilson Gilmore and Craig Gilmore, "Restating the Obvious," in *Indefensible Space: The Architecture of the National Insecurity State*, Michael Sorkin, ed. (New York: Routledge, 2008). A state is different from a government, or group of people who operate the state's institutions at any given time. According to the Gilmores, states are "ideological and institutional capacities" while governments are their animating force.

3. David Graeber and David Wengrow, *The Dawn of Everything: A New History of Humanity* (London: Allen Lane, 2021).

4. David Kaib, remarks at Abolition and the State Part II, hosted by Interrupting Criminalization, January 22, 2022.

5. The notion that a defining feature of states is their exercise of a monopoly on the legitimate use of violence within a given territory is attributed to sociologist Max Weber,

although Graeber and Wengrow credit German philosopher Rudolph von Ihering. Graeber and Wengrow, *The Dawn of Everything.*

6. Gilmore and Gilmore, "Restating the Obvious"; Graeber and Wengrow, *The Dawn of Everything.*

7. Graeber and Wengrow, *The Dawn of Everything.*

8. Gilmore and Gilmore, "Restating the Obvious." According to the Gilmores, states are "ideological and institutional capacities" while governments are their animating force.

9. Gilmore and Gilmore, "Restating the Obvious."

10. Dean Spade, remarks at Abolition and the State Part I, hosted by Interrupting Criminalization, September 11, 2021.

11. David Correia and Tyler Wall, *Violent Order: Essays on the Nature of Police* (Chicago: Haymarket Books, 2021).

12. Brendan McQuade, remarks at Abolition and the State Part II, hosted by Interrupting Criminalization, January 22, 2022.

13. Klee Benally, remarks at Abolition and the State Part I, hosted by Interrupting Criminalization, September 11, 2021.

14. Leanne Betamosake-Simpson and Robyn Maynard, *Rehearsals for Living* (Chicago: Haymarket Press, 2022).

15. Simpson and Maynard, *Rehearsals for Living.*

16. William C. Anderson, "A Note on the 'Failed State,'" *Offshoot Journal*, May 10, 2021, offshootjournal.org/a-note-on-the-failed-state. *See also* William C. Anderson, *The Nation on No Map: Black Anarchism and Abolition* (Chico, CA: AK Press 2022); Zoé Samudzi and William C. Anderson, *As Black as Resistance: Finding the Conditions for Liberation* (Chico, CA: AK Press, 2018).

17. Jackie Wang, remarks at Abolition and the State Part I, hosted by Interrupting Criminalization, September 11, 2021; *see also* Wang, *Carceral Capitalism.*

18. Jackie Wang, *Carceral Capitalism* (Pasadena: Semiotext(e), 2018).

19. Dean Spade, remarks at Abolition and the State Part I, hosted by Interrupting Criminalization, September 11, 2021.

20. Spade, remarks at Abolition and the State Part I.

21. Ruth Wilson Gilmore, "Understanding Capitalism: A Workshop for Abolitionist Organizers," hosted by Interrupting Criminalization, September 10, 2021; "Activists Say: Ruth Wilson Gilmore," July 22, 2021, www.youtube.com/watch?v=z0SOKx29e38.

22. Geo Maher, *A World Without Police: How Strong Communities Make Cops Obsolete* (Brooklyn: Verso, 2021).

23. Kelly Gillespie and Leigh-Ann Naidoo, remarks at Abolition and the State Part II, hosted by Interrupting Criminalization, January 22, 2022.

24. Dean Spade, remarks at Abolition and the State Part I, hosted by Interrupting Criminalization, September 11, 2021.

25. William Anderson, remarks at Abolition and the State Part I, hosted by Interrupting Criminalization, September 11, 2021; *see also* William C. Anderson, *The Nation on No Map: Black Anarchism and Abolition* (Chico, CA: AK Press 2022).

26. Maynard and Simpson, *Rehearsals for Living.*

27. Jackie Wang, remarks at Abolition and the State Part I, hosted by Interrupting Criminalization, September 11, 2021; *see also* Wang, *Carceral Capitalism*.

28. Nicos Poulantzas, *State Power Socialism* (New York: Verso, 1978), 123.

29. Graeber and Wengrow, *The Dawn of Everything*.

30. Angela Y. Davis, Gina Dent, Erica Meiners, and Beth E. Richie, *Abolition. Feminism. Now.* (Chicago: Haymarket Press, 2022); Angela Y. Davis, *Freedom Is a Constant Struggle: Ferguson, Palestine, and the Foundations of a Movement* (Chicago: Haymarket Press, 2016).

31. Ruth Wilson Gilmore, "Capitalism," Interrupting Criminalization, September 10, 2021.

32. Gilmore and Gilmore, "Restating the Obvious."

33. Jackie Wang, remarks at Abolition and the State Part I, hosted by Interrupting Criminalization, September 11, 2021.

34. Graeber and Wengrow, *The Dawn of Everything*; James C. Scott, *Against the Grain: A Deep History of the Earliest States* (New Haven: Yale University Press, 2017).

35. Christos Lynteris, "The State as a Social Relation," *Anthropology & Materialism* 1 (2013), doi.org/10.4000/am.291.

36. "Activists Say: Ruth Wilson Gilmore," July 22, 2021, www.youtube.com /watch?v=z0SOKx29e38; Ruth Wilson Gilmore, "Abolition on Stolen Land," October 9, 2020, challengeinequality.luskin.ucla.edu/abolition-on-stolen-land-with-ruth-wilson -gilmore.

37. Grace Lee Boggs, *The Next American Revolution: Sustainable Activism for the Twenty-First Century* (Berkeley: University of California Press, 2011).

38. Kelly Gillespie and Leigh-Ann Naidoo, remarks at Abolition and the State Part II, hosted by Interrupting Criminalization, January 22, 2022.

39. Gillespie and Naidoo. Gillespie and Naidoo point to writings on abolition pedagogy as guides to how we might begin to learn and teach in ways that support such a transition. *See, e.g.*, Kelly Gillespie and Leigh-Ann Naidoo, "Abolition Pedagogy: Force Fields of Critique," *Critical Times* 4 no. 2: 284–312, August 1, 2021, doi.org/10.1215/26410478 -9093094; Dylan Rodríguez, "The Disorientation of the Teaching Act: Abolition as Pedagogical Position," *Radical Teacher* 88, no. 10 (2010): 7–19, 10.1353/rdt.2010.0006. *See also* Paula X. Rojas, "Are the Cops in Our Heads and Hearts?" in *The Revolution Will Not Be Funded: INCITE! Women of Color Against Violence* (Boston: South End Press, 2009), available at: sfonline.barnard.edu/navigating-neoliberalism-in-the-academy-nonprofits -and-beyond/paula-rojas-are-the-cops-in-our-heads-and-hearts for a discussion of liberatory education strategies of the landless people's movement in Brazil (MST).

40. Grace Lee Boggs with Scott Kurashige, *The Next American Revolution: Sustainable Activism for the Twenty-First Century* (Berkeley: University of California Press, 2011); Grace Lee Boggs, *Living for Change* (Minneapolis: University of Minnesota Press, 2016).

41. Boggs, *The Next American Revolution*; Boggs, *Living for Change*.

42. Eric Stanley, remarks at Abolition and the State Part II, hosted by Interrupting Criminalization, January 22, 2022.

43. Maynard and Simpson, *Rehearsals for Living*; *Lorenzo Kom'Boa Ervin: Organizing Outside the System from the Black Panther Party Until Now: Original Interview with Robyn Maynard of No One Is Illegal Radio*, 2011, e-artexte.ca/id/eprint/32138/1/Lorenzo%20

Ervin%20Robyn%20Maynard.pdf; *Anarchists in the Black Panther Party and Black Liberation Army: Interviews from No One Is Illegal Radio*, 2010, e-artexte.ca/id/eprint /32161/1/ojore%20lutalo-ashanti%20alston-%20interview%20with%20robyn%20 maynard.pdf; Ashanti Alston, "Beyond Nationalism but Not Without It," *Onward*, Spring 2002, theanarchistlibrary.org/library/ashanti-alston-beyond-nationalism-but-not -without-it. *See also* Lorenzo Komboa Ervin, "Why I Am an Anarchist," June 5, 2017, blackrosefed.org/komboa-why-i-am-an-anarchist.

44. Klee Benally, remarks at Abolition and the State Part I, hosted by Interrupting Criminalization, September 11, 2021.

45. Benally, remarks at Abolition and the State Part I.

46. Anderson, *The Nation on No Map*; *see also* Mike Harman, "Huey Newton Introduces Revolutionary Intercommunalism," Boston College, November 18 1970," *Libcom*, February 15, 2018, libcom.org/library/huey-newton-introduces-revolutionary -intercommunalism-boston-college-november-18-1970.

47. Harsha Walia, remarks at Abolition and the State Part II, hosted by Interrupting Criminalization, January 22, 2022.

48. Robin D.G. Kelly, Afterword, *Rehearsals for Living*.

49. Harsha Walia, remarks at Abolition and the State Part II, hosted by Interrupting Criminalization, January 22, 2022.

50. Eric Stanley, remarks at Abolition and the State Part II, hosted by Interrupting Criminalization, January 22, 2022; Anderson, *The Nation on No Map*.

51. Maynard and Simpson, *Rehearsals for Living*.

52. Harsha Walia, remarks at Abolition and the State Part II, hosted by Interrupting Criminalization, January 22, 2022; Boggs, *The Next American Revolution*.

53. Che Gossett, remarks at Abolition and the State Part II, hosted by Interrupting Criminalization, January 22, 2022.

54. Maynard and Simpson, *Rehearsals for Living*; Correia and Wall, *Violent Order*.

55. Maynard and Simpson, *Rehearsals for Living*; *see also* Tiffany Lethabo King, *The Black Shoals: Offshore Formations of Black and Native Studies* (Durham: Duke Press 2019).

56. Life and Debt, "Life and Debt," lifeanddebt.org. *See also* Ugonna-Ora Owoh, "A Year After #EndSARS, Nigerian Youth Maintain That Nothing Has Changed," *Okay Africa*, October 27, 2021, okayafrica.com/protest-in-nigeria-end-sars; Boggs, *The Next American Revolution*.

57. Kenyon Farrow, remarks at Abolition and the State Part I, hosted by Interrupting Criminalization, September 11, 2021.

58. Eric Stanley, remarks at Abolition and the State Part II, hosted by Interrupting Criminalization, January 22, 2022.

59. Maurice BP-Weeks, remarks at Abolition and the State Part II, hosted by Interrupting Criminalization, January 22, 2022

60. Hall et al., *Policing the Crisis*.

61. Brendan McQuade, remarks at Abolition and the State Part II, hosted by Interrupting Criminalization, January 22, 2022.

62. Paula X. Rojas, "Are the Cops in Our Heads and Hearts?" in *The Revolution Will Not Be Funded*, INCITE! Women of Color Against Violence (Boston: South End Press, 2009), sfonline.barnard.edu/navigating-neoliberalism-in-the-academy-nonprofits-and -beyond/paula-rojas-are-the-cops-in-our-heads-and-hearts.

63. Rojas, "Are the Cops in Our Heads and Hearts?"

64. Raúl Zibechi, "Times of Collapse, Times of Possibilities: Latin American Societies in Movement," NACLA, June 10, 2021, nacla.org/latin-america-pandemic-movements -zibechi.

65. Wang, *Carceral Capitalism*.

66. Brendan McQuade, remarks at Abolition and the State Part II, hosted by Interrupting Criminalization, January 22, 2022.

67. Maynard and Simpson, *Rehearsals for Living*; King, *The Black Shoals*.

68. Charmaine Chua, "Abolition Is a Constant Struggle: Five Lessons from Minneapolis," *Theory & Event* 23, no. 4 Supplement (October 2020): S-127–S-147, muse.jhu .edu/article/775394.

69. Leah Lakshmi Piepzna-Samarasinha, *Care Work: Dreaming Disability Justice* (Vancouver: Arsenal Pulp Press, 2018).

70. Kaba, "To Stop Police Violence, We Need Better Questions—and Bigger Demands."

71. Brendan McQuade, remarks at Abolition and the State Part I, hosted by Interrupting Criminalization, September 11, 2021.

72. Jackie Wang, remarks at Abolition and the State Part I, hosted by Interrupting Criminalization, September 11, 2021.

73. Community Resource Hub Learning Communities, October 2021.

74. Dean Spade, remarks at Abolition and the State Part I, hosted by Interrupting Criminalization, September 11, 2021.

75. Jamel Campbell-Gooch, Building Beyond Policing Convening, October 2021.

76. "Why We Don't Make Demands," *Crimethinc*, crimethinc.com/2015/05/05 /feature-why-we-dont-make-demands.

77. Interrupting Criminalization, *Navigating Public Safety Task Forces*, 2021, inter-ruptingcriminalization.com/task-forces.

78. Orleans Parish Prison Reform Coalition, "Help Not Handcuffs," opprcnola.org /helpnothandcuffs.

79. Interrupting Criminalization, *Navigating Public Safety Task Forces*, 2021, inter-ruptingcriminalization.com/task-forces.

80. Sheila Nezhad, "Decisions That Point Minneapolis Toward Safety and Justice Must Be Made in the Open," *MinnPost*, January 27, 2022, www.minnpost.com /community-voices/2022/01/decisions-that-point-minneapolis-toward-safety-and -justice-must-be-made-in-the-open.

81. Interrupting Criminalization, *Navigating Public Safety Task Forces*, 2021, inter-ruptingcriminalization.com/task-forces.

82. "The Breathe Act," Breatheact.org.

83. Downstate Coalition for Crime Victims, "Procurement Justice," downstatecoali tion.org/procurement.

84. Adam Gabbat, "Felony Charges Against BLM Protestors Are 'Suppression Tactic,' Experts Say," *The Guardian*, August 16, 2020. *See also* Akela Lacy, "Protestors in Multiple States Are Facing Felony Charges, Including Terrorism," *The Intercept*, August 27, 2020, theintercept.com/2020/08/27/black-lives-matter-protesters-terrorism-felony-charges; Iveliz Orellano, "Black Lives Matter Protestors Are Facing Felony Changes a Year After

Uprisings," *Teen Vogue*, November 4, 2021, teenvogue.com/story/black-lives-matter-protesters-felony-charges; Neil MacFarquhar, "Why Charges Against Protestors Are Being Dismissed by the Thousands," *New York Times*, November 19, 2020; Mike Baker, "Corrosive Effects of Tear Gas Could Intensify Coronavirus Pandemic," *New York Times*, June 3, 2020; Lizzy Acker, "Kaiser Permanente Studies Effects of Tear Gas on People Exposed During Portland Protests," *Oregon Live*, August 5, 2020, oregonlive.com/health/2020/08/kaiser-permanente-studies-effects-of-tear-gas-on-people-exposed-during-portland-protests.html; Matthew Rozsa, "So Much Tear Gas Has Been Sprayed on Portland Protestors That Officials Fear It's Polluted the Water," *Salon*, August 24, 2020, salon.com/2020/08/24/so-much-tear-gas-has-been-sprayed-on-portland-protesters-that-officials-fear-its-polluted-the-water.

85. Reid Epstein and Patricial Mazzei, "G.O.P. Bills Target Protesters (and Absolve Motorists Who Hit Them)," *New York Times*, April 21, 2021; *see also* Shirin Yaseen, "USA: Rights Expert Decries Wave of Anti-protest Laws 'Spreading Through the Country,'" *Global Issues*, May 5, 2021, globalissues.org/news/2021/05/05/27752. In states like Texas, Florida, Arizona, Indiana, Illinois, North Carolina, Louisiana, and Utah, momentum toward reduction of police budgets was blocked by state legislators passing or threatening legislation that would penalize cities that did so.

86. Jeramey Jannene, "New Police Grant Approved with Little Scrutiny," *UrbanMilwaukee.com*, March 26, 2021, urbanmilwaukee.com/2021/03/26/city-hall-new-police-grant-approved-with-little-scrutiny.

87. *See, e.g.*, H.R.3098—Defund Cities That Defund the Police Act of 2021, H.R.3217—Lawless Cities Accountability Act of 2021; H.R.1465—Right to Remain Safe Act of 2021. The Senate Resolution introduced by Senator Bernie Sanders with respect to the 2022 federal budget also provided that federal funding may be limited to cities that defund the police. S.Con.Res.14 (2021).

88. "COPS Hiring Grants," www.ojp.gov/sites/g/files/xyckuh241/files/media/document/copsgrants.pdf.

89. Hans Nichols, "White House's Tough-on-Crime Message: Use COVID Funds," *Axios*, July 12, 2021, www.axios.com/white-houses-tough-on-crime-message-use-covid-funds-bb8d909f-4f35-4a37-9445-12aac98c2590.html.; *Ensuring That Federal Stimulus Funds Support Care Not Cops*, Community Resource Hub (2021), defundpolice.org/wp-content/uploads/2021/04/0407_CARES_ARPA_B.pdf.

90. Markasa Tucker-Harris and Devin Anderson, *Milwaukee Police Pension Impacts in FY2023 and Beyond* (African American Roundtable, 2021), static1.squarespace.com/static/600b57f5148d2b2280631e37/t/615716c5b49f71111da939e3/1633097414343/2021+Pension+Report+%28Final%29.pdf.

91. "COPS Hiring Grants," www.ojp.gov/sites/g/files/xyckuh241/files/media/document/copsgrants.pdf; Action Network, "No More COPS Funding in the 2022 Budget," actionnetwork.org/petitions/no-more-cops-funding-for-increasing-police-personnel.

92. Tracey L. Meares, "A Public Good Gone Bad," *Boston Review*, August 1, 2017, bostonreview.net/law-justice/tracey-l-meares-policing-public-good-gone-bad.

93. Evelyn Hockstein, "Biden's Passive Revolution: Using Gramsci to Understand Biden's 'Reformism,'" *Cosmonaut*, May 29, 2021, cosmonautmag.com/2021/05/biden-passive-revolution-using-gramsci-to-understand-bidens-reformism; Andrea J. Ritchie, *The Demand Is Still: Defund the Police, Fund the People, Defend Black Lives*, Interrupting Criminalization, January 2021.

94. Decriminalize Seattle, "Participatory Budgeting," decriminalizeseattle.com /participatory-budgeting.

95. Nichols, "White House's Tough-on-Crime Message: Use COVID Funds"; Community Resource Hub, *Ensuring That Federal Stimulus Funds Support Care Not Cops*, 2021, communityresourcehub.org/wp-content/uploads/2021/04/0407_CARES_ARPA_B .pdf.

96. Bryce Covert, "Where 'Defund' Isn't Dead," *The Nation*, November 16, 2021, thenation.com/article/society/police-reform-defund.

97. J. David Goodman, "A Year After 'Defund,' Police Departments Get Their Money Back," *New York Times*, October 10, 2021. *See also* Sara Cline, "Portland Among US Cities Adding Funds to Police Departments," *San Diego Tribune*, November 17, 2021, sandiegouniontribune.com/news/california/story/2021-11-17/portland-among-us-cities -looking-to-refund-police.

98. Davis et al., *Abolition. Feminism. Now.*

99. Harsha Walia, "Dismantle and Transform: On Abolition, Decolonization, and Insurgent Politics," *Abolition Journal*, May 22, 2016, abolitionjournal.org/dismantle-and -transform.

100. Dan Berger and David Stein, "Dismantle, Change, Build: Policies of Abolition," in Kaepernick, ed., *Abolition for the People*.

101. Kristian Williams, *Our Enemies in Blue: Police and Power in America* (Oakland: AK Press, 2015). Williams describes PFAs as "a semi-autonomous component of the state," claiming partial control over its capacity for violence. *See also* Ethan Fauré, "Reactionary Power in the Union," *Political Research*, January 20, 2021, politicalresearch.org /2021/01/20/reactionary-power-union; Stuart Schrader, "To Protect and Serve Themselves: Police in US Politics Since the 1960s," *Public Culture* September 1, 2019; 31 (3): 601–623, doi.org/10.1215/08992363-7532667.

102. NAACP Legal Defense and Education Fund, *Community Oversight of Police Union Contracts*, August 2020, www.naacpldf.org/wp-content/uploads /LDF_07242020_PoliceContractToolKit-12c.pdf; Williams, *Our Enemies in Blue*.

103. Amir Vera, "Texas Billboard Warns Drivers to Enter Austin 'At Your Own Risk' After City Reduces Police Budget," CNN, September 13, 2020, cnn.com/2020/09/13 /us/austin-texas-defund-police-billboard/index.html. *See also* Meagan Falcon, "Austin Votes Against More Police in Prop A: Election Results," *Patch*, November 2, 2021, patch .com/texas/downtownaustin/austin-votes-against-more-police-prop-election-results.

104. KFOR-TV and K. Querry, "Judge Says Norman Council's Meeting to Cut Police Department's Budget Violated Law," KFOR, December 3, 2020, kfor.com/news/local /judge-says-norman-councils-meeting-to-cut-police-departments-budget-violated-law.

105. For more information, see nomorecopmoney.com.

106. No More Cop Money, "No More Cop Money: Get Police Money out of Politics," nomorecopmoney.com; Color of Change, *Police Foundations: A Corporate Sponsored Threat to Black Lives* (2021), policefoundations.org/wp-content/uploads/2021/10/Color -Of-Change-Report-Police-Foundations-A-Corporate-Sponsored-Threat-to-Democracy -Black-Lives.pdf.

107. Odette Yousef et al., "Active-Duty Police in Major U.S. Cities Appear on Purported Oath Keepers Rosters," NPR, November 5, 2021, npr.org/2021/11/05/1052098059 /active-duty-police-in-major-u-s-cities-appear-on-purported-oath-keepers-rosters. *See also* Sharon Zhang, "Leaked Documents Show Police Officers on Supposed Oath

Keepers Rosters," *Truthout*, November 5, 2021, truthout.org/articles/leaked-documents
-show-police-officers-on-supposed-oath-keepers-rosters; Sharon Zhang, "Boston PD
Covered Up Police Union Head's Child Molestation Charges for 25 Years," *Truthout*,
April 13, 2021; Jasson Perez, "The Problem of Police Nationalism," *Dissent Magazine*,
Summer 2021, dissentmagazine.org/article/the-problem-of-police-nationalism; Naomi
Braine, "The Long and Tangled History of Law Enforcement and Right-Wing Violence,"
Political Research, January 25, 2021, politicalresearch.org/2021/01/25/long-and-tangled
-history-law-enforcement-and-right-wing-violence.

108. David Zahniser and Kevin Rector, "L.A.'s Deal with the Police Union Would
Guarantee $245 Million in Overtime Pay," *Los Angeles Times*, February 13, 2021.

109. Williams, *Our Enemies in Blue*; *see also* Maher, *A World Without Police*.

110. Kim Kelly, "Police Unions: What to Know and Why They Don't Belong in the
Labor Movement," *Teen Vogue*, June 25, 2020, teenvogue.com/story/what-to-know
-police-unions-labor-movement; Williams, *Our Enemies in Blue*.

111. Seattle DSA, "MLK Labor Council Kicks Out Police Union—Statement by
Seattle DSA," Seattle DSA, June 22, 2020, seattledsa.org/2020/06/mlk-labor-council
-kicks-out-police-union-now-step-up-the-struggle-to-transform-our-unions-into-anti
-racist-democratic-class-struggle-organizations. *See also* "MLK Labor Council Kicks Out
Seattle Police Officers' Guild," *Seattle Medium*, June 17, 2020, seattlemedium.com/mlk
-labor-council-kicks-out-seattle-police-officers-guild.

112. Refund Raleigh, "Projects," refundraleigh.org/projects. *See also* Durham Beyond
Policing, "Durham Beyond Policing for Community-Led Safety and Wellness," durham-
beyondpolicing.org/blog.

113. Kris LaGrange, "AFL-CIO: Police Unions Can Stay In," *UCOMM* blog, June 10,
2020, ucommblog.com/section/union/afl-cio-police-unions-can-stay. *See also* Kim
Kelly, "No More Cop Unions," *New Republic*, May 29, 2020, newrepublic.com/article
/157918/no-cop-unions; Dave Jamieson, "The Labor Movement Faces a Reckoning over
Police Unions," *HuffPost*, June 6, 2020, huffpost.com/entry/the-labor-movement-faces
-a-reckoning-over-police-unions_n_5eda9958c5b640424ef70cd2.

114. Whitlock and Heitzeg, *Carceral Con*, 46. *See also* Bill Fletcher Jr., "The Central
Issue Is Police Repression, Not Police Unions," *In These Times*, June 12, 2020, inthese-
times.com/article/the-central-issue-is-police-repression-not-police-unions.

115. Maher, *A World Without Police*.

116. Gabbriel Schivone, "Rebel Cops," *The Progressive*, December 8, 2020, progressive
.org/magazine/rebel-cops-schivone.

117. NAACP Legal Defense and Education Fund, *Community Oversight of Police
Union Contracts*, August 2020, www.naacpldf.org/wp-content/uploads/LDF
_07242020_PoliceContractToolKit-12c.pdf.

118. Project, "The Work," www.the490project.com/the-work.

119. The Prometheus Conspiracy, the peoplesfire.org.

120. Markasa Tucker-Harris and Devin Anderson, *Milwaukee Police Pension Impacts
in FY2023 and Beyond* (African American Roundtable, 2021), static1.squarespace.com
/static/600b57f5148d2b2280631e37/t/615716c5b49f71111da939e3/1633097414343
/2021+Pension+Report+%28Final%29.pdf.

121. Woods Ervin, Ricardo Levins Morales, Zola Richardson and Jonathan Stegall,
"The Fantasy of Community Control of the Police," *The Forge*, February 4, 2021, forge-
organizing.org/article/fantasy-community-control-police.

122. Movement for Black Lives, "Vision for Black Lives: Community Control," m4bl
.org/policy-platforms/community-control.

123. Ervin et al., "The Fantasy of Community Control of Police."

124. *See, e.g.*, Andrea J. Ritchie and Brit Schulte, "'Prostitution-Related' Loitering
Ordinance Promotes Racial Profiling in Chicago," *Truthout*, July 24, 2018, truthout.org
/articles/anti-prostitution-ordinance-promotes-racial-profiling-in-chicago.

125. Beth Richie, Dylan Rodríguez, Mariame Kaba, Melissa Burch, Rachel Herzing, and Shana Agid, *Problems with Community Control of Police and Proposals for
Alternatives*, defundpolice.org/wp-content/uploads/2021/03/Problems_w_CRBs
_and_Proposals_for_Alternatives-1.pdf.

126. Richie et al., *Problems with Community Control of Police and Proposals for Alternatives*.

127. Ervin et al., "The Fantasy of Community Control of Police."

128. Ervin et al., "The Fantasy of Community Control of Police."

129. Cops Are Flops Collective, *Reimagining Justice in South Africa Beyond Policing*,
2020, drive.google.com/file/d/1krNcg_saPFABqjuFkQvtVKUpIjivd8Es/view.

130. Kamau Franklin, "You Can't Abolish the States Institutions Without Abolishing
the State That Created Them," *Grassroots Thinking*, November 1, 2021, grassrootsthink-
ing.com/2021/11/01/you-cant-abolish-the-states-institutions-without-abolishing-the
-state-that-created-them.

131. Margaret Kimberley, "Freedom Rider: The Police Defunding Con Game," *Black
Agenda Report*, July 8, 2020, blackagendareport.com/freedom-rider-police-defunding
-con-game.

132. Kimberley, "Freedom Rider: The Police Defunding Con Game."

133. Andrea J. Ritchie, *The Demand Is Still Defund the Police, Fund the People, Defend
Black Lives*, Interrupting Criminalization, 2021, bit.ly/DefundPoliceUpdate.

134. Assata Shakur, *Assata: An Autobiography* (Lawrence Hill Books, 2001); *see also*
"Black Liberation and the Abolition of the Prison Industrial Complex: An Interview with
Rachel Herzing," *The Black Scholar*, September 6, 2016.

135. Candice Bernd, "'Defund Police' Doesn't Mean Hire Private Guns—but Cities
Are Doing Just That," *Truthout*, September 1, 2020, truthout.org/articles/defund-police
-doesnt-mean-hire-private-guns-but-cities-are-doing-just-that.

136. Stop LAPD Spying, "Defund Surveillance," stoplapdspying.org/defund
-surveillance.

137. Andrea J. Ritchie and Mariame Kaba, "We Want More Justice for Breonna Taylor
Than the System That Killed Her Can Deliver," *Essence Magazine*, December 6, 2020.

138. John Eligo and Shawn Hubler, "Throughout Trial over George Floyd's Death,
Killings by Police Mount," *New York Times*, November 30, 2021; Andrea J. Ritchie and
Mariame Kaba, "We Want More Justice for Breonna Taylor Than the System That Killed
Her Can Deliver," *Essence Magazine*, December 6, 2020.

139. Williams, *Our Enemies in Blue*.

140. Mariame Kaba and Andrea J. Ritchie, "A World Where George Floyd and Ma'Khia
Bryant Would Still Be Here Is a World Without Police," NewsOne, April 22, 2021, news
one.com/4143261/george-floyd-makhia-bryant-abolition-police; Ritchie and Kaba, "We
Want More Justice for Breonna Taylor."

141. Chicago Torture Justice Memorials, chicagotorture.org.

142. Movement for Black Lives, "Reparations Now," 2019, m4bl.org/wp-content /uploads/2021/06/Reparations-Now-Toolkit-FINAL.pdf.

143. Chicago Torture Justice Center, chicagotorturejustice.org. *See also* Movement for Black Lives, "Reparations Now," 2019, m4bl.org/wp-content/uploads/2021/06 /Reparations-Now-Toolkit-FINAL.pdf.

144. For more information about Chicago's struggle for reparations from police violence, please visit Chicago Torture Justice Memorials, chicagotorture.org; Chicago Torture Justice Center, www.chicagotorturejustice.org. The reparations for police violence conversation toolkit can be found at bit.ly/REPJuneConversationTK.

145. Rachel Herzing and Isaac Ontiveros, "Responding to Police Killing: Questions and Challenges for Abolitionists," *Centre for Crime and Justice Studies* 82, no. 1 (December 2010): 38–40, doi.org/10.1080/09627251.2010.525940.

146. Just Transition Alliance, "What Is Just Transition?," jtalliance.org/what-is-just -transition; *see also* Center for Story-based Strategy, "Just Transition," www.storybased strategy.org/just-transition.

147. Gabbriel Schivone, "Rebel Cops," *The Progressive*, December 8, 2020, progressive .org/magazine/rebel-cops-schivone.

148. Schivone, "Rebel Cops."

149. Schivone, "Rebel Cops."

150. Schivone, "Rebel Cops."

Experiment and Build

1. adrienne marie brown, *Emergent Strategy: Shaping Change, Changing Worlds* (Chico, CA: AK Press, 2017), 42.

2. Paula X. Rojas, "Are the Cops in Our Heads and Hearts?" in *The Revolution Will Not Be Funded*, INCITE! Women of Color Against Violence (Boston: South End Press, 2009), available at: sfonline.barnard.edu/navigating-neoliberalism-in-the-academy -nonprofits-and-beyond/paula-rojas-are-the-cops-in-our-heads-and-heartsfor a discussion of liberatory education strategies of the landless people's movement in Brazil (MST).

3. Rojas, "Are the Cops in Our Heads and Hearts?"

4. Rojas, "Are the Cops in Our Heads and Hearts?"

5. Rojas, "Are the Cops in Our Heads and Hearts?"

6. Rojas, "Are the Cops in Our Heads and Hearts?"

7. Rojas, "Are the Cops in Our Heads and Hearts?"

8. Roja, "Are the Cops in Our Heads and Hearts?".

9. Mijente, "¿SIN EL QUÉ?," El Comite, March 10, 2020, mijentesupportcommit-tee.com/post/sin-el-que.

10. Mijente, "¿SIN EL QUÉ?"

11. Mijente, "¿SIN EL QUÉ?"

12. Kia Smith, "Who Are the Organizers?" *South Side Weekly*, September 16, 2020, southsideweekly.com/who-are-the-organizers.

13. K. Agbebiyi, Kira Shepherd, and Danielle Sered, *Solutions to Violence: How to Create Safety Without Policing or Prisons* (New York: Common Justice, 2021), d3n8a8pro7vhmx .cloudfront.net/commonjustice/pages/477/attachments/original/1630695014 /Solutions_to_Violence_final.pdf?1630695014.

14. Ruth Wilson Gilmore, "Abolition on Stolen Land," Keynote Conversation, UCLA Luskin Institute on Inequality and Democracy, filmed October 9, 2020, vimeo.com /467484872.

15. Robyn Maynard, Leanne Betasamosake Simpson, Hannah Voegele, and Christopher Griffin, "Every Day We Must Get Up and Relearn the World: An Interview with Robyn Maynard and Leanne Betasamosake Simpson," *Interfere Journal* 2 (2021): 142–165.

16. Mariame Kaba, "Yes, We Literally Mean Abolish the Police," *New York Times*, June 12, 2020.

17. "Study Guide for *Invisible No More: Police Violence Against Black Women and Women of Color*," invisiblenomorebook.com/study-guide. *See also* Rachael Zafer, "Reading and Discussion Guide: *We Do This 'Til We Free Us: Abolitionist Organizing and Transforming Justice*," 2021, haymarketbooks.org/pdfs/10.

18. Interrupting Criminalization, "Abolition Imagination Cards," interruptingcriminalization.com/imagination, www.interruptingcriminalization.com/postcards

19. Angela Y. Davis, Gina Dent, Erica Meiners, and Beth E. Richie, *Abolition. Feminism. Now.* (Chicago: Haymarket Press, 2022).

20. Benji Hart, *Practicing Abolition, Creating Community*, Project NIA, issuu.com /projectnia/docs/practicing_abolition_creating_community_final_22.

21. *See also* Devin Anderson, "Imagine Yourself Free by Liberate MKE," *Issuu*, November 16, 2020, issuu.com/liberatemke/docs/zine__5_.

22. Black Visions, "Minneapolis Without Policing," blackvisionsmn.org/mnwithout policing.

23. "No Cop Academy," nocopacademy.com.

24. No Cop Academy, "#NoCopAcademy: The Report," nocopacademy.com/wp -content/uploads/2020/06/NCAReportFinal2018.pdf.

25. Devin Anderson, "Imagine Yourself Free by Liberate MKE," *Issuu*, November 16, 2020, issuu.com/liberatemke/docs/zine__5_.

26. Poder in Action, "Phoenix Futuro: A People's Report on Policing and Safety,"static1 .squarespace.com/static/5b2c1316697a982293b76310/t/604907c26227a5576fb60539 /1615398853088/Phoenix+Futuro-A+People%27s+Report+on+Policing+and+Safety .pdf.

27. Movement Alliance Project, "Safety We Can Feel," February 2021, amistadlaw.org /sites/default/files/attachments/2021-03/Safety_We_Can_Feel-Report.pdf.

28. Nasvhille People's Budget Coalition, "Survey," nashvillepeoplesbudget.org/peoples -budget-survey.

29. Visit the organizing resources section of defundpolice.org and select the "Community Research/Survey" filter on the left for more examples of community surveys, defundpolice.org/organizing-resources.

30. Defund CPD Research and Policy Toolkit, defundpolice.org/wp-content/uploads /2021/03/Defund-CPD-Research-Policy-Toolkit.pdf.

31. Jackson People's Assembly, jxnpeoplesassembly.org.

32. Black Nashville People's Assembly, facebook.com/blknshassembly.

33. Black Visions, "The Path Forward," blackvisionsmn.org/path-forward. Minneapolis organizers were inspired by the Southern Movement Assembly, southtosouth.org.

34. Participatory Budgeting Project, "Where Is PB Happening?" participatorybudgeting.org/case-studies.

35. Black Brilliance Research Project, Black Brilliance Research Report, February 20, 2021, seattle.legistar.com/View.ashx?M=F&ID=9210619&GUID=CA0CF864-7944 -4FDF-9EDC-64FC53CA3C46.

36. Black Brilliance Research Project, Black Brilliance Research Report.

37. Seattle Solidarity Budget, www.seattlesolidaritybudget.com.

38. Mutual Aid Hub, mutualaidhub.org.

39. Dean Spade, *Mutual Aid: Building Solidarity During This Crisis (and the Next)* (Brooklyn, NY: Verso, 2020).

40. Alexandria Ocasio-Cortez, *Mutual Aid 101: #WeGotOurBlock Toolkit*, 2020, cdn .cosmicjs.com/09a653b0-7545-11ea-be6b-9f10a20c6f68-Mutual-Aid-101-Toolkit.pdf.

41. Spade, *Mutual Aid*.

42. INCITE! Women of Color Against Violence, *The Revolution Will Not Be Funded: Beyond the Non-Profit Industrial Complex*, 2nd ed. (Durham: Duke Press, 2017).

43. Spade, *Mutual Aid*.

44. Spade, *Mutual Aid*.

45. Spade, *Mutual Aid*.

46. Equity and Transformation Chicago, "COVID19 LifeKit: We Keep Us Safe! Community Care and Mutual Aid," 2020, cf84fce6-8756-40c5-92ef-cd97cbc441f3.filesusr .com/ugd/9c611a_dc910e072ce943fb98e8b667a15139ba.pdf. *See also* eatchicago.org /campaigns-programs.

47. Maira Khwaja, Trina Reynolds-Tyler, Dominique James, and Hannah Nyhart, "Our Year of Mutual Aid," *New York Times*, March 11, 2021.

48. BigDoorBrigade, "Solidarity, Not Charity," bigdoorbrigade.com.

49. Spade, *Mutual Aid*.

50. Mariame Kaba, "9 Solidarity Commitments to/with Incarcerated People for 2021," docs.google.com/document/d/e/2PACX-1vRR6IALSI7L16B0AdDwQ4 EZ2W3cKhRh2jE_OFcli13S-G3mLy3DzTjRehXerTM7HP2rjcIR2SJpV5ML/pub.

51. Generation Five, "Transformative Justice," on file with authors.

52. Feminist Abolition and Transformative Justice, "18 Million Rising," youtube.com /watch?v=Zz6Yn_3rSAk&t=362s.

53. Mimi Kim, "Transformative Justice: A Brief Description," *Leaving Evidence*, leavingevidence.wordpress.com/2019/01/09/transformative-justice-a-brief-description/

54. Transform Harm, transformharm.org/transformative-justice.

55. Ann Russo, *Feminist Accountability: Disrupting Violence and Transforming Power* (New York: NYU Press, 2018).

56. The Audre Lorde Project, "Report of the National Gathering on Transformative Justice & Community Accountability Strategies for Women of Color and Lesbian, Gay, Bisexual, Two-Spirit, Trans & Gender Non-Conforming People of Color," 2010.

57. *See* New York Public Library, "Until We Reckon: Danielle Sered with Mariame Kaba," September 19, 2019, www.facebook.com/NYPLEvents/posts/231770 7288559035.

58. Shana Agid, Judy Park Lee, and Mariame Kaba, "Skills, Relationships and Structures Worksheet," Interrupting Criminalization, September 2021, static1

.squarespace.com/static/5ee39ec764dbd7179cf1243c/t/61564e2d250f1c4c98a59912
/1633046061304/Skill+Relationships+Structures+Worksheet.pdf.

59. Page May and Nate Marshall, "Toward the Unreasonable," in *The End of Chiraq: A Literary Mixtape*, Javon Johnson and Kevin Coval, eds. (Chicago: Northwestern University Press, 2018).

60. Advancement Project, "#AssaultAt map," policefreeschools.org/map.

61. Advancement Project, *We Came to Learn: A Call to Action for Police Free Schools*, 2017, advancementproject.org/wp-content/uploads/WCTLweb/index.html#page=1.

62. "People in Education," www.peopleineducation.org.

63. Naaz Modan, "Dive Brief: Pandemic Spurs State Investment in Community School Model," K-12 Dive, February 1, 2022, www.k12dive.com/news/pandemic-spurs-state-investment-in-community-school-model/618095; Coalition for Community Schools, www.communityschools.org.

64. Maya Schenwar and Victoria Law, *Prison by Any Other Name* (New York: The New Press, 2018); Oakland Power Projects, "Maybe You Don't Have to Call 911? Know Your Options," in *Beyond Survival: Strategies and Stories from the Transformative Justice Movement*, Ejeris Dixon and Leah Lakshmi Piepzna-Samarasinha, eds. (Chico, CA: AK Press, 2020).

65. Schenwar and Law, *Prison by Any Other Name*.

66. Oakland Power Projects, "Maybe You Don't Have to Call 911? Know Your Options."

67. Schenwar and Law, *Prison by Any Other Name*.

68. Madison Pauly, "Who Keeps Us Safe? Two 911 Calls, Six Years Apart, Reveal the Perils of Policing and the Promise of Alternatives," *Mother Jones*, October 14, 2021, www.motherjones.com/crime-justice/2021/10/police-killing-black-shooting-911-alternative-oakland.

69. "M.H. First: Community First Response," www.antipoliceterrorproject.org/mental-health-first.

70. One Million Experiments, "Mental Health First," files.cargocollective.com/c1000528/Mental-Health-First_Zine-Pages.pdf.

71. One Million Experiments, onemillionexperiments.com.

72. Megyung Chung, Diana Zúñiga, and Andrea J. Ritchie, *Navigating Public Safety Task Forces*, Interrupting Criminalization, 2021, www.interruptingcriminalization.com/task-forces.

73. Ruth Wilson Gilmore, "Making Abolition Geography In California's Central Valley," *The Funambulist*, December 20, 2018, thefunambulist.net/magazine/21-space-activism/interview-making-abolition-geography-california-central-valley-ruth-wilson-gilmore.

Black Feminist Musings

1. Audre Lorde, *Sister Outsider: Essays and Speeches* (New York: Crossings Press, 2007).

2. "Under the Tree: A Seminar on Freedom with Bill Ayers," Bill Ayers interview with Ashlee Woodard-Henderson, podcast audio, May 28,2021, open.spotify.com/episode/7d2rmjx2ssip3ODN1aVrlA?si=KCGHOTmrSzaIjhIgT4nJJA.

3. Blake Piffin, "Police Harassment Leads to Crowd Singing Kendrick Lamar's

Alright," YouTube video, July 28, 2015, youtube.com/watch?v=VUC_DOhfzwQ. *See also* Brittney Cooper, "A Chilling Reminder That Black Lives Matter Less to Police: I Won't Soon Forget the Sound of People Screaming from Pepper Spray," *Salon*, July 29, 2015.

4. Fannie Lou Hamer, speech delivered at the founding meeting of the National Women's Political Caucus in Washington, DC, on July 10, 1971.

5. Becky Thompson, "Multiracial Feminism: Recasting the Chronology of Second Wave Feminism," *Feminist Studies* 28, no. 2 (2002): 337–60, doi.org/10.2307/3178747.

6. Angela Y. Davis, Gina Dent, Erica Meiners, and Beth E. Richie, *Abolition. Feminism. Now.* (Chicago: Haymarket Press, 2022).

7. Patricia Hill Collins, *Black Feminist Thought: Knowledge, Consciousness, and the Politics of Empowerment* (New York: Routledge, 2000).

8. Sarah Haley, *No Mercy Here: Gender, Punishment, and the Making of Jim Crow Modernity* (Chapel Hill: University of North Carolina Press, 2016).

9. George Yancy, "Black Trans Feminist Thought Can Set Us Free," *Truthout*, December 9, 2020, truthout.org/articles/black-trans-feminist-thought-can-set-us-free.

10. Che Gossett, "Žižek's Trans/gender Trouble," *Los Angeles Review of Books*, September 13, 2016, lareviewofbooks.org/article/zizeks-transgender-trouble; Cathy J. Cohen, "Punks, Bulldaggers, and Welfare Queens: The Radical Potential of Queer Politics?," in *Black Queer Studies: A Critical Anthology*, E. Patrick Johnson, Mae G. Henderson, eds. (Durham: Duke University Press, 2005).

11. Talila A. Lewis, "Disability Justice Is an Essential Part of Abolishing Police and Prisons," in Colin Kaepernick, ed., *Abolition for the People* (Kaepernick Publishing 2021).

12. "Combahee River Collective Statement," in Keeanga-Yamahtta Taylor, *How We Get Free* (Chicago: Haymarket Books 2017).

13. INCITE!, "Dangerous Intersections," incite-national.org/dangerous-intersections/.c.

14. "Combahee River Collective Statement," in Keeanga-Yamahtta Taylor, *How We Get Free.*

15. Movement for Black Lives, "Vision for Black Lives," m4bl.org/policy-platforms.

16. Yancy, "Black Trans Feminist Thought Can Set Us Free."

17. Haley, *No Mercy Here*. See also Talitha LeFlouria, *Chained in Silence: Black Women and Convict Labor in the New South* (Chapel Hill: University of North Carolina Press, 2015).

18. Saidiya Hartman, "Saidiya Hartman on Insurgent Histories and the Abolitionist Imaginary," *Art Forum*, July 25, 2020, https://www.artforum.com/interviews/saidiya-hartman-83579.

19. Barbara Ransby, *Ella Baker and the Black Freedom Movement: A Radical Democratic Vision* (Chapel Hill: University of North Carolina Press, 2005).

20. "Combahee River Collective Statement," in Taylor, *How We Get Free.*

21. Hortense Spillers, "The Scholarly Journey of Hortense Spillers," *Brandeis Now*, February 1, 2019, brandeis.edu/now/2019/february/hortense-spillers-qa.html.

22. June Jordan, "Nicaragua: Why I Had to Go There," *Essence*, January 1984. *See also* M. Jaqui Alexander, *Pedagogies of Crossing: Meditations on Feminism, Sexual Politics, Memory, and the Sacred* (Durham: Duke University Press, 2006).

23. Audre Lorde interview on Grenada's 1983 invasion, www.youtube.com/watch?v=8SbKW-qTO8c.

24. *See, e.g.,* Davis et al., *Abolition. Feminism. Now.*; Harsha Walia, *Border & Rule: Global Migration, Capitalism, and the Rise of Racist Neoliberalism* (Chicago: Haymarket Books, 2019); Stuart Schrader, "Defund the Global Policeman," *NPlusOne,* 2020, www .nplusonemag.com/issue-38/politics/defund-the-global-policeman; William I. Robinson, "A Global Police State Is Emerging as World Capitalism Descends into Crisis," *Truthout,* November 28, 2020, truthout.org/articles/a-global-police-state-is-emerging -as-world-capitalism-descends-into-crisis; Marisol Lebrón, *Policing Life and Death: Race, Violence, and Resistance in Puerto Rico* (Chapel Hill: UNC Press, 2019); Robyn Maynard, "Trans-Atlantic Affinities: Post-Ferguson Freedom Dreams and the Global Reverberations of Black (Feminist) Struggle," *Scholar and Feminist Online* 15, no. 3 (2019), sfonline .barnard.edu/unraveling-criminalizing-webs-building-police-free-futures/trans-atlantic -affinities-post-ferguson-freedom-dreams-and-the-global-reverberations-of-black -feminist-struggle; Stuart Schrader, *Badges Without Borders: How Global Counterinsurgency Transformed American Policing* (Chapel Hill: UNC Press, 2012).

25. Grace Lee Boggs with Scott Kurashige, *The Next American Revolution: Sustainable Activism for the Twenty-First Century* (Berkeley: University of California Press, 2011).

26. This statement is based on a *New York Times* article that reported that half a million people turned out to protest the murder of George Floyd in nearly 550 places across the United States on June 6, and that an estimated 15 to 26 million had participated in protests over the preceding weeks, correctly describing this as the largest mobilization in *U.S.* history. Larry Buchanan, Quoctrung Bui, Jugal K. Patel, "Black Lives Matter May Be the Largest Movement in U.S. History," *New York Times,* July 3, 2020. To offer just one point of comparison, Paula Rojas describes participation in a single protest during a mass protest in Chile in support of the Socialist Populist government of Salvador Allende at 1 million people out of a population of 10 million, the equivalent of 28 million people in the U.S. Rojas, "Are the Cops in Our Heads and Hearts?" Millions mobilized in South Africa and beyond over decades as part of the resistance to the apartheid state. During the Salt Marches protesting British rule in India, hundreds of thousands participated over a two-year period and over sixty thousand people were *arrested* in a single year. These examples are not offered to diminish the importance and magnitude of the 2020 Uprisings, but simply to put them in the context of historical global resistance movements.

27. *See* Hilary Moore, *Beyond Policing: A Handbook for Community-Led Solutions to the Violence of Policing in Western Europe* (Belgium: Rosa-Luxemburg-Siftung), February 2022, www.rosalux.eu/en/article/2084.beyond-policing.html; *Disarm, Defund, Dismantle: Police Abolition in Canada,* Shiri Pasternak, Kevin Walby, and Abby Stadnyk, eds. (Toronto: Between the Lines, 2022); *Building the World We Want: A Roadmap to Police-Free Futures in Canada,* Robyn Maynard, ed., bit.ly/BWWWCanada; Cops Are Flops Collective, *Reimagining Justice in South Africa Beyond Policing,* 2020, drive.google .com/file/d/1krNcg_saPFABqjuFkQvtVKUpIjivd8Es/view.

28. Andrea J. Ritchie, "Police Responses to Domestic Violence: A Fact Sheet," Interrupting Criminalization (2020), static1.squarespace.com/static/5ee39ec764dbd7179cf1243c /t/615d2d8d53ef604bf219fa3f/1633496919504/Police+Responses+to+Domestic+Viole nce_English.pdf.

29. Ashley Bohrer, "No Selves to Defend," *Red Wedge Magazine,* August 19, 2014, redwedgemagazine.com/interviews/no-selves-to-defend.

30. Ritchie, *Invisible No More.*

31. Ritchie, *Invisible No More.*

32. Sasha Ann Panaram, "'So Much of the Work of Oppression Is Policing the

Imagination'—Saidiya Hartman #UnderTheBlacklight," @SashaPanaram (Twitter), August 5, 2020, twitter.com/SashaPanaram/status/1291173243169251328.

33. Tamara Kneese and Hi'ilei Julia Kawehipuaakahaopulani Hobart, "Radical Care: Survival Strategies for Uncertain Times," *Social Text* 38 (2020), 1–2.

34. Hortense Spillers, "The Scholarly Journey of Hortense Spillers," *Brandeis Now*, Feb. 1, 2019, brandeis.edu/now/2019/february/hortense-spillers-qa.html.

35. "Abolition. Feminism. Now." Haymarket Books, February 4, 2022, www.youtube .com/watch?v=xvJCjh9ZbRM.

36. Che Gossett, "Abolitionist Alternatives: Black Radicalism and the Refusal of Reform," *Cabinet Magazine*, December 15, 2020, cabinetmagazine.org/kiosk /gossett_che_15_december_2020.php.

37. Taylor-Corrine Benton, "I Am Totally Amazed by This Moment . . . I Never Imag-ined Abolition Discourse Entering the Mainstream," *USC Annenberg Media*, June 26, 2021, www.uscannenbergmedia.com/2021/06/25/i-am-totally-amazed-by-this-moment -i-never-imagined-abolition-discourse-entering-the-mainstream.

38. "Abolition. Feminism. Now." Haymarket Books.

39. Barbara Sostaita, "Free Radicals," Bitch Media, July 1, 2020, bitchmedia.org /article/abolition-healing-connected-essential.

40. Jubilee Closing Remarks by Mariame Kaba, www.facebook.com/blackfeminist future/videos/346300447354883.

41. Trinh T. Minh-ha, *Elsewhere, Within Here*: *Immigration, Refugeeism and the Boundary Event* (Abingdon: Routledge, 2010).

42. Audre Lorde, "The First Black Feminist Retreat, July 6 1977" in *I Am Your Sister: Collected and Unpublished Writings of Audre Lorde* (Oxford: Oxford University Press, 2011).

43. Tracey Ross, "The Abolitionist Project: Building Alternatives to Policing," *Essence*, November 4, 2020.

44. Julian Randall, "True Story," *Poetry Foundation*, June 17, 2019, www.poetry foundation.org/articles/150310/true-story.

45. Keguro Macharia, twitter.com/keguro_/status/1013709160536592384?s=20&t =Wamf2fDJ4mQVKGEtUjQgyw.

Index

ableism, 128–129, 156–157
abolition feminism, 249, 268–269, 273–274
abundance mindset, 189, 216, 217
accountability: of gender-based violence perpetrators, 74; of police, 44, 236–237; punishment compared to, 83, 179; self-accountability, 201; through transformative justice, 255–264
Advancement Project, 153
affective economy, 188
AFL-CIO, 228
African American Policy Forum, 2
African National Congress, 232
Agid, Shana, 231
Akbar, Amna, 120
Alexander, Amanda, 70
Alim, Malik, 271–272
Alliance for Educational Justice, 153
alternative to incarceration (ATI) drug programs, 154
American Public Health Association (APHA), 176
American Rescue Plan Act (ARPA),

12, 13, 59, 66, 221, 223–224
Anderson, William C., 206, 208, 212, 213
anti-Asian violence, 97–98
Anti Police-Terror Project, 8, 267
anti-rape movement, 90–92
arrest rates for violent crime, 41, 44, 54
art projects, 248–249
Atlanta, GA, 149
autonomous Indigenous mutuality, 211–212
aworldwithoutpolice.org, 196

Bailey, Moya, 145
Baker, Ella, 276, 286
Baker, Thomas Owen, 238–239
Baldwin, James, 189–190
Baltimore, MD, 2, 67
Bambara, Toni Cade, 284
Barrow, Kai Lumumba, 199
Bay Area Transformative Justice Collective, 82, 257, 266
Bayley, David, 54
Beam, Joseph, 284

Bell, Monica, 181–182
Ben-Moshe, Liat, 156, 164
Benally, Klee, 206, 211–212, 252
Bender, Lisa, 6
Benjamin, Ruha, 122, 140
Berger, Dan, 13, 204, 225
"Beyond Do No Harm" principles, 161
Bierria, Alisa, 187
Black Brilliance Project, 251
Black Codes, 46
Black feminism: culture of care, 97, 196, 215; defund demands as rooted in, 11; global scope of, 213, 277–278; histories of, 274–275; imaginative work of, 284–285; perspective of, 275–286; and the practice of radical care, 281–282; and practicing liberation now, 284; principles of, 21–22; resistance to false narratives, 279; roots of INCITE!, 98–99; telling the abolition story, 279–281
Black Panthers: community control demands of, 232; divest and invest demands of, 113; free breakfast programs of, 254–255; health issues and, 161; platform of, 22; "survival pending revolution" framework of, 198, 252
Black Visions, 5, 6, 7, 197, 249, 250
Blackstone, William, 143–144
Blanchfield, Patrick, 183
Bland, Sandra, 2, 20
Blow, Charles, 119
body cameras, 123–124
Boggs, Grace Lee, 211, 213, 277
Boykin, Asantewaa, 267
BREATHE Act, 25–26, 220
"broken windows" policing, 64
Brooks, Cat, 78
Brooks, Rayshard, 110

Brown, Anna, 162
Brown, Michael, 1, 4, 116, 123
Brownsville neighborhood, New York City, 126
Buffalo News, 3
Build the Block project, 267
"Building Beyond Policing" gathering, 203
Bumpurs, Eleanor, 1
Burch, Melissa, 231
Burge, Jon, 237
Bush, Cori, 26, 220
BYP100, 8, 271

California prison expansion, 22–23, 307n101
Camden, NJ, 122–123
Campaign Zero, 109–110, 111
Campbell-Gooch, Jamel, 218
Cantú, Francisco, 239
capitalism: abolition feminism and, 276; carceral, 28–29, 206–207, 309n130; Gorz's theories on dismantling, 131; policing and, 142–143. *See also* racial capitalism
carceral creep, 92
carceral feminism, 95
carceral medical systems, 156–157
carceral politics of safety, 190
carceral social work, 167–168
carceral state: affective economy and, 188; anti-violence groups' coalescence around, 92; Black feminism and the violence of the, 274; criminality and, 29; as death-making, 239; defined, 28, 309n131; dismantling, 204–214; dual-power strategy and, 244–245; global struggles against, 278; mutual aid programs and the, 254; as the organizer of racialized gender violence, 275; propaganda concerning safety

and the, 187, 280; repression and pacification of abolitionists by, 220–222; state institutions of, 202; system of order maintenance of the, 234–235; transformational justice and, 256, 257, 260, 264; undermining of defund campaigns by, 223, 224, 225

care, culture of, 191–192, 216, 265–269, 281–282

Caruthers, Jakeya, 187

caseworkers, 167–174

Castile, Philando, 4

Center for Policing Equity (CPE), 111

Center for Popular Democracy, 8

Central Park Five, 71–72, 85

Champaign, IL, 48

Chauvin, Derek: complaints against prior to George Floyd murder, 328n16; lack of accountability of, 236; murder conviction of, 121, 235; positional restraint use by, 110; reaction to murder by, 4; video of, 123

Cházaro, Angélica, 178–179

Chicago, IL: accountability for police violence in, 237; authors' experience of organizing in, 19–20, 24; "Becoming a Man" program, 69; Chicago Alternative Policing Strategy program, 125; discernment questions used by organizers in, 132–133; mayoral candidate on increasing police budget, 31; neighborhood noise problem resolution, 240–242; police spending as percent of budget, 8; police violence against people in the sex trade, 161; resident surveys, 249, 250; street harassment of girls in, 95–97; transformative demands, 133–136

Chicago Alternative Policing Strategy (CAPS), 125

Chicago Torture Justice Center, 237

child sexual abuse, 82, 256

"child welfare" systems, 169–174

chokehold bans, 110, 120–121

Chua, Charmaine, 194, 200, 216

civilian police accountability boards, 129

Clark, Jamar, 4, 5

Cleveland, OH, 271–273, 284

Cloud, Erin Miles, 17

Clyburn, James, 10

Code, Zoya, 328n16

coerced treatment, 147, 154, 157, 164, 166

Cohen, Rachel, 62

Cole, Teju, 117

collective care, 191–192, 216, 265–269, 281–282

collective experimentation, 247–248

collective imagination exercises, 248–251

collective living, 184

Collins, Patricia Hill, 47

colonialism, 205–206, 213

Combahee River Collective, 11, 274, 276

commoning and the commons, 214, 215–217

Communities United Against Police Brutality (CUAPB), 230

Communities United for Police Reform (CPR), 114

community control of police, 230–234

"Community Not Cops" campaign, 152–153

community policing, 124–126

community review boards (CRBs), 231–232

compensation for police harm, 129–130, 137, 237

conflict resolution, 66, 184,
240–242, 267
consent decrees, 115, 116–117, 119,
130–131
consequences for violence and harm.
See accountability
contracts, police, 226–227, 228–229
convictions for police violence, 235
convictions for violent crime, 41, 44,
84
Cooper, Anna Julia, 278
"copaganda," 182–187, 350n9
copspeak and cop knowledge, 185
Correia, David, 119, 180–181, 185
Cosby, Monica, 87
counselors, 152–153, 159–160
COVID-19 pandemic: effects of,
3–4; homicide rates during,
61–62; mutual aid projects,
253; organized abandonment
and deaths due to, 53; public
health policing, 175–176; racial
discrimination in enforcing
public health orders, 48. *See also*
American Rescue Plan Act
Creative Interventions, 266
credible messengers. *See* violence
interruption programs
crime, as construct, 45–46, 60
crime rates: adding community
nonprofits and reduction in,
65–66; number of police and, 54;
police control of, 49–53; polls on,
62–63; selective citation of, in pro-
police narratives, 59–64
crime-violence relationship, 44–53
criminal system. *See* prison industrial
complex
criminalization: challenging the
concept of, 186–187; of child
sexual abuse, 82; of domestic
violence, 83; of drug use, 155;
industrialization and, 45; of

medical care seekers, 160–163;
organized abandonment and,
27–30; as power, 46–49; of
people in the sex trade, 158–160,
344n106; of survivors, 78–79, 100
The Crisis of Criminalization (report),
29–30
crisis response, 149, 157–158, 219
Critical Resistance, 15, 24, 98–99,
197
culture of care, 191–192, 216,
265–269, 281–282
Cuomo, Andrew, 100
CURE Violence model, 66

Danziger Bridge shootings, 115
dashboard cameras, 123
"data-driven" policing, 56–58
Davis, Angela Y., 29, 31, 208, 238,
282, 283
Davis, Mike, 23, 31
de-commodification of resources,
215–216
de-escalation of violence, 79, 104,
199
d/Deaf communities, 128–129
Death in Custody Reporting Act,
300n4
decertification registry, 137–138
Decriminalize Seattle, 251
defund movement: backlash to, 182,
220–222; both/and approaches,
130–131; calls for reform as a
reaction to, 107–112; community
control debates and, 233;
contractual blocks to demands
of, 229; counter-narrative,
58–64; history of calls to,
22–26; mainstream Democrats'
discrediting of, 10; misinformation
concerning, 10–11; origins of,
8; police fraternal associations'
response to, 226; recapturing

resources from the state, 218–225;
as step toward abolition, 13–14
Defund Police, Invest in Community Care report, 157, 158
Diallo, Amadou, 1, 49, 114
Dignity in Schools Coalition, 152–153
Dior, Iyanna, 105
disability justice issues, 128–129, 164–167, 341n66
disabled people. See disability justice; marginalized people; mental health needs
disarming police, 196–197
discernment process for policy proposals, 132–133
discretion in police use of force, 118–121
disempower, disarm, disband framework, 196
Dismantle, Change, Build framework, 197–200
dismantling the carceral state, 204–214
divest/invest framework, 25–26, 113, 163, 177–178, 195, 197
domestic and sexual violence: failure of criminal justice system to stop, 84–85; grassroots rape crisis centers, 90; against incarcerated persons, 87–89; by police, 3, 72–73, 86, 324n67; police violence against survivors of, 77–78, 322n33, 328n16; policing and, 34–35; rates of, 75–76; root causes of, 83; state violence compared to, 87; "unfounded" rape case reports, 51–52; unreported, 76–77
DPH Must Divest, 162
Drug Abuse Resistance Education (D.A.R.E.) program, 151
drug policies, 47, 151, 153–155, 169–171, 342n77

Drug Policy Alliance, 154
dual power strategy, 214, 243–244, 245, 253
DuBois, W.E.B., 208

economic issues, 124, 163. *See also* budgetary issues; capitalism; racial capitalism
education. *See* schools
8CantWait proposals, 109–111
8toAbolition, 111
eligibility for social goods, 144
Ellis, Eddie, 22
Emanuel, Rahm, 31, 135
emergency medical treatment, 162–163
England, 143–144
Enough Is Enough (report), 5
Ervin, Woods, 9
Eterno, John, 51
evictions and COVID deaths, 53
Ewing, Eve, 285
experimentation: abolition and, 246–248; schools as sites of, 264–265; through collective care, 265–269; through transformative justice, 255–264
EZLN, 243–244

false narratives, 12, 118, 279–280
family policing, 169–174
Farrow, Kenyon, 214
fear mongering, 59, 62–64
federal crime bills, 115
federal government oversight, 115, 116–117
feminist approaches to violence interruption, 67–68. *See also* abolition feminism; Black feminism; carceral feminism
Fernandez, Fabián, 161
Fireweed Collective, 156, 344n96
Fletcher, Bill, 228

Floyd, George, murder of: increased support for abolition after the, 111; as catalyst for national reckoning on police violence, 3–8; Chauvin's conviction for, 121; Justice in Policing Act and, 26, 109, 110; lack of accountability for the, 236; Minneapolis police policies after the, 118; national conversation of the, 203; video of, 123
former cops, 238–239
fraternal associations of police. *See* police fraternal associations
Frazier, Darnella, 4, 123
Frederique, Kassandra, 163
Freedom to Thrive (Center for Popular Democracy), 8
Frey, Jacob, 7
Fukui, Elliott, 156, 191
funding: of community-based safety programs, 219–220; community needs and, 223–224; Community Oriented Policing Service grants, 221; of police in schools, 152; problems with, 219–220; Violence Against Women Act, 76. *See also* budgetary issues

Garner, Eric, 1–2, 116, 120
Gary, Ja'Tovia, 190–191
Generation Five, 256
George, Maddesyn, 78
George Floyd Justice in Policing Act (JPA), 26, 109–110, 112, 130, 137
Gillespie, Kelly, 208, 211
Gilmore, Craig, 204, 205, 208, 209, 218
Gilmore, Ruth Wilson: on abolition, 16; abolition as repeated rehearsals, 247; abolition's existence now, 269; on building on what already exists, 200; on changing everything, 39; Critical Resistance and, 24;

on organized abandonment, 27; post-colonial states, 207; on racial capitalism, 26; on "the state," 204, 205, 208, 209, 210, 218; on transformative demands, 131; on violence, 44
Gissler, Tom, 238
Global South, 27, 214, 243–244, 277, 278, 367n26
Goff, Phil, 112
Goodmark, Leigh, 76, 83, 92
Goodwin, Alyxandra, 28
Gorz, André, 131
Gossett, Che, 15, 213, 274, 282
governance, modes of, 211–214
government funding. *See* budgetary issues; funding
Graeber, David, 205, 208
Grant, Oscar, 1, 8, 238
Gray, Freddie, 2, 116
green space revitalization, 68
Gruber, Aya, 61
Guinea-Bissau, 207
gun sales, 62

Haggerty, LaTanya, 1
Haley, Sarah, 46, 274
Hall, Stuart, 43, 182
Hamer, Fannie Lou, 273
Hansberry, Lorraine, 281
Hansford, Justin, 125
"Harm Free Zones," 199–200
harm reduction-based practices, 166, 194
Harris, Daniel, 110
Hart, Benji, 249
Hartman, Saidiya, 262, 276, 280
Harvey, David, 27
Hassan, Shira, 127
Head Start programs, 254
Headly, Jazmyne, 147
Health Alliance for Violence Intervention (HAVI), 66

health care. *See* medical care
Heitzeg, Nancy, 29
Hemphill, Prentis, 30
Herzing, Rachel: on abolition, 131, 204; Build the Block project, 267; on community control, 231; on fighting on multiple fronts, 198; on new ways of reducing harm, 217; on options beyond policing, 64; on punishing agents of the state, 238; on reforms, 116, 117; on the term "officer," 185; on the transition to abolition, 138
"high crime" area policing. *See* "hot spot" policing
Holtzclaw, Daniel, 95
homicides: arrests for and rates of, 54; causes of rise in, 61–62; statistics, 52–53, 59–60; unsolved, 56
hospital care. *See* medical care
"hot spot" policing, 56–58
housing needs, 103, 194
Hurricane Katrina, 115

Iannelli, Jerry, 183
Illinois, prison spending in, 23
impact zones, 316n93
implicit-bias training, 110, 116
INCITE!, 19, 24, 98, 274
income support programs, 145–147
Indigenous people, 45, 85, 206, 211–213
intercommunalism, 212
Interrupting Criminalization: "Beyond Do No Harm" principles, 161; community control debate, 233–234; millionexperiments.com, 246; on nonpolice mental health crisis responses, 157, 158; strategy session, 128
intra-community conflict resolution examples, 240–242

invest/divest framework. *See* divest/invest framework
involuntary commitment, 157

James, Kirk, 168
Jenkins, Andrea, 6
JMac for Families, 172
"job readiness" classes, 159
John Jay College of Criminal Justice, 49, 54, 68
Jones, Monica, 105
Jordan, June, 277, 281
just transition framework, 238–239
Justice in Policing Act (JPA). *See* George Floyd Justice in Policing Act (JPA)

Kaepernick, Colin, 22, 118
Karakatsanis, Alec, 45
Karisa, Mia, 16
Kaur, Mallika, 104
Kelley, Robin D.G., 28, 212
Kelling, George, 64
Kerala, India, 207
Kerner Commission, 113
Kilgore, James, 176
Kim, Mimi, 92, 167
Kimberly, Margaret, 232
King, Rodney, 1, 114
King, Rosamund, 110
Kohler-Hausmann, Julilly, 29
Kundnani, Arun, 28

Landauer, Gustav, 210
Law, Victoria, 108, 150, 154
Law for Black Lives, 8
lawsuits, police brutality, 129–130
LeFlouria, Talitha, 46
Lenoi, Tiffany, 283
Lewis, Lisa, 123
Lewis, Talila A., 80–82, 128–129, 156–157, 166
Lexow Committee, 112–113

LGBTQ people: barriers to social
welfare benefits for, 146–147;
survivors of violence, 74, 78. *See
also* Black feminism
Li, Emma, 249
liability insurance for police, 129
Locke, Amir, 118–119, 121
Lord of the Flies (book and film), 184
Lorde, Audre, 277, 282, 284, 286
Louisville, KY, 110, 229
Lumumba, Chokwe, 250
lure of reform, 126–130
Lyles, Charleena, 123

Macharia, Keguro, 286
Macias, Moki, 149
Maher, Geo, 207, 228
mainstream Democrats, 10
mainstream media: Central Park
Five case, 71–72; "copaganda,"
183–184, 350n9; crime reporting,
60–61, 62–63; on death of defund
movement, 225, 282; police-
related violence statistics, 2–3
making power and taking power. *See*
dual power strategy
mandated treatment programs, 154,
159, 160
mandatory arrest policies, 78
manipulation of crime data, 51–52
marginalized people: COVID-19
mortality rates, 4; COVID-19
order enforcement disparities,
48; criminalization of, 47; in the
current public safety narrative,
181; drug policies and, 153–154,
155, 342n77; mandatory arrest
policies and, 78; police response
to emergency calls from, 33;
police sexual violence against,
73; response to call for help for,
41–42; sexual violence against,
75, 87–88; social policing and,

167–168, 171; structural roots
of violence, 98; transformative
justice roots and, 257–258. *See also*
specific groups
Marikana massacre, 232
Marroquin, Jacquie, 102
Martensen, Kayla, 167
Martin, Shauntrice, 77
mass movements in the Global
South, 278, 367n26
Mathiesen, Thomas, 15
May, Page, 262
Maynard, Robyn, 15, 206, 208, 212,
213, 247
McBride, Michael, 62
McCants-Turner, Johonna, 103
McCray, Antron, 71
McDonald, Laquan, 132
McDowell, Meghan, 188
McMillan, Joyce, 172
McQuade, Brendan, 119, 122, 143,
206, 214, 217
Meares, Tracey, 222
media reports. *See* mainstream media
medical care, 160–163, 164–167,
347n137
Meiners, Erica, 23, 132
Mental Health First, 167, 267
mental health needs, 149, 155–158,
166–167, 219, 267
MeToo movement, 100, 101
Mexico, 244–245
migrant experiences, 189
Mijente, 244–245
Miller, Reuben Jonathan, 181
Miller, Tyisha, 1
millionexperiments.com, 246
Mingus, Mia, 243, 257
Minh-ha, Trinh T., 284
Minneapolis, MN: calls for reform
in, 109; community control debate
in, 230, 232; community outrage
at police violence, 4–8; complaints

made against Derek Chauvin,
328n16; discretion in use of force,
118–119; experience of building
safety in, 194, 216; "hot spot"
policing, 57; police department
size mandate, 6–7, 226, 302n26;
task forces, 219

Mirror Memoirs, 74

model of care, 166–167

Mogul, Joey, 198

"A Moment of Truth" statement,
99–100

Montgomery, Kandace, 6

Moore, Hilary, 74

Moore, Tiawanda, 95, 135

Movement for Black Lives (M4BL),
25–26, 197, 220, 231, 270

Movement for Family Power, 169,
174

MPD150 (community initiative), 5,
180

municipal budgets. *See* budgetary
issues; funding

municipal task forces, 218–219

Murakawa, Naomi, 22, 36, 117, 121,
124, 138

mutual aid, 194, 210, 248, 252–255

mutuality, 211–212

Naidoo, Leigh-Ann, 208, 211

nation-states, 206, 212

National Association of Social
Workers (NASW), 168

National Initiative for Building
Community Trust and Justice,
328n16

nations vs. nation-states, 212

Natural Helpers initiative, 104, 266

Neocleous, Mark, 120–121, 143

neoliberalism, 26–32, 92, 113,
144–146, 163

New Orleans, LA, 115, 123, 218–
219

New York Police Department, 51,
114, 120–121, 126

New York Senate Lexow Committee,
112–113

New York Times, 9, 30–31, 33, 41,
248

news media. *See* mainstream media

Newton, Huey P., 212

Nezhad, Sheila, 180, 219

911 calls: domestic violence calls
as percent of, 76; example of
response to in Louisville, KY, 77;
for nonemergency or noncriminal
issues, 199; police killing of caller,
183; police response to, 33, 55,
193–194; response and alternatives
to, 267

nonpunitive consequences for harm.
See accountability

Oakland Power Projects, 267

Obama, Barack, 10, 107–108

"officer-involved shootings"
terminology, 183

Okafor, Krystle, 192

Ontiveros, Isaac, 238

Operation Legend program, 221

Oregon, 163

organized abandonment: in Black
and Brown neighborhoods, 58;
in Chicago, 249; death by, 53;
family regulation policies and, 171;
mutual aid to counter, 254, 255;
neoliberalism and, 27; soft policing
and, 149–150; violence of, 268,
275–276

organized labor and police fraternal
associations, 227–228

pandemic relief funds. *See* American
Rescue Plan Act

Pantaleo, Daniel, 2, 120, 121

participatory budgeting, 245, 251

Pasternak, Shiri, 196
Pelot-Hobbs, Lydia, 115–116
People's Movement Assemblies, 7, 192, 250
People's Response Act, 26, 220
perceptions of safety, 189–191
Perez, Jasson, 233
Peterson, Ky, 78–79
Petrella, Christopher, 118
Pfaff, John, 61
Philadelphia, PA, 68
Philly Stands Up, 257
Piepzna-Samarasinha, Leah Lakshmi, 256
Pittsburgh Police Department, 115
police accountability boards, 129, 134, 233
police budgets: misinformation on effects of police budget cuts, 60–64; participatory budgeting, 245, 251; police fraternal association influence on, 226–227; problem with singularly focusing on, 224–225; shifting of policing funds to other government departments, 222–223; violence prevention programs vs. police costs, 67. *See also* funding
police contracts, 228–229
police control of crime rates, 49–53
police department size mandates, 226
police fraternal associations (PFAs), 120–121, 225–230, 359n101
police-free schools, 5, 9, 151–153, 264
police science, 143
police unions. *See* police fraternal associations
Policing Alternatives and Diversion Initiative (PAD), 149
policy discernment process, 132–133, 137–138

politics of police power, 190, 225–230
popular culture police depictions, 183–184
post-colonial states, 207, 208, 210–211, 232
Poulantzas, Nicos, 208
Pressley, Ayanna, 26
Prince William County Police Department, 52
principles of abolition, 195–201
privatization, 234–235
pro-policing narratives, 12, 58–64
"problem-oriented policing," 58
profit and police technology, 124
Project NIA, 93, 240–241, 246, 249
Prometheus Conspiracy, 229
ProPublica, 51–52
prostitution. *See* sex trades
protests, state response to, 192–193, 220–222
psychiatric hospitals, 156–157
public health: "Beyond Do No Harm" principles, 161; orders, 48; police in health care facilities, 162; policing approach, 174–177; violence interruption models, 66
public opinion polls, use of in crime reporting, 62–63
public safety: as goal of police abolition, 17–19; perceptions of, 189–191; reimagining, 179–181, 248–255, 265–269, 281
Pulley, Aislinn, 233–234
punishment vs. accountability, 179, 238, 258, 259

qualified immunity, 136–137

racial capitalism: "civilization" and, 181; defined, 308n127; neoliberalism and, 26–32; social policy and, 150–151; soft policing use in maintaining, 36–37, 148; in South Africa, 232; the state and, 205–206, 208, 209, 210, 212, 213; sustainable economies vs., 202; vulnerabilities as structured by, 189

racial profiling, 114

racialized criminalization, 309n140

radical care, 281–282

rape. *See* domestic and sexual violence

Rasmussen, Cameron, 168

"reasonable" use of force, 118–121

rebuilding the commons, 214, 215–217

Reclaim the Block (organization), 5, 7, 180

red light cameras, 124

reform: both/and approach, 130–131; community policing calls, 124–126; failure of, 138–139; history of efforts to, 112–117; logic of reformism, 332n92; lure of, 126–130; as more rules that won't mean less violence, 118–121; police training measures, 149–150; problem with, 36, 107–112; as reentrenchment of failed system, 117–118; task forces, 218–219; technological, 122–124; transformative demands vs., 131–138

reimagining policing. *See* reform

Rekia's Law, 130

reparations, 237, 260

residential mental care facilities, 156–157

resignations and retirement of police, 238–239, 316n104

resources: commoning and the commons, 214, 215–217; de-commodification of, 215–216; recapturing from the state, 210, 217–225

restorative justice, 67, 257

Reynolds, Diamond, 4

Rice, Tamir, 4, 110

Richardson, Kevin, 71

Richie, Beth, 21, 29, 87, 167, 231, 268–269

Roberts, Dorothy, 173

Robinson, Cedric, 28

Rodriguez, Dylan, 117, 231

Rojas, Paula X., 214, 244, 367n26

Roman, John, 63

Russo, Anne, 257

Sacramento, CA, 47–48, 267

Safe Streets, 67

safety. *See* public safety

Salaam, Yusef, 71

Sanders, Bernie, 109

Sangoi, Lisa, 169, 171, 174

Santa Cruz Women Against Rape (SCWAR), 90–92, 93

Santana, Raymond, 71

Schenwar, Maya, 108, 150, 154

schools, 5–6, 23, 24, 151–153, 264–265

Seattle, WA, 55, 104, 227, 251

self-accountability, 201

self-defense, criminalization of, 78–79, 100, 275

self-fulfilling prophecies, 56–57, 58, 62–63

Sered, Danielle: on accountability vs. punishment, 259; on the causes of violence, 82, 260; on the criminal punishment system, 83; myths about violence, 70; on safety, 69; on unreported violence, 76

settler colonial states, 205–206, 213

sex trades, 94–95, 158–160, 161, 344n106

sexual violence. *See* domestic and sexual violence

Shahidah-Simmons, Aishah, 74

Shakur, Assata, 234
Sharkey, Patrick, 61
Sharpton, Al, 121
Sheraton, Minneapolis occupation, 194, 216
Simpson, Leanne Betasamosake, 212, 213, 247
slave patrols, 329n30
slavery, 45–46, 85–86
slowed police response times, 55
smart policing. *See* reform
Smith, Barbara, 273
social policy, 144–151
Social Service Workers United, 176
social workers, 152, 167–174
soft policing: actors and institutions of, 140–142; by caseworkers, 167–174; disability justice and, 164–167; in the health care system, 160–163; history of, 142–148; privatization and, 234–235; public health approaches, 174–177; in schools, 151–153; "someone else, somewhere else" logic of, 148–151; war on drugs as, 153–155
"someone else, somewhere else" logic, 148–151, 157, 165
South Africa, 210–211, 232
Spade, Dean: community discernment process and, 132; on mutual aid, 253; on sexual violence for incarcerated people, 89; on the state, 206, 207, 208, 218; on violence, 84
Spillers, Hortense, 277, 281
Srinivasan, Amia, 190
Stadnyk, Abby, 196
Stanley, Eric, 16, 211, 214
the state: defining, 204–205, 206, 353n2, 353n5; liberation from, 211–212; recapturing resources from, 210, 217–225
statistics: Death in Custody

Reporting Act, 300n4; homicides, 59–60; media reporting of police-related violence, 2–3; police control of crime rates, 49–53; unreliability of, 44–45; unsolved crimes, 56
Stein, David, 13, 204, 225
Stinson, Phil, 239
"stop and frisk" policies, 114, 134
street harassment, 95–97, 325n87
structural racial oppression. *See* racial capitalism
surveillance, 96–97, 122–124
surveys and research, community-based, 249–250
Survived and Punished NY, 49, 79, 100
survivors: calls for police alternatives by, 74–75; criminal justice system experience of, 76–82, 83–84; criminalization of, 49; demand for community-based safety programs, 102–103; direction of anti-carceral policies, 103–106; "A Moment of Truth" statement, 99–100; needs and wants of, 79–80; police abolition roots, 90–103; of sexual violence by police, 72–73; of unreported violence, 76–77
Swadhin, Amita, 74

Taller Salud, 67–68
Tasers, 124
Task Force on 21st Century Policing, 109, 110, 127
task forces, municipal, 218–219
Taylor, Breonna, 26, 110, 235
Taylor, Keeanga-Yamahtta, 112
technological reforms, 122–124
"thin blue line" ideology, 180–181, 184, 226, 350n9
three-strikes laws, 22–23
Time's Up, 100–101

Tlaib, Rashida, 26
Tongan teens, stranded, 184
Torres, Jenna, 159–160
Tourmaline, 89, 146–147
trans people, 42, 76, 89, 105, 154, 166. *See also* Black feminism; LGBTQ people; marginalized people
transformative demands, 131–139, 198–199
transformative justice, 255–264
transitional period, 238–239, 243–245
transnational politic of Black feminism, 277
treatment, not punishment policies: disability justice and, 164–167; medical care and, 160–163; for people with mental health needs, 155–158; for people in the sex trades, 158–160; in war on drugs, 153–155
Tubman, Harriet, 283

underreporting of police-related deaths, 3
"unfounded" criminal complaints, 51–52
United Kingdom, 196
unreported crime, 76–77
unsolved crimes, 55–56
U.S. Department of Justice, 60, 61, 114, 115, 221
use of force policies, 115, 118–121

Van Dyke, Jason, 132
violence: celebrated, 48–49; community nonprofits' effects on, 65–68; and crime, 44–45; de-escalation of, 79, 104, 199; domestic compared to state, 87; media framing of police violence, 183; myths surrounding, 70; as

percentage of police calls, 41; by police, 18, 43, 86–87; police discretion in use of, 118–121; police failure at preventing, 42–43; police killings, 2–3, 54, 235–238; police response times and, 55; police self-justification and, 43–44; transformative justice and, 255–264. *See also* domestic and sexual violence
Violence Against Women Act (VAWA), 75–76
violence interruption programs, 66–68
violence matrix, 87–88
violence workers, police as, 18, 43, 86–87

wage labor, 142–143
Walby, Kevin, 196
Walia, Harsha, 212, 213, 277
Wall, Tyler, 119, 180–181, 185, 206
Wang, Jackie, 28, 206–207, 208, 209–210, 217–218
war on drugs. *See* drug policies
Warner, Mark, 10
Washington Post, 2, 69, 116
Webster, Daniel, 61
"welfare queen" trope, 145–146
Wells-Barnett, Ida B., 183, 279, 280
Wengrow, David, 205, 208
Wet'suwet'en nation, 212
Wexler, Chuck, 61
white collar crime, 56–57, 258
Whitlock, Kay, 29
Wickersham Commission, 113
Williams, Damon, 245–246
Williams, Kristian, 235
Williams, Toni-Michelle, 105
Wilson, Darren, 1
Wilson, James Q., 64
Wise, Kharey, 71
Wun, Connie, 98, 118

Yale Justice Collaboratory, 130
Yes 4 Minneapolis campaign, 7
Young Women's Action Team
    (YWAT), 96–97, 325n87
Youth Mandate for Education and
    Liberation, 153

Zapatistas, 243–244

About the Authors

Mariame Kaba is a leading prison and police abolitionist. She is the founder and director of Project NIA and the co-founder of Interrupting Criminalization. She is the author of the *New York Times* bestselling *We Do This 'Til We Free Us* and lives in New York City.

Andrea J. Ritchie is a nationally recognized expert on policing and criminalization, and supports organizers across the country who are working to build safer communities. She is co-founder of Interrupting Criminalization and the In Our Names Network and the author of *Invisible No More: Police Violence Against Black Women and Women of Color.* She lives in Detroit.

Publishing in the Public Interest

Thank you for reading this book published by The New Press. The New Press is a nonprofit, public interest publisher. New Press books and authors play a crucial role in sparking conversations about the key political and social issues of our day.

We hope you enjoyed this book and that you will stay in touch with The New Press. Here are a few ways to stay up to date with our books, events, and the issues we cover:

- Sign up at www.thenewpress.com/subscribe to receive updates on New Press authors and issues and to be notified about local events
- Like us on Facebook: www.facebook.com/newpressbooks
- Follow us on Twitter: www.twitter.com/thenewpress
- Follow us on Instagram: www.instagram.com/thenewpress

Please consider buying New Press books for yourself; for friends and family; or to donate to schools, libraries, community centers, prison libraries, and other organizations involved with the issues our authors write about.

The New Press is a 501(c)(3) nonprofit organization. You can also support our work with a tax-deductible gift by visiting www.thenewpress.com/donate.